Managing Conflict through Communication

Fifth Edition

DUDLEY D. **CAHN**

Professor Emeritus
State University of New York, New Paltz

RUTH ANNA **ABIGAIL**

Professor Emeritus
Azusa Pacific University

PEARSON

Boston Columbus Indianapolis New York San Francisco Upper Saddle River
Amsterdam Cape Town Dubai London Madrid Milan Munich Paris Montreal Toronto
Delhi Mexico City São Paulo Sydney Hong Kong Seoul Singapore Taipei Tokyo

Editor in Chief: Ashley Dodge
Senior Acquisitions Editor: Melissa Mashburn
Editorial Assistant: Megan Hermida
Executive Marketing Manager: Kelly May
Marketing Coordinator: Theresa Rotondo
Senior Digital Media Editor: Paul DeLuca
Digital Media Editor: Lisa Dotson
Production Manager: Fran Russello
Full Service Project Coordination: Shylaja Gattupalli / Jouve India Private Limited
Art Director: Jayne Conte
Cover Designer: Karen Salzback
Cover images: Fotolia: © Michael Brown
Printer/Binder: LSC Communications

Credits and acknowledgments borrowed from other sources and reproduced, with permission, in this textbook appear on the appropriate page within text.

© Ruth Anna Abigail/Pearson Education, pages 18, 33, 180; © Dudley D. Cahn/Pearson Education, pages 20, 58, 62, 99; allesalltag/Alamy 136; SW Productions 189; mediaphotos/Getty Images, 272.

Library of Congress Cataloging-in-Publication Data
Cahn, Dudley D.
    Managing conflict through communication / Dudley D. Cahn, Ruth Anna Abigail.—5th ed.
        p. cm.
    Ruth Anna Abigail appears as the first named author on the previous edition.
    ISBN 978-0-205-86213-9 — ISBN 0-205-86213-6
    1. Conflict (Psychology)   2. Interpersonal conflict.   3. Conflict management.   I. Abigail, Ruth Anna.   II. Title.
    BF637.I48L85 2013
    303.6—dc23

                                                    2012037218

ISBN 13: 978-0-205-86213-9
ISBN 10: 0-205-86213-6

17 2023

CONTENTS

PART III Broadening Our Understanding of Conflict Processes

CHAPTER 10
Managing Win–Lose Conflicts through Negotiation 226

CHAPTER 11
Managing Others' Disputes through Mediation 247

CHAPTER 12
Managing Conflict in the Workplace 267

CHAPTER 13
Managing Social Conflict   296

PREFACE

DEALING WITH CONFLICT REMAINS CHALLENGING

As we coauthors worked on revising our textbook for the fifth time, we reflected on all that has gone on in our lives since we started collaborating so many years ago. A lot has happened to each of us over these many years. These significant events jolted us into reality and forced us to consider our subject from new perspectives resulting in the fifth edition of our textbook.

While much has changed for us in recent years, one principle has held steadfast throughout all editions of our book: Many people still have a strong need to study conflict. People tend to feel negatively about conflict, and they do not handle confrontations well. We believe that the common mismanagement of conflict explains the bad name given to the subject. We intend to help you learn more constructive attitudes and more positive conflict management and resolution skills, so that you feel less apprehensive about engaging in interpersonal conflict and better able to manage and resolve it.

Conflict continues to be one of the "grand challenges" of our time, occurring because of deep divisions in our society that carry over into our interpersonal relationships. There are cultural divides between ethnic, racial, and religious groups. There are political and value barriers that separate conservatives and liberals. There are gender gaps between the sexes. There are economic and power divides between upper and lower economic and social classes. There are age barriers between our younger and older citizens. When these divides carry over into interpersonal relations, even people of similar backgrounds find differences difficult to overcome.

Where there is a divide, we communication teachers and researchers look for bridges. It is no surprise then that we have identified communication as the essential bridge in overcoming conflicts. As a first step the conflicting parties must meet to deal with the issues that divide them. They must take time out of their busy schedules, allocate resources they may find limited, pay attention to matters they may consider unimportant or frustrating, and listen in order to learn how to bridge the gap that separates them. Meeting together and paying attention to the issues and each other is an important first step, but more is needed. In this next step, the conflicting parties must communicate. How do they do that? What do they say? How do they say it? Because they have thoroughly researched the communication processes in conflict situations, communication scholars have a great deal to offer students interested in studying conflict. They

- offer a wide variety of tools for successfully managing conflict situations.
- are sensitive to ethical concerns as they create solutions to challenges such as conflict.
- view communication, conflict, the management of conflict, anger, stress, forgiveness, negotiation, and mediation as processes.

- study the role of stress and negative attitudes as key contributors to conflict—anger as an escalator of conflict and emotional residues as barriers to reconciliation.

The purpose of this textbook is to apply these contributions to the effective management of conflict. While the challenge of conflict initially appears enormous, the subject is divisible into more manageable parts or learning modules. Moreover, as a discipline, communication has identified many principles and techniques that prevent conflicts from turning violent and damaging the conflicting parties and their relationship. Some of these principles and techniques are preventive in nature; others repair channels of communication and restore relations.

WHAT IS NEW IN THIS EDITION?

If we just consider all that has happened to us since our last edition, we are surprised at how much we wanted to change and add for this edition. Meanwhile, our students have caused us to realize that revising is necessary to better relate to them. They wanted more clarification, less redundancy, and longer treatment of some topics and less on others. They expressed their confusion to us and need for our help as they waded through the complex and challenging subject of interpersonal conflict. So what is different this time around? A lot!

- We have added a new chapter on interpersonal violence (titled Chapter 5: Managing Violent Tendencies), a topic that is receiving more attention in the study of communication and conflict.
- The theory chapter has been moved forward in the book and is now Chapter 3.
- The chapters on negotiation and mediation have been moved to Part III as Chapters 10 and 11.
- We combined the previously separate chapters on anger and stress into Chapter 8.
- Many chapters have been strengthened by adding theories and the findings of recent research studies that relate specifically to that topic.
- To make the text more useful to instructors who use classroom activities or teach in a discussion format, most chapters now include an exercise that captures the key idea of the chapter and a discussion assignment that applies the chapter's key ideas to a case study.

Our readership presents a challenge. While most college students continue to fall into the 18–22 single group who are interested in conflict issues related to dating, teachers, parents, and roommates, there are increasingly more "nontraditional" students taking college courses online and who reflect an older group, married or divorced, with children, and long-term employment, planning soon to retire, or presently serving our country in the military. They are more interested in issues related to their marriage, family, retirement, and military or workplace. We have tried to include issues and conflict examples that reflect the diversity of our students.

However, regardless of their age and marital status, we are struck by the fact that our students continue to come to us with little previous conflict training. Students of all ages would like to know exactly how to confront someone they know personally and how to better manage their present conflicts. They want to know specifically what to say and exactly how to say it. Introducing the S-TLC system for responding to conflict, six steps to successful confrontation, and how to create effectively worded I-statements in Part I of the text responds to the students' need to learn immediately how to effectively deal with problems and issues they are presently facing.

As in the previous edition, Part I is intended to serve as an introduction to the study of conflict. Part II continues to emphasize the factors that escalate conflict and techniques for de-escalating it. However, we changed Part III to the idea of broadening the study of conflict to include negotiation, mediation, workplace conflict, and social conflict. Thus, the new edition addresses a wider variety of social contexts of interest to our students.

Throughout the textbook, we continue to provide practical advice concerning conflict along with theoretical notions about it. Each chapter is a learning module, beginning with specific objectives, followed by instruction including a summary clearly tied to the opening objectives, and finally ending with practical exercises that apply key ideas in the chapter to learners' lives and case studies. Our thinking is that successfully doing the exercises is an indication that our students have mastered the content.

As you use this book, remember that conflict often results in personal change. Expect to question thoughts, feelings, and behaviors that you have taken for granted in the past and to add new ideas and actions to your ways of thinking and behaving.

LEE'S ACKNOWLEDGMENTS

Although I am officially Dudley Cahn, I am known to my students, colleagues, and friends by the nickname of Lee. As in previous editions, I have my students to thank for their help and input. This is probably due to the fact that I now teach this course entirely online, which is quite a different experience from teaching face to face. Students seem more open to express themselves online, revealing what they don't know as much as what they do. From their comments, I am able to determine their needs and problems reading the text, doing the assignments, and discussing the key ideas. Because I found myself explaining more to my online students, I feel that there is a better way to organize the chapters and explain some of the key concepts and principles. Thanks to my students for their input and encouragement, the end result is a clearer work with a broader perspective than our earlier editions.

As I have done in earlier works, I would like to express my appreciation to the many scholars who have shared with me over the years their ideas on interpersonal conflict. Among them (in alphabetical order) are William Benoit, Nancy Burrell, Daniel Canary, Steve Duck, Sally Lloyd, Loreen Olson, Michael Roloff, Ray Ross, Teresa Sabourin, Stella Ting-Toomey, Steve Wilson, and Dolf Zillmann. Although my mentors have passed on, I want to acknowledge the important role they played in my life: Charles Brown, Donald Cushman, and Clare Danielsson. A day doesn't go by that I don't reflect on the influence these people had on me.

As a result of recently editing a scholarly book on family violence for SUNY Press, I learned a lot about conflict from my contributors. I would like to thank

Nancy Brule, Jessica Eckstein, SuZanne Enck-Wanzer, Loreen N. Olson, Felicia Roberts, Angela Swanson, Mari Elenar Villar, and Steven R. Wilson for helping me better understand how interpersonal conflict can lead to violent behavior.

Obviously, I have my coauthor to thank for her willingness to again work with me. The first edition was her textbook alone, but I have been privileged to work with her starting with our second and subsequent editions. We alternate the role of senior author, so that each of us has an opportunity to take the work in a little different direction and run with it. I am pleased that Ruth Anna let me pilot the ship this time around, while she monitored and approved the changes I proposed. Although we alternate senior authorship, we continue to collaborate and take mutual responsibility for each revision.

I also have my spouse to thank for her patience, understanding, and willingness to put up with my mood swings and occasional fuzziness she could see in my eyes as I would swing from attention to inattention, which occurred as I reflected on what I had recently written or realized that I should have written instead. Sharon has strongly encouraged my writing efforts and allowed me a lot of time and the necessary space to accomplish this project as she did for the ones before. I appreciate the fact that, while we have learned how to collaborate as our marriage evolved, she did not see these revisions as issues for family conflicts.

Finally, I would like to acknowledge the role our adult children, Leanne Richards, Cort Happle, and Katherine Karpinski, have played in our lives and our four grandchildren, Jessica and Daria Richards, and Ethan and Kolby Karpinski.

RUTH ANNA'S ACKNOWLEDGMENTS

I want to first say thank you to Lee for his hard work on this edition. He really made it possible. It would not have happened if I were leading the task this time.

I'd also like to thank the many students who used this book in my classes and offered suggestions for revisions, as well as letting me use their stories to illustrate important points. I'd also like to thank Barbara Baker and Shelley Lane. We all met at USC in 1979 and it would be hard for me to estimate the impact both have had on my life. Thanks, my good friends!

Thank you to the members of the School of Adult and Professional Studies at Azusa Pacific University, and Fred Garlett (EJ), my dean, who have all been a great support to me in my scholarly endeavors. Thanks especially to the "hall people" who help me maintain sanity and perspective: Frank Berry, Brent Wood, Stephanie Fenwick, and Sarah Visser, and colleague Gordon Jorgenson, who loves to make me laugh. Special thanks also to the Circle of Friends: Julia Underwood, Trish Hanes, Leah Klingseis, Rebecca Knippelmeyer, Caron Rand, Gillian Symonds, Joyce Kirk-Moore, and Melanie Weaver, and to my friends David Esselstrom, Doug Campbell, Joseph Smith, and Murray Flagg—you all know why.

Finally, I thank my family for all they do to help me be the person I am: my adult children, Kathy and David Lulofs, my dogs, Elisa and Jacques, and my sister, Vicki McGuire.

Introduction to the Study of Conflict Communication

OBJECTIVES

At the end of this chapter, you should be able to:

- Define interpersonal conflict and give examples of conflict situations.
- Define conflict management and explain how it has the potential to convert potentially destructive interpersonal conflicts into productive ones.
- Explain why the transactional model of communication is preferable to the linear model for managing conflict situations.

- Define process and pick a successfully resolved conflict to describe in terms of the five stages of constructive, successful conflict.
- Explain why many people view conflict negatively and how they could view it positively.
- Define civility and explain why it is a problem today and what can be done about it.

KEY TERMS

accuracy
adversely affect
    relationships
civility
communication
conflict communication
conflict management
conflict metaphor
conflict resolution
cycle
destructive conflict
differentiation phase

incompatible goals
incompatible means
inevitability of conflict
    principle
initiation phase
interdependence
interpersonal conflict
linear model of
    communication
meta-conflict perspective
negative view of conflict
positive view of conflict

prelude to conflict
problematic situation
process
process view of conflict
    communication
productive conflict
resolution phase
sense of urgency
transactional model of
    communication
triggering event

Conflict is one of the grand challenges of our time. It occurs because there are deep divisions in our society that carry over into our interpersonal relationships. There are cultural divides between ethnic, racial, and religious groups. There are political and value barriers that separate conservatives and liberals, gender gaps between the sexes, economic and power divides between upper and lower economic and social classes, and age barriers between younger and older citizens. While we typically think of these divides as the source of conflict in interpersonal relations, even people of similar backgrounds find it difficult to overcome their differences.

Where there is a divide, we must look for bridges. A common bridge for barriers in interpersonal relations is communication. As a first step in communicating, the conflicting parties must meet to deal with the issues that divide them. They must take time out of their busy schedules, pay attention to matters they may consider unimportant, perhaps spend money and allocate often-limited resources, and listen to people they would like to ignore. In so doing, the conflicting parties create or repair channels of communication and thus lay a foundation for bridging the gap that separates them. Sometimes it takes outside intervention to bring the conflicting parties together and help them communicate.

WHAT THIS TEXTBOOK OFFERS YOU

For the longest time, I thought conflict was like having a big wave come at me on the beach. If I moved fast enough, I might be able to dive under it. Sometimes I could just stand my ground against it. And other times, it knocked me on my rear. But until recently, I didn't really think I could ride that wave, to turn it into something useful. I'm not sure I can do that with all my conflicts—I am better off diving under some, but they don't knock me down as often as they used to.

If you are like most people, you probably would rather not have conflict knock you down or make you dive out of the way to avoid it. On the contrary, you probably want to know how to confront someone you know personally and how to better handle your present conflicts. You want to know what you can say and how you can say it. To meet this need, we designed this textbook to help you learn how to use effective communication behavior to manage your everyday conflicts.

Our approach to managing conflict provides solid information at the outset that prepares you to start dealing with your conflicts immediately, followed by information that deepens your understanding of conflict. In Part I, we define interpersonal conflict and conflict management, describe interpersonal conflict as a process, and provide an overview to the different means or cycles of communicating in a conflict situation. We introduce theories that can be applied to conflict to help us better understand what is going on beneath the surface. In addition, we demonstrate useful techniques for communicating in conflict situations: assertiveness, steps to effectively confront conflicts, and our S-TLC system for effectively managing conflicts. In Part II, we discuss violent tendencies and how to manage them, the ways in which people's communication behaviors contribute to the climate of the conflict, and we demonstrate how to better manage your handling of various factors that contribute to conflict escalation and containment—namely, loss of face, stress and anger, and emotional residues needing forgiveness. In Part III, we discuss various ideas that broaden your understanding of conflict to include negotiation, mediation, workplace conflicts, and social conflict.

In this chapter we define interpersonal conflict and discuss some of the different ways people view it. We believe that conflict is not simply a part of life; conflict is life—an everyday occurrence. People regularly experience times when their wants and desires are contradictory to the wants and desires of people important to them. Equally important, we can see no reason for conflicts to ever evolve into violent behavior. Conflicts exist as a fact of life, but we believe that they do not have to escalate out of control. When we effectively manage our conflicts, we can convert destructive conflicts into productive ones. These ideas make it worth your time and effort to learn how to more effectively manage your interpersonal conflicts.

At the end of this chapter is an "Introductory Exercise" that you may wish to begin right away, because you need to observe your conflict behavior over several days or more. The exercise is designed to make you aware of the key concepts we discuss in this chapter as they actually apply to you.

THE NATURE OF CONFLICT

One challenge we often encounter is that people are not aware of all the conflicts they are having with other people. The stereotype of conflict is screaming, yelling, throwing dishes, and/or swearing, if not actually punching or pushing each other. However, we are in conflict when not speaking to each other, too. To grasp the full extent of our conflict activity, we need to explore the meaning of the term and people's perception of it.

The English language uses many different terms as synonyms for interpersonal conflict or our experience of it: *confrontation, verbal argument, disagreement, differences of opinion, avoidance of confrontation, avoiding others, changing the topic, problem-solving discussion, interpersonal violence, physical abuse, sexual abuse, verbal abuse, silent treatment, stonewalling, glaring at one another, making obscene gestures, expressions of anger, hostile reactions, ignoring the other, unhappy relationships, simply giving in, accommodating, going along reluctantly, not making waves, competition, negotiation, bargaining, mediation, disputing, quarreling, threatening,* and *insulting.* Even though this is a long list, you can probably add to it. Because there are so many events people refer to as conflict, we think it is important that we have a common reference point in the form of a definition for interpersonal conflict as we begin this text.

Defining Interpersonal Conflict

We define **interpersonal conflict** as a *problematic situation* with the following four unique characteristics:

1. the conflicting parties are *interdependent,*
2. they have the perception that they seek *incompatible goals or outcomes* or they favor *incompatible means* to the same ends,

3. the perceived incompatibility has the potential to *adversely affect the relationship* if not addressed, and
4. there is a *sense of urgency* about the need to resolve the difference.

If you are like a lot of us, when you first read a definition of a key term, you don't realize all that the definition entails. So, let's consider what is interesting, unique, and useful about the way we define interpersonal conflict. First, our definition focuses on the idea of those **problematic situations** that arise because partners perceive that they seek different outcomes or they favor different means to the same ends. We view conflict as two or more competing responses to a single event, differences between and among individuals, mutual hostility between individuals or groups, or a problem needing resolution.

Instead of narrowly defining interpersonal conflict as an expressed struggle or a verbal exchange,[1] we recognize that some conflicts are not overt, apparent, or open. Just as one can claim that "we cannot not communicate," a conflict may exist even when people are not arguing or even talking to each other. We can recognize that we are experiencing a conflict long before we actually say anything about it. By emphasizing the notion of a conflict situation, we can include people who are not speaking to each other, purposely avoiding contact, giving each other the silent treatment, using nonverbal displays to indicate conflict, or who are sending mixed messages to each other. For example, one study found that when people experienced negative emotions, they became more evasive and equivocal.[2] Thus, it is likely that when people are first thinking about a conflict, they may not even say anything about it; rather, they may evade the topic or communicate about it in ambivalent terms.

By emphasizing the interdependence between or among the conflicting parties, we focus on conflict in interpersonal relationships. **Interdependence** occurs when those involved in a relationship characterize it as continuous and important, making it worth the effort to maintain. We want to underscore the fact *that interpersonal conflicts occur with people who are important to us and who we expect to continue seeing or working with in the future*. We may argue with a stranger, have a difficult time returning a defective product to a store, or endure the bad driving habits of another on the road, but these are not examples of interpersonal conflict because the conflicting parties do not have an interpersonal relationship. Having said that, some of the skills involved in arguments with strangers overlap the skills taught in this book. If you have to return a product to a store, for example, and you expect resistance or difficulty, explaining the situation carefully using the skills outlined in later chapters should boost your chances of success. However, in this book we want to emphasize the importance of using principles, concepts, and skills that improve our ability to handle conflicts with the important people in our lives— family, roommates, romantic partners, friends, neighbors, and colleagues at work.

An incompatibility lies at the heart of a problematic situation. **Incompatible goals** occur when we are seeking different outcomes; for example, we each want to buy a different car, but we can only afford to buy one. Incompatible goals may also entail personal habits that clash, as when one person in a living situation is less bothered by clutter than the other. **Incompatible means** occur when we want to achieve the same goal but differ in how we should do so; for example, we agree on the same car, but not on whether to finance it or pay cash.

Mismanaged conflicts could **adversely affect relationships,** meaning that conflicts can make people feel uncomfortable when together, dissatisfied with their partners, and lead them to desire change. If people dominate their partners and always win their arguments, the partners may want to exit the relationship. If conflicts leave people feeling dissatisfied, they may refuse to forgive, seek revenge, or become abusive. If people feel helpless in a relationship, they may grow apathetic, uncaring, or uninterested in it. If people avoid dealing with issues, their relationship may stagnate because problems are not getting resolved. The point is that our relationships generally deteriorate when we manage them poorly. Rather, people should look for opportunities to make their partners feel better and cause their relationship to grow. If they perceive that they cannot do that, they may look elsewhere for relationship satisfaction.

Our definition emphasizes that the issue or problem underlying the conflict has a **sense of urgency,** defined as reaching a point where it needs effective management sooner rather than later. Although letting problems mount up is usually not a good idea, people often let unresolved issues fester and grow until they can't take it any longer and explode. The interpersonal conflicts that interest us most are those that have this sense of urgency because they are approaching the point where they must receive attention or else. This is why there is a potential for adverse effects on the relationship if the issues are not addressed.

The Inevitability of Conflict

Conflict should be accepted as a fact of life. Simons wrote over 40 years ago that at one end, conflict is seen as a disruption of the normal workings of a system; at the other, conflict is seen as a part of all relationships.[3] A number of recent studies have demonstrated that conflict is a "common and inevitable feature" in close social relationships.[4] We encounter it at home, at school, and at work.

> I never thought that I would have "roommate" problems after graduating
> from college. Actually, the problems are with my new husband, but they
> remind me of what I went through in college—when to do the dishes, how
> to sort the mail, who should take messages, when does the trash go out,
> who picks up after his (!) dog, who does the housework. I am amazed at the
> number of issues that arise when living with another person.

Think over years past and recall the conflicts, complaints, or grievances you had with these three types of people: (1) neighbors living a few houses away, (2) next-door neighbors, and (3) family members (or teammate, close friend, roommate, or romantic partner). With the more distant neighbors, the appearance of their home and yard, noise, or their pets and children trespassing on your property may have upset you. These problems can also happen with a next-door neighbor, but now you may also encounter disagreements over property lines, dropping in on you too often, borrowing tools and not returning them, unsightly fences, invasions of privacy, making noises far into the night, blinding lights, talking to you every time you go out into your yard (especially when sunbathing). What about your family members? Here you could probably write a book. You may have had disagreements over study habits, sleeping habits, smoking, snoring, messiness, household chores, use of a car, friends who are noisy or sleep over, paying bills, buying furniture, TV, tools, and borrowing clothes. If you substitute a teammate, close friend, or romantic partner, you have likely accumulated a list of disagreements.

Undoubtedly, you can add many examples to these lists. The question is this: What happens to conflicts as relationships become closer, more personal, and more interdependent? The answer is that conflict becomes increasingly more likely, hence inevitable. We call this the **inevitability of conflict principle**. If you compare the lists you created for the three types of relationships above, you will probably find that as the relationship becomes closer and more interdependent (from a distant neighbor to a next-door neighbor and from a next-door neighbor to a roommate, teammate, close friend, or romantic partner):

- the more issues are likely to occur,
- the more trivial (minor) complaints become significant ones, and
- the more intense your feelings are.

As we go from our relationship with a distant neighbor to that of a roommate, we are not only becoming physically closer, but we also feel emotionally closer. In addition, the behavior of someone close to us usually has more consequences for us than the behavior of those more physically and emotionally distant. This interdependence means that the individuals involved can become problematic by interfering with each other's goal achievement or means to reaching those goals whether the goals are emotional, psychological, or material.

Researchers have identified seven types of emotional, psychological, and material resources that produce satisfaction in long-term romantic relationships.[5] As you might have guessed, those aspects that provide satisfaction in relationships have the potential to create conflict when people perceive they are lacking. In order of importance, they are:

- love—nonverbal expressions of positive regard, warmth, or comfort
- status—verbal expressions of high or low prestige or esteem
- service—labor of one for another
- information—advice, opinions, instructions, or enlightenment
- goods—material items
- money—financial contributions
- shared time—time spent together

In the best kind of long-term romantic relationship, partners believe that they get what they deserve. Although the above list focuses on romantic partners, many of these seven resources are relevant to other types of interpersonal relationships, including roommates, neighbors, friends, coworkers, and family.

The point is that we can expect more conflict as we become closer to and more interdependent with some people. No wonder Stamp found that conflict plays a role in the creation and maintenance of interpersonal relationships.[6] The inevitability of conflict principle runs contrary to the idea that, if we look long and hard, we can find people with whom we can share conflict-free lives. It means that we should cease our efforts to find perfect people and learn how to manage the conflicts we are sure to have with those closest to us. We need to learn how to deal with minor as well as major conflicts, how to maintain our objectivity when engaged in conflict, and how to keep our self-control. The narrative below illustrates these ideas:

> Before I started keeping track, I didn't think that I was involved in many conflicts. Now, I see that I have a lot of them, and that I could have handled them differently. Acquaintances, outsiders, and strangers make me angry, but I choose not to get into a verbal conflict with them. It just isn't worth the time or effort. Basically, I just walk away or change the topic.
>
> I also noted that I deal with my conflicts differently with people closest to me. I have the greatest difficulty reaching an agreement usually with the people that I care most about. It frustrates me when the people closest to me cannot understand how I feel. Such is the case with my father. He is home alone all day and does nothing to keep himself busy. In my opinion I think he enjoys getting into conflicts with me just to have something to do and to make me communicate with him.

Although conflict is inevitable, we argue that it need not get out of hand and perhaps turn violent. Unfortunately, too many people see violence as a necessary way to deal with conflict, but other options exist. By teaching nonviolent solutions to problems, setting an example in our daily lives, and raising our children to resolve interpersonal conflicts peacefully, we are helping to reduce violence as a serious social problem. Thus, learning to avoid escalation (i.e., learning de-escalation) is an important goal of this textbook. We next turn our attention to the idea of managing our conflicts.

CONFLICT MANAGEMENT

Defining Conflict Management as a Skill

Everyday language reflects the variety of ways in which we regard conflict: We talk about handling conflict, dealing with it, avoiding it, or resolving it. We define **conflict management** as the communication behavior a person employs based on his or her analysis of a conflict situation. Another concept, **conflict resolution**, refers to only one alternative in which parties solve a problem or issue and expect it not to arise again. Conflict management involves alternative ways of dealing with conflict, including resolution or avoiding it altogether.[7] Effective conflict management occurs when our communication behavior produces mutual understanding and an outcome that is agreeable to everyone concerned.[8]

Note that we define conflict management as communication behavior because behaviors can become skills, suggesting that we can learn from our past mistakes and improve the way we handle conflicts. In recent years, communication scholars have focused on the idea of "communication competence," describing communication skills that are useful in conflict situations. When we can successfully perform a communication behavior (such as listening without interrupting) and repeat that behavior when the situation calls for it, we have a communication skill. Competent communicators not only try to repeat the skill when need be; they also are able to perform that skill without hesitation.[9]

One way to understand communication competence is to refer to a television dance competition, where one of the judges made a distinction between moving and dancing. He accused one contestant of merely moving around the stage. Dancing, he said, requires experience, good training, and practice. When one dances, the person engages in a performance. Those who simply move about do not express any feeling or engage others. We can use this analogy to compare communication behaviors to communication skills.

Skills are not innate; they are learned. We develop them through experience. The only way you learn how to handle conflict situations more competently is to work through the conflicts you encounter—that is, learning from this book and trying to practice your new skills. Due to the complexity of the task, few successfully ride a bicycle the first time. Most fall off. Sometimes they are lucky and stop before hurting themselves. Soon, with a great deal of concentration, riding a bike is manageable, and then it becomes something that is almost second nature. The problem is that most of us are more willing to learn how to ride bicycles than we are to learn conflict management skills. Communication competence takes knowledge about the way conflict works, knowledge of the skills that are used in conflict situations, and practice. This book discusses the skills associated with framing messages in conflict situations—specific message behaviors that have proven effective in various kinds of conflicts. The goal is to connect thinking about conflicts with acting in conflicts so as to choose the most effective behaviors possible.

In addition to focusing on behaviors that can become skills, our definition of conflict management has two more important implications. First, our definition implies that you have choices to make when in a conflict situation such as how to communicate. You can choose among various options to deal with conflicts. You may avoid or confront conflicts. You may react peacefully or violently. You may treat others politely with respect or verbally abuse others. You may simply give in or insist on "having everything your way."

Second, our view suggests that, in order to effectively manage conflict, you must analyze it by taking a meta-conflict perspective. You may recall that one of the fundamentals of interpersonal communication is the idea of meta-communication, where one tries to objectively look at interaction between people and talk about it intelligently. We might sit back, observe a couple of friends interact, and then describe their interaction pattern to them. Perhaps we observe that one person dominated the conversation, that is, talked the most and controlled the topic of discussion. In conflict, the ability to take a **meta-conflict perspective** means that you can look back on the conflicts you have experienced, analyze what you did well and what you did poorly, and learn from your mistakes. Eventually, you may even monitor your present interpersonal conflicts, realize what is going on, alter your behavior, and better manage the conflicts.

Linear and Transactional Approaches to Communication

Communication competence has changed from teaching the linear approach to communication to the transactional approach. In basic communication courses, you probably learned that communication was once viewed as one person sending a message to another person (receiver) through some channel. Such a view of communication also contained a provision for noise (interference) and for receiver feedback, so that the receiver could indicate to the message sender that she or he received the message as intended. We can apply this view of communication as managers of conflict. One conflicting party (the message sender) may send any of the following messages to the other party of the conflict (the message receiver):

I am not speaking to you.
I don't want to talk about that.
I disagree with you.
I want to fight.
I don't like you.
I don't like what you said.
I don't want to see you anymore.
I want something to change.

The sender of such messages may use any of the following channels:

Face-to-face
Synchronous via some medium like a cell phone or instant messaging
Asynchronous via an email, text message, or a relay person as the message
   carrier

Noise may consist of distractions in the face-to-face environment (such as TV, other people, or loud sounds) or technical difficulties that delete messages via the Internet or cut off contact on a cell phone.

In a conflict, feedback from others may consist of nonverbal reactions, such as facial cues (anger, hurt, sadness), body movements (standing up or walking out), gestures (making a fist, becoming more dynamic and lively), tone of voice (screaming, yelling), or verbal responses (name-calling or swearing).

In the above paragraphs, we described a **linear model of communication**, using the words sender, receiver, channel, noise, and feedback. For the most part, this model emphasizes **accuracy**: Is what was "received" the same meaning as what was "intended or sent"?

While this approach can be helpful to our understanding, it is a narrow view of communication. When applied to conflict, the linear model limits our view of interpersonal conflict as something we do to someone. For example, we might take a position and try to convince the other of our view.

While the above description of conflict and communication may sound familiar to many of us, interpersonal conflict is a lot more complicated than the simple sending and receiving of messages. When conflicts arise, they arise because of the way both people act with respect to one another. In essence, we make our conflicts together; it is rare that a conflict is entirely the fault of one person in the relationship. Recognizing that, we would hope to create and manage a more productive conflict—one that begins with a problem and ends when conflicting parties agree on what to do about it.

From a linear point of view, our focus is on the end result, which means getting the other to change his or her mind or behavior to coincide with our position. In addition, using a linear model to explain conflict often results in trying to fix the "blame" of the conflict situation on one person or another, not recognizing that both people in a conflict situation contribute to the emergence of the conflict. In the extreme, this mode of thinking might lead us to go so far as to accuse the other of being stupid, making a bad decision, or doing something wrong behaviorally. We may yell and scream until the conflict tilts in our favor. Obviously, this can do damage to our relationship with others. Fortunately, there are other ways to manage conflicts. Our need for an alternative approach leads us to the "transactional" model of communication.

While the linear view emphasizes the end product of communicating (convincing, persuading, controlling, or dominating the other), the **transactional model of communication** emphasizes managing and coordinating. Given this view, **communication** may be defined as the exchange of verbal and nonverbal messages in an attempt to better understand one another's perspective and create shared meaning.[10] Such an approach recognizes that this view of communication (and by extension, conflict) isn't something we do to one another, but something we do with one another (like teamwork).

Similarly, a conflict is not seen as something that happens when one person "sends" a message to another indicating that he or she is unhappy with some behavior of the other. Rather, conflict is seen as the behaviors of each person, in response to one another, exchanging messages, hearing each other out, cooperating, and conjointly creating an understanding in which both people perceive themselves as being in conflict with one another, mutually sharing responsibility for the conflict situation, and working together to better deal with it. One student described it as "trying to build a sandcastle by directing someone else's hands."[11] Conflict is viewed as giving and taking, working together for a solution to a problem, discussing and arriving at mutual understandings, consensus, agreement, and resolution. Both conflicting parties have a responsibility toward empathizing with each other, avoiding judgment, keeping an open mind, welcoming feedback, and realizing that both may have to adapt to resolve the issue.

One implication of this approach is that we view communicators as working together to create meaning. The advantage is that we begin to recognize the importance of both people's behavior in the conflict situation. One person acting "competently" in a conflict situation, using effective communication skills, usually cannot bring the conflict to a mutually satisfying resolution all by himself or herself. It takes two people to make a conflict, and it takes two people to manage or resolve it in a mutually agreeable manner. The way people talk about the conflict together, the way they express messages in response to one another, and the way they "read" each other's nonverbal messages as the conflict is being enacted all create the conflict situation as well as manage it or move it to resolution. Moreover, it is not simply that the actions we choose are a result of the way we interpret situations; instead, what happens in this conflict affects how we think about future conflicts.

The primary difference between the linear and transactional focus in communication is seen in the visual metaphors we might use to explain each. While the primary visual metaphor for the linear model is a conveyor belt (messages sent and received in a linear fashion), in the transactional model, communication (and hence conflict as a type of communication) is seen more as a dance that two people do together (messages co-created by managing and coordinating).

Destructive and Productive Conflict Communication Processes

What does it mean to take a process view of something? A **process** is dynamic, ongoing, and continuous (not static, at rest, or fixed). It is evolutionary in nature. Viewing objects, people, events, and social situations as processes means that we understand:

- Processes have stages or phases of development through growth or deterioration.
- They have a history in which a distinctive pattern emerges.
- They consist of continual change over time.
- They have ingredients that interact (affect one another) that may or may not lead to the next stage (depending on the ingredients).
- At any given point in time and space, they represent some outcome, stage, or state of being (like a picture or a single frame in a film).

The way we talk about something often fails to reflect a process view—such as "the happy couple," "a divorced person," or "an ex-convict"—which suggests that people do not change, are not at one stage of a developing life cycle or relationship, or do not learn from their experiences and grow. We forget that communication is a process when we focus on simply getting our message understood by others without trying to see their point of view, adapting to it, and co-creating meaning. Failing to see a conflict as a process explains why some people are not interested in learning how to manage it. So, we don't take a process view:

- when we see something as unchanging (e.g., he was a naughty child, so he is probably a problem adult),
- when we see something as having no history (e.g., nothing in your past is important or affects you today),
- when we see something at its present age only and not as a stage in development (e.g., you are always this way and will never change), or
- when we do not consider the ingredients that make up something (e.g., you do not consider how your goals, fears, and abilities, others' expectations of you, and your deadlines or time limits interact to create how you view yourself).

We do not want to take such a static approach when discussing communication and conflict. Instead, we see them as dynamic, changeable, and moving toward some end. By combining the terms, we can define **conflict communication** as a process of exchanging verbal and nonverbal messages in a conflict situation that starts with antecedents, moves through steps, and ends with consequences.[12] We know that resolving conflict through communication does not end conflict forever, however much we might want that to be the case. We engage in conflict again and again, and we have a pretty good idea how these conflicts unfold.

A **process view of conflict communication** has implications for how we view a conflict situation and conflict management behavior. Both are embedded in a series of instances that follow one another (as in a video of people meeting, talking, and departing). Such a view of reality reflects awareness that our lives consist of events influencing subsequent events.[13] When we learn to take this view, we begin to see situations and behaviors as phases or stages, reflecting a switch to a process orientation. If the series continues to repeat itself (like a perpetual motion machine), it becomes a **cycle.** In some cases, conflict situations become cycles because they get bogged down in particular stages and repeat themselves. Effective conflict management consists of converting potentially destructive messages into productive conflict communication. Later, in Chapter 2, we elaborate on dysfunctional and functional cycles of conflict communication to help us identify the behaviors that make conflict destructive, and, it is hoped, choose behaviors that keep the conflict from becoming so.

As depicted in Figure 1.1, a process view suggests that a successfully resolved conflict moves through a series of five recognizable stages, steps, or phases, with each stage affecting the next.

The **prelude to conflict** consists of the variables that make conflict possible between those involved. The prelude comprises four variables:

- the participants in the conflict situation (number, age, sex, etc.)
- the relationship between them (which may vary in closeness and distribution of power) and their conflict history

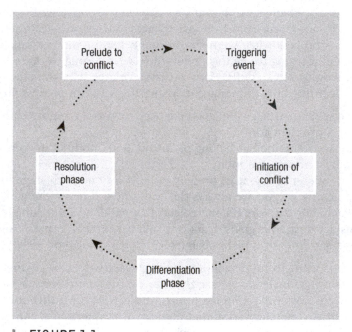

FIGURE 1.1

A Process View of Conflict. The process view of conflict assumes that all we have experienced prior to a particular conflict forms the group for the conflict we are currently experiencing. Prior experiences comprise the prelude to the conflict. A triggering event causes us to perceive that we are in a conflict with another person. After a triggering event, we (or the other person) will initiate the conflict through nonverbal means (withdrawal, silence, slamming doors, etc.) or verbal means ("we need to talk"). The differentiation phase includes working out the conflict, including the identification of the issue and feelings about it. The resolution phase includes the outcome to the conflict and becomes part of the prelude to the next conflict experienced.

- other interested parties to the conflict (including bystanders)
- the physical and social environment of the conflict situation (a party in someone's home, a meeting at work, dinner with family or friends)

In the prelude to conflict, the potential for manifest conflict exists because of the people involved and the other social and physical factors that define the situation. Like the first block in a line of dominoes, these variables affect the course of conflict.

The **triggering event** or conflict stimulus is a behavior that the parties in the conflict point to as the issue, problem, or focal point of the conflict. Examples include saying something upsetting, doing something offensive, or not doing something one is expected to do by others.

An important point to understand about triggering events is that the parties involved don't always point to the same behavior as the trigger for the conflict. For example, you may have experienced some long-term dissatisfaction with the way your roommate leaves his or her clothes and objects all over the house. For you the trigger of your conflict is the roommate's messiness. You finally say something to the other person and, in doing so, trigger a conflict for her or him about the other's perception of you as controlling. For that person, a conflict exists in which the trigger is your attempt to influence her or his behavior. While you both are experiencing one conflict situation, the behavior that each of you see as the trigger to it is sometimes different. In effect there are really two conflicts going on simultaneously each with its own trigger, one involving a roommate's messiness and another dealing with your dominant behavior. Your discovering this would be a good example of meta-conflict analysis. Having said that, we often engage in a single conflict where the parties can agree on the trigger. For example, a daughter is issued a ticket for texting while driving and her parents confront her about it. Both might agree in this case that she should not be texting while driving. So, sometimes the parties can agree that a particular event triggered the conflict.

The **initiation phase** or response occurs when the conflict becomes overt. This happens when at least one person makes known to the other that a conflict exists, such as reacting to another's upsetting comment, pointing out the offensive nature of the other's behavior, or reminding the other that she or he is expected to do something the person is not doing.

The **differentiation phase** or ongoing interaction pattern occurs when the participants use constructive or destructive strategies and tactics, presenting both sides of the story, moving back and forth, and escalating and de-escalating the conflict. Lasting anywhere from a few minutes to days or even weeks, this is the stage where the conflict becomes quite obvious. Although parties may view the open disagreement as "the conflict," from a communication point of view, the revelation of differences is the fourth stage in the interpersonal conflict process.

This phase serves a useful purpose by allowing both parties to explain how they see the situation that gives rise to conflict and what they want to happen as a result of the conflict. Sometimes, only one participant wants to address the conflict; the other person avoids confronting the issues. The relationship, the conflict history of the participants, and their preferred styles in doing conflict all act as ingredients that affect how the conflict proceeds.

The **resolution phase** or outcome occurs when those involved accept some outcome to the conflict. Ideally, a successful conflict results in a win–win outcome, where the participants are both satisfied with the outcome and put the matter to rest. Less ideal, the participants may decide that the issue is settled for the time being while recognizing that it may arise again in the future. The worse case occurs when a dominant partner decides the matter for both partners and acts as though the matter is resolved when in fact the partner is dissatisfied with the result.

In this textbook, we argue that conflict management may result in resolution or it may not. In some cases, the best decision may be to accommodate or avoid confrontation. In all of these cases, one is managing the conflict process. One manages the conflict process whether effective or not and whether the conflict is resolved satisfactorily or not. This book explains how to effectively manage conflicts to the mutual satisfaction of the parties concerned.

Regardless of the outcome reached, the way in which a conflict is managed affects the way future conflicts are managed between the affected parties. Thus, we illustrate the conflict process as a cycle, where the management of one conflict becomes part of the prelude of the next conflict. Again, this book focuses on constructive conflict management approaches.

When people are able to bring their conflicts to successful resolution, it reinforces positive thinking about conflict. Each successful conflict we engage in increases the chances that future conflicts are productive because we learn that conflict isn't dreadful and something we must avoid.

You should realize not all conflicts are exactly alike. Some may follow the five-step sequence of events faster or slower, and there is often an uneven distribution of time within the model. For example, the prelude to conflict may occur over several months and the actual overt manifestations of conflict happen in a matter of minutes or vice versa.

Moreover, as we show in the next chapter, from a process perspective, an unsuccessful conflict is one that becomes diverted at one of the stages. A conflict may begin to progress through the phases and stop, or it may return to a previous stage when new issues are introduced and added to the conflict. As in examining any communication event, the process steps may illuminate but also distort our expectations. The steps are used for explanation and analysis, not as a Procrustean bed into which all conflicts must fit exactly.[14]

Conflict communication is destructive or dysfunctional when it leaves the participants dissatisfied. Perpetual conflicts can produce perpetual problems in a relationship.[15] According to researchers, there are at least three ways in which conflicts may escalate and do harm to a relationship. First, the more excited and heated the conflict communication (in terms of physiological arousal, especially for men), the more likely the partners are to disengage from their relationship during the next few years. Second, some patterns of conflict communication (such as appeasing the other rather than engaging in conflict) are more disastrous to the relationship in the long run even if they appear more desirable at the beginning. Third, certain nonverbal behaviors during conflict communication (e.g., woman's disgust, man's miserable smile, etc.) predict relationship breakups later. The fact that certain communication behaviors and ways of dealing with conflict are associated with relationship dissatisfaction and breakups necessitates a better understanding of conflict communication and are discussed in detail in Chapter 2.

On the other hand, conflict communication is productive or it serves a useful purpose when the participants are all satisfied and think that they have gained as a result of the conflict. However, feelings about the outcome are not enough to determine the productivity of a conflict. Some conflicts, although uncomfortable in the short run, may serve the needs of those in the relationship in the long run, or may even serve others outside the parties' relationship or society at large.

This makes sense, particularly for people who are uncomfortable engaging in conflict communication at the outset. If, for example, you have a new roommate, and you find almost immediately that your personal habits are diametrically opposed, you might feel uncomfortable as you confront your roommate in order to find some point of agreement on your habits. Because you do not know the other well, the conflict communication may seem strained and awkward. Afterward, you may think you did not respond verbally in the best way possible. However, if you see improved changes in behavior over time, then we can conclude that the conflict was productive. You need to enlarge your view of a conflict to include not only the outcomes or results but also you and your partner's feelings about one another's actual behavior within the conflict itself as measures of effective conflict management. The following are two examples of how effectively managed conflicts move through the five stages:

Example 1

Prelude.   For the first time in about two weeks, my dad, brother, and I were all in the same place at the same time. We went to dinner together, giving us our first chance in weeks to talk together. We had just ordered dinner when the inevitable question came up. What am I going to do after I graduate? When the question came up this time, I had an answer. I told my dad about the progress I had made in job contacts and other possibilities I was considering. I especially wanted to travel during the summer with a sports team as a sports information director, but I had made no specific plans. Pop asked if I had sent in my application yet. I said that I hadn't.

Trigger.   My older brother, Stuart, chimed in that I'd better do it soon. This is when the conflict started. The tone in Stuart's voice was what set me off. He was using a condescending attitude toward me, which I hate.

Initiation.   I told him that it was none of his business; that he need not tell me what to do.

Differentiation.   Stuart got mad, as usual, and told me that I was interpreting the situation wrong. He basically told me that I shouldn't feel the way I do because they were only showing that they care. This rubbed me the wrong way because I've had enough of people telling me how I should feel. I tried to explain how I felt but was interrupted several times with the response that I was wrong to feel that way. I told him that I thought I was being more than fair in telling my family my plans and feelings.

Resolution.   At this point, my father intervened and made us both apologize to each other for making such a scene. We did and moved on to other topics that were safer to discuss.

Example 2

Prelude.　Our daughter is not a morning person. My husband is one, but I am usually the one who drags her out of bed for school. The other morning I was having a hard time waking up, and I didn't worry too much about it because my husband was up and I didn't have to get up early. I finally got up just before my daughter had to leave.

Trigger.　My husband remarked "I got Jenny up for you." That really irritated me, because when he says that it sounds like taking care of our daughter is a favor he does me instead of an obligation we both have.

Initiation.　I remarked that it really bothered me when he said that.

Differentiation.　He said that he realized that it would be easier for all concerned if he got her up this morning. I said I didn't like the way he said it.

Resolution.　He apologized and said he didn't mean it the way it sounded. He appreciated that I usually got her up. He was just trying to reassure me that I didn't have to worry about getting Jenny to school. I told him I appreciated being reassured, but really needed to believe we were in this together. He agreed, and we dropped it.

We believe that **destructive conflict** occurs when the parties do not manage a conflict in a way that is mutually satisfactory and does harm to their relationship. Moreover, when participants in the conflict lose sight of their original goals, when hostility becomes the norm, when mismanaged conflict becomes a regular part of the interaction between people, conflict is destructive. Most importantly, we characterize destructive conflict as a tendency to expand and escalate the conflict to the point where it often becomes separated from the initial cause and takes on a life of its own. Consider this person's account of poorly handled conflicts.

> I gave one friend, Jason, an incorrect reason why another friend, Tim, was not going to have a drink. I told Jason that Tim had a problem with alcohol, which wasn't really true. When Tim found out what I told Jason, he got upset (understandably) with me, and we had a nasty argument, which continued to the following night. I remember yelling, swearing, flaying my arms in the air, kicking a chair, and accusing him of being from an alcoholic family (which wasn't true).

According to our view, destructive conflict occurs when there is an increase in the number of issues, number of people involved, costs to the participants, and intensity of negative feelings. It includes a desire to hurt the other person and to get even for past wrongs. Destructive conflict occurs when there is escalation and parties fail to consider their options. Lastly, destructive conflict places heavy reliance on overt power and manipulative techniques.

We believe that **productive conflict** occurs when a conflict is kept to the issue and to those involved. It reduces the costs to the participants and the intensity of negative feelings. It includes helping the other person and letting go of past feelings. Productive conflict occurs when there is no escalation and loss of control. It features an awareness of options in conflict situations. Productive conflict does not rely on overt power and manipulative techniques. Along with these characteristics, we think that a productive view of conflict situations includes flexibility and a belief that all conflicting parties can achieve their important goals.

Productive conflict is distinguished from destructive on the basis of mutually favorable or unfavorable outcomes. We need to say more about the idea of outcomes, or the results people are seeking to achieve when they engage in conflict. Sometimes, these goals are clear at the outset, and at other times they develop as the conflict continues.

We realize that the term "outcomes" may suggest the resolution of some issue or solution of some problem. However, many people are satisfied even when these goals are not achieved. All they want from the conflict situation is for the other party to show interest in the problem; show concern for their feelings; and pay attention to their wants, needs, or interests, even if their wishes are not fulfilled. These are more personal, emotional outcomes that are associated with perceived fairness, acceptance as a person, and justice. There is a common understanding that complaints need attention from those responsible. In conflicts, both parties are anxious to tell their side of the story and want others to hear them out. If you take the time and make an effort to meet with me and show interest in my concerns, I may leave a conflict situation at least somewhat satisfied or feeling better than if you continue to ignore me or treat me badly. Better yet, you may make future decisions based on my recent input.

Negative View of Conflict

Unfortunately, many conflicts fail to make it through all five stages and end with mutual satisfaction with the outcome. Our experience with conflict has made us wary of it. One of the challenges in getting people to learn more about conflict management is that people often do not even like to use the word conflict to describe their experiences, as this narrative demonstrates:

> I don't have conflicts, because to me, a conflict is when you have no place left to go. I'm right; you're wrong, so let's forget it. Up to that point, I bargain or argue, but I don't have conflicts.

Even when we are able to recognize one when we are in the middle of it does not mean that we have begun to think about conflict as something that is potentially helpful. Conflicting parties often experience a curious tension; that is, they expect (logically and intellectually) to experience conflict but want to settle it as soon as possible so that their lives can return to "normal."

What comes to mind when you think of interpersonal conflict? How would you complete this sentence: To me, conflict is like. . . . Would you describe conflict as like a war, battle, or fight? Would you say conflict is more like a struggle, an uphill climb, or a contest of wills? Is it like feeling sick to your stomach? Do you think of conflict as like being on trial, a day in court? Perhaps you see it as a game, match, or sport? Or would you describe it more as a communication breakdown, a barrier between you and another? Photo 1.1 shows one person's view of conflict: It is something that makes her feel bound and gagged.

Conflict is almost always associated with negative feelings. We know that many people do not feel confident about handling a conflict. In a study, researchers asked people to describe past interpersonal conflicts and found that they overwhelmingly used negative terms to describe their conflicts: "It is like being in a sinking ship with no lifeboat," "like a checkbook that won't balance," or "like being in a rowboat in a hurricane."[16] The participants in the study described their conflicts almost uniformly as destructive or negative, suggesting that when they effectively managed an interpersonal conflict, respondents did not think it was a conflict at all.[17] This is typical of a **negative view of conflict**: The idea that conflicts are painful occurrences that are personally threatening and best avoided.

To say what conflict is like is an exercise in creating a **conflict metaphor**, where you are asked to compare one term (conflict) with something else (struggle, exploding bombs, being on trial). Metaphors are not only figures of speech but also a reflection of how we think.

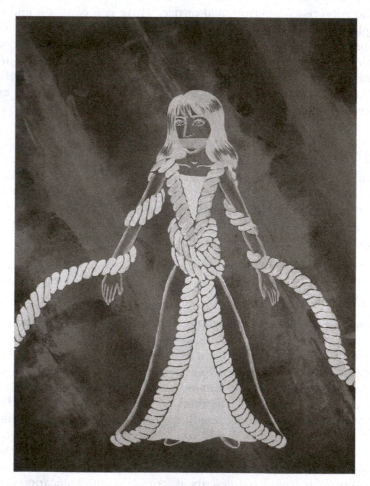

Photo 1.1. Bound. Amy Munive's conflict art reflects her negative perceptions of conflict as something that renders her helpless and speechless.

How we think about something like conflict and the metaphors we may create for it create an expectation as to what can, will, or should happen, and the sort of emotions that might occur. How people think about conflict in general terms affects how they see their current situation, how they see the conflict issue, what choices they think are available to them, and how they view the other person's actions. You can know a great deal about conflict management, but if you hold a negative view of conflict your behaviors may be less competent when faced with one.

What do we learn from a collection of metaphors people give when asked what conflict is like to them? First, interestingly, we find that not everyone uses a metaphor to describe a conflict unless they are prompted to do so.[18] However, those who do so often use metaphors that are associated with the strategy used to respond to conflict: People who use negative strategies use more negative metaphors and others who are more passive use metaphors that reflect powerless feelings.

Second, we learn that not all people choose the same adjectives when describing what conflict means to them. People choose different adjectives to describe their perception of interpersonal conflict. These words reflect somewhat different views, which are themselves in conflict. Quite often a person who sees conflict as a "battlefield with relationships being the casualties" does not compare it to being on trial or a day in court, as another might. Probably, neither person thinks of conflict as like a basketball game, a tennis match, or some other sport. Although people vary in their perceptions of conflict, most seem to reject the idea that interpersonal conflict is a positive, healthy, and fortunate event—one they should welcome.

This common but negative attitude toward conflict hinders us from learning how to better manage our conflicts. Although people often think that they can learn new communication skills to improve the way they handle interpersonal conflicts, they do not realize that their attitudes, beliefs, and emotional reactions may have to undergo change as well.

Just as one can view a glass of water as half empty but another sees it as half full, so can we switch from a negative view of interpersonal conflict, where we see it as threatening, to a positive view. One woman reports her change in attitude toward conflict.

> The most valuable lesson I have learned is that conflict is not necessarily bad. I no longer see conflicts as a danger to relationships. My acceptance of conflicts as the result of relationships has helped minimize the discomfort I feel in conflict situations.

This is a **positive view of conflict**, where *the effective conflict manager does not view conflict negatively, but rather sees opportunities to resolve problems and improve relationships with the people who mean the most in conflict situations.* The important first step in managing conflict is to adopt a mind-set that embraces conflict as an opportunity while recognizing the risks involved in it. Your other skills in conflict depend on your ability to transform how you think about conflict in general. Cloke remarks:

> We can all recognize that in order to resolve our conflicts we have to move towards them, which is inherently dangerous because it can cause them to escalate. It is somewhat more difficult for us to grasp that our conflicts are laden with information that is essential for our growth, learning, intimacy,

and change, that they present us with multiple openings for transformation and unique opportunities to let go of old patterns.[19]

This mind-set recognizes the importance of personal responsibility for one's actions and encourages flexibility in oneself and in others within the conflict situation. It also recognizes that communication works no miracles but that it usually helps when managing many of our conflicts. Most important, this mind-set rejects easy solutions and recognizes the complexity of conflict situations and their outcomes.

The conflict art in Photo 1.2 illustrates the Ideal Conflict Manager mind-set. It recognizes the inherent danger in conflict—there are thorns, and there are places where a person can get trapped. At the same time, it demonstrates the positive outcomes that can arise from conflict handled well.

Learning to Respect Others: Civility as a Response to Conflict

Perceiving conflict as an opportunity to solve problems and improve a relationship should help us better manage many of our conflicts. Another challenge is getting people to realize that an important means of responding to conflicts across all contexts is mastering the habit of civility. Civility is not to be confused with simple

Photo 1.2. This watercolor painting by Lynn Palmer titled "Every Conflict Tells a Story" reflects a healthy view of conflict. There may be some painful spots involved, and there may even be places where the conflict is derailed or stalled, but overall, conflict yields positive results.

etiquette. **Civility** is constituted by an attitude of respect toward others manifested in our behavior toward them; that respect is not predicated on how we feel about them in particular. Civility requires that we are mindful of others around us and aware of the impact our behavior has on them.[20]

Is civility really a problem for us? The answer, unfortunately, is yes. One needs only to drive on an interstate, stand in a long line, deal with a government agency, or listen to people in a shopping mall to realize that civility is lacking in our society. The use of profanity is at an all-time high; according to a recent radio station's "guess what" game, the average American curses 70–80 times a day. Incivility is no stranger to the workplace, either. As Sutton points out, "many workplaces are plagued by 'interpersonal moves' that leave people feeling threatened and demeaned, which are often directed by more powerful people at less powerful people."[21] Sometimes, incivility becomes so intense that it is better characterized as bullying, a set of behaviors we discuss in Chapter 12 or violent social groups we discuss in Chapter 13.

Carter's seminal work on *Civility* provides a perspective on why we have become so uncivil toward one another. He traces the historical development of books of etiquette, developed to help people get along in close quarters. Some of the earliest American writings on civility were proposed as guidelines to help people get along on railway cars, where they were in the company of strangers for long periods of time. The early writings were reminders to passengers that they were not alone on the train. They affect others by untoward behavior. As Carter points out, in many ways, we have become unaware of the fact that we are not solitary passengers through life. The relative isolation of our lives today, whether in our cars, our homes, or our communities, often leads us to act in ways that are rude to others.

Carter also indicates that attitudes and behaviors constitute civility, but he takes the idea a bit farther. Civility, Carter argues, "is the sum of the many sacrifices we are called to make for the sake of living together."[22] These sacrifices may include giving up the need to be right or the need to be heard in order to attain a greater good for the relationship, group, family, or organization as a whole. This does not mean we suppress needed and helpful conflict, but that we stop and think about whether speaking up really is necessary for the good of all. Carter argues that "a nation where everyone agrees is not a nation of civility but a nation withered of diversity. . . . When we are civil, we are not pretending to like those we actually despise; we are not pretending to hold any attitude toward them, except that we accept and value them as every bit our equals . . ."[23] In other words, how we treat others should be independent of what we think of them. Sometimes, it takes a while for people to catch on to this notion, as the narrative below indicates:

> I have to work with someone who has been a thorn in my side for a long time. We have been on the opposite sides of most issues, and he has done some things that would get him fired anywhere else. To my dismay, I found that I would have to attend the same conference as he and be in his company for a week! I was not happy about it, and spent some time bad-mouthing him to one of my colleagues who was also attending the conference. He finally told me that if I was going to continue like that for the week, he

was going to ask for hazardous duty pay when we returned. I realized at that moment that I was turning into the kind of jerk I thought the other person was. I decided to try something different. I was nice to him the whole conference. I'm not going to tell you that I like him any better now, but being civil did have its own rewards. I wasn't anxious, I wasn't irritated, I was just polite. The colleague who formerly had said he wanted hazardous duty pay was amazed.

Given the importance of civility, what are the behaviors a person should adopt that reflect it? To begin with, civility is a way of being attentive, acknowledging others, thinking the best of others, listening, being inclusive, speaking kindly, accepting others, respecting their boundaries, accepting personal responsibility, and apologizing when necessary.[24] Troester and Mester offer five specific rules for civil language at work:

1. The best words to choose when caught in an unexpected, emotionally charged situation are no words at all.
2. Use words respectful of the specific listener to whom they are addressed.
3. Respect the reality of the situation by choosing temperate and accurate, not inflammatory, words when describing or commenting on ideas, issues, or persons.
4. Use objective, nondiscriminatory language that respects the uniqueness of all individuals.
5. Respect your listeners by using clean language all the time on the job.[25]

We close with some of the principles that Carter lays out in his book, as they provide the most wide-ranging set of assumptions that can help us to engage in civil behavior. As we discussed previously, the decision to be civil to others should not depend on whether we like them. Further, since civility is seen as sometimes sacrificing one's own wishes, that sacrifice must be extended to strangers as well as people we know. Civility is both a commitment not to do others harm and a commitment to do good for others. When we disagree, civility requires that we be honest about our differences and do our best to manage them rather than suppressing them or ignoring them. Finally, as Carter argues, civility requires that we come into the presence of others with a sense of awe and gratitude, rather than a sense of duty and obligation.

Civility is an important skill in our conflict management toolbox. Along with the other tools covered in later chapters, we believe civility should be the primary skill people learn in order to function more effectively.

MANAGE IT

Because you want to know how to confront someone you know personally and how to better handle your present conflicts, we designed this textbook to help you use effective conflict communication behavior. Our goal in this first chapter is to introduce you to the study of interpersonal conflict, defined as a problematic situation that occurs between interdependent people who seek different goals or means to those goals, which has the potential to adversely affect the relationship if not addressed and that there is a sense of urgency about the need to resolve the differences. Our definition broadens the study of conflict because nonverbal messages such as not speaking to one another can adversely affect relationships as much as verbal ones.

Although many people may not admit it, most people encounter conflict quite frequently. Conflict is inevitable—as relationships become closer, more personal, and more interdependent, more conflicts occur, trivial (minor) complaints become more significant, and feelings become more intense. Although conflict is inevitable, it does not need to get out of hand and perhaps turn violent because other options are available. We always have choices (or options) in conflict situations, and we are all responsible for our own actions.

Conflict management is the communication behavior we employ based on our analysis of a conflict situation. Productive management of conflict situations includes flexibility and the belief that all conflicting parties can achieve their important goals.

Competent conflict managers must recognize that communication is not linear and not simply saying what's on one's mind. Communication (and, by extension, conflict) isn't something we do to the other person, but something we do with one another (like teamwork or like a dance). The advantage of the transactional model is that we recognize the importance of both people's behavior in the conflict situation. One person acting competently in a conflict situation and using effective communication skills usually cannot bring the conflict to a resolution. It takes two people to make the conflict, and it takes two people to manage or resolve it. By taking both parties' behavior into consideration, we can better determine what communication option we should exercise in a given conflict situation. We can respond by avoiding the conflict, sitting down and discussing it with the other person, or reacting with aggressive speech or violent behavior. The best of these options is communicating about the conflict.

We may not realize it at the time, but constructive conflict communication is possible in most if not all problematic situations. Conflict communication is a process of exchanging verbal and nonverbal messages in a conflict situation that starts with antecedents, moves through steps, and ends with consequence.

The process view suggests that productive conflict communication goes through five stages. The prelude to conflict sets the stage by identifying the people, place, and time of the conflict. At the next stage, a triggering event functions as a stimulus, often leading to the initiation of conflict, followed by the initiation phase, which is the response to a triggering event. The subsequent differentiation phase is the ongoing interaction pattern in which most of the conflict communication occurs. Finally, in the resolution phase conflict participants ideally come to a mutually satisfactory agreement or outcome.

The problem is that not many conflicts result in mutually satisfactory outcomes or make it through all five stages. Therefore, conflict holds a kind of dread for us—because we know we have often mishandled it in the past. This negative view of conflict may lead us to avoid improving situations and interpersonal relationships; thus, we urge our students to adopt a more positive view of conflict.

An important part of communication to others is civility, which is constituted by an attitude of respect manifested in our behavior toward others. Remember that this form of respect is not predicated on how we feel about them personally. The various ways to approach conflict are discussed in the next chapter.

EXERCISES

INTRODUCTORY EXERCISE

This exercise asks you to observe the conflicts you encounter over a week or more (see conflict records that follow). You may include recent conflicts that occurred prior to this assignment if you remember them in detail.

When recording your conflicts, keep in mind our definition of a conflict situation. Some students say they cannot do this exercise because they have no conflicts. This means that they do not understand this chapter. Remember that unexpressed conflicts do exist. For example, according to the way conflict is defined in this textbook, a conflict exists any time we would prefer to do something but give in to others and do something else, or we may simply avoid confronting others, which is a type of conflict. So, we actually may have more conflicts than we may think. In your essay, address the following topics:

a. What do you think of the authors' definition of interpersonal conflict? (For example, you might start out giving the authors' definition and explain how well it fits with the conflicts you are presently observing in your life.)
b. Would you say that it is inevitable to experience conflict with these individuals?
c. In what ways were the conflicts productive and in what ways destructive?
d. Conclude with a paragraph on how satisfied you are with the way you and the others handled these conflicts and any problems you have when attempting to manage your interpersonal conflicts.

CONFLICT RECORDS

Instructions: Make 10 copies of this record. Over the next week or so, observe your conflicts and fill out a record for each one. After you accumulate 10 or more, you should review them to see how they compare with each other.

Interpersonal Conflict Record

Date: _____ Time: _____ (AM/PM) Length of argument (time): _____

Topic/Issue of conflict:

How often has this issue come up in the past?

Rarely 1 2 3 4 5 6 7 8 9 Very Often

What actually started/triggered the conflict?

Description of the conflict: verbal argument, physical abuse, silent treatment/

stonewalling, changed subject/made light of conflict, etc.:

Emotions you experienced:

How did it end?

Intensity of disagreement:

Low 1 2 3 4 5 6 7 8 9 High

Degree of resolution:

Resolved 1 2 3 4 5 6 7 8 9 Unresolved

THINK ABOUT IT

1. In what ways do you take a non-process view of communication, relationships, or conflict? How can you change your thinking?
2. Define process and pick a successfully resolved conflict and describe it in terms of the five stages or phases of constructive, successful conflict.
3. Describe your family. With whom in your family do you have the most conflict? What can we conclude after hearing about family conflicts from a number of people?
4. Some argue that humans have an instinct for conflict. Do you think it is an inborn trait? Does it make us more or less human? If it is innate, is it a valuable asset?
5. Is it possible to view interpersonal conflicts positively? Can you give examples of positive outcomes from your own experience?
6. In problematic situations, how do you respond to the important people in your life? Do you deny that a problem exists, change the subject, or avoid the problematic person? What prompted you to take a class in conflict management?
7. Do you believe that if you have the right partner the two of you will live conflict free? Is it possible to find someone who presents no problems? Do you expect others to respect your property and privacy? What do you do when they don't?
8. What are the real-world implications of saying "conflicts need not get out of hand"? Under what conditions would you see escalating conflict as acceptable? Why?
9. Before reading this chapter, how did you feel about confronting others when a conflict arises? Did you feel positive or negative about it? How did that affect the way you handled past conflicts? Do you think you would be more successful if you felt more positively about conflict?

APPLY IT

1. Imagine representing your attitudes toward conflict visually rather than through language. What would your conflict art look like? What materials would you use? What kinds of colors would you use? What kinds of images would best represent your feelings about conflict? Write down a description of what you would do, or better yet, take some time to actually make your conflict art.
2. Ask your friends to describe their feelings about conflict. What kinds of words do they use? Do they tend to think of conflict as negative or positive?
3. Take a piece of paper and draw two columns on it. On one side, describe an unproductive conflict. On the other, describe a productive conflict. What are the differences between the two conflicts? How can you apply your learning to the next conflict you face?
4. Take a sheet of paper and draw three columns on it. Describe three recent conflict-triggering events that happened to you that involved people you know well. For example, a person at work is always borrowing your materials without permission. Compare the way you responded to each of these triggers. Did you respond the same way in each case? If so, why? If not, why?

WORK WITH IT

1. Using the process approach, identify each of the phases of the conflict communication cycle in the following narrative (prelude, triggering event, initiation, differentiation, and resolution).

"I was having dinner with my parents. When the topic of politics arose, I made a negative comment about the current U.S. president, in response to which my father called me an idiot. I felt my dad wasn't even listening to my point of view but rather looking for ways to criticize me. I told him that he wasn't listening. This in turn angered him and he told me that I'm someone impossible to carry on a conversation with. I told him that he was regressing to the way he treated me when I was a child. He then said, 'When is your attitude going to change? Are you going to ever grow up?' I told him I was trying but felt that he was too demanding in his expectations of my maturity. As usual, my mother was eating without saying anything."

2. Using the process approach, identify each of the phases of the conflict communication cycle in the following narrative (prelude, triggering event, initiation, differentiation, and resolution).

"There are four secretaries where I work. Two of us have the same title because we are designated as the company 'president's secretaries' and part of our job is to manage the workflow for the entire team of four. My coworker and I have to come to many agreements about phone schedules, work schedules, meetings dates, and lunch schedules. We both try to come up with ideas of our own to put to use for the team, and at times we have had arguments. We can sometimes come to an agreement and use one or the other's ideas.

Recently, he and I met to talk about our new lunch schedule because we went from six secretaries down to four after layoffs. We both came up with our ideas on how to work lunch schedules and phone coverage. He liked his idea and I liked mine, but this time we really didn't want to use the other person's ideas. After a few rounds of rethinking what to do, we finally made a new schedule together. We needed to work together in order to see that there were times that the other was missing and unfairness in certain areas of phone coverage. We had to do the schedule five times to get it right. It sounds a lot easier, but it's not. Everyone gets a day off phones but still has to cover phones during lunch time, even if it's her or his day off because we don't have enough people. Two people go to lunch at 12 pm and two go at 1 pm and when you aren't at lunch you cover phones. We had to swap times through the week to make sure at least two days a week two people are going to lunch at 12 and that everyone has a chance to go to lunch with a different person at least one day a week. Wow, what a project it turned out to be, but we finally got a working schedule in place, after we did it together."

DISCUSS IT

1. Read the following conflict narrative and in a group of 5–7 colleagues answer the questions following it.

"There are three of us presently living together. The conflict is with an ex-roommate who lived with two of us last semester. She moved in with a friend for the free room and board. Sometimes she decides she doesn't want to drive the 12 miles home, so she stays the night with us. This went on just about every night last week. When here, she wore my clothes every day (without asking first), slept on our couch (which gave us no place to study), ate our food, and used our personal items like shampoo and makeup. I finally had enough when she walked by me after class wearing my brand new wool coat with the sleeves rolled up and said, 'Hi! I'm wearing your coat!' I don't mind if people borrow my clothes, but I prefer that they ask first and that I get them back in the condition I lent them. Also, I'd like it if she would plan when she is spending the night so she could bring her own clothes, makeup, and food. As the saying goes, 'I love her but I can't afford to keep her!' After a week of this, I finally had it with her and really blew up! I screamed and yelled at her, and she burst into tears, packed up, and left. It felt good letting off all that pent-up anger, but I somehow wish it hadn't worked out this way."

As a way to apply what you learned from reading this chapter, after reading the above case study, participate in a class discussion by answering the questions below:

a. How would you apply the author's definition of interpersonal conflict to this narrative?

b. What do you think the friend's view of conflict is (positive or negative) and why?

c. Are conflicts like these expected among friends? Have you had similar conflicts?

d. Was there potential for violence here? Why or why not?

e. How would you apply the author's definition of conflict management and conflict communication to this narrative? Was it managed or mismanaged, and why?

f. Based only on the material presented in this chapter, how could the friends have converted this interpersonal conflict into a more productive conflict?

NOTES

1. See, for example, Linda L. Putnam, "Definitions and Approaches to Conflict and Communication," in John G. Oetzel and Stella Ting-Toomey (Eds.), *The Sage Handbook of Conflict Communication: Integrating Theory, Research, and Practice* (Thousand Oaks, CA: Sage Publications, 2006), pp. 1–32.

2. Joseph P. Forgas and Michelle Cromer, "On Being Sad and Evasive: Affective Influences on Verbal Communication Strategies in Conflict Situations," *Journal of Experimental Social Psychology* 40 (2004), 511–518.

3. Herbert W. Simons, "Persuasion in Social Conflicts: A Critique of Prevailing Conceptions and a Framework for Future Research," *Speech Monographs* 39 (1972), 227–247.

4. Fran C. Dickson, Patrick C. Hughes, Linda D. Manning, Kandi L. Walker, Tamara Bollis-Pecci, and Scott Gratson, "Conflict in Later-Life, Long-Term Marriages," *Southern Communication Journal* 67 (2002), 110–121.

5. Uriel G. Foa and Edna G. Foa, *Societal Structures of the Mind* (Springfield, IL: Thomas, 1974); Katherine D. Rettig and Margaret D. Bubolz, "Interpersonal Resource Exchanges as Indicators of Quality of Marriage," *Journal of Marriage and the Family,* 45 (1983), 497–509.

6. Glen H. Stamp, "A Qualitatively Constructed Interpersonal Communication Model: A Grounded Theory Analysis," *Human Communication Research,* 25 (1999), 543.

7. Dudley D. Cahn, *Intimates in Conflict* (Hillsdale, NJ: Erlbaum, 1990), p. 16.

8. Stephen C. Yungbluth and Stephen E. Johnson, "With Respect to Emotion in the Dominion of Rationality: Managing Conflict Through Respectful Dialogue," *Atlantic Journal of Communication,* 18, 2010, 211–226.

9. Brian H. Spitzberg and Michael L. Hecht, "A Component Model of Relational Competence," *Human Communication Research* 10 (1984), 577.

10. Youngbluth and Johnson, "With Respect to Emotion in the Dominion of Rationality," p. 213.

11. Timothy Phillips, unpublished reflection paper (MLOS 561), Azusa Pacific University, May 22, 2008.

12. Dudley D. Cahn, "Conflict Communication," in V.S. Ramachandran (Ed.), *Encyclopedia of Human Behavior,* 2nd Edition (San Diego, CA: Academic, 2012), pp. 571–579.

13. Kenneth W. Thomas, "Conflict and Conflict Management," in M. D. Dunnett (Ed.), *The Handbook of Industrial and Organizational Psychology* (Chicago, IL: Rand McNally, 1976), p. 893.

14. In Greek mythology, Procrustes was an innkeeper with only one bed. If his guest was too short for the bed, he stretched the guest to fit; if the guest was too long, he cut off the guest's legs to fit.

15. Courtney W. Miller, Michael E. Roloff, and Rachel S. Maris, "Understanding Interpersonal Conflicts that Are Difficult to Resolve: A Review of Literature and Presentation of an Integrated Model," in Christian S. Beck (Ed.), *Communication Yearbook*, Vol. 31 (Hillside, NJ: Lawrence Erlbaum, 2007), pp. 118–171.

16. Suzanne McCorkle and Janet L. Mills, "Rowboat in a Hurricane: Metaphors of Interpersonal Conflict Management," *Communication Reports* 5 (1992), 57–66.

17. Ibid., p. 63; see also Jacqueline S. Weinstock and Lynne A. Bond, "Conceptions of Conflict in Close Friendships and Ways of Knowing among Young College Women: A Developmental Framework," *Journal of Social and Personal Relationships* 17 (2000), 687–696.

18. Suzanne McCorkle and Barbara Mae Gayle, "Conflict Management Metaphors: Assessing Everyday Problem Communication," *The Social Science Journal* 40 (2003), 137–142.

19. Kenneth Cloke, *Mediating Dangerously* (San Francisco: Jossey-Bass, 2001), pp. 3–4.

20. Giovinella Gonthier, *Rude Awakenings: Overcoming the Civility Crisis in the Workplace* (Chicago, IL: Dearborn Publishing, 2002), p. 13.

21. Robert I. Sutton, *The No Asshole Rule* (New York: Warner Business Books, 2007), p. 20.

22. Steven Carter, *Civility* (New York: Harper Perennial, 1998), p. 11

23. Carter, *Civility*, p. 23.

24. P. M. Forni, *Choosing Civility: The Twenty-Five Rules of Considerate Conduct* (New York: St. Martin's Griffin, 2002).

25. Rod L. Troester and Cathy Sargent Mester, *Civility in Business and Professional Communication* (New York: Peter Lang Publishing, 2007), pp. 78–85.

Communication Options in Conflict

OBJECTIVES

At the end of this chapter, you should be able to:

- Define and give examples of intangible conflict issues.

- Distinguish among behavioral, personality, and relationship issues.

- List the steps in the dysfunctional cycles, namely avoidance/accommodation, competitive, and passive–aggressive conflict communication.

- List the steps in the functional cycles, namely compromising and collaboration conflict communication.

- Describe the differences between compromising and collaboration.

- Explain the three factors you should consider when choosing among the five conflict communication options.

- Describe the three primary considerations that should influence your choice of a conflict communication option.

- Explain the advantages of collaboration.

KEY TERMS

accommodating
avoidance
behavioral issues
collaboration
communication
    apprehension
communication
    considerations
competitive conflict
    escalation cycle

compromising
conflict communication
    options
conflict issues
confrontation avoidance/
    accommodation cycle
gunny-sacking
intangible conflict issues
passive–aggressive
    communication

personality issue
personal stress
relationship issues
relationship stress
schismogenesis
scripts
undesired repetitive pattern
    (URP)

As discussed in Chapter 1, **conflict issues** are the focal point of the conflict, the "trigger" that people point to when they are asked what the conflict was about. In this chapter, we consider a broad class of conflict issues: those that concern intangible issues. The first nine chapters of this textbook emphasize various communication principles and techniques that are most useful for resolving conflicts over intangible issues.

INTANGIBLE CONFLICT ISSUES

Unlike tangible issues (to be discussed later in Chapter 10), which involve hard, physical, or observable assets that are usually scarce resources so they cannot be shared by all parties concerned, **intangible conflict issues** center on gut feelings like love, respect, and self-esteem as well as other topics like power, cooperation, and other beneficial behaviors such as attention and caring. Conflicts over issues that are intangible, and, thus, not truly scarce resources (even though conflicting parties may think otherwise), include situations like these:

- One partner has not been paying enough attention to the other partner (ignoring her or him).
- One person offends another by using sexist, racist, stereotyped, or otherwise offensive language.
- One person's behaviors, habits, or actions annoy or upset another person.
- One partner needs time alone or time out with friends.

Note that the common feature of these examples is that they all involve non-material issues. Usually, we do not lose in situations where we are asked to spend more time with a partner. So in situations like this, being aware of the effects of one's behavior on others is not a win–lose situation. Asking one's relational partner to allow time for other friends or to leave one alone should not threaten the partner or take away from the relationship. Although these resources are often initially perceived as being scarce, this is a misperception, because conflicting parties can share them. When one is involved in situations like these, careful diagnosis of the conflict is needed. Except in cases involving major personality issues, conflicts involving resources that are not scarce are often resolved through interpersonal communication because assertiveness and cooperation can result in mutually satisfactory outcomes.

As depicted in Table 2.1, a more detailed analysis of intangible conflicts shows that they usually involve personality, relationship, or behavioral issues. **Personality issue** conflicts focus on a whole constellation of behaviors such as being dominating, introverted, selfish, or achievement oriented. "Alanna always does this." A lazy person presents problems for a highly productive, motivated individual. A shy person may make social life difficult for an outgoing, extroverted person. Behaviors are involved, but there is more going on. In cases involving distrust, power imbalance, or defensiveness, we offer advice in Chapter 6, where we discuss how to manage these aspects of one's personality. Conflicts over intractable issues involve disagreements over value-based beliefs, such as the ethics of stem-cell research; foreign policies of the U.S. president; and so on. Such disagreements need not affect a relationship, but sometimes people are so committed to their positions that they are unwilling to "live and let live." We discuss intractable issues in detail in Chapter 13.

In cases where the conflicting parties differ on a way of life or values, they need to make deep-seated changes, seek therapy, or make major life changes, which are possible, but difficult and unlikely. Often personality conflicts do not result in mutually satisfying outcomes. How many times have we heard people saying, "I believe she or he will change after we marry"? While some do, many

TABLE 2.1

Issues in Conflicts

Tangible Issues	Intangible Issues		
Concern material resources that cannot be divided up equally. "I think we need new windows this year, even if we have to borrow the money to pay for them."	Involve immaterial resources that we value, such as esteem, power, love, etc.		
	Personality Issues	**Relationship/ Normative Issues**	**Behavioral Issues**
	"I wish you weren't so selfish."	"Because we are friends, you can depend on me for help when you need it."	"Why did you buy a new stereo we cannot afford?"

don't. Hopefully, your involvement with problematic personalities that refuse to seek help or change is only temporary and you can soon move on to others who can provide a more satisfying relationship.

Conflicts over **relationship issues** involve rules, norms, and boundaries that partners have tacitly or overtly agreed on.[1] Sometimes one friend decides to change the nature of the relationship to a romantic one, but the other person is caught completely off guard and finds the other's advances offensive or inappropriate because she or he wants them to remain "just friends." At other times one is upset with a romantic partner's lack of commitment. In Chapter 9, we examine violation of relationship rules and the relationship repair process when they are violated. Still other intangible conflicts involve **behavioral issues**, which concern specific and individual actions we can observe such as the way we handle money, time, space, and so on. The issue concerns *how* we have done something or what we have done. Later, in Chapter 7, we discuss a special case of behavioral issues, often viewed as embarrassing moments, where one may lose face in a social situation.

We should not confuse behavioral issues with personality and relationship issues, which also consist of behaviors. Behavioral issues are generally specific to a situation and do not constitute a whole constellation of behaviors that make up a personality or a relationship. When Mike is late to meet Sara, she might object because she was worried about him. If Mike is always late, undependable, and lazy, she finds herself dealing more with a personality issue. If Alex wants to push Kelly into a more serious relationship before she is ready, they end up dealing with a relationship issue. However, if Melody says Jordan should be more considerate of her feelings, as part of a request she is making, she is dealing with a behavioral issue.

Intangible issues may be resolved through communication. However, not all communication behavior is productive. In the remainder of this chapter, we compare and contrast the conflict communication options available to you.

CONFLICT COMMUNICATION OPTIONS

Could you imagine having the idea that your behavior has no consequences? Probably not, because you see the effects of what you choose to do. If you believe as we do that our actions have consequences, that we do in fact have the ability to choose among alternatives, and that people should take responsibility and be accountable for their actions, then you need to know what alternatives exist in conflict situations and reflect on the different outcomes, so that you can better manage your conflicts. The following sections explore some of the implications and factors that are relevant when considering communication options in conflict situations, based on the assumption that with some instruction and practice you can modify your behavior to better adapt to your circumstances. It is our desire that you learn to recognize when each of the orientations might be preferable in a given situation and strive for collaboration whenever possible.

Communication scholars often look for patterns of interaction, both functional and dysfunctional. In Chapter 1, we defined interpersonal conflict, conflict management, and the five stages for the successful resolution of conflict. In this chapter, we provide a bird's eye view of the various choices available to people in conflicts and the choices we see as most desirable.[2] Each option leads in turn to a particular combination of outcomes (results of the conflict): lose–lose, lose–win, win–lose, or win–win. And each outcome contains within it strategies (verbal and nonverbal behaviors) people can enact to get the outcome they desire. When faced with a conflict, people find themselves caught up in a dysfunctional conflict cycle because of the communication option they have chosen.

DYSFUNCTIONAL CONFLICT CYCLES

As we think about conflicts as processes with recognizable phases, it's important to consider them in the context of the many routine activities we perform. For example, you probably arise about the same time each day, have a breakfast similar to the one from the day before, put on your clothes in the same order, and engage in family, work, or school activities as usual. Sometimes routines are nearly unconscious behaviors. Routinized events are **scripts** that we perform with little deviation each time we do them. People repeat similar behaviors each time they encounter the event. Without scripted events, it is more difficult getting through the day. Imagine having to make a new decision for each choice that confronts you! The unfortunate truth, though, is that sometimes our conflict behavior becomes scripted. When we behave automatically, without consciously contemplating our alternatives or realizing that we have options and can choose among them, we are using scripts.

Dysfunctional conflict cycles are scripted. Cronen and colleagues call a negative scripted event an **undesired repetitive pattern (URP)**,[3] or the feeling of being trapped in a set of circumstances beyond one's control. Those involved in URPs can have automatic "knee-jerk" responses to one another: Something one of them says triggers an automatic response in the other, and the episode quickly escalates out of control. It happens when those involved have a pretty good idea of what the other is going to say next, or at least they think they do. URPs recur, are unwanted, and generally occur regardless of the topic or situation. Those in the URP have a feeling that the pattern is difficult, if not impossible, to enact.

There are three common dysfunctional conflict cycles:

- the confrontation avoidance/accommodation cycle
- the competitive conflict escalation cycle
- the passive–aggressive cycle

A key point is that issues are not resolved in these dysfunctional cycles, which stem in large part from the negative attitudes people have about conflict and from the way those attitudes are confirmed by mismanagement of their conflicts.

Avoiding/Accommodating Conflict Communication as an Option

I was raised to be submissive. I obeyed my parents and other elders/authority figures; I never questioned what I was told. I believe this is because of my parents' culture and because of their ages (my mom is 41 years older than me and my dad was 53 years older than me). I am breaking free of the submissiveness (if you knew me about 6 or 7 years ago compared to now you would know I have changed), but I have A LOT more of breaking free to do. I have a hard time being vulnerable to people and admitting when I am angry. I have a tendency to accommodate people and avoid the situation and forgetting about it. I don't stay angry (and keep it in) for long. It usually passes after a little bit.

This is an example of a dysfunctional cycle called **confrontation avoidance/accommodation cycle,** which is characteristic of those people whose first impulse is

Hiding in the Sand. Bobbi Foot's conflict artwork depicts her desire to avoid conflict and pretend it doesn't exist by keeping her head in the sand. Nevertheless, she does keep an eye out for problems coming her way.

to avoid initiating conflict or to quickly give in (accommodate) when conflicts arise. Behaviors indicative of this strategy include choosing to withdraw, leaving the scene, avoiding the discussion of issues, or remaining silent.[4] It's important to distinguish this from what some might consider humility or embrace of others.[5] **Avoidance** means that people do their best not to engage in conflict. This is similar to the communication styles of shyness or reticence because such individuals allow others to interrupt them, subordinate them, or "walk all over them like a doormat." Sometimes they have poor eye contact, poor posture, and a defeated air about them. We may recognize the avoiding/accommodating communicator by her or his indecisiveness. People complain that when they confront someone who responds in this way, the other often apologizes too quickly, refuses to take the conflict seriously, becomes evasive, stonewalls (avoids or ignores them), or walks out. Such a communicator may sound sarcastic, but when confronted the person denies any wrongdoing.

We would classify as examples of avoidance statements like these:

"I don't dare say anything."
"I want to avoid creating unpleasantness for myself."
"What good would it do to speak up?"
"I went along because I didn't want to offend anybody."
"I don't want to make waves."
"It's okay for you to take advantage of me. I don't mind."
"I don't want to say anything that makes you uncomfortable, upset, or angry."
"Whatever you decide is okay with me."

Some people may prefer to avoid conflict situations because they experience what researchers call **communication apprehension,** or the level of anxiety a person feels in response to interpersonal, group, or public communication situations. Both terms describe people's failure to engage in conflict with others. For example, people who describe themselves as high in communication apprehension in interpersonal relationships prefer avoidance/accommodation as a conflict style.

Similar to avoidance, **accommodating** means smoothing over conflicts, obliging others, and not making waves. People may say what they want or feel but are quick to give in to the other. Those who simply give in try to maintain the illusion of harmony. As a result, they suppress the conflict issue in this situation because they do not want to risk ill feelings. Perhaps one is so concerned about the relationship and the other person that he or she suppresses personal needs, interests, and goals, and thus does not make waves. While the partner of the one who is avoiding or accommodating may derive considerable personal growth and satisfaction, the one who avoids or gives in is not deriving similar benefits.

When people engage in avoiding or accommodating behavior, they may find themselves in a dysfunctional conflict cycle. The steps in the confrontation avoidance/accommodation cycle are these:

1. The cycle begins with the belief that confrontation is bad and we should avoid if at all possible.
2. Because we would like to avoid confrontation, experiencing one makes us nervous.

3. Generally, something that makes us nervous is something we put off as long as possible.
4. Unfortunately, many issues worsen when left alone, so eventually we have to confront them.
5. Our anxiety causes us to handle the confrontation badly.
6. Our negative perception of conflict is confirmed, and the cycle starts again.

If we apply the five-stage model of successfully resolved conflicts from Chapter 1 (see Figure 1.1) to the conflict avoidance/accommodation cycle, we see that a conflict has a prelude stage (e.g., one or more of the participants has a past history of poorly managing conflicts), followed by a stage two triggering event (e.g., one partner forgets an important date), but instead of progressing to stage three, initiation, the offended individual does not initiate the conflict because she or he prefers to avoid or give in to most confrontations. Either the conflict isn't resolved, which hurts the relationship, or issues build up until one eventually erupts, resulting in a mismanaged conflict. This reinforces negative attitudes because the pain associated with the previous conflict discourages one or both partners from wanting to address future issues.

By not addressing their concerns, people may engage in **gunny-sacking,** or storing up hurts and anger until they explode. The strategy is harmful because one eventually explodes, and the conflict gets out of hand.

> My husband played his video games too much and this became a real problem after our daughter was born. My husband played his video game for a good six hours a day after work. Because I didn't say anything to him, he must have felt it was ok. One day our daughter got hurt playing in the house. I got home and when I saw what was going on I grabbed his video game and threw it hard right down on the floor. I really had stored up a lot of hurt and anger until I couldn't take it anymore. My husband was upset with me for wrecking his game and that made it even worse.

Gunny-sacking can destroy a relationship. All too often, people say, "If only he (or she) had said something; I never knew there was a problem." We shouldn't wait until it is too late or lose our self-control as it isn't fair to our partners or us. By getting troubles off our chests, we can monitor one another, adapt as needed, and avoid little problems turning into bigger ones. Thus, we identify this cycle as a win–lose. By giving in, the avoiders/accommodators lose the fight, but their partners win. A person who gives in time after time may eventually believe that he or she has "had enough" and leave the relationship.

Generally, people who avoid confrontation or accommodate do so because they have a bad history of dealing with conflict in general. We can add that they are *not* sufficiently concerned about solving a problem to risk confrontation or do not care enough about their relationship to confront others to improve or clarify the situation.

Probably the most widespread misassumption about conflict, and the one that has the greatest chance of creating a confrontation avoidance/accommodation cycle, is the notion that conflict is abnormal. People who experience conflict want to end it as soon as possible so that their lives can "return to normal"—harmony being the norm. The truth is that both excessive conflict and excessive harmony are abnormal. Harmony and conflict are processes in life; people move back and forth between them. Harmony in a relationship is desirable, but it does not allow growth because it does not allow change. Rummel noted that "the desire to eradicate conflict, the hope for harmony and universal cooperation, is the wish for a frozen, unchanging world with all relationships fixed in their patterns—with all in balance."[6] This misassumption affects the way people approach the study of conflict management. They are motivated to learn about conflict so they can do it better, and faster; their motivation is not to gain a true understanding of the process while they are in it.

Related to the notion that conflicts are abnormal is the idea that conflicts are pathological: They are symptoms of a system that is functioning incorrectly. Some conflicts are indeed pathological. We have all had the experience of observing people who continued a conflict long after it made any sense to do so. For the most part though, conflict is a sign that a system (an interpersonal relationship, a task group, or an organization) is functioning well and testing itself to make sure the boundaries are clear and understandable to those involved. We pursue this idea of conflict as a normal part of relationship growth when discussing systems theory in Chapter 3.

Sometimes people believe that if they ignore an issue long enough, it may go away on its own. Often when we avoid conflict or simply give in, though, the problem continues and sometimes gets worse. In any case, it eventually demands some kind of action. In fact, if you think about the definition of conflict we offered in Chapter 1, you may realize that if an issue is important enough to be thought of as an interpersonal conflict, it is unlikely that time alone can resolve it.

In Chapter 1, we noted that the bulk of conflict management advice is slanted toward open conflict or confrontation, largely because people would rather avoid it altogether or accommodate others. But we now know that not every conflict requires engagement. Some issues *are* better left alone. Either they are unimportant or taking the time to address them can create more problems in the future than simply not addressing them. Constructive avoidance requires that we effectively analyze the situation and choose an appropriate response, rather than react out of fear of confrontation.

> Previously, I saw conflict as a situation that needed to be addressed immediately. As I became more comfortable in how I handle conflict, I grew more discerning. I starting trusting my intuition, and I felt comfortable in not always addressing conflict. I learned that there are occasions when people just really have a "bad day" and instead of always addressing conflict and being too concerned about what is going on, I learned that opting to just "let it go" works for me.

As this case illustrates, some topics may not require a confrontation. In such cases, confrontation avoidance or accommodation may be an effective way to manage a conflict. In Bill's case, presented below, avoidance is appropriate for this particular issue, but not as a general habit for the couple.

Prelude.   This is a second marriage for both of us, and my wife brought three kids with her. Her oldest daughter seems really wacky to me.

Trigger. Her daughter's nutty behavior is a problem. Last week, she ran over her monthly texting limit by a large amount. However, I didn't comment on it or my wife would get real defensive and upset with me.

Using the five-stage model from Chapter 1, we see that there was no initiation stage (or differentiation or resolution), because Bill chose to avoid confronting his wife or her daughter. Thus, the issue is unresolved and may continue for years to come. Interestingly, this avoidance behavior is more typical of husbands than of wives in marital relationships.[7]

Roloff and Ifert claim that confrontation avoidance/accommodation can serve useful purposes, as long as it eliminates arguing and does no damage to the relationship.[8] Sometimes, avoidance/accommodation in the present allows for the reintroduction of a difficult topic later at a more appropriate time.[9] However, if any participant in a conflict believes that leaving an issue unresolved is problematic, then that person should confront the other person about the issue as soon as possible.[10]

Competitive Conflict Communication as an Option

Some dysfunctional conflicts or URPs often have an escalation effect, in which each exchange between those involved gets increasingly intense. **Schismogenesis** (the escalation of the cycle) occurs when the behaviors of one person intensify the behaviors of another person.[11] Schismogenesis is complementary in nature when the exchanges balance each other (e.g., as one person becomes more dominant, the other becomes more submissive; as one person shows off, the other becomes more admiring, which leads to more exhibitionism). Schismogenesis is symmetrical when each person tries to outdo the other's behavior. Seeking revenge often leads to symmetrical schismogenesis, as blood feuds escalate through retaliation after retaliation.

There are a number of behaviors that contribute to the escalation of a conflict, which can cause it to get out of hand.

- talking louder; yelling
- standing up
- getting into the other's face, space invasion
- making a threatening gesture (fist, finger)
- pushing/shoving/poking with finger/hitting
- swearing/cursing
- attacking the other's face with insults, name calling, putdowns, racial/ethnic slurs, etc.
- disconfirming the other
- making verbal threats
- pushing sensitive buttons (i.e., bringing up unrelated sensitive issues)
- increasing competition and encouraging rivalry
- damaging the other's possessions
- mocking the other
- shutting the other out or walking away
- being egged on by bystanders

A dysfunctional conflict cycle is the **competitive conflict escalation cycle,** in which the conflict bogs down in the differentiation stage when competitive interests lead to divergence rather than integration.[12] In this cycle, the participants are so concerned with winning that they are unable to respond to integrative messages, if indeed those messages even make it into the conflict interaction. Consider this example:

Prelude. I already knew where my favorite blouse was—it was in my sister's room. She seems to have this habit of borrowing whatever she wants without my permission. I went into her room and...

Trigger. Under her bed was where I found my blouse. I was so angry that I had KILL written on my forehead. I went searching for my sister throughout the house, like a lion searches for its prey. When I found her...

Initiation. I brought up all the past times that she had taken something from me without permission, and then I accused her of "stealing" my blouse.

Differentiation. She started screaming at me, and I called her a kleptomaniac. Neither of us was trying to de-escalate the conflict. She stormed off to her bedroom and I went to mine. We haven't spoken for two days. But like past occurrences, we eventually get over it. At least until something like this happens again!

Resolution. There was none because the conflict did not make it to this stage.

In this narrative, you can see how the cycle operates. One sister has unresolved grievances concerning the borrowing of clothes, and it affects the way she views the current emerging conflict. As she communicates her anger about having her clothes borrowed, she not only talks about this incident but all the past grievances as well, reflecting the belief that she is in the right and her sister is in the wrong. As it might be expected, the sister also takes a right/wrong position and yells back. One person has the sense that he or she has won (typically, the one who walks out first), and the other person feels as though he or she has lost, creating yet another grievance that colors the perception of future conflicts.

The steps in competitive conflict escalation cycle are as follows (Figure 2.1):

1. The cycle is fueled by previously unresolved grievances that color the perception of the current conflict.
2. The conflict is initiated with competitive messages that indicate "I'm right— you're wrong" stance on the part of the initiator.
3. The cycle is intensified when the other responds with a win–lose orientation.
4. The outcome is generally that one person wins, and the other loses.
5. The person who has lost has an unresolved grievance that affects future conflicts.

Because the winner takes all, the competitive communication approach tries for an "I win–You lose" outcome. We need not fall into this pattern. Conflicting parties may view an argument as the rational exchange of claims about some ideas or may view argument as competition. When we take the first view, we may argue about politicians, politics, whether a movie is worth seeing, whether being a vegetarian is reasonable, and so on. Life gives us many opportunities to express our opinions by stating claims and offering reasons for making those claims. Many of us find people who are reluctant to express an opinion to be boring. On the other

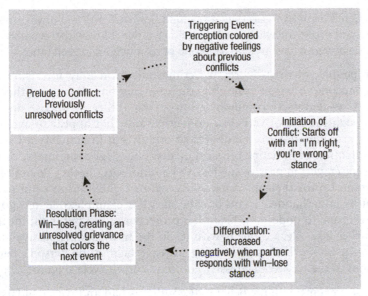

FIGURE 2.1
The Competitive Conflict Escalation Cycle.

hand, an argument becomes competitive when one person's desire to express an opinion becomes a need to win an argument without space for anyone else's opinion to receive equal consideration. A controlling partner who always has to win arguments uses conflicts to serve his or her personal needs. Competitive argument occurs when one has a desire to win no matter what harm it does to a relationship. It becomes problematic when one can't take losing or "never loses" an argument. We are turned off by either type. It is no fun engaging in conflict with them. In extreme cases, competition has the potential to adversely affect the relationship, if either person finds the competition upsetting.

Pruitt and Rubin argue that competition in a conflict creates a pattern of interaction that intensifies the competition and the desire to outdo the other. Whereas the competition may start with more friendly competition, later moves become more unfriendly, increasing the number of issues in the conflict. As issues are introduced, the conflict is less likely to focus on a particular issue and is more likely to result in an irritating universal level such as "You're always bugging me." Moreover, although the conflict may have started with one person's desire to simply win, the desire to win is distorted into a desire to win coupled with a desire to hurt the other with the loss. More parties may become involved as the conflict escalates. The most difficult part about this process, though, is the fact that each competitive move creates a difficult to reverse transformation in the conflict situation, making it more and more difficult for those in the conflict to de-escalate because they see it as "backing down."[13]

Passive–Aggressive Communication as an Option

When I didn't like the way my team at work felt about something, I would go directly to the boss and win her over to my position. That way, it would look like the boss didn't like the group's idea. Admittedly, I did get nasty sometimes when

I would tell her what was going on behind her back. She was always interested and would probe me whenever I was in her office. I know that members of my team suspected what I was up to. None of us much liked each other.

To other people, passive–aggressive communication may look similar to the avoidance/accommodation cycle, but the one enacting it knows otherwise. We define **passive–aggressive communication** as the ability to impose one's will on others through the use of verbal or nonverbal acts that appear to avoid an open conflict or accommodate to the desires of others, but in actuality are carried out with the intention of inflicting physical or psychological pain, injury, or suffering. When people engage in passive–aggressive communication, they do not openly and directly stand up for their interests, concerns, or rights, but attempt to get what they want by underhanded means or sabotage. For example, one may go behind a co-worker's back to undermine his or her project at work, but in the meantime tell the co-worker how pleased one is with it. So the individual is passive (accommodating) to the co-worker's face but is aggressive behind the person's back. These are the steps in the passive–aggressive communication cycle (Figure 2.2):

1. The cycle begins with the belief that conflict is bad and we should avoid if at all possible.
2. Because we would like to avoid conflict, experiencing one makes us nervous.
3. Generally, something that makes us nervous is something we put off as long as possible.
4. Rather than confront the person, one goes over the person's head or behind the person's back to get one's way.
5. If the person gets his/her way, one's behavior is confirmed, and the cycle starts again.

The passive–aggressive communicator is trying to win a conflict while making it appear that he or she is being cooperative. The passive–aggressive communication behavior is a type of its own with some characteristics from both the avoiding/accommodating and the competing types.

What communication behaviors do passive–aggressive communicators use? They may

- spy on others to get information to use against them.
- withhold something the other person wants, such as approval, affection, or sex, in order to get what they want.
- operate behind the scenes in an attempt to undermine others or to motivate outsiders to act against their adversaries.
- spread lies behind their adversary's back and engage in back stabbing.
- disclose some personal information to people they shouldn't after it was told to them in confidence.
- encourage attacks from outsiders.
- simply refuse to defend the adversary when others are attacking her or him.
- give away to others something of value to their adversary to make them think that they are perceived as friends when they are not.
- deny to one's face that a problem exists while at the same time fail to cooperate.

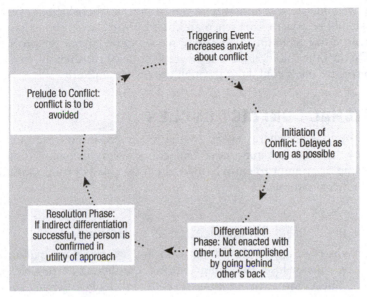

FIGURE 2.2
The Passive–Aggressive Communication Cycle

- forget promises, agreements, and appointments.
- make unkind statements and then quickly apologize.
- engage in anger displays such as playing a stereo too loudly or slamming doors while denying that there is a problem.
- do things more slowly than necessary, such as taking more time than usual to get ready.
- get confused, sarcastic, helpless, or tearful without saying why.
- get sick when they have promised to do something.
- schedule too much at once.
- evade meetings so that others are inconvenienced.

On occasion, we all get sick, make noises, fail to do a chore, or over-schedule activities, but the passive–aggressive communication behavior is done with malicious intent. Initially, passive–aggressive communication behavior is of the win–lose variety. It may result in one getting what he or she wants while "doing in" the other. However, when the victimized individual discovers the truth, he or she may end the relationship and have nothing more to do with the abuser.

Like the competitive communication style, the passive–aggressive person is oriented toward an "I win–You lose" outcome. In the passive–aggressive option, a person tries to win through subversion.

There are times when we might try to convince ourselves that passive–aggressive behavior is a good option. For example, if your neighbors are having a noisy party and it is late, you might choose to call the police rather than simply ask them to turn down the music. Or if you discover that your acquaintance has cheated on an exam, you might just report the incident anonymously rather than confronting the person with your knowledge. Such choices seem reasonable under the circumstances, but ultimately we abdicate responsibility in the situation. Choosing passive–aggressive behavior should be a last resort when all other options have been exhausted. If we have no reason to fear harm to ourselves, we should confront the problem person directly. On the other hand, if the other person appears threatening, then perhaps it is safer to register one's complaint through the proper authorities.

FUNCTIONAL CONFLICT CYCLES

Functional options are characterized by the recognition that both our needs and the needs of the other are important. One can partially recognize these needs by compromising or attempt to entirely meet them by collaborating. Both have their place in conflict situations.

Compromising Conflict Communication as an Option

A middle-of-the-road approach is **compromising**, which means making sure that no one totally wins or loses. By compromising, conflicting parties are settling for a workable solution rather than finding a totally mutually satisfying solution. The steps in the process of compromising conflict communication are as follows:

1. Determine the needs of the conflicting parties.
2. If everyone has a legitimate claim, examine the outcome to determine whether everyone can receive an equal or fair share of the claim.
3. If dividing the claim works, give everyone involved his or her share of the claim.

We are reminded of stereotyped depictions of the siblings arguing over inherited property. Compromising would involve selling the property, with the proceeds evenly distributed to each of the siblings.

There are occasions where compromising can contribute positively to the outcomes in a conflict situation, especially in situations in which all parties cannot have everything they want. However, compromising can also contribute negatively to the outcomes if all parties exchange offers and make concessions, and walk away from the conflict feeling dissatisfied with the outcome. In the case of an inheritance, some siblings may believe that they did more to help their parents, especially in their later years, and should receive more than those siblings who did not contribute as much. As a strategy favoring trade-offs involving "give and take," compromising is designed as a realistic attempt to seek an acceptable (but not necessarily preferred) solution of gains and losses for everyone involved. This strategy is not ideal because regardless of the initial objective, in the end neither party may win everything using it, as they both lose at least some of what they would have liked to achieve.

Collaborating Conflict Communication as an Option

Collaboration means using integrative behaviors and developing mutually satisfying agreements to solve the problem once and for all. Collaboration, then, has two essential ingredients. First, it consists of integrative behaviors such as cooperation, collective action, and mutual assistance. When people collaborate, they work together toward the same ends in compatible roles. We call this teamwork. To an observer, the collaborators appear to work side by side and hand in hand. This approach is in direct contrast to opposing or competing individuals who counteract, antagonize, and work against one another.

Secondly, collaboration means that the partners have in mind the same goal, which is to strive for a mutually satisfying solution to the conflict. Mutually satisfying solutions are win–win outcomes. Collaboration not only emphasizes one's own self-interests but also respects the other's interests, needs, and goals. While collaboration may involve confronting differences, it requires a focusing on the problem and includes sharing information about everyone's needs, goals, and interests.

Avoiding Early Compromising

All too often, conflicting parties are too quick to try compromising, when greater effort would produce a solution that completely satisfies both of them. For example, conflicting parties might settle for the following:

Examples of Compromising	Examples of Collaboration
Alternate driving the car or	Go together to events
Split driving 50:50 or	Take a bus/train
Split housecleaning chores or	Hire a housecleaning service
Alternate watching TV programs or	Watch one and tape the other
Alternate holidays with family or	Spend part of the holiday with each family
Divide the money between them or	Increase the amount so that both get what they want

COLLABORATION: THE PREFERRED APPROACH

Most writers favor the collaboration strategy for managing conflicts. It requires that a person believe that the concerns of the other person are as important as one's own and adopts the goal of finding mutually satisfying solutions to problems and resolutions of issues, which takes time and effort. Gross and colleagues demonstrated that people in temporary task-oriented dyads preferred a problem-solving approach and were critical of a controlling approach to the problem.[14] Research by Manning and Robertson suggests that "skilled negotiators tend to use low avoidance and high collaboration modes of conflict handling . . . [they] also show a preparedness to use accommodation and compromising, whilst avoiding competition."[15]

Collaboration is necessary for genuine and mutual understanding. With training, people can adopt a strategy of collaboration and find ways to develop mutually satisfying solutions to conflicts. The steps in the process of collaboration are these:

1. The partners clarify their points of view to one another.
2. They commit themselves to the rigid goal of developing mutually satisfying solutions, but they are flexible with respect to the means for achieving them.

3. They strive for a mutual understanding by increasing their range of perspectives, solutions, or alternatives.
4. They implement their mutual understanding by undertaking the solution as agreed on.

When conflicting parties decide to confront one another in an effort to solve a problem, they need to *clarify their points of view* to one another. Collaboration calls for understanding the other as well as one's own position and respecting one another. To do this, we need to understand that good, well-intentioned people may hold opposing views, which do not diminish their humanity in any way. This narrative reports one person's frustration with a friend who cannot accept other points of view.

> I don't know why, but often my friend and I get into huge arguments when we're driving somewhere. The other day he was talking about how repressed the U.S. is compared to Europe, and how we shouldn't have so many laws restricting our "natural inclinations." I replied that laws are often there to protect others from what we'd like to do, and he got really loud and said no reasonable person could see it any other way than his. This is what he usually says when he's tired of trying to make his point and doesn't want to listen to what I have to say, so I dropped it.

When people collaborate, they are *rigid in terms of the goal of developing mutually satisfying solutions, but they are flexible with respect to the means for achieving them.* They are committed to a win–win outcome and are able to devise alternative ways to achieve it. Thus, they accept only high personal gains for themselves and their partners and tend to pursue many alternative paths in an effort to achieve a mutually satisfying outcome.

Resolving differences in opinion or points of view, in a manner that is mutually advantageous to everyone involved, the partners strive for a *mutual understanding* by increasing their range of perspectives, solutions, or alternatives. Understanding the perspective of another person does not necessarily mean agreeing. It means only that you make an effort to see the problem as the other defines it, without deciding on the validity of the other person's perspective.

While the discovery of a mutual understanding is often a challenging task, all the time and effort spent on its pursuit is wasted if appropriate measures are not taken to put the solution into effect. To *implement a mutual understanding* means to undertake the solution as agreed on. Quite often, this requires a trial period. Sometimes minor adjustments are needed to make matters work out as intended.

In sum, Daniels and Walker describe the key aspects of collaboration as follows:[16]

1. Collaboration is less competitive.
2. It features mutual learning and fact finding.
3. It allows for exploration of differences in underlying values.
4. It resembles principled negotiation, focusing on interests rather than positions.
5. It allocates the responsibility for implementation across many parties.
6. Its conclusions are generated by participants through an interactive, iterative, and reflexive process.

7. It is often an ongoing process.
8. It has the potential to build individual and community capacity in such arenas as conflict management, leadership, decision making, and communication.

To illustrate the collaborative strategy in a real conflict situation, the following extended example is offered.

CASE STUDY

Oganna and Adrian were married soon after graduation four years ago and each has worked ever since. This year they received a $20,000 inheritance (left to both of them). Now Oganna wants to take a year off from work and use the inheritance to pay for a year of her schooling. However, Adrian is against her taking a year off from work and favors banking the inheritance instead.

After giving the matter considerable thought and preparing for a possible conflict situation, Oganna decides to discuss her idea with Adrian, so she suggests that they talk about it after supper. She begins the confrontation by telling Adrian that she is unhappy with her present job and realizes that he would like her to continue working, but she would like to quit her job. She then listens to Adrian, who says that he realizes that she doesn't like her job, he is concerned about their future finances, and would prefer they both continue to work while they invest the inheritance, so that it would grow into a sizable nest egg.

Oganna states that she wants to take a year off from work to attend a local university to acquire a master's degree in Business Administration, which she says may advance her career in the long run. Adrian, who likes his job, is adamantly opposed to her taking a leave of absence because after four years of their paying off debts for an automobile and furniture for their apartment, he says that he would like to put the money in a bank to earn interest.

Both Oganna and Adrian indicate that they must resolve these differences of opinion because the issues are creating a strain on their marriage. They also say that a completely satisfactory understanding must not break up their marriage, but at the same time, must not result in either one having to give up ambitions, needs, and goals. In other words, they are rigid in their goals of achieving a mutually satisfying solution but flexible in how they might go about achieving it. At this point in the confrontation, they also shift from sticking to their positions or wants (I want to quit and go to school; I want you to make money) to a discussion of their interests or needs. While Oganna says she wants to have a job that is more satisfying, Adrian points out his need for future financial security. So, they agree that a solution must enable Oganna to advance in her career; and yet it must provide greater financial security for Adrian.

While Adrian and Oganna appear rigid with respect to goals, they report that they are willing to entertain a wide variety of means for attaining them. Here they begin to brainstorm a variety of options. Oganna could earn her degree on a full-time basis, on a part-time status, or not return to college at all and do something else instead. Adrian, meanwhile, could bank all $20,000 or $10,000 or $5,000 or none at all. At this point, however, a premature understanding that consisted solely of

Oganna agreeing to return to school on a part-time basis and Adrian banking $10,000 would be an example of compromising with both persons receiving less than they desire. They agreed that they would rather find a solution that is more satisfying to them both.

In addition to increasing the range of perspectives, the partners would benefit by trying to discover new perspectives, solutions, or alternatives that are related to the matter at hand, such as time, money, interests, security, and status or other factors that were not considered at first. Perhaps, in the case of Oganna and Adrian, they may introduce a time dimension in at least two ways. Oganna could attempt to complete the degree in one year or spread it out over two years or more. Adrian could invest the entire inheritance for an indefinite period or invest all of it now and some of it later. Moreover, because Oganna expressed a desire to do something different, she could consider not doing some aspect of her work that is especially bothersome to her. Perhaps a vacation or a change in her job situation such as a different task, new co-workers, or a different department (or even a new job) would satisfy her need for a change.

An idea occurs to Oganna that might help Adrian view the situation in a different light. She decides to go so far as to suggest that she could not remain in a marriage where a husband was not more interested in her happiness, needs, and interests. In fact, she states that obtaining a master's degree may make her more valuable to her employer and better guarantee her tenure and advancement in the long run. However, she adds that Adrian needs to realize that neither Oganna's desire for time off nor Adrian's desire for financial security is achieved in the event of a marital breakdown, especially if it means

divorce. The threat of severe financial loss at this time which neither party wants may motivate the couple to see the value of the newly discovered alternatives to the problem, to realize that there may be a way to reach mutual understanding, and to make an even greater effort to achieve it.

It is hoped that Oganna and Adrian use interpersonal communication skills that are collaborative. Both are analytic, conciliatory, and problem solving in focus, attempt to clarify the issues and facilitate mutual resolution of the problem, describe behavior, disclose feelings, ask for disclosure from the other person, ask for criticism from the other person, qualify the nature of the problem, support the disclosures or observations the other person has made, and accept responsibility for each one's part in the conflict. Using the acceptable elements of the possible alternative opinions, points of view, and solutions, the partners work together to find a choice that meets the needs of everyone involved.

In the case of Oganna and Adrian, an example of an understanding that is mutually advantageous is as follows. As soon as possible, they could take a three-week camping trip that they both want. Oganna could return to her job after the vacation and enroll part-time at the university for one year at which time she could request a leave of absence to attend to her studies full time, and then she could earn any remaining credits on a part-time basis. In the meantime, Adrian could bank most of the inheritance to draw interest for one year at which time Oganna could spend half of the inheritance on her education and the remainder could stay in the bank indefinitely. This solution has the potential of completely satisfying both Oganna and Adrian because while on a vacation with Adrian, Oganna is "getting away for a while" and on return she commences work on her degree and looks forward to a semester of full-time graduate student status next year, while Adrian banks most of the money for one year and half after that.

Although other agreements are possible, this is an example of how the collaborative strategy may actually enhance a relationship. During the confrontation and development of a mutually satisfying outcome, Oganna and Adrian have a greater understanding of each other's needs, desires, and beliefs. Each may believe that his or her position has a valuable contribution to make in the long run to their relationship, and that each needs to take the other's ideas into account in any decision the couple reaches. They may take pride in the fact that they asserted themselves and employed the collaboration strategy. As a follow-up, the partners need to reinforce these attitudes during the next few months to guarantee the successful implementation of the mutual understanding.

When you don't have the time or effort or find collaboration to be a problem, you can consider using an alternative strategy. However, as a general rule, we would like to see you adopt the collaboration strategy more often because it contributes less toward long-term personal and relationship stress and most toward personal and relationship growth and satisfaction.

Low Personal and Relationship Stress

In general, stress "comes from demands and pressures of the recent past and antici-pated demands and pressures of the near future."[17] Stress can be personal or rela-tional in nature, or a combination of both.

Personal stress occurs within a person and refers to wear and tear on one emo-tionally and physically. While a little stress is positive and pleasurable as when one experiences an uplift associated with falling in love, seeing a great performance, or watching an exciting athletic event, other stressors such as strong feelings of anxiety, frustration, and anger that are associated with life crises such as a death of a family member, a divorce, a marriage, a new job, or a change in one's location may con-tribute to ulcers, heart disease, hypertension, migraines, and even suicide. Loneliness is also stress producing. Psychologists have long argued that stress improves perfor-mance, but only up to a point, at which efficiency drops off sharply. We have more to say about personal stress in Chapter 8 on managing anger and stress.

Relationship stress occurs outside the individual and refers to wear and tear on a relationship. Whereas personal stress goes on within the individual, relationship stress goes on between two or more persons. In long-term relationships, negotiat-ing partner roles (such as who housecleans, who does the dishes, and who gets up at night for a crying baby) is frequently mentioned as a relationship stress pro-ducer. Because of the omnipresence of interpersonal conflict, a little relationship stress is normal and unavoidable, but in the extreme, relationship stress becomes synonymous with relationship dissatisfaction and deterioration, which eventually may result in social disengagement such as breaking up, divorcing, or losing a job. Frequent reliance on collaboration to manage conflicts is the most advantageous alternative because it alone reduces one's emotional and physical stress as well as the stress on the relationship.

High Personal and Relationship Growth and Satisfaction

By failing to include one's self interests, both avoidance and accommodation create conditions characterized by low feelings of self-worth and relationship satisfaction, and no opportunities for personal or relationship growth. By considering one's self-interests (but at the expense of others), competition creates conditions one may describe as high in personal growth, feelings of self-worth, and relationship satisfaction for the dominant party but low in personal and relationship growth for the other party to the conflict. Thus, it may happen that people who frequently use accommodation and those who tend to choose to compete are attracted to each other initially, but find that the stress and strain on the relationship as they grow apart often leads to relationship dissatisfaction for the one who gives in and eventual disengagement. By gaining some and losing some of one's interests, needs, and goals, compromising as a strategy contributes to moderate feelings of self-worth and relationship satisfaction, and moderate personal and relationship growth. Finally, *by allowing for self-interests, encouraging effective listening, and promoting an integrative approach to problem solving, collaboration, if enacted often enough, is the only strategy that contributes to high feelings of self-worth and relationship satisfaction for both partners and maximum personal and relationship growth.* When successfully utilized as a mode for resolving interpersonal conflict aimed at developing an integrated consensus through argumentation and perspective-taking, collaboration not only ends conflict but modifies the perspective of the individuals involved to a consensus framework that respects individual differences.

COMMUNICATION CONSIDERATIONS: CHOOSING THE APPROPRIATE COMMUNICATION OPTION

The idea we would like to foster is that flexibility, openness to alternatives, and adaptability are important interpersonal communication skills. However, we also favor a tendency toward the collaborative conflict strategy, which is proactive in nature and incorporates cooperative, integrative, and assertive behavior.

Although many advocates of nonviolence claim that physical aggression is never an appropriate response, it would seem that it is justified in a few specific cases (involving self-defense). However, we are unable to imagine a situation in which verbal aggression is appropriate. A passive-aggressive response is only appropriate when one fears a violent retaliation. Effective communicators are assertive when it is appropriate and nonassertive when the situation justifies it. When is it appropriate for us to engage in assertive or nonassertive communication behavior? Three **communication considerations** are the occasion, the other person, and your needs.

The Occasion (Including Time and Location)

In many respects, an occasion is like a situation. Recall from Chapter 1 that we said a "situation" exists when people play out particular roles in a given context that consists of a familiar setting at a particular time. You can think of a situation as being like a type of book—novel, nonfiction, collection of short stories, mystery, and so on. Just as there are many mysteries, novels, and nonfiction books, an occasion would be the equivalent of a particular book—this mystery, this romance, this thriller, where the time and place create unique expectations that guide our behavior. Like situations, occasions tend to recur—one mystery may seem similar to another. But just as different books call for different readings, so do different occasions call for different behavior.

The Other Person

Although the people involved and affected by your behavior are part of any situation, we want to call special attention to these elements because they must be taken into account in a conflict. We treat our parents, grandparents, significant others, siblings, children, employers, employees, and friends differently simply because of who they are and what they mean to us. Because they are important to us we must focus on the needs of the other person. The realization that people are motivated by their own self-interests means that we have to take them into consideration if we are to gain agreement on solutions to problems and resolution of conflicts.

Your Needs

You are an important element in every conflict situation. You should consider your own needs and how you have prioritized them. Not all our needs constitute a life or death situation. We must satisfy at least some of our needs if we want to live a life worth living, but some needs are better put off at least temporarily or reduced to a less prominent position.

Consider collaborative conflict communication:

- when a conflict is over something that is important to you
- if you "hate yourself" later for not letting your feelings, ideas, or opinions be known
- when a long-term relationship between you and the other person is important
- when the other person can handle your assertiveness without responding with aggression or passive–aggression
- when the other person is cooperative
- when a win–win solution to a problem is possible

Consider avoiding/accommodating conflict communication:

- when you aren't sure of your facts or confident of your idea
- when the emotional hurt offsets any benefits that might result
- when something has occurred that is more important to the others than it is to you
- when a long-term relationship between you and the other person is important

Consider competing conflict communication:

- when you have exhausted the other options, and you are in a physically threatening situation in which you must defend yourself to avoid being seriously injured or killed. Even then, use the minimum force necessary to overcome the threat. Let the police and the courts take the matter further.

- when a physically threatening situation exists for others and you choose to intervene on their behalf.

Consider passive–aggressive conflict communication:

- when you are in a physically threatening situation. You may have to go behind the other person's back and secretly report him or her in order to avoid direct confrontation where the other might seriously harm you.

MANAGE IT

This chapter identified the choices we can make in conflict situations. Many people do not realize that they have options and can freely choose among them, with differing results. The way we view our relationship with the other person, our past successes and failures in enacting conflict with the other, how we identify an issue, how we assign blame, and how we voice our complaint all affect our pattern of conflict communication. Potentially productive conflict behavior exists somewhere in the maze of options. In each stage of conflict communication we can choose to spin off into the avoidance/accommodation, competitive, or passive–aggressive conflict communication cycles.

Often people get caught up in destructive cycles that do not allow their conflict to progress to some satisfactory outcome. The conflict avoidance/accommodation cycle is characteristic of a relationship between people whose first impulse is to avoid initiating conflict or to quickly withdraw or give in when conflicts arise. They serve as examples of how unsuccessful conflicts become mired down early on and do not make it to the initiation stage. Generally discouraged because we run the risk of ignoring important issues until they overwhelm us, this cycle may be useful when the emotional hurts offset any benefits that might result.

The competitive conflict escalation cycle has a prelude stage (e.g., one or more of the participants has a past history of poorly managing conflicts) followed by a stage two triggering event (e.g., one partner forgets an important date) and moves through stage three initiation, but gets locked into stage four differentiation, instead of progressing to the final stage five resolution. We again discourage the use of this form of conflict communication because of its win–loss outcome, except when you have exhausted the other options, and find that escalating the conflict is the only way to get the other person to take it seriously.

The passive–aggressive conflict communication cycle starts out like the conflict avoidance/accommodation cycle but then one resorts to sabotage and going behind the other's back to resolve the conflict. As for the other dysfunctional cycles, we discourage you from using this one except when you are in a physically threatening situation. You may have to go behind the other person's back and secretly report him or her in order to avoid direct confrontation where the other might seriously harm you physically.

When we see conflict as a normal part of relationships and when we listen to others and assert ourselves, we are less likely to become mired down in a destructive conflict cycle. Sometimes we choose to split the difference by compromising with the other person. In important conflicts, though, our best option is to choose collaboration because it is the only one that encourages personal and relationship growth without producing personal and relationship stress.

How does one determine when to choose one option over another? Three factors everyone should consider when choosing among the four conflict communication options are the occasion/time/location, the other person, and one's own needs. The communication considerations described in this chapter can help us conflict communication option is best.

In addition to learning about the communication options that exist in conflict situations, we need to know relevant theories that can help us better understand interpersonal conflict. We present these theories in the next chapter.

EXERCISES

THINK ABOUT IT

1. How have your conflicts typically played themselves out? Do you sense that there are patterns in your conflicts?
2. Think of a time when you felt that you handled a conflict well. What did you do that seemed competent to you? How do those behaviors contrast with a time when you felt you handled a conflict poorly?
3. Have you ever experienced a conflict where you and the other person disagreed on the trigger event? How were you able to resolve the conflict?
4. What has happened in the past when you or the other person have avoided or accommodated in the conflict? Were you satisfied with the outcomes? What would you have done differently?
5. What has happened in the past when you and the other person have competed against each other in the conflict? Were you satisfied with the outcomes? What would you have done differently?
6. What has happened in the past when you or the other person were passive–aggressive in the conflict? Were you satisfied with the outcomes? What would you have done differently?
7. Based on your experiences with conflict, what would you say are your assumptions about conflict? How do they affect the way you make choices when you are faced with a problematic situation?

APPLY IT

1. Write out a description of a recent conflict that you experienced or observed. What would have happened if there were more or less individuals involved as parties to the conflict? How would the addition or subtraction of interested third parties or bystanders affect the conflict outcome? What effect would changing the time or place have had on the conflict?
2. Compare two conflicts in which avoiding worked in different ways—one conflict you avoided eventually resolved itself, and another you avoided that ended up getting worse because you put off confronting it.
3. Compare two conflicts, one that escalated and another that did not. What was the difference between the two? What were the outcomes?
4. Write out a description of a conflict you recently experienced or observed. If you had attempted the collaborative style, what actions would you have taken at each step of the conflict?

5. Take a piece of paper and write a description of a conflict you recently experienced or observed. Below your description, draw three columns and label them the occasion, the other person, and my needs. How does each aspect of the conflict impact the way you should react to the conflict you've described?

WORK WITH IT

Answer the questions following the description of the conflict.

A and B married this past year, and A wants to spend the holidays with his/her side of the family. B wants them to go to his/her parents for the holidays. Neither wants to visit his/her relatives alone.

a. What phases of collaboration should they employ?
b. What additional techniques could they use?
c. What might their final agreement look like if it attempts to satisfy both of their needs or interests?

DISCUSS IT

1. Read the following conflict narrative and the instructions that follow it.

"I live on my own and only visit my parents every year or two for a holiday. Recently, we were all sitting down to Mom's holiday dinner when the topic of politics arose. I made a negative comment about the current U.S. president, in response to which my father called me an idiot. I felt he wasn't even listening to my point of view, but rather looking for ways to criticize me like he always did when I lived at home. I told him that he wasn't listening. This, in turn, angered him, and he told me that it is impossible to carry on a conversation with me. I told him that he was regressing to the way he treated me when I was growing up. He then said, 'When is your attitude going to change? Are you ever going to grow up?' I told him I was trying but felt that he was too demanding in his expectations of my maturity. As usual, my mother was eating without saying anything."

As a way to apply the concepts that you have learned from reading Chapter 2, read the above case study and participate in a class discussion by posting an answer to one of the questions below.

a. What type of dysfunctional conflict cycle is illustrated by this case study? Explain your response.
b. What do you think happens later in this situation? What makes you think so?
You can participate in one or more discussions of the above questions.

2. Read the following conflict narrative and the instructions that follow it.

"I was trying to teach a class when a student came in to remove some audiovisual equipment. He didn't explain why he was there. I had to ask him. I then asked him if it could wait until the end of the class. He said, 'No.' I said, 'Okay,' rather reluctantly. He left, and then came back about five minutes later. I said nothing. When he came back the third time (all the while making noise and making it difficult for me to continue the class discussion), I finally said, 'You are disturbing my class, and I must ask you to stop coming in. This really bothers me.' He replied, I'm having a bad day.' One of my students said after class that I 'went nuclear' on the student!"

As a way to apply the concepts you learned from Chapter 2, participate in a class discussion by posting an answer to one of the questions below.

a. Which of the five conflict strategies are illustrated in this narrative?
b. What conflict communication option is preferable in the above narrative, as presented? Which is most likely? Which is the worst, and why?

c. Change some part of the case study to use a different conflict communication option, and explain the likely outcome of the conflict situation.

You can participate in one or more discussions of the above questions.

NOTES

1. Dudley Cahn, "Friendship, Conflict and Dissolution," in Harry Reis and Susan K. Sprecher (Eds.), *Encyclopedia of Human Relationships* (Thousand Oaks, CA: Sage, 2009).

2. We also want to emphasize that this is not intended as an exercise in labeling people as personality types such as nonassertive or aggressive. Nor is this a psychological approach that digs for deep emotional problems that account for personality disorders. Our goal is to identify certain conflict communication behaviors that are viewed as good or bad habits or behaviors learned from good or poor models and apply them in problematic situations.

3. Vernon E. Cronen, W. Barnett Pearce, and Lonna M. Snavely, "A Theory of Rule-Structure and Types of Episodes and a Study of Perceived Enmeshment in Undesired Repetitive Pattern ('URPs')," in Dan Nimmo (Ed.), *Communication Yearbook 3* (New Brunswick, NJ: Transaction Books, 1979), pp. 225–240.

4. An interesting counterpoint to this idea is found in Julia Richardson, "Avoidance as an Active Mode of Conflict Resolution," *Team Performance Management* 1 (1995), 19–23, who argues that the lack of confrontation between management and teams can actually be an active strategy on the part of a less powerful team to accomplish their goals more covertly.

5. See, for example, Miroslav Volf, *Exclusion and Embrace* (Nashville, TN: Abingdon Press, 1996).

6. Rudolph J. Rummel, *Understanding Conflict and War: The Conflict Helix,* Vol. 2 (Beverly Hills, CA: Sage Publications, 1976); "A Catastrophe Theory Model of the Conflict Helix, with Tests," *Behavioral Science* 32 (1987), 238.

7. Ann Buysse, Armand DeClercq, Lesley Verhhofstadt, Else Heene, Herbert Roeyers, and Paulette Van Oost, "Dealing with Relational Conflict: A Picture in Milliseconds," *Journal of Social and Personal Relationships* 17 (2000), 574–597.

8. Michael E. Roloff and Danette E. Ifert, "Conflict Management through Avoidance: Withholding Complaints, Suppressing Arguments, and Declaring Topics Taboo," in Sandra Petronio (Ed.), *Balancing the Secrets of Private Disclosures* (Mahwah, NJ: Lawrence Erlbaum Associates, Publishers, 2000), pp. 151–163; Denise Haunani Solomon, Leanne K. Knobloch, and Mary Anne Fitzpatrick, "Relational Power, Marital Schema, and Decisions to Withhold Complaints: An Investigation of the Chilling Effect on Confrontation in Marriage," *Communication Studies* 55 (2004), 146–171.

9. Michael E. Roloff and Danette Ifert Johnson, "Reintroducing Taboo Topics: Antecedents and Consequences of Putting Topics Back on the Table," *Communication Studies* 52 (2001), 37–50.

10. Ibid., pp. 57–58.

11. Gregory Bateson, *Naven,* 2nd Edition (Stanford, CA: Stanford University Press, 1958).

12. Several authors have noted that once a conflict is initiated, the greatest pressures are toward escalation rather than toward containment and management. See, for example, Morton Deutsch, "Conflicts: Productive or Destructive?" *Journal of Social Issues*

25 (1969), 7–41; Louis Kriegsberg, *The Sociology of Social Conflicts* (Englewood Cliffs, NJ: Prentice Hall, 1973); Dean G. Pruitt and Jeffrey Z. Rubin, *Social Conflict: Escalation, Stalemate, and Settlement* (New York: Random House, 1986); R. D. Nye, *Conflict among Humans* (New York: Spring Publishing, 1973).

13. Pruitt and Rubin, pp. 7–8.

14. Michael A. Gross, Laura Guerrero, and Jess K. Alberts, "Perceptions of Conflict Strategies and Communication Competence in Task-Oriented Dyads," *Journal of Applied Communication Research* 32 (2004), 249–270.

15. Tony Manning and Bob Robertson, "Influencing, Negotiating Skills and Conflict Handling: Some Additional Research and Reflections," *Industrial and Commercial Training* 36 (2004), 108.

16. Steven E. Daniels and Greg B. Walker, *Working through Environmental Conflict: The Collaborative Learning Approach* (Westport, CT: Praeger, 2001), p. 124.

17. American Psychological Association, "The Different Kinds of Stress," retrieved October 26, 2005, from http://apahelpcenter.org/articles/article.php?id=21.

Managing Conflict from a Theoretical Perspective

OBJECTIVES

At the end of this chapter, you should be able to:

- Explain the key concepts and assumptions that identify factors that play an important role in interpersonal conflict according to each theory.

- Explain key principles that describe how conflicts develop according to each theory.

- Identify the type of conflict explained by each theory.

- Demonstrate how one should manage or resolve interpersonal conflicts according to each theory.

KEY TERMS

anxiety
attribution theory
attribution error
blaming
comparison level (CL)
comparison level for
    alternatives (CL$_{alt}$)
displacement
displaced conflict

external attribution
false conflict
frustration
holistic
homeostasis
internal attribution
misplaced conflict
overblown conflict
psychodynamic theory

repression
skill
social exchange theory
system
systems theory
theory
uncertainty

How do you explain that on some days, a triggering event doesn't provoke any conflict? Or, suppose the presumed conflict turned out to be not a conflict at all, how would you explain that? This is why theories are important to us.

In everyday terms, a theory means speculation as in a hunch or guess. Not so in social science, where the word theory refers to a comprehensive explanation of how or why, based on an identification of causes and their effects, supported by facts (data) gathered over time. For our purposes, we define **theory** as a means of explaining how something works. Theories also enable scientists to make predictions about as yet unobserved events. So, if we can explain how something works, we should also be able to prevent that something from happening. Therefore, theories lead to important insights, followed by social experiments, as researchers attempt to prove them.

Theories also enable us to carry skills from one situation to another and to apply them appropriately within situations. As you learned earlier, a **skill** is a communication behavior that you have learned and can apply when it is called for. You have learned to carry that skill into different kinds of conflict communication situations. But you can have a skill without understanding why it works. You may have the skill of nodding your head and looking at the other person when he or she is speaking, but perhaps you would need to study theories to better understand why such skills work as they do.

Some prefer to identify theory as thinking about a conflict, and practicing theory as doing conflict. You want to behave effectively and constructively—that is, practice good conflict management. But how should you think about conflict? Theory helps us think about conflict in ways that improve our ability to manage it effectively.

In this chapter, we apply to conflict situations various theories that social psychologists and communication researchers created to explain why people in conflict behave the way they do. Each theory adds an additional set of factors to explain more precisely the causes and effects of interpersonal conflict. A more encompassing view of the conflict situation appreciates the role played by factors beyond the conflicting parties caught up in the moment. The parties bring baggage to the conflict, and external factors impinge on the conflicting parties, who may also be uncertain as to why their partners behave as they do. Theories may help us to better understand the role played by these factors that affect the conflicting parties.

While the theories in this chapter pertain to a broad range of everyday conflicts, in later chapters we add other theories that apply to specific types of conflicts. For this chapter, though, we concentrate on those theories that best explain everyday conflicts.

INTRAPERSONAL THEORIES OF CONFLICT

When looking for the cause of a conflict, it is important to consider expanding our awareness of the problematic situation to include the feelings, beliefs, and attitudes of those who engage in the conflict. Psychodynamic, attribution, and uncertainty conflict theories, generated by researchers in psychology, social psychology, and communication, have focused on individual psychological processes, or what individuals bring to the interpersonal conflict situation and how that impacts the conflict process. The key concept that unifies these theories is their assumption that the way people act in conflict situations is due, in large part, to their individual dispositions or ways of thinking. The theories remind us that the individuals, themselves, in a conflict play a large part in determining the direction that the conflict takes. As we learned in Chapter 1, the prelude to a conflict includes the parties themselves and what they believe, feel, want, and how they view the world.

Psychodynamic Theory

Do you ever wonder why another person won't talk about an issue, or wants to drop it after you bring it up, or engages in a conflict over some issue that is not the real problem? Have you experienced the brunt of someone's anger when you believe you didn't deserve it? Have you wondered why other people exploded over a minor issue, blowing the conflict all out of proportion? To answer these questions, we need to turn to one of the most historically significant psychological theories.

Based on the work of Sigmund Freud and his followers, **psychodynamic theory** says that people experience conflict because of the tension arising from their intrapersonal (internal, psychological, emotional, and mental) states.

From a Freudian perspective, three aspects of the human mind affect the way in which frustration, or more generally, psychic energy, is released. The principal component of the mind is the id, the unconscious aspect that "contains everything that is inherited, present at birth, or fixed in the constitution."[1] The id contains the libido, the source of instinctual energy, which demands discharge though various channels. The id operates on the "pleasure principle," a tension-reduction process in which tension from a bodily need is translated into a psychological wish in order to reduce the tension. The id seeks pleasure and avoids pain; it seeks only to satisfy its needs without regard for the cost of doing so.

Opposing the id is what Freud called the superego, containing both the ego ideal and the conscience. The ego ideal is an internalized idea of what a person would like to be. The conscience contains morals and other judgments concerning correct and incorrect behaviors. As a parent does, it tries to punish a person for "immoral" behavior and reward a person for "moral" behavior through feelings like guilt or pride.

Mediating between the id and the superego is the ego, governed by the "reality principle," which attempts to "postpone the discharge of energy until the actual object that will satisfy the need has been discovered or produced."[2] The ego, in mediating between the id and the superego, plays a significant role in conflict situations—it tries to reconcile the desires of the id ("I want it all, and I want it right now") with the constraints of the superego ("Nice people don't throw temper tantrums"). The ego must constrain aggressive impulses and control the level of anxiety conflict creates.

Anxiety is a tension that occurs when people perceive danger in a situation. People can become anxious when they think that someone may interfere with their goals, when they fear their own impulses in a situation, or when they disapprove of their own actions. Psychodynamic theory explains how individuals respond to conflict situations, particularly in light of their anxieties.

Anxiety, in turn, may lead us to suppressed issues. **Repression** is another defense mechanism that occurs when we try not to think about our situation. Scarlett O'Hara vocalized this process in *Gone with the Wind* when she would say, "I won't think about that today. I'll think about that tomorrow." Repression can explain **misplaced conflicts**, which occur when people argue about issues other than the ones at the heart of the conflict. We engage in conflict with the right person, but the conflict occurs over the wrong issue. For example, you may be upset by the way your boss treats you. Perhaps your boss is demeaning, withholds appropriate praise, or treats you differently than other employees. That's not an

In her artwork, Ania Mulka was dealing with a situation where she felt that she was hearing too much information about a negative situation that she could not control.

easy topic to talk about with someone in authority over you. So you may engage in conflict over your work schedule, the pace of the work, or benefits, because these issues are easier to talk about.

The following story, told by a wife about her marriage, is an example of misplaced conflict with serious implications for the relationship:

> We've been seeing a marriage counselor for several weeks now, and we deal with all sorts of issues like my husband's problem with my playing the Vampire War game on the computer (even though I work full-time) and my concern that he doesn't put enough time and energy into his business. But I get the impression that we're just putting out little brush fires when the forest is burning down. The heat of the real conflict is so intense we keep going around it. I think the real problem is that he treats me more coldly and cruelly than he would treat a stranger. He never touches me or shows me any kind of affection.

In the preceding example, the husband's concern over the computer game and the wife's concern about the effort put into the business are legitimate issues. The suppressed issues, however, are masked by these "safer" issues. The wife uses the computer game as a weapon against a husband who emotionally abuses her:

It bothers him that she is so involved in a time-consuming computer game, so she has less time to spend with him. It helps that she works outside the home. She can legitimately say that there is not enough time to do everything. She does not really want to deal with his lack of respect, so talking about his lack of business efforts is a safer issue. Because they keep dealing with the small, visible conflicts instead of looking at the pattern of their conflict behavior, the small conflicts continue to multiply until one or the other leaves or until they learn how to deal with the conflicts. Deutsch argued that manifest or overt conflict is difficult, if not impossible, to resolve unless the underlying conflict has been dealt with in some way or unless the overt conflict is separated from the underlying conflict and treated in isolation.[3]

Since misplaced conflicts revolve around "safe" rather than the "real" issues, they are often difficult to diagnose. A conflict issue that comes up repeatedly may mask a deeper issue between those involved. However, you need to understand that, where conflicts are managed rather than resolved, the same issues may arise frequently with no other underlying meaning. For example, if you are a person of tidy habits rooming with a messy person, the issue of cleanliness is likely to arise often, but it probably does not mask a deeper issue other than the fact that you have different habits. Misplaced conflicts concern relational issues such as expectations for behavior, respect, abuse and threats, and so on. Because these issues are central to the way people relate to one another, people often find it easier to focus on visible issues, such as money or work habits, where any difference in action is observable.

Freud theorized that the ego experiences frustration when trying to constrain aggressive impulses. **Frustration** results from the internal battle between the id and the superego that often erupts into conflict with others. Frustration can originate from many sources, for example, tension, stress, insecurity, anxiety, hostility, sexual urges, or depression.

Frustration can lead to an **overblown conflict**, which occurs when people get carried away and exaggerate a conflict, generally using a relatively unimportant issue as a focal point. The parties seem to invest far more emotion and energy than the situation deserves. These conflicts are discussed in detail in Chapter 8 on the topic of stress. For example, if you have been trying to finish an important project at work and a smaller one has slipped past you, a request to complete the smaller project, particularly from a peer or a subordinate, may result in you blowing up rather than simply saying you'll get to it as soon as you can. This narrative illustrates an overblown conflict.

> I had been having a really bad day. I felt overburdened by homework and job responsibilities, and to top it off, I had a huge paper I was working on that was due in two days, which I had barely even started. Mary chose this particular time to enter the room and discuss the positioning of our bathroom towels on the rack. She seemed frustrated that the four of us, who were sharing the bathroom, had taken to haphazardly pushing and stuffing our towels through the narrow metal rods, thus having them all scrunched up together, which did not allow them to dry properly. I felt that this was such an inane discussion, I suddenly erupted and really told her off.

Although the towels represent a conflict issue the roommates should discuss rationally at some point, in this overblown conflict they have served the person trying to study as a way to release her frustration about her lack of progress. Overblown conflicts are often resolved when the person who has done the ranting and raving apologizes, usually making some excuse for the untoward behavior (e.g., "I was stressed out") that the target of the conflict accepts as a reasonable excuse.

The ego also deals with aggressive impulses by suppressing them or redirecting them through a process of **displacement,** which occurs when people take out their frustrations on those perceived as less dangerous to them rather than those persons who caused the original feelings. In displacement, the aggressive impulse is often redirected "toward a more vulnerable or socially acceptable target than the actual source of frustration . . . . Displacement is more likely when the true source of frustration is powerful or particularly valuable to the individual."[4]

Displaced conflict occurs when people direct a conflict toward the wrong person, avoiding a confrontation with the appropriate person.[5] This type of conflict almost always happens with people with whom we have an interpersonal relationship, and whom we think of as a "safe target" for our frustration. The person we avoid is someone we do not want to offend or provoke because that person has greater power (rank, physical strength, or nasty reputation). Like the chilling effect we explain in Chapter 5, a person avoids confronting someone who has greater power (rank, physical strength, or nasty reputation) and who could use that power to harm him or her. The common example of displaced conflict is Dan, who is angry at his boss but doesn't say anything to him, then comes home to his loving wife or children, whom he abuses with his anger.

A key point to remember about psychodynamic theory is that it explains those conflicts that, from the target's vantage point, often arise out of nowhere. The following narrative is an example of a displaced conflict due to internal frustration.

> I work in a retail store and I am often in charge of ringing people up at the register. I always make sure that when I ask for the next person in line that in fact the truly next person in line comes over or at least has a chance to. But when I asked for the *next* person in line, another lady who was not the next person in line came over. When I tried to get the proper person to come over, the woman that had come over started yelling at me. I calmly explained to her that it was part of my job to make sure that the next person in line had a fair chance to come over. She did not like this and went so far as to throw her credit card at me when paying. This made me absolutely furious and the worst part about it was there was nothing that I could say.
>
> So after I got off work I met my boyfriend at my apartment. Everything was going along smoothly until suddenly we got into a disagreement about whether we would go out that night or stay in. I was tired from working all day, but he wanted to go out. Well I ended up blowing the whole situation out of proportion and I know that it was due to the tension I had held on to all day from the irate customer that I had dealt with earlier in the day.

This retail salesperson needs to learn how to deal more effectively with offensive customers so that she doesn't have so much pent up frustration. Using some of the stress reducing activities covered in Chapter 8 on stress and anger would probably help her quite a bit. Unfortunately, too many people do not do anything until after they have ruined one or more relationships with those who were the safe targets of their frustrations.

In sum, according to psychodynamic theory the reason another person won't talk about an issue, or wants to drop it after you bring it up, is because she or he is suffering from anxiety and reacts by repressing issues or misplacing them by arguing over issues other than the real problem. You may have to drop the issue, and consider that it is not something the two of you can sit down and discuss in a meaningful, rational way. Hopefully, this is something you can live with and that there aren't too many issues like this in your relationship. In addition, the other person may deal with aggressive impulses by redirecting them from the real source of their frustration to safer targets, like friends, romantic partners, or family members, which may be you when you don't believe you deserve their wrath. Or, the other person may blow a conflict all out of proportion because of pent up frustration due to stress, insecurity, anxiety, or other urges. In both cases, it helps to call this behavior to the other's attention and explain how it upsets you, with the goal of finding other ways for the person to vent their frustrations without doing damage to your relationship. Meanwhile, hopefully, you understand what pressures the person is under, and that she or he apologizes to you.

Attribution Theory

What causes others to blame you for problems? Why do they seek revenge and retaliate against you? To answer these questions, we need to learn about attribution theory.

An attribution is an inference or assumption made about the causes of our own or another's behavior. In everyday interaction, we believe other people act as they do because they want to (internally motivated) or because they are pressured to by others (externally motivated). If I think that your behavior is internally motivated (based on your attitudes, needs, wants, beliefs), and I don't approve of what you did or said, I could say that you acted that way because you are evil, angry at me, anxious, unmotivated, depressed, unintelligent, or a cheat (as though you are a bad person who intended to cheat me)—all **internal attributions**.

If I approve of what you did or said, I might attribute the behavior to an external source such as a run of luck, God, your parents, and so on—all **external attributions**. For example, I might credit your spouse for your success at your job.

Sillars argued that in a conflict situation, one makes conclusions about our own or the other person's behavior and that those conclusions lead to theories to explain the conflict.[6] **Attribution theory** states that people act as they do in conflict situations *because of the inferences they make about others based on their behavior*. Attributions are internal, related to the person's general personality, or external, related to the other person's circumstances.

Sillars claimed attributions affect the way people define conflicts, interpret the other's behavior, and choose strategies to achieve their goals effectively within conflict situations. Furthermore, the process of making attributions about the other

What kinds of attributions might be made about a person who dresses a dog in this manner?

may discourage the selection of collaborative conflict strategies, because the process of attribution may shift the blame from oneself to the other. **Blaming** others is saying they are at fault. The act of blaming is a characteristic of negative conflict behaviors and is often associated with verbal and physical abuse, which increases the likelihood of escalating conflict.

People are most likely to perceive the other as aggressive and respond with anger and retribution when three conditions are met. First, the action the other person has taken is seen as a constraint to one's own alternatives or outcomes. Gabriel cannot act in the way he wishes because of Javier's actions. Second, not only has Javier taken action that constrains Gabriel, but Javier appears to have done so in order to intentionally harm Gabriel. Third, the action taken by Javier is seen as abnormal or illegitimate. Gabriel sees no action on his part that might have provoked Javier into acting as he did. Anger or retribution is less likely on Gabriel's part if Javier is seen as having acted without choice and because forces moved him in the direction taken. Anger and retribution are more likely if Gabriel sees Javier's action as arbitrary or whimsical.

As you consider attribution theory, an important aspect to remember is that it explains retaliatory behavior. When we make internal attributions about another person (she wanted, he hates, she's stupid, he's evil, she's angry, etc.), it often results in name calling (you cheat, idiot, lazy, good for nothing, etc.) and assigning blame (it's all your fault). Making external attributions for oneself is a way to avoid blame (it's my parents' fault that I am this way, I can't help that I didn't go to the right school) and to avoid giving credit to others where it is due (your spouse must have done it for you, you got the job because you graduated from the right school, you must have had connections, etc.).

Interestingly, we tend to make internal attributions to explain others' behavior when we don't like it and external attributions when we are impressed.[7] Meanwhile, we do the opposite for our own behavior. If I do something impressive, I like to take the credit for it (aren't I great!), but when it is nasty, I try to blame it on someone else (she made me do it). This is called the **attribution error.**

> The other night my three friends and I played a card game called Spades. My partner and I were not doing as well as the other team. I figured that somehow they were giving each other some kind of signals; so I finally stopped the game and accused them of cheating us. One of them responded by saying, "We are winning simply because of the luck of the draw." But the conflict escalated into a yelling match. Luckily, someone suggested that we change partners, which solved the problem. We went back to playing cards, but I still ended up on the losing side.

One interesting study looked at the way attributions were made about the use of humor by participants in a conflict episode. When humor was attributed to internal motives (e.g., "that person just enjoys jokes"), it had a negative outcome on the conflict resolution, but when humor was attributed to an external motive (e.g., laughing at the situation), it had a more positive effect on conflict resolution.[8] In another study, Sillars and colleagues found that conflicting spouses saw their own messages in more favorable terms than their partner's.[9]

To summarize how attribution theory explains some of our conflicts, others may make an attribution error by blaming you personally for problems because they think you were internally motivated to act as you did. If you explain that there were other, external, factors that actually account for your actions, you may convince them that you should not be held responsible for what you did. In addition, if they no longer blame you personally, they may not want to seek revenge and retaliate against you.

Uncertainty Theory

Have you ever experienced a conflict, but later discovered that there was no disagreement after all? Perhaps, you thought you did something that upset another person only to discover later that they were not upset with you at all. A theory that helps us understand how this can happen is known as uncertainty theory.

Uncertainty can occur at two levels. Conflict creates uncertainty within the relationship in which it occurs (e.g., romantic partners contemplate what happened and how they are supposed to relate to each other), and uncertainty also exists to different degrees within the particular conflict process itself. **Uncertainty** in the conflict process occurs when we have insufficient information to understand another's motives, goals, or behaviors or when we do not know the reasons for another's actions.

Many events are capable of creating uncertainty in relationships: changes in the other person's behavior, the breaking of a confidence, a friend breaking off contact, and a romantic partner going out with someone else. Interestingly, nearly all the events recalled by people as those causing uncertainty are classified as conflict episodes.[10] Most people cannot recall anything that might have been a clue to events causing uncertainty, or they can recognize clues only in retrospect. Uncertainty in a relationship generally leads to increased communication with the other person, and when people communicate about events causing uncertainty, they are more satisfied. Those who do not talk about uncertainty-causing events generally express regret about avoiding talking about them. As time passes, feelings about uncertainty-causing events become less negative.[11] Communication with the other, "doing" the conflict, is generally the best way to reduce uncertainty within a relationship. But there is a deeper level of uncertainty—that within the conflict itself.

Conflicts are inherently messy and filled with ambiguity. "The characteristic of conflict that is most difficult to capture in research is the chaos that pervades a heated argument or a long-simmering conflict."[12] There are three sources of ambiguity and disorder in conflict: the source of the conflict, the complexity of conflict patterns, and the omnipresence of conflict in daily activities.

Issues in conflict are rarely singular or straightforward. Rational views of conflict assume that both people are able to identify the issue, develop straightforward goals about it, and move toward resolution through compromise or collaboration. However, the real case is that people may not share the same perception about the issue or may not agree on the conflict issue at all. They may think the conflict has arisen due to different causes; they may interpret the other's behavior differently than the other intends; and so on. Further, conflicts may exist simultaneously at different levels—superficial issues may also involve deeper relational implications. Mild conflicts generally reflect agreement concerning the deeper relational issues involved; in bitter and destructive conflicts, relational issues are entangled and difficult to resolve.

The complexity of conflict may also affect the level of ambiguity present. Whereas casual conversation is characterized by adherence to a set of cooperative principles, these principles are often violated in conflict when it is not in one's best interest to converse in a succinct, relevant, and orderly manner. In addition, patterns in conflict (beyond the broad stages of prelude, initiation, differentiation, and resolution) are difficult to identify. Most conversation shows a reciprocal pattern, in which message types are generally followed by similar types, but when people are in conflict, they often alternate between aggression or assertiveness and withdrawal—they move forward but then back depending on what the other person is doing.[13] Further, participants in conflicts often introduce, drop, reintroduce, and expand topics in an unpredictable pattern, making it difficult for the other person to know where the conversation might lead.

A final source for the situations of uncertainty created by conflicts is the omnipresence of conflict in our everyday lives. They can occur anywhere, at any time. Often we may feel surprised by them. It's rare that we can make an appointment for a conflict!

When a person is in an uncertain relationship, they tend to "test the waters," so to speak, in order to reduce the uncertainty they feel. They are alert and observe the other person's behavior. They'll look for positive behaviors, but may overestimate the meaning of a negative behavior (e.g., she looks upset—she's probably thinking about breaking up with me). Indeed, in a situation of uncertainty, this overemphasis on the meaning of the behaviors the uncertain person observes makes it harder to reduce the uncertainty. This conflict narrative demonstrates how uncertainty makes interaction between both people difficult.

> After a terrible conflict in which I felt physically endangered, I asked my partner to move out. She promised to reform, but the difficulty is that she doesn't really think she did anything wrong. So she'll say things that indicate she doesn't trust me. In the meantime, I'm worried about her losing her temper again, and I'm watching all the time to see what's going to happen. It's pretty hard for both of us to simply relax when we are around each other.

Uncertainty theory helps explain **false conflicts**, which occur when at least one person in an interdependent relationship thinks that there is a conflict but after talking to the other(s) involved, finds there is no conflict. This narrative demonstrates a false conflict.

> I was hanging curtains in my daughter's room, her kitten was pulling at the material, so I picked it up and put it behind me without looking. I should have known better—there were objects all over the floor and apparently it landed on something the wrong way. I heard a meow-spit-hiss, and turned around to see it favoring one leg. Horrified, I picked it up and rushed it to the vet to find that its leg was broken.
>
> When I picked my daughter up from school, I tried to find some way to explain gently that it was my fault her kitten was injured. She simply looked at me and asked, "Is Sheba okay?" I replied that she was, although she would wear a cast for four weeks. My daughter said, "Well, accidents happen, Mom. You didn't mean to hurt her." I thought I would drive the car onto the sidewalk in amazement. I expected fireworks, but nothing happened.

Because we may assume that we are in a conflict due to the limited knowledge we have, false conflicts are generally resolved with sufficient information. Asking, and being told, leads to resolution fairly easily. Other false conflicts have to do with what people think that the other person might have done before they get their facts straight. Conflicts concerning beliefs, facts, or perceptions generally arise from a lack of information or distorted information. Imagine thinking you are in conflict with someone only to find that you are not. This is one reason why we need to talk to the other party. Otherwise, we may fret for nothing.

> I have this problem with my husband. When I talk to him, he usually makes no response. I wish he would just nod his head or comment or utter something like OK, right, good, or not if he objects. I really don't know where he stands when I am talking with him. By responding, I'll know if he is paying attention, understands what I am saying, or agrees or disagrees with me. Just an "un uh" would be great!

Sometimes opening a channel of communication is something as simple as acknowledging what the other is saying. By giving feedback, you can let others know what you are thinking.

In the absence of feedback, people reduce uncertainty in conflict situations in one of three ways. First, they may choose to trust the other, although the ability to trust depends on past behaviors. Second, they may reduce uncertainty by taking the perspective of the other person. And third, they may reduce uncertainty by engaging in "imagined interactions," or thoughts about what they might say and what the other might do in a conflict situation.[14] We discuss imagined interactions in Chapter 4, but here is an example of how one person is using them.

> With the economy in such bad condition, people have been laid off from my work. We're all getting pretty paranoid around here, and it's hard not to read things into the messages we hear. I keep thinking about what I will say if I am laid off. I have all this stuff I'd really like to tell them about this crappy job. I think about it at night before I go to sleep and it actually makes me feel better.

In conclusion, according to uncertainty theory, people who lack necessary information may engage in false conflict over ends or means to an end on which they actually agree. By expanding their channels of communication and explaining more to each other, they can clear up these misunderstandings. Many potential conflicts can be avoided by maintaining open channels of communication between you and people who are important to you.

RELATIONSHIP THEORIES OF CONFLICT

While the theories in the first section focused on the individual as a key element in conflict, this section considers theories that explain conflicts on the basis of the nature of the relationship between the people involved. Recall from Chapter 1 that the relationship of the conflicting parties is an important part of the prelude to a conflict. The two dominant relationship theories are social exchange theory and systems theory.

Social Exchange Theory

How might experience in previous relationships affect your conflicts in your present relationship? How might alternatives to your relationship affect your conflicts in your present relationship? If you haven't considered these questions, you should. Moreover, you should read about social exchange theory.

Developed by Kelley and Thibault, **social exchange theory** states that people evaluate their interpersonal relationships in terms of their value, which is created by the costs and rewards associated with the relationship.[15] A person's feelings about a relationship, according to this theory, depend on assessments of the amount of effort put into the relationship (costs) compared to what is received as a result of the relationship (rewards). People assess the costs and rewards associated with their relationships through what is termed the comparison level (CL) and the comparison level for alternatives (CL_{alt}). People enter into conflict when they believe that the rewards they are receiving are too little in comparison with the costs they must pay in the relationship.

According to social exchange theory, people in relationships (interpersonal, group, or organizational) ask "What does the relationship have to offer me? How valuable is it? Am I better off with or without the other person?" Social exchange theory explains how people rate their relationships in terms of how much they are giving to a relationship and what they are getting in return.

Rewards are resources of exchange (money, goods/property, love, sex, affection, companionship or shared time, status, services, information), while costs detract (pain/suffering, loneliness, abuse, loss of self-esteem, loss of resources of exchange, loss of investments). Based on costs and rewards, people make two comparisons (CL and CL_{alt}) to determine their level of relationship satisfaction and relationship commitment.

The **comparison level (CL)** is a standard with which people determine how satisfactory or attractive a relationship is. This standard also reflects what people think they deserve. If the rewards exceed the costs, then the CL raises because a person considers the relationship satisfying; if the outcome falls, then the CL also falls because the person is dissatisfied with the relationship.[16] A person's CL is created by considering all the possible outcomes a relationship might have, either from direct experience in the relationship or by observation of other relationships.

For example, in an interpersonal relationship, a person might think that, although he or she has fun with another person, the aggravation of waiting for that person to show up on time is getting too costly. In this case, the individual's previous experience makes one expect the other to show on time. There is now a conflict, even if not expressed, between the person and the one who is always late. There is a great deal we expect from new potentially romantic partners and friends based on our previous experiences.

The **comparison level for alternatives (CL_{alt})** is applied when a third party enters the picture. The addition of a third party may lead a person to examine the current relationship and perceive inequity in it, in turn creating conflict. A person compares the rewards and costs of the present relationship with those of the alternative relationship, and if the current relationship's rewards exceed the alternative, he or she remains committed to the current relationship.

This narrative illustrates how a person begins to make changes in a relationship through a consideration of the rewards and costs.

My mother graduated from high school early in order to marry my biological father and move with him to Germany, where he was stationed in the service. I was born a year later, and they divorced a few months after I was born. My mom then married Harry when I was about two. For the next 14 years, I lived with my mom and Harry, seeing my dad on the weekends. I felt like I lived two separate lives. Home was where Mom and Harry were—in fact, I didn't call him my stepfather, I called him "Dad." My biological father didn't like that.

My relationship with my biological father got worse over the years. I never enjoyed spending time with him and I even dreaded seeing him because he bad-mouthed my mom and Harry. My biological father resented the relationship I had with Harry and he kept trying to make me think Harry was a bad guy. He would use gifts as a way of making me visit him. He bought me lots of toys, took me fun places, and as I got older the gifts got more expensive—a television, a stereo, the promise of a car. I accepted these gifts with a clear conscience because I figured he "owed" me for the miserable weekends I spent with him.

When I was 16 my biological father and I had a major confrontation over this pattern we had developed. I basically stood up to him and told him how I hated the way he bad-mouthed my mom and how I didn't want to spend any more time with him if he was going to be like that. My father comes from a culture where you don't argue with your parents, so when I stood up to him, he got upset and told me never to come back to his house. That was five years ago, and I have never spoken to him since that time.

The narrator in this conflict has a clear CL when she evaluates the relationship she has with her biological father. She has a good relationship with her stepfather and wants only one family, not two. Her father appears satisfied with the relationship they had, but her dissatisfaction grows as the expensive gifts no longer are enough to make up for the unpleasantness of each weekend visit.

This conflict also illustrates the idea of CL_{alt}, which is the lowest level of outcomes a person may accept in a current relationship in light of available opportunities in other relationships. The more the outcomes in a relationship exceed the CL_{alt}, the more a person is committed to the current relationship, and the more dependent that person is on the relationship for psychological rewards. As time wears on, the rewards of the narrator's relationship with her father are too low for her to accept. The emotional cost of staying in the relationship is higher than the value of any gift her father can give her.

Social exchange theory assumes that people choose their behaviors due to self-interest and a desire to maximize rewards while minimizing costs. However, choices are made with respect to rules of fairness: People generally expect rewards proportionate to contributions they make to the relationship, based on their perceptions of the rewards and costs involved. So, even if a relationship is unsatisfactory at a particular point in time, if people think that it was a good relationship in the past and believe it might satisfy them in the future, they do not immediately abandon the relationship when problems arise.

From a social exchange point of view, conflict arises when one person in the relationship thinks that the outcomes are too low and perceives that the other may resist any attempt to raise the outcomes. This is precisely what happened in the narrative. It is possible that the narrator could have convinced her father that continuing to bad-mouth her mother (particularly 16 years after the divorce) was not appropriate. Such an outcome would have been the result of what social exchange theory terms *cooperative joint action*, where both people agree together to make changes in the relationship. Through independent action, the narrator could simply have continued her relationship with her biological father without expecting him to change, although this was unlikely as his behavior really bothered her. The actual outcome of the conflict was *imposed joint action*, where the narrator's father discontinued their relationship.

How people choose to alter their outcomes depends on the power held by each person in the relationship. Kelly and Thibault argued that the dependence of person A on person B constitutes person B's power over A. In the preceding narrative, the biological father believed he held the power in the relationship, which he exercised by discontinuing it. But the daughter also held power in that she was willing to lose the relationship if it didn't change.

Overall, social exchange theory leads to four insights about conflict behavior. First, the theory recognizes that people are often quite rational about the way they "do" conflict, calculating the costs of various options and weighing those costs against the potential rewards the options might bring. This strategic calculation is illustrated by the following conflict account.

> For the last two years, I have grown increasingly dissatisfied with my boss because she has doubled my workload. In addition, there are two of us doing the same job, but she did not distribute the tasks fairly between us. My frustration was growing, but I knew I couldn't get a job anywhere else for the same amount of money I was making. On the other hand, my life was getting so overwhelming that I was beginning to think that maybe the money wasn't that good. I started looking at jobs similar to mine online. I thought my boss would see how the tasks were allocated, but she seemed oblivious. I also know that she really hates it when I point out stuff like this to her, so I was hesitant to go talk to her. I finally screwed up the courage, but all she said is that she would think about the allocation of tasks. I didn't feel confident about any change in the future, but two weeks later she announced a change that made it much fairer for the two of us.

The preceding account also illustrates a second concept emphasized by social exchange theory: the interdependence of those in the conflict. It is not possible, according to social exchange theory, to take steps to resolve a conflict without reactions from the other person involved.

The third social exchange theory concept is that conflict is a situation in which moves and countermoves take place. It helps us understand how people explain conflicts—when narrating a conflict episode most people use a move–countermove format: He did this, so I did that, and so on.

The fourth concept of social exchange theory is that people in conflicts choose actions based not only on their particular rewards but also on their costs for the relationship. People may deliberately avoid a conflict because the current costs of initiating one are too high. Conversely, they may engage in a conflict because the costs of not doing so are too high.

Although some people initially react to social exchange theory negatively, thinking it is wrong to use an economic model to explain relationships, social exchange theory does make sense. We don't like believing that we put more into a relationship than we receive. If we have hope of staying in the relationship, we work to increase our rewards relative to our costs. On the other hand, if the costs continue to rise without some increase in rewards, people tend to cycle out of the relationship—as they see conflict as creating too high a "cost" with respect to the "reward" they might receive, they do not communicate their concerns and eventually do not communicate on other matters as well.

Here is another example of a conflict that illustrates social exchange theory.

> Before college began, a high school friend and I had a great relationship. We would hang out all of the time together and knew all of each other's secrets. We promised that even though we'd be going away to different colleges, we'd always stay in touch and be the best of friends. After graduation, we both got

absorbed in our own college life and lost our close ties. She eventually got bored with college and decided to take some "time off," while I remained in school where I am extremely busy with work, family issues, and my boyfriend.

Over the past three months she has been trying to get me to come back home for a weekend and go out partying at the local bars with her. She won't give up and insists that I spend more time with her, and she says that, after all of this time, I'm not living up to my promise. Recently we lost touch again when I was too involved with my local obligations to call her back or spend a weekend partying. When I finally did call her, she never returned my phone calls and I haven't heard from her since. I think that she must have compared the lack of satisfaction of our present relationship to all the dissatisfaction she must be feeling and it is less satisfying than she expected. She had put a lot of time and effort into maintaining our present relationship, while I did not. She was clearly putting more into the relationship then she was receiving, and so she must have decided to end our relationship.

What should we take away from social exchange theory? First, we better understand how our experience in previous relationships can affect conflicts in a current relationship. A high CL (based on previous experience with others) makes us demand more from someone who wants a relationship with us, and conversely, a low CL (based on previous experience with others) results in our being more likely to tolerate our circumstances in a less satisfying relationship. Second, we also better appreciate the role alternatives can play in our present relationships. Partners with fewer or no alternatives are more likely to stick with problematic relationships, but those with alternatives may demand more improvements or consider exiting a relationship. This means that we must work to make our friends, romantic partners, and family members happy, or other alternatives may appear more attractive and threaten our relationship (such as moving out, running away from home). We should also note that investments of time and energy in a relationship increase partner satisfaction and commitment. This helps explain why some long term relationships are harder to breakup than shorter term ones. Overtime, partners spend a lot of time together, share many memorable moments, give each other sentimental gifts, and do favors for one another. The more investments they make, the more difficult is to terminate the relationship. Thus, partners should make such investments to strengthen their commitment to the relationship.

Systems Theory

As we learned in Chapter 1, interdependent people—that is those in close, personal relationships—engage in more conflict than with others who are less interdependent. Why do you have more conflicts with friends, romantic partners, and family members than with acquaintances? What environmental changes increase conflicts among people who are important to each other? We learned in Chapter 1 that the situation (or environmental influences that surround us) is also a part of the prelude to conflict. Systems theory helps us get a better grasp of the big picture.

According to system theorists, a **system** is a set of interrelated components acting together as a unit. A **holistic** perspective suggests that the system (couple, family, team, organization, society, etc.) is key, not the individual. That is, while it helps to know what elements (people) are in a system (relationship), it is the system itself that is most important in helping us understand the behavior and conflicts within it. We know that people often behave a certain way because they are part of a system. We can expect certain people to act a certain way because they are married (marital system), members of a family (family system),[17] friends (friendship system), or members of a group or organization (organizational system). As they say about systems, the "whole is greater than the sum of its parts." The difference between a smooth running system and one not functioning at a 100 percent is often due to the willingness of people to work together for the good of the whole.

A system also has some purpose—it is goal-directed and adapts to its environment through self-maintenance and regulation. **Homeostasis** means that the system maintains itself in pursuit of a goal. The goal in a marriage is to stay married—and it is much harder than it sounds! There are environmental changes that come in many forms: income reductions, in-law interference, job demands, and more. Conflict arises as these external factors make keeping the relationship stable and growing problematic. From a practical point of view, conflict occurs within a relationship because a person in that relationship needs to adapt to demands of the other person or to demands in the environment surrounding the relationship.

Systems theory is best summarized by Ruben, who argued that, if human relationships are thought of as systems, communication, and therefore conflict, are not only inevitable but also continual.[18] According to Ruben, rather than being a disruption in the normal state of affairs, conflict is the normal state of affairs within any system. Conflict is the primary way in which a system adapts to the demands of its environment. So, conflict encourages growth and adaptation of a system. Without conflict, a system faces the possibility of stagnation and decay.

Let us illustrate how systems theory can explain conflict by considering Mike and Lori, who fight constantly. They dropped out of college to get married young and have a baby. Lori's parents were so much against the marriage that they cut off contact and support to the young couple. Mike has only one parent, his mother, who is living on welfare, is an alcoholic, and depends on Mike for some support. She wants to live with them, but Lori is against the idea because she doesn't get along with her. Mike lacks both a college degree and employment skills and continues to have trouble holding a job.

Meanwhile, Lori claims that she can't get a job and wants to stay home to raise their daughter. Mike wants her to go back to school and get a job after graduation, while his mother could move in and take care of their daughter. During the first year, Mike felt that he had to locate and tear up all the credit cards in their home, because Lori was buying things for him, herself, and the baby, which he felt they couldn't afford. They argue constantly over lack of money, his mother, her not working, credit cards, and his working off and on.

Mike and Lori's family, viewed as a system, is not adapting well to environmental pressures (Mike's mother, outside school and work possibilities or lack of them, and insufficient funds). One could expect disagreements to occur, but the family members are not making necessary changes to adapt to outside pressures. Obviously, they should go back to school and graduate. Then they need to get additional schooling or training beyond college to qualify for good jobs. Lori needs to learn how to set up a family budget and stick to it. Mike or Lori's mother could help watch the children while they are taking classes, but Mike's mother would also need to stop drinking (and get help with her problem). Mike and Lori need to realize that other families are struggling, but they make necessary sacrifices to restore homeostasis and survive as a unit.

In sum, we learn from systems theory that interpersonal conflict is a relationship's way of adjusting to changes in our environment. Since our environment is always changing, we can expect conflicts in our relationships as we decide on (discuss and debate) how to adapt to these changes.

MANAGE IT

As we state at the beginning of this chapter, understanding theories can help us understand our conflicts better so that we can adapt to them more easily. Table 3.1 illustrates the relationship between the type of conflict we observe, its root causes, and the theory that best explains that type of conflict. Psychodynamic theory, for example, helps us understand that aggressive impulses result from internal conflict between the id and the superego, which produces tension, stress, insecurity, anxiety, hostility, sexual urges, or depression that may lead to frustration. Psychodynamic theory explains misplaced conflict as when we are anxious about the issue at hand so we repress it, displaced conflict as when we fear taking our conflict to the person who is responsible for our frustration and instead take it out on safer targets like friends, partners, and family, and overblown conflicts as when we can no longer contain all the aggressive energy that has been building up for some time.

Attribution theory helps explain retaliatory behavior—we respond the way we do because we assume we understand why other people behave as they do. Making internal attributions for others' actions often results in name-calling and assigning

TABLE 3.1

The Relationship of the Type of Conflict to Its Cause and Theoretical Explanation

Type of Conflict	Cause	Explanation
Displaced, misplaced, or overblown	Stress, hostility, sexual urges, depression, insecurity, or anxiety	Psychodynamic theory
Retaliation/revenge	Misattribution error	Attribution theory
False conflict	Misunderstanding due to lack of information	Uncertainty theory
Unhappy/conflictual relationship	Imbalance in the resources of exchange	Social exchange theory
Conflict over how to adjust to a new situation	Environmental change or influence	Systems theory

blame. We make external attributions for ourselves to avoid blame or to avoid giving credit to others. We tend to make internal attributions to explain others' behavior when we don't like it, and external attributions when we do like what we see. Meanwhile, we do the opposite for our own behavior. This is known as the attribution error.

We can discuss uncertainty theory at two levels. Conflict creates uncertainty within the relationship in which it occurs when we have insufficient information to understand another's motives, goals, or behaviors or when we do not understand another's behavior. Uncertainty theory helps explain false conflicts which may be easily resolved by providing the necessary information.

According to social exchange theory, partners determine the value of their relationships. This theory explains how people rate their relationships in terms of what they are giving to them and getting in return. Partners make two comparisons to determine their level of

1. relationship satisfaction (based on experiences in previous relationships) and
2. relationship commitment (based on rewards/costs of alternatives).

How much and for how long a person can tolerate certain aspects of an interpersonal relationship (costs) depends on these two comparison levels (rewards, alternatives to the present relationship, and investments in the relationship).

Systems theory also deals with relationships. A system has some purpose—it is goal-directed and adapts to its environment—a type of self-maintenance or self-regulation. Thus the system maintains itself (homeostasis) in pursuit of a goal. Conflicts are natural as people decide how best to adjust to the demands from outside their relationship.

Sometimes people say that a theory sounds reasonable but doesn't work in practice. In fact, good theories are those we can put to use. The theories presented in this chapter are part of a conflict manager's toolbox—they help to make sense of conflict behavior and guide us in the competent choice of conflict management strategies.

EXERCISES

THINK ABOUT IT

1. Are there situations in your life where you are more likely to displace your anger or conflict with the other person than to deal with it directly? What characterizes those situations?
2. Have you ever experienced a misplaced conflict? What was the root cause? What was the safe issue? How did you determine that you were experiencing a misplaced conflict?
3. When have false attributions you have made about another exacerbated a conflict situation? Have there been times when making accurate attributions about the other has helped you?
4. What conflicts can you identify that were motivated by uncertainty? How could you have obtained more information before engaging in the conflict?
5. What conflicts can you identify that were motivated by a desire to increase your rewards or to decrease your costs in a relationship? Were you successful? Why or why not?
6. What conflicts can you identify that were motivated by systems theory principles? How best might you deal with such conflicts?

APPLY IT

1. This exercise is something you can start now and add to throughout the chapter. Take a piece of paper and draw two columns on it. In the left column, list your theoretical tools, starting with psychodynamic theory. In the right column, describe what your tool does in analyzing conflicts.
2. Add to the paper you started above. Write attribution theory in the left column, and explain how it helps you to analyze conflicts in the right column.
3. Add to the paper you started above. Write uncertainty theory in the left column, and explain how it helps you to analyze conflicts in the right column.
4. Add to the paper you started above. Write social exchange theory in the left column, and explain how it helps you to analyze conflicts in the right column.
5. Add to the paper you started above. Write systems theory in the left column, and explain how it helps you to analyze conflicts in the right column.

WORK WITH IT

1. Label the following statements by selecting either (a) internal attributions or (b) external attributions. Check your answers against those at the end of the exercises.
   a. "He did this to me because he wants to get even."
   b. "She did this to me because she hates my guts."
   c. "He did poorly because his parents expect the worst from him, so he delivers accordingly."
   d. "He didn't show for the test because he is probably afraid he will fail."
   e. "He made the test too hard, so I flunked it."
   f. "Of course she didn't return the laptop. She is an idiot. What do you expect from an imbecile?"
   g. "They keep tearing up the parking lots and that is why I was late to class."
   h. "I've been in a slump, which is why I am not doing well these days."
   i. "She's immoral and only wants you for your money."
   j. "He treats you badly because you are so tall. He has a rotten attitude toward others taller than he is."
   k. "Luck is against me. Maybe next time I will get lucky."
2. Identify the theories that best explain the following conflicts. Check your answers against those at the end of the exercises.
   a. Conflict situation: I blame my roommate for our current feud. All I can think about is getting even. Yesterday, he took my car and returned it on empty. I thought I had plenty of gas so when I took off today I was shocked when I ran out on the way to classes. I had to walk into town and carry a can of gas back to the car three miles each way. I also missed my test. You want to know what makes me mad? I know that he had the money to buy gas, and he must have driven by at least three stations when going through town. He just wanted to get me into trouble with my professor and mess up my grades. He must hate my guts. I am going to retaliate. He has to meet an important study group tonight, and I am going to wait till he is ready to go to tell him he can't use my car. Let's see how he feels about flunking a test.
      1. Which conflict theory discussed in this chapter best explains this conflict?
      2. What is really the cause of the conflict?
      3. How could or should one resolve this conflict?
   b. Conflict situation: I am anxious before flying on a trip; so I become irritable and wind up fighting with my partner before I go over insignificant but overblown issues.
      1. Which conflict theory discussed in this chapter best explains this conflict?
      2. What is really the cause of the conflict?
      3. How could or should one resolve this conflict?

c. Conflict situation: I am unhappy in my relationship because I have to do all the housework and my partner won't agree to do more. It seems unfair that I have to do more than my share. Why won't she help out?
   1. Which conflict theory discussed in this chapter best explains this conflict?
   2. What is really the cause of the conflict?
   3. How could or should one resolve this conflict?

ANSWERS TO EXERCISES:

Work with It #1

a. a
b. a
c. b
d. a
e. b
f. a
g. b
h. b
i. a
j. a
k. b

Work with It #2

a. *Attribution theory.* Misattribution is the cause of the conflict. I can overcome such conflicts by being more aware of my biases.
b. *Psychodynamic theory.* Tension, feelings, or anxiety is the cause of the conflict. I can overcome such conflicts by stress reduction therapy.
c. *Social exchange theory.* An imbalance exists in the resources of the exchange. My partner needs to restore the balance by helping out more or by paying for her share if we hire a housekeeper.

DISCUSS IT

Read the following conflict narratives and the instructions that follow them.

Conflict situation #1:
"I realize we made a serious commitment when we married, but I am unhappy with the way things are going, because I am holding down two jobs to make ends meet, and you can't even find a part-time job. I also come home and find the house a mess. I don't understand why you can't do more to pull your weight in this relationship. It seems unfair to me."

1. Which conflict theory discussed in this chapter best explains this conflict?
2. What is really the cause of the conflict?
3. How could or should one resolve this conflict?
4. Have you (or someone you know) had a conflict that illustrates this theory? How was it handled?

Conflict situation #2:
"I realize I am under a lot of pressure at work. I am worrying about losing my job if I'm not more productive at work. That's why I've been so difficult lately and easily upset. I realize that we fight a lot when I am under pressure at work. I expect you to understand that I can't

say anything at work, so sometimes I come home and take it out on you. I am sorry I really erupted last night and got carried away. I am not usually like that, you know."

1. What conflict theory discussed in this chapter best explains this conflict?
2. What is really the cause of the conflict?
3. How could or should one resolve this conflict?
4. Have you (or someone you know) had a conflict that illustrates this theory? How was it handled?

Conflict situation #3

"I was really upset with my partner, Sarah, yesterday, but she deserved it. I am getting tired of her putting me down in front of my friends. I wanted to get even for all the pain she has caused me. Yesterday, I got my chance because her parents joined us for dinner. When I was alone with her mom, I told her that Sarah is a terrible housekeeper, so I do all the house-work. Then, we aren't embarrassed when people visit. I told her she said her father did all the housework when she was growing up (which I knew wasn't true). Later, her mother must have said something to her because Sarah went to bed early and locked the bedroom door. I must have hit a nerve. I had to sleep on the couch, but it was worth it. I felt good about getting even with her for all the nasty things she tells my friends."

1. Which conflict theory discussed in this chapter best explains this conflict?
2. What is really the cause of the conflict?
3. How could or should one resolve this conflict?
4. Have you (or someone you know) had a conflict that illustrates this theory? How was it handled?

As a way to apply the concepts that you have learned from reading Chapter 3, participate in a class discussion by answering the questions that follow each of the conflict situations.

NOTES

1. Calvin S. Hall, *A Primer of Freudian Psychology,* 2nd Edition (New York: World, 1979), p. 28.
2. Ibid.
3. Morton Deutsch, "Conflicts: Productive or Destructive?" *Journal of Social Issues* 25 (1969), 7–41.
4. Hall, *Primer*, p. 14.
5. Jeffrey W. Kassing and Rachel L. DiCioccio, "Testing a Workplace Experience Explanation of Displaced Dissent," *Communication Reports*, 17 (2004), 114.
6. Alan L. Sillars, "Attributions and Communication in Roommate Conflicts," *Communication Monographs* 47 (1980), 180–200; Alan L. Sillars, "The Sequential and Distributional Structure of Conflict Interactions as a Function of Attributions Concerning the Locus of Responsibility and Stability of Conflicts," in Dan Nimmo (Ed.), *Communication Yearbook* 4 (New Brunswick, NJ: Transaction Books, 1980), pp. 217–235.
7. Stacy L. Young, "What the _____Is Your Problem? Attribution Theory and Perceived Reasons for Profanity Usage during Conflict," *Communication Research Reports* 21 (2004), 338–347.
8. Amy M. Bippus, "Humor Motives, Qualities, and Reactions in Recalled Conflict Episodes," *Western Journal of Communication* 67 (2003), 413–426.
9. Alan Sillars, Linda J. Roberts, and Kenneth E. Leonard, "Cognition During Marital Conflict: The Relationship of Thought and Talk," *Journal of Social and Personal Relationships* 17 (2000), 479–502.

10. Sally Planalp and James M. Honeycutt, "Events that Increase Uncertainty in Personal Relationships," *Human Communication Research* 11 (1985), 593–604.
11. Sally Planalp, Diane K. Rutherford, and James M. Honeycutt, "Events that Increase Uncertainty in Personal Relationships II," *Human Communication Research* 14 (1988), 516–547.
12. Allan L. Sillars and Judith Weisberg, "Conflict as a Social Skill," in Michael E. Roloff and Gerald R. Miller (Eds.), *Interpersonal Processes: New Directions in Theory and Research* (Newbury Park, CA: Sage Publications, 1987), p. 148.
13. Ibid., p. 153.
14. James M. Honeycutt, Kenneth S. Zagacki, and Renee Edwards, "Imagined Interaction and Interpersonal Communication," *Communication Reports* 3 (1990), 1–8.
15. John W. Thibault and Harold H. Kelley, *The Social Psychology of Groups* (New York: John Wiley, 1959); Harold H. Kelley and John W. Thibault, *Interpersonal Relations: A Theory of Interdependence* (New York: John Wiley & Sons, 1978).
16. Amy M. Bippus, Justin P. Boren, and Sabrina Worsham, "Social Exchange Orientation and Conflict Communication in Romantic Relationships," *Communication Research Reports,* 25(3) (June 2008), 227–234.
17. Paul Schrodt, "Family Communication Schemata and the Circumplex Model of Family Functioning," *Western Journal of Communication,* 69 (2005), 359–376.
18. Brent D. Ruben, "Communication and Conflict: A System-Theoretic Perspective," *Quarterly Journal of Speech* 64 (1978), 205–206.

Responding to Conflict: A Practical Guide to Managing Your Own Conflicts

OBJECTIVES

At the end of this chapter, you should be able to:

- Briefly explain the S-TLC system for dealing with conflict situations.

- Define assertiveness and explain its role in the confrontation process.

- List the six steps in constructive confrontation.

- Correctly create a four part I-statement.

- Explain what it means to take a creative approach to resolving conflicts.

- Apply at least two different creative methods to the analysis of a particular conflict you are experiencing.

KEY TERMS

assertive communication
attention point
basic communication rights
confrontation
confrontation steps
consequences statement
creativity
defensiveness
empathy
entry point
feelings statement
goal statement
gunny-sacking

identity goals
imagined interaction
informational reception
    apprehension
instrumental goals
I-statements
lateral thinking
listening
mind-mapping
personalized
    communication
problematic behavior
    statement

process goals
relational goals
reversal
self-talk
Six Hats
S-TLC
stopping
thinking
trained incapacity
vertical thinking
visual journal

When those involved in a conflict choose not to engage in avoiding/accommodating, competing, or passive–aggressive conflict communication and instead choose collaboration as explained in Chapter 2, they may both win. As professors who regularly teach conflict management, we often hear "I am in a conflict right now, what exactly should I say and how should I say it?" In an effort to supply an answer to these often asked questions, we responded with this chapter that includes practical or applied information to help you implement a collaboration approach to managing your own conflicts. In this chapter, we explain our S-TLC system for dealing with conflicts, assertiveness, I-statements, and the six-step approach to confronting others in conflict situations.

At the end of the chapter, you are invited to participate in two-person role plays that are designed for you to implement the principles and techniques discussed in this chapter. Remember that practice makes perfect.

THE S-TLC SYSTEM

We use the hyphen in *S-TLC* to differentiate it from the common TLC—which we all need in our lives. Note, however, that our TLC stands for something different from Tender, Loving Care. The **S-TLC** system is an acronym for Stop, Think, Listen, and Communicate. By following these four steps, you can often resolve interpersonal conflicts through basic communication skills. Let us begin with "stopping."

Stopping: Taking Time Out

Stopping is like taking a time out. When you realize that a conflict exists, begin by saying: "Stop!" For many people this is not too difficult. For others acquiring skills for slowing down the conflict is imperative. Some suggestions are as follows:

1. Exit temporarily to calm yourself. It is helpful to let the other person know that you are not abandoning the situation and will return.
2. Get a glass of water or some other beverage and take sips of the beverage before you respond to the other person.
3. Count backward from 100.
4. Change the problematic topic for a while to allow time for the air to clear.

It would help at this point for us to ask you to list as many ways as you can for stopping and taking time out in a conflict situation. Try to compare your list with as many people as you can. You are likely to find that there are a variety of ways to *Stop*. What is important about this step is that it forces us out of a reactive stance into a proactive one. We now turn your attention to thinking about the conflict.

Thinking about the Conflict

Think before you act! **Thinking** about the conflict means that you consider its cause and possible outcomes before you take action. At an elementary level, try not to take the conflict personally. Effective conflict managers effectively think about the situation. You are more likely to have satisfactory outcomes when you think about a conflict ahead of time instead of going into it without thinking.[1] We discuss two ways you can think about a conflict.

Thinking about Doing Nothing or about Changing the Other Person, Situation, or Self The first step in thinking about a conflict is to understand that we have at least four options to contemplate: While not advisable, we can do nothing and try to live with the situation. Sometimes that is our best choice, but usually it leaves a situation unchanged, continually eating away at us, and making us more miserable. Many times, better options are these: we can try to change the other person, we can try to change ourselves, or we can try to change the situation.

How can one person change another? Can or should we persuade the other to change his or her wants or needs? Sometimes it is in the best interests of the other person to do so. At other times, our desire to change the other has more to do with our own needs, which may seem selfish to the other. While this is an option, don't be surprised when other people resist your efforts to get them to change.

How can people change themselves? Can or should they change their wants or needs? You might decide that the best course of action is to adapt to the situation. You may find that it is not as difficult as you imagined. Sometimes we even acquire new interests, beliefs, or actions because we tried doing something different.

How can a person change the situation? This is a drastic step because it involves changing the environment, context, or relationship. It may mean finding new roommates, partners, or friends. It may mean moving to a different location that better meets everyone's wants and needs. A change in situation includes the possibility of breaking up with someone or changing jobs. Because changing a situation is a major undertaking, it generally only occurs when the other options don't work out and more drastic measures need to be taken.

Thinking about Your Goals A key factor to think about prior to confronting another person is your and the other person's goals. To do this, you need to understand the four types of goals that are relevant.

Instrumental goals are those that require the opponent to "remove a specific obstacle blocking completion of a task."[2] If you want a professor to change a grade, for instance, your instrumental goal is the actual changing of the grade as a result of your interaction with the professor. **Relational goals** involve attempts to gain power and to establish trust as the relationship between those in the conflict is established. Relational goals would include establishing your right to question the grade you received while not infringing on the professor's power. **Identity goals** concern how those in the conflict situation view each other. While people are generally motivated to maintain and support each other's self-image, they sometimes desire to attack the image of the other in a conflict situation. In questioning a grade, for example, you would want to make sure that you do not personally attack the professor; comments such as "your grades are unfair" or "you never give consideration to what I say" are attacks on identity. A more supportive comment is "I believe I met the requirements because I . . ."

The fourth type of goal people might pursue in conflict situations is **process goals**, which refer to alternative ways to manage conflict communication. One party may prefer openness, consensus, and fairness, while the other prefers to keep feelings and wants private, maintain control, and win every argument. Parties need to first agree on their process goals before engaging in a conflict over an issue. The conflicting parties might raise and discuss such questions as, "Is their relationship important to them both? Is there one style of communication and conflict that would enhance their relationship more than others? What happens to the relationship if only one person gets his or her way now or most times? Are both parties skilled in constructive conflict management techniques?" Competing process goals make conflicts over issues difficult to manage or resolve.

Thinking about the conflict means that you also think creatively about the way you should manage the conflict. Creativity is such an important part of the "thinking" step that we want to explore the subject in greater depth later in this chapter. At this time, in the next section, we move on to the next step in the S-TLC model and discuss some means for improving your listening.

Listening in Conflict Situations

Listen before you say anything! The tendency of most people is to justify themselves the moment they hear criticism, rather than really listening to what the other person is saying. We believe that the ability to truly hear what the other person is saying is as important as what we say in a conflict.

Most popular advice on conflict is more linear than transactional in its approach to conflict because it emphasizes speaking skills: "Say it this way, at this time." But as we learned in Chapter 1, communication is transactional, consisting of the *interaction* of two or more people, and conflict occurs because the people have different and incompatible unmet needs and goals (or differ on the means for achieving the same goal). No one likes to hear "I can't believe you feel that way," or "You're wrong," when one is trying to explain his or her feelings.

Listening consists of focusing one's attention on the other person. It is characterized by openness to the other person's views, willingness to suspend judgment during the discussion, and patience to hear the other out. Listening involves both an empathic response to the other person, and a commitment to hear to all the other person has to say.[3] Listening does not come naturally, but it can be learned and the skills can be retained.[4] Rogers noted the following:

> Our first reaction to most of the statements, which we hear from
> other people, is an immediate evaluation or judgment, rather than an
> understanding of it . . . . Rarely do we permit ourselves to understand
> precisely what the meaning of his statement is to him. I believe this is because
> understanding is risky. If I let myself really understand another person, that
> understanding might change me. And we all fear change.[5]

We typically feel defensive when others have something critical to say about us. We do not want to know that we are not doing well or not doing all we should do. We want to think everything is fine. **Defensiveness** is a state of emotional arousal that occurs when we believe that the other person is attacking us, which in turn affects our behavior. As a result, we have difficulty hearing what the other is saying and reject outright the other person's ideas.[6]

Defensiveness arises from the interaction of people in a situation and occurs when people have a perceived flaw that they do not want to admit, and they are sensitive to that flaw. When sensitive people believe that another has attacked their flaw, they respond by defending themselves.[7] People who think they are listened to are less likely to feel attacked. Listening is a way of reducing both our own and others' defensiveness.

Effective listening consists of several skills, some of which may seem obvious to you, and some that may seem new. Listening cues, such as head nods and "uh-huh," are important. These "response tokens" show that you are interested and willing to let the other continue.[8]

In addition, you can engage in these behaviors to help to make you a better listener in conflict situations.

1. Shift your attention from whatever you are doing and to the other person.
2. Look at the other person.
3. Try to understand the other person's feelings rather than focusing on arguing with the other person.

Remember that listening to and understanding others does not mean you have to agree with what they say. You are only trying to hear the person out before agreeing or disagreeing. Listening is a way to affirm the value and worth of others. One author wrote that the feeling of being truly heard is so close to the feeling of being loved that most people cannot tell the difference.[9] Next, we turn to the topic of communicating.

Communicating in Conflict Situations: Asserting Yourself

When engaged in conflict, there are many ways to respond. You could react with violence or not. What are the outcomes if you react violently? What would happen if you don't? You could respond by communicating in a destructive way, such as yelling, swearing, accusing, blaming, and name calling. You could respond by avoiding the conflict altogether or by simply giving in. Finally, you could sit down and discuss the problem with the other person in a collaborative manner. If you choose the latter, assertiveness plays an important role.

Assertive Communication When people choose not to engage in avoiding/accommodating, competing, or passive–aggressive conflict communication and instead choose assertiveness by speaking up about their concerns, interests, and needs, they and their partners may both win, which is the essence of the collaborative approach to conflict management. **Assertive communication** is defined as the ability to speak up for one's interests, concerns, or rights in a way that does not interfere with the interests or infringes on the rights of others. Assertiveness is a means of avoiding gunny-sacking, which we introduced in Chapter 2. Of course, this also means that one must allow others to communicate their own feelings, beliefs, and desires. Assertive communication behavior gives others a chance to improve the situation, which is a good idea when a relationship is important to you. She or he says what the problem is so that the other may choose to do something about it. The other person may not respond in a manner that the assertive person would prefer, but at least the other is given a chance to do so. By getting troubles off our chests, we can monitor one another, adapt as needed, and avoid little problems turning into bigger ones. People who are assertive with one another have the greatest chance of achieving mutual satisfaction and growth in their relationship.

Central to assertiveness is the idea that we all have **basic communication rights.** Think about your present relationships at home, school, work, and free time and consider whether these rights are being respected. You have the right to

1. be listened to and taken seriously
2. say no, refuse requests, and turn down invitations without feeling guilty or being accused of selfishness
3. be treated as an adult with respect and consideration
4. expect that others do not talk to you in a condescending way
5. not feel what others want you to feel, not see the world as they would have you perceive it, and not adopt their values as your own
6. have your own feelings and opinions as long as you express them in a way that doesn't violate the rights of others
7. have and express your interests, needs, and concerns as long as you do so in a responsible manner
8. change your opinions, feelings, needs, and behaviors
9. meet other people and talk to them
10. privacy—to keep confidential or personal matters to yourself
11. have others leave you alone if you wish
12. ask others to listen to your ideas
13. ask for help or information from experts and professionals, especially when you are paying for it
14. not assert yourself, confront someone, or resolve a conflict
15. ask others to change their behavior when it continues to violate your rights

Do some of these items surprise you? Are you violating the rights of others? There may be other rights that you could identify. With these rights comes responsibility. Moreover, to expect fair treatment from others, you must also respect the communication rights of others and treat them "as you yourself would like to be treated." As we enter into relationships, it becomes our task to help all involved to recognize and protect those rights. This is why in Chapter 2 we said we favor collaboration over compromise, which goes further in protecting the communication rights as well as other needs, interests, and concerns of both parties.

While we are generally in favor of assertive responses to conflict situations, we need to point out that confronting others is not always advisable. You need to choose to assert yourself when the situation calls for it, however. Sometimes others cannot handle your assertiveness, and they may be someone who has a lot of influence over you or your future, such as your boss, teacher, parent, or romantic partner. Insecure people may become aggressive or passive aggressive. One of the authors, Lee, likes to tell his students that the romantic, dating period is a good time to determine whether a potential mate can handle one's assertiveness. When a problem occurs in your relationship, you can test your partner's ability to deal with conflict situations by confronting him or her. If that person turns abusive, walks out on you, becomes rigid and uncooperative, and you find yourself having to avoid or accommodate on all important concerns, you need to realize that such a person is likely to continue to mismanage conflict situations. On the other hand, if the person is not turned off by your assertiveness, takes you into consideration, and cooperates with you, then you may have discovered someone who is an effective conflict manager. The moral to the story is to try to surround yourself with people who are open with you and who can handle your assertiveness.

As you have discovered by reading about conflict communication processes in Chapter 2, it is regrettably too easy for conflicts to spin off into dysfunctional cycles. In the next section, we describe a series of steps for effective confrontation, which can help you manage your conflicts without, it is hoped, diverging into a destructive cycle.

THE SIX-STEP CONFRONTATION PROCESS

We begin by defining **confrontation** as an interpersonal conflict communication process in which the parties call attention to problems or issues as they occur between them and express their feelings, beliefs, and wants to one another.

Because of the potential benefits, we need to know how to effectively confront others about conflicts that eat away at our relationships. There are six **confrontation steps** to move through as you manage a conflict with another person. They are as follows:

1. Preparation: Identify your problems/needs/issues.
2. Arrange for a time and place to meet and talk.
3. Interpersonal confrontation: Talk to the other person about your problem.
4. Consider your partner's point of view: Listen, empathize, and respond with understanding.
5. Resolve the problem: Make a mutually satisfying agreement.
6. Follow up on the solution: Set a time limit for reevaluation.

Although we would like to avoid giving the impression that all conflicts, large and small, are resolved by following six easy steps, it helps to know what to do and what not to do when confronting someone with whom you disagree. Also, keep in mind that when you find yourself stopped at one step, we advise backtracking one or more steps to allow for a more thorough discussion before attempting moving forward. That being said, let's begin with the first step, preparation for confrontation.

1. Preparation: Identify Your Problems/Needs/Issues

The first step is preparation, where you identify your problems, needs, and issues. "Preparation is the most extensive and, in many ways, the most important stage of the confrontation process."[10] This process is the stop and think portion of the S-TLC model. At this stage, self-talk is important. **Self-talk**, as you can guess, is verbalizing, either out loud or to ourselves, inner messages. People can talk themselves out of confronting others, they can talk themselves into it, or they can talk themselves into handling confrontation in negative, destructive ways. Asking yourself, "who, what, where, when, and how," enables you to examine many more aspects of a situation to determine what the problem is, how it affects you and the relationship, and how you feel about it. You need to determine what you want (your goal). Ask yourself what is likely to happen if you don't receive what you want or what could happen to the relationship if you do. Once you have determined that you need to confront the other person, you need to try to think positively and encourage yourself to go through with it.

Self-talk may lead to imagined interactions, which we discussed in the previous chapter. **Imagined interaction**, which serves a planning function, is a form of intrapersonal communication in which you think about what you might say and another might say in response to you in a particular conversation.[11] People who imagine interactions with others do not actually think about the interaction as they expect it to occur. Rather, they think about the interaction in an "if-then" kind of way: If he says "x," I will tell him "y"; if she says "a," I will say "b." In this sense, imagined interactions are much like cartoon strips. They are both visual and verbal, they happen sequentially, and the imaginer can rewrite the script if desired. Imaginers also have powers similar to comic strip creatures: They can control a conversation to their satisfaction, they can read the minds of characters, and they can travel through time or backup action if they want to replay it.[12]

There is a downside to imagined interactions. When people are asked about thoughts they have concerning conflict situations, only 1 percent report thinking about the other person's view in the conflict situation.[13] People do try to make sense of conflict situations, however, by answering the following questions: Who or what is responsible for the conflict and how serious is the conflict? Unfortunately, simply focusing our thoughts on a conflict often makes it worse. People who dwell on a particular conflict tend to place the blame on the other person involved and overestimate the seriousness of it.[14] We find it useful to not simply ponder the conflict, but to think competently about what the other person might say about it, and what you would like to say. It is important not to mimic the findings of one study, where results indicated that people imagine interactions with significant levels of verbal aggression and physical violence.[15] Imagining yourself acting competently in the conflict situation is most likely to result in competent behavior. After preparing for the confrontation, now is the time to arrange for it.

2. Arrange with the Person for a Convenient Time and Place to Talk

You might tell the person that "we need to talk about . . ." Most people understand that the statement, "We need to talk about . . ." is an invitation to confront, creating the *initiation stage* of the successful conflict process as described in Chapter 1. If you are uncomfortable using the phrase, "We need to talk," you may use words of your choosing to arrange to meet at a particular time and place. To us authors, this step is like making an appointment with a colleague or a reservation for dinner. We are simply saying that you both need to agree on a time to sit down and talk about what is bothering you.

Personally, we think you need to provide a little bit about the subject so that the other person has some idea about the topic of discussion, otherwise she or he may worry about something that has nothing to do with the meeting.

- You need to pick a time and place that is appropriate, but usually not over 24 hours from the time when you ask the other person to meet and talk.
- Pick a place that is relatively private and free of distractions.

3. Interpersonal Confrontation: Talk to the Other person about Your Problem

Stage three is the actual interpersonal confrontation, where you talk to the other person about your problems, needs, or issues. This is the stage where assertiveness plays an important role because you call attention to a problem or issue and give voice to your wants, interests, or needs. When you want to assert yourself, follow these suggestions:

- Stand tall, or if sitting, lean slightly forward, but don't crowd the other person.
- Keep at least a couple of feet between you both.
- Look at the person, but don't stare (suggestion: focus on her or his forehead).
- Look serious, but don't frown, glare, or appear menacing.
- Speak firmly, calmly, slowly, and don't allow yourself to become verbally aggressive.
- Use open gestures, and avoid any threatening gestures such as arm waving, pointing, standing up, or making a fist.
- State your own point of view in terms of your needs, wants, interests, and concerns, but find something on which you both agree.

Later in this chapter, we describe "I-statements" because they are an excellent way to assert yourself in a conflict situation.

4. Consider Your Partner's Point of View

At stage four, you need to consider your partner's point of view. Researchers claim that empathy is an essential aspect of communication competence. **Empathy** is the ability to consider another person's beliefs or feelings, so that we can see the situation from the perspective of the other. Empathy does not require that we agree with the other's perspective, but it does allow us to understand it.[16] Put yourself in the other's position and ask yourself how you would feel if requested to make the same change. Would you resent it? Would you think that such a request is reasonable? If you do not think it is, chances are the other doesn't either.

According to researchers, some individuals suffer from **informational reception apprehension**, which is an emotional state in which a person finds it difficult to respond to what is being said. A person experiencing this apprehension may not be able to even hear what the other is saying, much less process or interpret the meaning of the message.[17] This concept is particularly relevant because people often fear what others may say in a conflict situation. They may blame us, bring up undesirable information, or remind us of past incidents. However, it is important that you open yourself to the other's point of view. Hopefully, you can see that the need to "hear the person out" outweighs the unpleasantness of what the other may have to say.

When we listen to another's feelings, sensitivity is important. Perhaps one of the most disconfirming actions we can take is to tell others that they have no right to feel the way they do. Instead, focus on why others feel the way they do and what role those feelings play in the conflict. If a listener responds to a statement like "I get angry when I think you are taking advantage of me," by disparaging the feeling ("You can't really be angry over this"), the speaker will be less likely to continue the conflict episode to a mutually satisfactory ending. More likely, the person raising the issue will shut down and say something like, "Never mind. It doesn't matter," leaving both people feeling that the issue is unresolved.

Another disconfirming action is the response many people make when listening to others: "I know exactly how you feel." This is one message that does not belong in conflict language. You make such a statement to someone close to you when you're sharing an excited exchange or discovering mutual interests. But in conflict, such a statement belittles others because it negates the uniqueness of the listener's experience, and, in essence, represents a play for power. Rothwell refers to this as a "shift" response, as opposed to a "support" response.[18] The emphasis is on "I" (my wants, needs, desires, and importance), not on "you" (your wants, needs, desires, and importance). If you tell me how angry you are with me because I was on the phone when you expected an important call and I say, "I know just how you feel. Last week I didn't get an important call, either," whose feelings become the focus of attention? Mine do. How is it different if I respond, "I didn't realize that you were expecting a call" or "You're really angry, aren't you"? This response makes your feelings the focus of my attention and, in doing so, acknowledges my responsibility in the conflict and my willingness to make amends. After determining how the other feels about the issue or problem, you can do the next step, resolve it.

5. Manage the Problem: Come to a Mutual Understanding and Reach an Agreement

An important step in managing conflict is coming to a mutual understanding and reaching an agreement. We sometimes find it helpful to put the agreement in writing for future reference ("You say I agreed to what?"). We need to request specific actions. The reason we request the action is shown in the expression of needs. Through the expression of specific wants, and having reached an agreement, conflicting parties can give the outcome a try, and attempt the last step, review and reevaluation. Many interpersonal conflicts are resolved with rather simple agreements ("OK, I agree to do the dishes on days you work"). For more complicated ones, we make a number of suggestions for written agreements in Chapter 11, when we look at formal agreements that result from mediation.

6. Follow Up on the Solution: Set a Time Limit for Reevaluation

The entire confrontation process does not stop with an understanding, agreement, or resolution; it ends only after successful performance overtime, which is determined (and more likely guaranteed) by a review at a later date, because a true resolution or an agreement is one that works or is actually carried out. We suggest that you set a date with the other to return to the issue at hand to evaluate the progress made, reward yourself if successful, or to revise your agreement if not. After a few weeks, discuss to what extent the necessary changes have actually occurred.

I-STATEMENTS: AVOIDING DEFENSIVENESS

Key to a productive conflict is the ability for grieving individuals to effectively communicate their desires for change without offending the other person so much that he or she stops listening. Clearly, the way we state problems in a conflict situation affects the other person's response.

We need to avoid arousing defensiveness in other person.

One of the ways, we can avoid arousing defensiveness is through I-statements. **I-statements** personalize the conflict by owning up to our feelings rather than making them the responsibility of the other person.

I-statements are also an important part of being assertive. They call attention to both our rights as a communicator (to express our feelings) and our responsibilities (to communicate those feelings in a way that reflects ownership of them and doesn't infringe on the rights of others). Central to the notion of assertiveness is responsibility—for your actions, for your feelings, for your words, and for the consequences of all of them. This suggests that when we take responsibility for how we feel and act, we start to realize that in every conflict situation all parties to the conflict have contributed to it in some way.[19] As the examples in Table 4.1 show, when you own up to your statements and feelings, you take responsibility for them.

In addition to taking responsibility for what one thinks, feels, and wants, saying "I feel" and "I think" is far less threatening to the other person than

TABLE 4.1

Statements Demonstrating Responsibility

Escaping Responsibility	Taking Responsibility
He made me do it.	I did it.
She upset me . . . she made me angry . . . she got me all riled up.	I was angry.
The professor is too hard and insensitive.	I think that the professor is . . .
That was a great movie!	I liked the movie a lot.
Everyone knows that isn't true.	I don't believe it.
Adults don't behave like that.	I don't approve of your behavior.
Nobody likes her.	I don't like her.
Anyone with any sense at all would not.	I don't understand why you would not.
This is the way it has always been.	I don't want to change it.

saying "you said . . ." and "You're wrong . . ." When we say "I think or I feel," we own our thoughts or feelings. We are not trying to make them the responsibility of the other person. If we speak in generalities (e.g., "Everybody knows you're wrong"), it sounds like we have nothing to do with the situation.[20]

Resorting to the use of You-language is a common way to avoid responsibility. We often resort to blaming the other person for our behavior and feelings, but again we need to strive for the truth, accuracy, and take responsibility. You can see the difference between the statements in Table 4.2.

Two "misassumptions" about others lead us to prefer depersonalized communication over communication that owns our feelings. First, we tend to confuse our perceptions of the other person with their qualities. Suppose, for example, your roommate frequently leaves a wet towel on the bathroom floor and hair in the sink after bathing. Which are you more likely to say to the other person (be honest!): "You're such a slob," or "It bothers me when you leave your towel on the floor and hair in the sink." The first statement puts all the blame on your roommate and implies that the other is a bad person. With the second statement, you run the risk that your roommate may not care if it bothers you. And so the first statement seems less risky, but that is an illusion. Say to your roommate, "You're such a slob," and you create defensiveness. Even when joking, negative language creates an unsafe feeling for the other, resulting in defensiveness. Defensiveness, in turn, causes people to tune out your ideas.

Another misassumption that seduces us into depersonalized communication is thinking that others do not change much, and so we can predict their behavior. We can make some educated guesses about the way others react, and the better we know them, the better those guesses become. But making sweeping statements about the other person's behavior to make him or her "pay attention" belittles the other and indicates a lack of trust. We can say only that people respond to situational demands; we can estimate how they might perceive those demands and respond to them.

We need to overcome these misassumptions. Accepting responsibility is less likely to result in defensiveness from the other person. We need to express our feelings about the situation as specifically as possible and link them to behavior in some way. Only then is the other person likely to understand what is meant. Even

TABLE 4.2	
"You" Statements versus "I" Statements	
You	I
You are too hard and insensitive	I think that you are . . . .
Your hair, hat, shoes are terrible	I don't like your hair, hat, etc.
You have a warped sense of humor	I don't think you're being funny
You're too sarcastic	I don't like sarcasm

TABLE 4.3

Examples of "I-Statements"

Feelings Statement	Problem Behaviors	Consequences	Goals
I feel annoyed	When I have to put gas in my car after you use it	Because I end up having to take the time to get gas	I'd like you to get gas after you use my car
I feel depressed	When I hear about all the fun others are having	Because the doctor says I have to remain inactive	I'd prefer to talk about other topics
I feel frustrated	When I study but still get a poor grade on a test	Because this could hurt my grade in this course	I would like to go over the chapters with you

if you first state the observation that your roommate left towels on the bathroom floor before declaring, "You're a slob," the other person is likely to become defensive and tune you out.

Components of I-Statements

To make effective I-statements, we have devised the following form to guide you:

I feel . . . when I . . . because I (think, believe) . . . I'd like (want, wish) . . .

Table 4.3 contains examples of the four parts of three types of descriptive statements:

1. *Feelings statement:* a description of your feelings (e.g., feeling angry, neglected, offended, surprised, depressed, or unhappy). It is important to link our feelings to particular situations; vague feelings often create frustration in the listener.
2. *Problematic behavior statement:* a description of the offensive, upsetting, incorrect, selfish, problem-producing behavior (e.g., the other saying something insulting, nasty, or sarcastic, leaving clothes all over the room, or forgetting an important date).
3. *Consequences statement:* a description of the consequences the problematic behavior has for you or others (e.g., wastes your time, you have to expend the effort, you could lose friends, or your parents may get angry). The statement contains the word "because." Ask yourself *why you want* the other person to change his or her behavior. What adverse impact does that behavior have on you? This may seem like stating the obvious but others do not always think about how their behavior impacts on you, so they need to be reminded.
4. *Goal statement:* a description of what you want specifically (e.g., one may want the other to appear on time in the future or call if delayed). It states what you want, would like, prefer, hope for, expect, or ask (avoid using words such as "demand," "require," and "or else"). A major challenge is identifying what you really want and stating your position in a clear way that specifically describes what it takes to satisfy you.

Notice that every part includes "I," and ideally, none contains "you." While in theory, the best I-statements do not contain "you," you may find it difficult to avoid saying "you" when describing the problem. Test your recognition of specific need/feeling statements in the following application at the end of this chapter.

We need to point out that you can make longer I-statements than the above examples. You may choose to talk for a while about how you feel, and then discuss what it was that made you feel this way and why. Because confrontation is a challenge for many, it may take a while before you eventually say what you want. This four-part format is presented only to ensure that you address all four components of an I-statement when presenting your side of the conflict.

Finally, I-statements won't work unless they are accompanied by a calm, non-threatening tone of voice and facial expression. If one is to avoid being perceived as judgmental, one must sound nonjudgmental in both what is said and how one says it. Otherwise, even the best worded I-statements won't work because they are accompanied by upset and anger, which contradict the words.

Advantages of Using I-Statements

By asserting yourself in this way, you provide much needed information, demonstrate honesty, and reduce defensiveness in others.

- You provide necessary information because the other person doesn't need to "read your mind" to determine what you are thinking, feeling, and wanting.
- You reveal your honesty by telling others what is on your mind, what you prefer, or what is upsetting you.
- You reduce defensiveness in others because you are not assigning blame or blurting out accusations.

Challenges Associated with I-Statements

I get too mad to be nice. Instead of using I-language, it is tempting to hit the other person where it hurts. This option seems particularly tempting when the other person has already hurt us. If you value your interpersonal relationship, you owe it to yourself and the other person to resolve the problem in a constructive and positive way. Owning your feelings, using the words "I think," "I feel," and "I want," minimizes the possibility of regret over what is said. I-statements make one more assertive without producing ill feelings and provoking retaliatory behavior.

Moreover, remember that the S-TLC system reminds us to stop, think, listen, and then communicate. You may need to stop and wait a few minutes, hours, or days until after you have "cooled down." Then, you may find it possible to express yourself using I-statements rather than abusive language.

It doesn't sound right or normal for me to talk that way. Many people have bad habits; they avoid conflict, simply give in, or respond to conflict in aggressive ways. The problem is that overtime, one's habits eventually seem "normal," and any new behaviors seem "artificial" at first and require effort to learn as new habits. However, what one learns, one can unlearn. You need to give them a try and see how they improve your interpersonal relationships.

Remember, you can take a time out. If you find yourself overwhelmed by the situation, unable to remain in control of your emotions, and unwilling to listen to the other, tell the other person you need to leave and talk later about the situation. This gives you time to calm down and compose an appropriate "I-statement." Walking away is not wrong if the alternative is losing control of yourself and ruining any chance to bring the conflict to resolution.

The S-TLC model and the use of I-statements are basic tools available to the conflict manager. While they seem straightforward, there are many potential ways in which individuals can manage their conflicts. Too often, they favor one way rather than consider the many means they have available for dealing with a conflict. The next section on creativity shows how we can look at conflicts from different points of view providing us with many more tools for better managing them.

Learning to be Creative When Managing Conflicts

Learning the conflict management skills covered so far in this chapter can produce many satisfying outcomes. However, we can enhance those outcomes by being creative in our approach to managing and resolving conflicts.

Defining Creativity

What is creativity? Creativity is not the same as intelligence—creative people need not have high IQs and vice versa.[21] **Creativity** is a process of making sense of some problem in a new way.[22] Why is creativity important? Perhaps the most important reason creativity is important is a self-serving one: You are more likely to develop mutually satisfying outcomes in conflict situations when you and the other party approach your conflicts creatively.

Most authors identify four stages of the creative process:

- *The preparation stage* includes all your previous learning as well as any information you gather to address the problem at hand.
- The *incubation stage* is a period of thinking about the problem—giving it time to take shape and form.
- The *illumination stage* occurs when a particular idea finally appears in response to the problem.
- The *verification stage* allows you to test whether the creative response you have come upon truly works.

Can we learn to be creative? Generally speaking, the answer is yes. One of the most stunning findings in all the work on creativity is this: There are not a lot of innate differences between people who are creative and people who are not. Most important to becoming more creative is the decision to do so.[23] However, one barrier to creativity is our trained incapacities.

Trained Incapacities

We could more easily think about our problematic situations if it were not for our trained incapacities. What are they? **Trained incapacities** refer to a person's abilities and talents that actually limit the person's thinking. Because the behavior has become generally beneficial (in nonconflict situations), the person expects it to work in all situations, but sometimes the ability may interfere with creativity. Two such trained incapacities are task-oriented/goal-centeredness and critical thinking.

On the one hand, being a *task-oriented and goal-centered leader* is generally viewed as a positive trait in American mainstream culture: People identify the end point they hope to reach and then push and pull others to get there as quickly and efficiently as possible. In many cases, the outcome is necessary or beneficial. However, in other cases people are so eager to achieve the end point that they do not adequately think about all the implications of what they are doing.

If you are task-oriented and goal-centered, you need to realize that your approach may have some limitations. You want to stop occasionally to ask if everyone is "on board" or feeling rushed. You might plan in some time for reflection. "Let us not make a decision today but sleep on it and meet again tomorrow. Let's take time to try to think of alternatives, imagine the possible outcomes of our decision, and determine whether we can live with this decision."

As a second trained incapacity, *critical thinking* is the ability to evaluate and challenge an idea that other people take for granted. Critical thinking may generate new ideas and insights and enable a more complete discussion of an issue. However, critical thinking can also stifle the introduction of new ideas or issues, leading to situations in which individuals fear voicing their own opinions and ideas for fear of rejection. When critical thinking is seen as attacking others' ideas, they may no longer want to participate in the discussion.

We must recognize some limitations to creative thinking. Beware of faultfinding and too much criticism of others and their ideas. We all need to "cut one another some slack" in life, or a relationship becomes too stressful. Some people think they are always right, know what's best for others, and think their ideas are always better than others'. They may have some good ideas, but there are times they are wrong and should have the stomach to admit it. It would also help to withhold your opinions until after you have heard from the others so as not to stifle their creative efforts.

Not Recognizing Your Creativity

A primary reason people don't behave creatively is because they don't think they're creative. Beyond that, though, there are other reasons that prevent people from taking chances with ideas. While some of these may not seem applicable to the creative management of conflict situations, most are.

According to Crosby, these factors arise from society and educational processes. Where there is peer pressure, for example, people tend to value conformity, and that constrains creativity. In addition, being curious may be seen as disruptive to the status quo. Where people are success-oriented, failure is something to be feared and so the risk of acting creatively doesn't seem worth it. People may also believe that acting creatively is a kind of playing that doesn't belong in a work situation. Finally, people may view acting creatively in a negative sense because they buy into the stereotype that creativity is associated with craziness.[24]

While the ability to be creative is present in all of us but not encouraged as much as it could be, it is also quite easy for creativity training to fade if not supported by others important to the one trained (e.g., teachers, supervisors, etc.).

Creativity training is most effective when people receive training that can be applied across a number of problem-generating situations.[25] The techniques we discuss in the remainder of this chapter are of that nature.

Creativity as Thinking Differently

In the S-TLC model, we explained the role of "T" (Thinking), noting the importance of being creative in your analysis of the problem. To approach problems creatively, we often have to think of them differently. One way to do this is to start asking questions that we don't normally ask. For example, we can ask "what if" in silly ways. "How would I respond if the other person were the president of the United States?" "How would I respond if the other were a gorilla?" "What would I do if I knew I only had 10 days to live?" The point is to ask questions that may not even be related to the conflict in order to think about it differently.

> I was upset with how my boss assigned my work schedule. I was about to barge into his office and let off some steam. However, I decided to think instead that the boss was a Martian with antenna sticking out of its head. This alien visitor cannot understand what it is to be a human being. So I really had to rethink what I was going to say and do. I figured the boss couldn't do anything about the schedule now that it was published. I decided that it was best to just let the boss know that I would have preferred a different work schedule and wished I'd be consulted more in the future, but I didn't make a scene about it.

Second, we can imagine how others might handle the conflict. How would your sister, brother, mother, father, aunt, uncle, or friend handle it? As one writer says:

> I have a good friend, Stevan, who teaches in the philosophy department. In the past I have shared my writing projects with him because I value his feedback. He always looks at the paper from a macro view and comments on my overall logic and organization. So now, after I finish writing a paper, I consciously ask myself, what would Stevan say about my paper. I immediately look at the organization of the paper, especially focusing on the overall logic. Do I move clearly from problem to solution? Do my examples and data prove the points I am making? Are my generalizations in need of toning down? It amazes me how I suddenly now see problems in my paper that Stevan would have caught. I don't normally think like my friend, but I know him well enough that I can look at my paper from his point of view and realize errors in my thinking.

To take the idea of thinking differently further, de Bono has identified two ways of thinking differently, vertical and lateral.[26] In **vertical thinking,** we move through a series of steps, making sure that one is completed before the next one is started. If we were to take a vertical thinking approach to the process of conflict as we do in Chapter 2, we would analyze everything about the prelude before thinking about the triggering event, everything about the triggering event before the initiation, and everything about each of the other steps before moving on to the next. This is a good way to begin thinking about a conflict. But it may not give us all the information we need if the conflict is complex or ambiguous. The danger inherent in vertical thinking is that, if we believe we have drawn all the right conclusions as we go along, the final conclusion is inevitable. We won't reconsider how we got there.

Lateral thinking "is concerned with restructuring . . . patterns (insights) and provoking new ones (creativity)."[27] Brainstorming is one way to engage in lateral thinking. To utilize brainstorming, we would permit every group member's contribution regardless of how ridiculous it might seem. We will have more to say about brainstorming in Chapter 10. Whereas in vertical thinking we search for the "right" pattern, in lateral thinking we search for all the patterns we can see. Lateral thinking does not require that we be right; it only requires that we consider a number of different options. Sometimes a bad option causes one to think of a much better one, or causes one to see ways to combine bad and good options into a superior one.

Another means of lateral thinking is **reversal,** or working backwards from the goal or end result. What would it take to get from here to there? What would it take to get to some intermediate point? What would it take to get to the next step? For example, what do we teachers of conflict management hope students learn by studying a unit or a chapter? Once that is known, what readings, exercises, and activities would contribute to that result? Thinking this way helps us to see some of the precipitating factors we might not have seen before. The end result of reversal is that we can identify where you are and then list the steps it would take to get you to a point where you can better manage conflicts on your own.

A third means of lateral thinking is changing the choice of entry point and attention area. Whereas the **entry point** is the part of the problem or situation that is first examined, the **attention point** is often the triggering event we identified back in Chapter 1 and is the part of the problem that is usually focused on. For example, suppose you realize that your romantic partner or roommate or friend isn't speaking to you without considering why. We would call this the entry part of the problem because this is the first time you realized that there is a problem of some kind. Back in Chapter 1, we identified the "initiation stage" of the conflict process as the point at which one lets the other know that a conflict exists. At this point, one may not remember or realize that something he or she did or forgot to do may have "triggered" the conflict. However, once the offended or upset person pointed out that the other did something that offended or upset him or her, our perspective of the conflict takes a dramatic shift. The conflict trigger now becomes the attention point because it was the cause of the problem or conflict. The trigger is something the offended or upset person is unlikely to quickly get over, so the issue may linger on for that person. The other may have to admit some wrongdoing, offer restitution, or make an apology, so the triggering event may linger for that person as well. This is why we call this the attention point, which differs from the entry point of the conflict.

Suppose I realize that you are not speaking to me (entry point). When asked, you say it is because I didn't call when you thought I should (attention point). Whereas normally a lot of the conflict would now center around the fact that my not calling you upset you, we might suggest that you consider the following: (1) Why were you so upset or offended when I didn't call (focus more on the entry point)? (2) Why did I forget to call (focus more on the attention point)? These questions create different views of the conflict to make available more ways for resolving it.

A fourth means of lateral thinking is the Six Hats method. **Six Hats** refers to another problem-solving approach created by de Bono, which is a method for pulling together a variety of ways to more creatively manage conflicts in one's life. In this approach, you ask questions from different vantage points. The various hats and their questions are as follows:

White Hat—calls for information known or needed. Using the white hat approach, you would list everything you know about the conflict—who is involved, why they are involved, what the issues are, when the conflict started, and so on.

Red Hat—signifies feelings, hunches, and intuition. Using the red hat approach, you would list the feelings you have about the conflict. What do you think is going on that might not be evident?

Yellow Hat—symbolizes values and beliefs. From this perspective, you want to think about whether the solution you're seeking is consistent with the person you believe yourself to be. Is it something that can work for you? Is it something you can live with? Is it something you can be proud of?

Black Hat—stands for a contrarian judgment, the devil's advocate. Now you focus on why something may not work or why it could go wrong. The black hat approach is pessimistic. When everything is going well, what are you overlooking that could go wrong?

Green Hat—focuses on creativity: unforeseen possibilities, imaginative alternatives, and new ideas. The green hat asks for different ways of looking at the problem. This is the lateral thinking approach.

Blue Hat—takes a macro approach to managing the thinking process. Using a blue hat perspective is a way of keeping yourself honest in the whole process. Have you really thought of all the angles? Are there other ways of achieving the same goal? Is the goal worthwhile?

While the hats appear as a list, you are free to begin with any one of them: there's not a right or wrong way to start. You can also go back and forth among the various hats.

Essentially, lateral thinking is a way of turning problems on their sides or upside down in order to think about them and see them in a new way. Such thinking can be help us better manage our conflicts.

Creativity as Seeing Differently

Some methods in creative thinking are visual in nature; "right-brain" approaches to analysis using colors and images instead of logical relationships between words. One of the foremost is called **mind-mapping,** which uses existing ideas to generate new ones. By linking existing ideas together, you can often think of a better way to deal with a problem than you would have otherwise. First created to help people take notes more effectively, mind-mapping is a process that was popularized by Tony Buzan. Several computer programs have been created to help people make mind-maps.

Unlike outlining, which presumes a linear relationship between the elements of a problem (i.e., vertical thinking), and which also requires that we know how those elements are related before starting, mind-mapping (i.e., lateral thinking) does not require a starting point. For example, we encourage our students to think about conflicts in terms of steps beginning with prelude and ending in resolution as in Chapter 1. Sometimes, though, it's really hard to figure out where a conflict has begun or why the other is upset or offended. Useful for identifying issues, the mapping technique helps us analyze conflicts. Mind-mapping has several rules:

- There is always a central image or graphic representation of a problem, which is always placed in the center (of the page).
- Ideas flow freely—there is no censorship.
- Only one or two words are used as labels to represent key ideas.
- Color is important to the map—it gives emphasis to different ideas.
- Lines (solid/dotted) are used to make connections between ideas.[28]

To make a mind-map, you should have a large piece of unlined paper and something to write with. You can make your mind-map smaller and without color, but colors help you see relationships between concepts. Start in the middle of the paper and write down what you think the conflict is about (using one or two words as a label). Now, write down everything about the conflict that comes to your mind (again using one or two words as labels). Write quickly and don't restrict your thinking. The first step is getting everything on paper.

Figure 4.1 illustrates a simplified, finished map. A complete map would have sub-branches for each topic that derives from the center of the map. We have limited the detail here to two of the six branches.

For this person, the problem concerned time management and her family. Having just started a master's degree program, being married, having four children, and holding a full-time job was beginning to look too difficult to manage. By mind-mapping, she saw more clearly the various issues and how they were related to one another. A lot of the conflict management has to come from balancing the various demands and getting others to help in addressing them.

Once the working mother identified the conflict issues, she was in a better position to prioritize them: What is the most important issue here? What issues exceed her ability to control them? For this person, family emerges as most important—giving them enough time and energy and making sure they know that they are her top priority.

The mind-mapping technique shows how many issues are really present in a conflict and how they affect each other, at least from one person's point of view. It can also serve other uses like a diary, for self-analysis, to prepare for teaching and presentations, and for management of tasks.[29]

While mind-mapping visually gives us the big picture, visual journaling is a fairly recent phenomenon, with ties to scrapbooking and collage. It is a way of making sense of things without using large amounts of text. Generally, it puts incongruent images together and looks for patterns and possibilities among them.

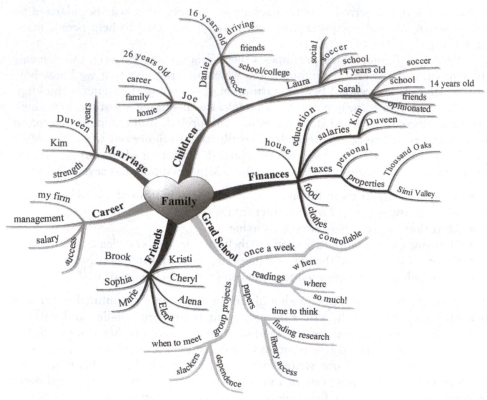

FIGURE 4.1
Example of Mind Mapping

Just as a journal is a written record of what we experience, a **visual journal** is an image-filled response to events that are happening in your life.[30] Since a visual journal is indeed a picture (or a group of pictures), the best way to understand it is to examine two examples.

In the following photo, the person who made the journal was experiencing a conflict in her dating relationship. She was finding that her boyfriend was rather controlling and she felt as though too often she was losing a part of what she valued in herself. As you can see, visual journaling is a sort of self-talk, much like a written journal, but nonverbal.

To use this technique effectively, you must first realize that it is guided by the process of creativity—preparation, incubation, illumination, and verification. To prepare, you need to first put aside any idea that you are going to create "art." You may in fact create it, but it is safer to begin by thinking that you are simply going to explore ideas using a visual medium. Second, have many more images at hand than you think you need. You can use all kinds of found images, such as those in old magazines or what you download from the Internet. It helps to have five or six different types of magazines that you can mutilate. Cut both images and interesting text, and don't worry about always cutting neatly or in a square. Cut around objects that you find interesting.

"How Far" by Ania Mulka.

Incubate your ideas by placing images in different places on the page. Put more on the page than you intend to use. Don't think about what you are using; simply reach for images as you feel led to them. Look at them upside down. Rearrange them at least three times. When you are satisfied, glue them in place.

Next, seek illumination by studying the array of images and text you have chosen. What is it saying about the conflict? What is it saying about your feelings? Finally, verify your conclusions by showing the journal to a trusted friend. Ask that person what they see in it. They may help you see the conflict even more differently than you thought.

Visual journaling can be a great way to work through problems when we simply have no words to describe them. When our emotions threaten to overcome us, images can help us focus so that words might come later.

I create art to help me understand problems in my own life as well as to help unblock my writing. One of the questions I found that really opened up some possibilities was a simple one that occurred in the middle of a piece of art—"Where would I be without my fear?" Answering that question helped me later on.

We're not suggesting that everyone start creating art (but it wouldn't hurt if we did); we are suggesting moving beyond the obvious to deal with conflicts in new ways that might ultimately be more fruitful.

We, the authors of this textbook attempted to blend together tried and true techniques for managing conflict with some new and different ideas of our own. To ensure that you are not lost in the details of any one chapter, we conclude this chapter with a summary of the main principles that should guide you as you manage your conflicts.

MANAGE IT

This chapter introduced you to one of the most important tools in conflict management—the S-TLC system. The S-TLC system teaches us to stop, think, listen, and then communicate with the other person. By following these four steps, we can often resolve interpersonal conflicts through basic communication skills.

The effective conflict manager knows when and how to appropriately confront others. Confrontation is a conflict process in which the parties call attention to problems or issues by assertively speaking up for their interests, concerns, or rights in a way that does not interfere with the interests or basic communication rights of others. There are six steps to confronting interpersonal problems. They are as follows:

- Preparation: Identify your problem/needs/issues.
- Arrange for a time and place to meet and talk.
- Interpersonal confrontation: Talk to the other person about your problem.
- Consider your partner's point of view: Listen, empathize, and respond with understanding.
- Resolve the problem: Make a mutually satisfying agreement.
- Follow up on the solution: Set a time limit for reevaluation.

To help students create assertive messages for expressing their feelings, wants, and needs during the third step of the confrontation process, we encourage them to use **personalized communication**—language using I-statements (i.e., I think, I feel) rather than "you" or depersonalized statements (i.e., "you always," "most people think"). These I-statements consist of four parts: I feel (feeling statement), when I (problematic behavior statement), because I (consequences statement), and I'd like (goals statement).

Learning conflict management skills can produce satisfying results. However, we can enhance those outcomes by being creative, especially in the thinking stage of confrontation. Creativity occurs when a person makes new and insightful connections between what he or she knows, the problem at hand, and possible solutions to that problem. It is important to realize that there are not a lot of innate differences between people who are creative and people who are not; creativity can be learned but it means listening to your intuition more closely. Can we learn to be creative? The answer is "yes."

One way to think differently is to ask questions that we don't normally ask. Second, we can imagine how others might handle the conflict. Third, you can try thinking vertically so as you move through a series of steps, you make sure that one is completed before the next one is started. Fourth, you can think laterally, which is a way of turning problems on their sides or upside down in order to think about them and see them in a new way. One means of lateral thinking is reversal, or

> **TABLE 4.4**
>
> **The Relationship of Type of Conflict with the Creative Method for Dealing with It**
>
> | Type of Conflict | Creative Method |
> | --- | --- |
> | Displaced, misplaced, or overblown revenge/retaliation | Visual journaling |
> | Arguing due to needed adjustments to changes in the environment | Mind-mapping |
> | Uncertainty due to lack of information | Vertical thinking, brainstorming, and Six Hats |

working backwards from the goal or end result. Thinking this way helps us to see some of the precipitating factors we might not have seen before. Other approaches to creative thinking are more visual. Mind-mapping, Six Hats, and visual journaling are "right-brain" approaches to analysis using colors and images instead of logical relationships between words. As depicted in Table 4.4, each may be used when dealing with certain types of conflict.

EXERCISES

THINK ABOUT IT

1. Think of a time when you felt that you handled a conflict well. What did you do that seemed competent to you? How do those behaviors contrast with a time when you felt you handled a conflict poorly?
2. How hard is it for you to stop a conflict? If you find it easy to not respond automatically, what advice can you give others who have trouble with this step? Whether you find this step difficult or not, what ways do you prefer if you try to take a "time out"?
3. What are you thinking about when others talk? Do you concentrate on what they are saying or do you think about your own ideas instead? After listening to someone, can you write down most of what that person told you? If not, why not?
4. In what kinds of situations are you most likely to be assertive? Were there disadvantages for you? Under what conditions is assertiveness advantageous?
5. How would you explain the importance of creativity in conflict management to another person?
6. Can you think of a time when a trained incapacity such as goal-centeredness or critical thinking got in the way of mutual understanding of a conflict situation? How did you determine that you were hampered by a trained incapacity?
7. What kinds of conflicts would be best analyzed using (a) the Six Hats method, (b) mind-mapping, and (c) a visual journal?

APPLY IT

1. Take a sheet of paper and make three columns. In each column, describe a conflict in which you thought the other person should change, you were able to change the conditions (or social environment) of the conflict, and you thought you should change in yourself. Which of the changes was easiest to implement? Why?

2. Take a sheet of paper and make three columns on it. Label the columns instrumental goal, relationship goal, and identity goal. In each column, describe a conflict you experienced or observed with that goal. What made it a conflict? How did you resolve the conflict?

3. Take a piece of paper and write a description of a conflict you recently experienced or observed. Below your description, list the actions you took that you would label as assertive. If you discover that none were taken, list the assertive actions you could have taken.

4. Look at the following statements. Which are correctly stated needs or feeling statements?

   a. I feel disappointed that you are backing out of this show after you agreed to help me with it.
   b. You really irritate me when you don't show up for a date with me.
   c. I need assurance I am loved in a language I understand.
   d. I need for you to tell me where a class is going so that I can get excited about it.
   e. I feel like a single parent around here.
   f. You don't seem to contribute anything to our group project.
   g. I feel frustrated when it seems that I have sole responsibility for planning our dates.
   h. I feel like I am going crazy.
   i. I feel insecure when we don't have at least the equivalent of a month's salary in the bank.
   j. I am not the only person who's having trouble in your class.

5. Look at the following statements. Which statements are goal statements specifying a clear want?

   a. Let's get together for lunch.
   b. I want us to spend more time together with the kids.
   c. I want you to attend this class with me.
   d. I wish we could play different kinds of music around here instead of yours all the time.
   e. I want to stop feeling overwhelmed.
   f. I don't want your pity!
   g. I wish you'd get off my case!
   h. I would like us to have one night a week, Wednesday, just for ourselves.
   i. I want you to exercise more.
   j. I want you to put your dirty clothes in the laundry instead of on the floor.

6. Fill in the blanks with words that complete the sentence using the formula:
   I feel . . . when . . . because . . . I want . . .

   • I feel _____ when I have to wait and wait because I hate waiting around and wasting time. I want to leave at the time we agreed on.
   • I feel frustrated when _____ because I don't know what is expected of me. I would like some help on how to improve my grades.
   • I feel angry at myself when we stay out too late and drink too much because_____. I want to get more sleep and cut down on my drinking.
   • I feel frustrated when I am the only one who cleans up this place because it's not fair to me. I want_____.

   Create your own I-statements:
   • I feel afraid when _____ because_____. I want _____.

   • I feel _____ when _____ because_____. I want _____.

7. Use the mind-mapping technique to analyze a conflict you have experienced recently. After you are done, write the answers to these questions: What were you thinking when you started? Is it still the same? When you see the whole picture, how is your thinking affected? What was surprising? Are there any parts out of balance? Do you need to fill anything else in?

8. Use the Six Hats problem-solving method to analyze a conflict you have experienced recently. Be sure to write the names of each hat and the conclusion that perspective brings to you.

WORK WITH IT

Read over the following actions, and identify any that you think are good examples of asser-tive communication.

   a. I not only have a high regard for the other, I also have a high regard for myself and my own personal goals.

   b. I allow other persons to interrupt me as much as they want. I believe that I am sensitive and subordinate to them. I am extremely indecisive and need time to think before settling a conflict. I often accommodate to the other person's view.

   c. I find that I use this behavior a lot at work and with the people with whom I work. I find myself forgetting promises, appointments, and agreements; making unkind statements about others when they are not around; scheduling too many tasks to do at once; gossiping about the people I am in a conflict with. I continuously deny that something is wrong, but then fail to cooperate.

   d. I don't let a lot bother me up to a certain point. Because of this, I do think I am letting other people get what they want and accommodating them. I know that I avoid serious conflicts in this manner. But when I am pushed past my limit my automatic system takes over and I shake like a leaf. It scares me into a sweat.

   e. I always seem to try to impose my will onto others. I know that I need to chill out at times but sometimes my anger takes over when I am in a heated argument. I bring up topics that the other person wasn't expecting. I use this style in situations where I need to win. I am highly competitive.

   f. I resort to swearing and other forms of verbal intimidation.

   g. Conflict can just be unproductive. I just save my breath rather than trying to explain my point of view.

   h. I make sure that my opinion is known and do the best I can to make sure my interests are known. But I also do not like anyone else to feel left out in a conflict situation. I am clear and concise in telling others what I believe the problem to be and possible ways to remedy it. Another behavior I have in a conflict situation is to be listened to and taken seriously. I believe everyone should be taken seriously, especially in a conflict situation.

   i. I try to be careful not to hurt anyone else's feelings with anything I say. I like to express myself in a responsible manner so as to not offend others.

DISCUSS IT

1. Read the following case study and answer the questions that follow it.
   When engaged in conflict with my brother, Carl, we usually begin with a period of silence where we both contemplate our reasons for feeling as we do. We usually think the problem over thoroughly before we say anything. Then comes the verbal argument (I prefer to call it a discussion). We try to be compromising and focus on the problem. We are supportive, encouraging, direct, and honest. We express positive feelings for each other to let each other know that we care and want things to work out. We are careful about letting the other express himself while trying to understand

his point of view. If you asked either of us, we could summarize the other's concerns quite accurately. I would say we believe in equal power. Finally after we get everything off our chests and get the matter resolved, we poke fun at each other and feel like a weight has been lifted off our shoulders.

    a. Did the parties use the S-TLC system for dealing with this conflict situation? How so?

    b. What do you think the parties probably did to "stop"?

    c. What do you think the parties probably did during the "thinking" step?

    d. What techniques do you think the parties probably used during the "listening" step?

2. Read the following case study and answer the questions that follow it.

My friend and I both struggle with our emotional problems. Lately, we have both worked on areas in our lives. She is trying to assert herself more, and I am to the point where I cannot take any more advice on how to run my life. I need to start thinking about what I want to be, not what everyone else tells me I should be. Unfortunately, these two areas have run into each other. She feels she needs to tell me how she feels about everything, including how I act. For example, she told me the other day that I should just say, "I can't go with you today," instead of giving a long explanation. She told me when I give a long explanation it seems that I am trying to make up an excuse and that I just don't want to go with her. I told her I really couldn't handle that kind of criticism right now, and she said "no problem." Two days later, we got into it again when she got mad at me for something that wasn't my fault. She still believes she should assert herself and tell me exactly what is on her mind, and I still cannot handle it right now. It's a stalemate.

    a. Regarding the S-TLC system, do you think the parties tried to "stop"? According to the text reading, what could/should they have done? If you are good at doing this step, what advice can you give to others?

    b. What do you think the parties probably did during the "thinking" step? According to the text reading, what could/should they have done? If you are good at doing this step, what advice can you give to others?

    c. What techniques did the parties use during the "listening" step? According to the text reading, what could/should they have done? If you are good at doing this step, what advice can you give to others?

    d. Did the parties try using I-statements? According to the text reading, what could/should they have done? If you are good at doing this step, what advice can you give to others?

    e. In what ways could the narrator change her friend, the situation, or herself?

3. In the following case study, how might you use the ideas in this chapter to produce a creative and more insightful resolution to the conflict?

An interesting situation is occurring with another tenant and my roommate and me in our apartment building. We have assigned parking spaces, and the tenant that parks next to my roommate has a tendency to pull his car in and park it in half of her space. She has asked him to move over because she has trouble opening her car door. He becomes upset because his car is soaked by the sprinklers located on the other side of it. Two nights ago when we came home, he was over his line and into our space. My roommate parked close to his car because she thought it might make him realize how close he was parking. However, he got angry and left a nasty note on her windshield. Both parties are not happy. I see the situation as petty, and I think that the neighbors need to work out some kind of agreement instead of exchanging unpleasant words or nasty notes.

    a. Before attempting to be creative, what would be a more obvious, straightforward application of the six-step confrontation model?

    b. How might you think differently in this situation? Ask unusual questions, imagine how someone you know might view the situation, and/or try thinking laterally.

    c. How might you apply visual methods of creative thinking: mind-mapping, Six Hats, and visual journaling?

    d. Using any or all of the above methods, describe a creative approach that produced a preferable, constructive solution to the problem that was different from initial attempts to resolve the conflict.

4. In the following case study, how might you use the ideas in this chapter to produce a creative and more insightful resolution to the conflict?

    My husband and I went out for an early dinner at a nice restaurant. The restaurant was practically empty, but we were seated next to a table that had a recently stained cover. The table had been cleared but had not been re-set for dinner. My husband, who once worked as a server in a 5-star restaurant, was horrified that the cloth was there—he felt that it should have been removed immediately even if the table wasn't set. He told the person who seated us that is was disgraceful, he told our server, and when the manager came over to ask if she could be of help, he told her. He was not appeased by their report that the busboy had not come in and it would be taken care of when he arrived. And no one was taking his "hint," if you could call it that, that the cloth simply be removed regardless of whether the table would be immediately re-set. The manager finally took it off but I could tell she was completely exasperated by his disgust at the tablecloth. Even after it was removed he kept saying that being forceful was the only way to get things done, and he was convinced he was right because everyone gave in to his demand. I was so embarrassed by his behavior that I left the waitress a *very* good tip.

    a. Before attempting to be creative, what would be a more obvious, straightforward application of the six-step confrontation model?

    b. How might you think differently in this situation? Ask unusual questions, imagine how someone you know might view the situation, try thinking laterally.

    c. How might you apply visual methods of creative thinking: mind-mapping, Six Hats, and visual journaling.

    d. Using any or all of the above methods, describe a creative approach that produced a preferable, constructive solution to the problem that was different from initial attempts to resolve the conflict.

EXERCISE: "MANAGING AN INTERPERSONAL CONFLICT"

OBJECTIVE

The goal is to apply the key concepts and principles taught in this chapter in a role play consisting of two conflicting parties and possibly one or two observers.

TIME

    Ten minutes to select a scenario, discuss the roles to be played.

    Fifteen minutes to discuss and resolve the conflict.

    Twenty minutes for the role players and observers to discuss their conflict with the rest of the class.

INSTRUCTIONS

Form groups of three or four persons. Two are to role play a conflict with the other one or two acting as observers and then complete Form #1 below. The two role players select one of the scenarios below (or make up another if you prefer) to serve as a conflict. Try to apply the principles and techniques taught in the chapter. Assume that you have thought about the conflict ahead of time (preparation—engaging in positive self-talk and imagined interaction), made a date to sit down and talk (at a convenient time and place). Now it is time for you to engage in interpersonal confrontation. Try to use S-TLC, assertiveness, and I-statements. After you explain the problem to the other, try to consider the other person's point of view, try to reach agreement that you can both feel good about (win–win), and set a time for a follow-up to ensure that the agreement is working out. Note to role players: It is fun to really get into the scene and add to it. You can supply details. You can start out angry, have to take a time out, say something rude, and see how the other responds. Maybe start out being difficult, but then slowly come around to the other's point of view. Maybe shake hands or hug at the end to show that all is well that ends well. Role plays can be done one at a time for the benefit of the class as an audience, or several done simultaneously in different parts of the classroom. They may or may not be videotaped for later viewing.

ROLE PLAYS

a. Family members: Brother and sister (or two sisters). You think that your sister took an expensive piece of furniture from your father's house after he passed away without discussing it with you. Your sister took care of your father in his final days and had a key to his house. Your sister was also in control of your father's finances and you think she took all his money from the bank during his final days. Now you are angry at your sister.

b. Two roommates are living in a house, with one television. You try to treat each other equally. Recently your roommate decided that he/she wants to watch some TV programs that are on at the same time as sporting events. Meanwhile, you want to watch sports on the weekend and some weekday nights. The negative atmosphere is so bad in the house that you decide to confront your roommate about it.

c. Two romantic partners are having a conflict overtime management. You want to spend time with your buddies and even invite one or two to join you and your woman friend when you go out together. She doesn't approve of all of your friends and finds two to be particularly offensive and a bad influence on you. She also wants to spend more time with you without your buddies hanging around.

d. A friend left her boyfriend and asked to move in with you. Kristi spends too much money. She likes to buy a lot of clothes. She never has enough for meals or gas, so she is always asking you for money to buy food or gas. She wants "a loan" from time to time and sometimes doesn't have enough to help pay the apartment rent and utilities. You are fortunate to have enough money, but think it is unfair that she isn't pulling her share and needs money from you so often. Kristi often doesn't pay back the money she owes you.

e. Two resident hall roommates: Bryon comes home late and rowdy from the local bars on Thursday, Friday, and Saturday nights. Sometimes he brings guys with him. On occasion one has even slept over because he was too drunk to drive. You have Friday classes and need to go to work early every weekend.

f. Two sisters: Tiffney borrows your clothes without your permission. She also occasionally snoops through your room and tries to find your diary, cell phone, and other personal items.

g. Married seniors: Husband recently retired and now spends all his time in the house. He doesn't do any household chores and gets in his wife's way.

h. Two neighbors: Pearson's dog barks, and when loose makes messes in his neighbor's yard. Recently the dog ripped open the garbage container when the neighbor placed it at the end of the drive for pickup.

FORM 1: OBSERVATION OF INTERPERSONAL CONFLICT.

1. How well did the conflicting parties use S-TLC? Did anyone stop and take a time out? Would it have been useful?

2. How might the conflicting parties have improved their "thinking" about the conflict?
3. How might the conflicting parties have improved their "listening" during the conflict?
4. How might the conflicting parties have improved their "communicating" during the conflict? (Did they use I-statements, assertiveness?)
5. How well did the parties use the six-step confrontation model? How well did each listen to the other?
6. Did the parties reach an agreement that both were satisfied with?
7. Did the parties set a date to return for a follow-up on how well the agreement was working out?
8. How well did the parties use their creativity? Did they try to look at the problem from different angles (use lateral or vertical thinking)? Did they use mind-mapping or visual journaling?
9. On a scale of 1–10 (worst–best management), how would you rate the management of this interpersonal confrontation? Which conflicting party attempted to be the most productive?

NOTES

1. Rory Remer and Paul de Mesquita, "Teaching and Learning the Skills of Interpersonal Confrontation," in Dudley D. Cahn (Ed.), *Intimates in Conflict: A Communication Perspective* (Hillsdale, NJ: Lawrence Erlbaum Associates, 1990), pp. 225–252.
2. Steven R. Wilson and Linda L. Putnam, "Interaction Goals in Negotiation," in James A. Anderson (Ed.), *Communication Yearbook 13* (Newbury Park, CA: Sage, 1990), p. 381.
3. William H. Baker, "Defensiveness in Communication: Its Causes, Effects and Cures," Journal of Business Communication 17 (1980), 33, 35.
4. Erik Rautalinko and Hans-Olaf Lisper, "Effects of Training Reflective Listening in a Corporate Setting," *Journal of Business and Psychology* 18 (2004), 281–299.
5. Carl R. Rogers, *On Becoming a Person* (Cambridge, MA: The Riverside Press, 1961), p. 18.
6. Baker, *Journal of Business Communication,* 33, 35.
7. Glen H. Stamp, Anita L. Vengelisti, and John A. Daly, "The Creation of Defensiveness in Social Interaction," *Communication Quarterly* 40 (1992), 177–190.
8. Nigel G. Ward, Rafael Escalante, Yaffa Al Bayyari, and Thamar Solorio, "Learning to Show You're Listening," *Computer Assisted Language Learning* 20 (2007), 385.
9. David Augsburger, *Caring Enough to Hear and Be Heard* (Ventura, CA: Regal Books, 1982).
10. Remer and de Mesquita, *Intimates in Conflict*, p. 229.
11. James M. Honeycutt, Kenneth S. Zagacki, and Renee Edwards, "Imagined Interaction and Interpersonal Communication," *Communication Reports* 3 (1990), 1–8.
12. Renee Edwards, James M. Honeycutt, and Kenneth S. Zagacki, "Imagined Interaction as an Element of Social Cognition," *Western Journal of Speech Communication* 52 (1988), 23–45.
13. Denise H. Cloven, "Relational Effects of Interpersonal Conflict: The Role of Cognition, Satisfaction, and Anticipated Communication," Master's thesis, Northwestern University, Evanston, IL, 1990.
14. Denise H. Cloven and Michael E. Roloff, "Sense-Making Activities and Interpersonal Conflict: Communication Cures for the Mulling Blues," *Western Journal of Speech Communication* 55 (1991), 134–158.
15. Terre H. Allen and Kristen M. Berkos, "Ruminating about Symbolic Conflict through Imagined Interactions," *Imagination, Cognition, and Personality* 25 (2005–2006), 307–320.

16. Amy S. Ebesu Hubbard, "Conflict between Relationally Uncertain Romantic Partners: The Influence of Relational Responsiveness and Empathy," *Communication Monographs* 68 (2001), 402.

17. Paul Schrodt and Lawrence R. Wheeless, "Aggressive Communication and Informational Reception Apprehension: The Influence of Listening Anxiety and Intellectual Inflexibility on Trait Argumentativeness and Verbal Aggressiveness," *Communication Quarterly* 49 (2001), 57.

18. J. Dan Rothwell, *In Mixed Company,* 6th Edition (Wadsworth, 2007).

19. Walter Isard and Christine Smith, *Conflict Analysis and Practical Conflict Management* (Cambridge, MA: Ballinger Publishing, 1982).

20. Herbert J. Hess and Charles O. Tucker, *Talking about Relationships,* 2nd Edition (Prospect Heights, IL: Waveland Press, 1980), pp. 13–14.

21. Howard Gardner, *Creating Minds* (New York: Basic Books, 1993).

22. Robert Weisberg, *Creativity: Genius and Other Myths* (New York: W. H. Freeman and Company, 1986).

23. Robert J. Sternberg, "Creativity as a Decision," *American Psychologist* 57 (2002), 376.

24. Andrew Crosby, *Creativity and Performance in Industrial Organization* (London: Tavistock Publications, 1968).

25. Ginamarie Scott, Lyle E. Leritz, and Michael D. Mumford, "The Effectiveness of Creativity Training: A Quantitative Review," *Creativity Research Journal* 16 (2004), 361–388.

26. Edward de Bono, *Lateral Thinking: Creativity Step by Step* (New York: Harper and Row, 1970).

27. Ibid., p. 14.

28. Joyce Wycoff, *Mindmapping: Your Personal Guide to Exploring Creativity and Problem Solving* (New York: Berkeley Books, 1991, p. 43).

29. Tony Buzan and Barry Buzan, *The Mind Map Book* (New York: Plume Books, 1993).

30. Some good references are Sharon Soneff, *Art Journals and Creative Healing* (Beverly, MA: Quarry Books, 2008) and Kelly Rae Roberts, *Taking Flight* (Cincinnati, OH: North Light Books, 2008).

Managing Violent Tendencies

OBJECTIVES

At the end of this chapter you should be able to:

- Explain why people are violent.
- Define interpersonal violence.
- Explain the steps in the violence and chilling effect cycles.
- Identify the three most common communication approaches to the study of interpersonal violence.

- Explain why violence is not a fact of life.
- Explain the role of alcohol and jealousy in the escalation of violence.
- Describe the factors that contribute to violence in the workplace.

KEY TERMS

aggressive communication
Alternatives to Violence
    Project (AVP)
Batterer Intervention
    Programs (BIPs)
chilling effect
common couple violence
communication cognitions
communication competence
communicator personality
    trait
culture of violence theory

dialectical
dialectical tensions
ethnography
general aggression model
interpersonal violence
interpersonal violence cycle
intimate terrorism
narratives
nonverbally aggressive
    communication
organizational culture
participant observation

patriarchal violence
physical aggression
qualitative methods
relational
    control-motivated
    aggression
social construction theory
unstructured interviews
verbal abuse
violence
workplace violence

W hen an interpersonal conflict gets out of hand, there is a likelihood of it turning violent. Violence is becoming increasingly prevalent in American social life, making the effective management of conflict an essential social skill. Researchers report that as many as 35 percent of high school students experience a physical altercation in a year's time.[1] Some of you have suffered painfully at the hands of a friend, partner, family member, bully, or work colleague. But suppose you have not? Interpersonal violence still affects you. Taking a broader view to include violent acts between acquaintances and strangers, the World Health Organization reports that the cost of people doing violence to each other reaches 3.3 percent of the U.S. gross domestic product.[2] This translates into a drag on the economy, costing us jobs, higher expenses, and lower pay. Due to its ubiquitous nature, violence in interpersonal conflict has received a significant amount of attention from social scientists in communication and other disciplines.[3] In this book, we do not include acquaintances and strangers, but it is clear that a great many partners in interpersonal relationships would benefit from learning how to prevent their conflicts from getting out of hand.

WHY ARE PEOPLE VIOLENT?

A number of different theories attempt to explain why people choose violence in conflict situations. We examine two of them in this chapter—the culture of violence theory and the general aggression model.

Culture of Violence Theory

Articulated by Wolfgang and Ferracuti,[4] the **culture of violence theory** argues that in large societies such as the United States, people form subgroups that develop values and norms justifying the use of physical force that exceeds the level that the larger culture might tolerate. Gang violence, for example, occurs due to subgroups that have come to see violence as the primary alternative when faced with an opponent. Commentary surrounding the Trayvon Martin case in Florida, where an older, heavier white male (George Zimmerman) killed a younger, smaller black male (Martin), has included many voices that justified the use of deadly force by Zimmerman. Advocates of the culture of violence theory could claim that Florida's law that allows a person who feels threatened "to stand his or her ground" even when retreat is possible is creating a culture of violence in that state.

General Aggression Model

A second theory that attempts to explain violence is the general aggression model,[5] which adds to our understanding of the prelude stage of the conflict process (see Chapter 1) by calling attention to the inclinations of the participants who later engage in conflict. The model argues that violence is chosen, or not chosen, based on the way the following factors interact: personal and situation variables, the present internal state of the actor, and the appraisal and decision process. Personal variables include personality qualities such as trait anger, past experiences of violence, and attitudes toward violence. Situational variables include alcohol use and physical or mental exhaustion. The present internal state of the actor may depend on recently experienced negative emotions such as anger, frustration, and disappointment. The appraisal and decision process requires the actor to have the mental resources available for reflection on potential anger. Thus, if a person is inclined to be angry, thinks of violence as an acceptable alternative, has recently experienced an emotional conflict with someone, and is mentally exhausted, he or she is much more likely to automatically choose violence than resist using it. Under the right conditions, all of us may turn violent; however, must we? The model implies that people who practice self-control can increase their ability to resist engaging in violent acts against others.

Both theories suggest that people may choose violence as they reflect on their experiences and react to their current affective states. The important point we want to make is this: violence is still a matter of choice, and not a good one.

INTERPERSONAL VIOLENCE DEFINED

Interpersonal violence is not difficult to recognize; it occurs when a person imposes his or her will (i.e., wants, needs, or desires) on a friend, romantic partner, family member, or work colleague through verbal or physical intimidation.[6] Violence has physical, emotional, and mental effects.

The degree of violence can range from relatively minor (verbal threats, threatening gestures) to extreme acts of physical aggression, torture, and bodily harm.[7] Violent behavior also ranges from carefully planned attacks to sudden emotional outbursts that injure others. Some persons may choose aggressive behavior in only one situation for a particular reason (such as revenge), while others choose it in many situations for many reasons.

According to our view, interpersonal violence, physical aggression, and abusive relationships are types of conflict communication, albeit extreme and unhealthy types, sometimes referred to as the dark side of interpersonal communication.[8]

Identifying the Potentially Violent Conflict Communicator

We may know physically violent behavior when we see it, but what communication cues do *potentially* violent communicators give off? The cues are many. They tend to interrupt, dominate, and stereotype others. They may engage in intense, glaring eye contact, put forward an invading posture as they bear down on others, and emit an arrogant air about them. They may try to dominate others by being loud, abrasive, blaming, intimidating, and sarcastic. They may make statements like the following:

"I have never lost an argument."
"His stereo was so loud, I had to go over and pull the plug out of the wall. Then, he got the message."
"I try to make others look bad, so that I look good. I try to get my way at all costs."
"I am the boss. I know what's best."
"I don't care what you think."

In Chapter 2, we listed a number of behaviors that contribute to the escalation of a conflict, which can cause it to get out of hand, such as making a threatening gesture (fist, finger), pushing/shoving/poking with finger/hitting, making verbal threats, and damaging the other's possessions. If abusers don't start a fight by getting physical, they react with violence the instant the other party "provokes them." They often get nasty in an argument by using intimate knowledge against the other, bringing up unrelated issues, making promises they don't intend to keep, using other people (attacking through friends or family), and demanding more than they should. Sometimes they display their battles in public.

> I sat in on a trial of an abusive husband. When the wife was on the witness stand, she said that she was fleeing from her husband when she got in their pick up truck and started out of the driveway. She claimed that he ran behind, jumped on the side of the truck, reached through the open window, and tried to grab the steering wheel. While they swerved this way and that, she drove over a bridge high above the water while he held on to the truck sometimes swinging out over the bridge railing. That is when the police saw them and pulled her over. It was a wonder he didn't fall to his death or force her to have an accident.

People who resort to violence or threats of violence often win conflicts at the expense of their partners, because they care less about relational goals than their own personal goals. Over time, the abused partner may eventually "get fed up" and leave the relationship, so both partners end up losing in the long run. Violent communication may take two forms: verbal abuse and physical aggression.

Verbal Abuse

In communication research, **verbal abuse** is defined as attacking the self-concept of another person in order to cause psychological pain for the other.[9] Verbal abuse is a form of psychological intimidation and takes the form of character attacks, insults, ridicule, profanity, and threats. It can also include making stereotypical and prejudicial comments.

A large body of research in a variety of settings demonstrates the importance of avoiding verbal abuse. Students are less likely to want to attend college classes taught by verbally abusive professors.[10] A study of health workers found that incidents of verbal abuse caused as much or more stress on the job as incidents of physical aggression.[11] Parental verbal abuse is linked to adolescent dissociative experiences.[12] College students describing patterns of aggression in their homes demonstrate the link between verbal abuse and physical aggression. As the frequency of the verbal abuse between their parents increases, so does the incidence of physical aggression. Parents who attempt to solve conflicts through "rational" means (i.e., talking it over) are much less likely to engage in physical aggression in conflict situations.[13] Men who were raised in violent families are more likely to be verbally aggressive, domineering, and negative with their dating partners, showing potential for physical aggression.[14]

Verbal abuse often plays a role in conflicts that turn physically violent. Researchers have found that verbal abuse is a part of a pattern of escalation that frequently leads to physical aggression.[15] In actuality, physical (nonverbal) aggression and verbal abuse often occur together, sequentially or simultaneously. While not all verbal abuse leads to physical violence, nearly all physically violent episodes are preceded by verbal abuse. Next we discuss nonverbal or physically aggressive communication.

Nonverbal Aggression (Physical Violence)

Physical aggression usually starts early in life. It consists of physical harm to others. A study of sixth-grade schoolchildren found that physical aggression is seen as a natural response to certain kinds of verbal abuse, particularly those associated with attacks on physical characteristics, ethnicity, or race.[16] Studies by Infante and his colleagues established that physically abusive husbands are more verbally abusive than non-physically abusive spouses. They are also less argumentative, in that they are less able to verbally defend their position and refute the positions that others take. The inability to argue verbally to establish and support different positions is a major contributor to physical and verbal violence.[17]

Although, research on violence in the family mostly focuses primarily on romantic couples or parent–child abuse, there are instances of adolescent-to-parent abuse. Of the thousands of articles written on domestic violence over the past 20 years, only a few dozen are on child-to-parent abuse.[18]

One of the biggest difficulties in examining physical violence is the effect that the presence of other people has on violent offenders. In many cases, people see violent behavior as necessary and appropriate; indeed, sometimes they believe that it is the only acceptable solution.[19] In addition, the presence of bystanders egging on the conflicting parties may encourage it to escalate into violence or good Samaritans may step in to stop it. Feld and Robinson found that the presence of bystanders decreased the use of violence by men toward women, but increased the use of violence of women toward men.[20]

Gender Differences

Intimate partner violence, particularly physical assault, rape, and stalking, are gender based. Research shows that men are more likely to resort to physical violence toward their female partners than vice versa. According to Marshall, males are more likely to hit or kick a wall, door, or furniture; drive dangerously; act like a bully; hold and pin; shake or roughly handle; grab; and twist an arm. Females are often the target of these acts.[21] Research also shows that male partners and fathers are more likely to physically harm their women and children than vice versa.[22] In the United States during 2005, 1181 women and 329 men were killed by an intimate partner (p. 3). The National Survey on Violence Against Women found that as many as 25 percent of surveyed women but only 8 percent of men reported that they had been sexually and/or physically assaulted by an intimate partner. Women also reported more severe violence such as having an intimate partner beat them up, choke or try to drown them, or threaten them with a knife or gun.[23] Moreover, more women than men reported feeling fearful because of a stalking experience.[24]

While interpersonal violence is usually viewed from a female-victim perspective, not all the threats or violent acts are done by men.

> I used to live next door to a young couple who had a large window in their kitchen right across the driveway from our kitchen window. We observed several loud confrontations between our neighbors that always went the same way. We would hear her yelling at him, and then she would grab one

of the large pans and try to swing it at him, which was a rather comical sight because he kept trying to get close to her and hug her. He would say, "Just let me hug you, let me make it up to you, I want to be nice to you," but she would swing the pan back and forth and yell, "Get away from me, don't touch me, I hate you . . ." It was always the same bizarre scene.

In cases where men are injured by their female partners, they may not report these violent acts to authorities because of the male stereotype as dominant over others or "taking it like a man," and the stigma attached to appearing weak.[25] According to privacy management theory,[26] the possibility of losing face may explain why men would be less likely than women to admit or report that they are victims of abuse.

The reports of male abuse that do exist suggest that roughly a third of women have physically attacked their male dating partners.[27] However, the way in which male-victim violence is reported differs from the way female-victim violence is reported. Violent acts by men are usually attributed to internal personality factors, such as the desire to dominate and control; violent acts by women were often labeled as self-defensive or retaliatory. Recall from our discussion of attribution theory in Chapter 3 that internal attributions included personality factors and external attributions included environmental factors (outside the individual) that impinged on the person. So, male violence may be seen as internally motivated (mean, controlling) and subject to blame, but female violence as externally motivated (he was trying to attack me) and more likely justified.

In both intimate partner violence and parent–child violence, verbal abuse may escalate into physical aggression. Verbal abuse and physical aggression are not recommended and often characterize problematic relationships in need of help, although the partners may not think so. There are two cycles that involve violence or the threat of violence: the interpersonal violence and the chilling effect cycles.

TWO TYPES OF INTERPERSONAL VIOLENCE

The Interpersonal Violence Cycle

The following steps comprise the **interpersonal violence cycle** (Figure 5.1):

1. Violence cycles begin with perceptions of unresolved conflict that color the perception of a current triggering event.
2. The cycle may begin in disagreement, but escalate into verbal abuse.
3. The conflict may end here, unresolved, and leaving a bad memory.
4. In some cases, verbal abuse may escalate into physical aggression, when one or both parties physically attack the other.
5. At some point, physical aggression stops, either by the participants themselves or by a third party.
6. Such behavior results in the individual feeling victimized.

For example, a couple with a history of unresolved conflicts may start by disagreeing over where to place fruits and vegetables in the refrigerator ("they should go over here"; "no they should go there"), but escalate into insults, name calling, and the like, and may even wind up screaming and throwing objects.

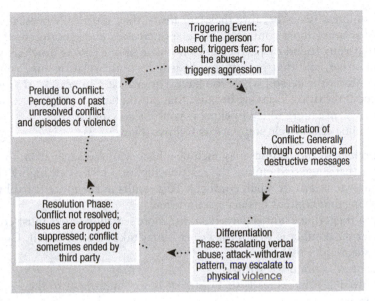

FIGURE 5.1

The Interpersonal Violence Cycle.

The violence cycle shows how an unsuccessful conflict may become mired down in one of the first four stages of a successful conflict cycle (see Chapter 1), namely at stage four—differentiation. Here, the conflict has a prelude stage (e.g., one or more of the participants has a past history of poorly managing conflicts), followed by a stage two triggering event (e.g., one person does something that the partner objects to). The conflict moves through stage three, initiation, where the abuser threatens or takes abusive or aggressive action, but gets mired down in stage four, differentiation, which may be an exchange of verbal abuse leading to physical fighting instead of progressing to the final stage, resolution, where both parties would have been satisfied with the outcome.

In other cases, a conflict may turn physically violent with one partner forcing his or her decision on the other, which may temporarily resolve and end the conflict by leaving one partner dissatisfied and unhappy with the result. If the victim accepts the outcome, then it could be said that the conflict reached the fifth stage, resolution, even if she or he is unhappy about it. On the other hand, the conflicting parties may still be stuck in the differentiation stage if the victim refuses to accept the outcome and resorts to passive–aggressive behavior to get his or her way.

The "Chilling Effect" Cycle

In Chapter 2, we described the avoidance/accommodation cycle. A special case of this is called the **chilling effect**, in which one person in a relationship withholds grievances from the other, usually due to fear of alienating the other person or fear of the other person's severe reaction.[28]

The chilling effect is distinctive because it includes an element of fear. Those who engage in it may fear that the other may turn physically violent. Moreover, they may suppress issues because they fear losing their partner, whereas in strong, committed relationships, conflict is more spontaneous and emotional. If you are worried that your friend or partner does not care about you as much as you care about him or her, and that person could easily leave the relationship, you are not likely to confront the person when you have a grievance. Conversely, if you are not worried about the other's leaving because that person has no alternatives and cares about you, you are more likely to express your dislikes and desires.

The chilling effect cycle steps are as follows (Figure 5.2):

- The prelude to the conflict may include a history of messages from the feared partner that suggested ending the relationship, or a history of highly charged responses to relatively small conflicts. This results in the more fearful partner perceiving that conflict has negative effects.
- When a triggering event is perceived, the more fearful partner must consider whether the conflict is worth the effort it may take to deal with it. Generally, he or she decides that it is not.
- The conflict is not dealt with.
- Unresolved grievances leads to a decrease in a commitment to the relationship.
- After several cycles of unresolved conflicts and decreased commitment, partners may simply cycle out of the relationship altogether.

The chilling effect shows how unsuccessful conflict becomes mired down in one of the first four stages of a successful conflict, as presented in Chapter 1. In this case, the conflict has a prelude stage (e.g., one or more of the participants has reason to fear the reaction of the other person based on a past history of abuse during

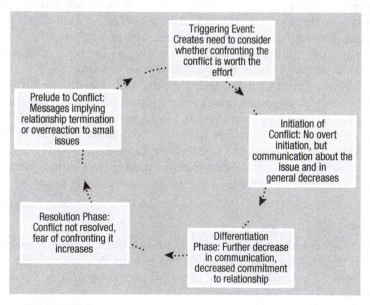

FIGURE 5.2
Chilling Effect Cycle.

conflict), followed by a stage two triggering event (e.g., one partner does something that upsets the other), but instead of progressing to the stage three initiation (or later stages), the offended individual does not initiate the conflict because he or she again fears the outcome. Meanwhile, a chilling effect puts communication barriers between those involved, which undermine the relationship and mutual happiness for the partners.

When a chilling effect occurs due to a fear of alienating the other and possibly causing the termination of the relationship, it's important for the partner perceiving the conflict to engage in reflection about both the conflict issue and the relationship itself. By not communicating about the issue, a barrier is created that ultimately may bring about what is feared—the end of the relationship. In reality, the person who does not confront for fear of the other ending the relationship is simply prolonging the inevitable.

When a chilling effect arises, there are two ways to respond to a threatening partner. First, in cases where one merely lacks the habit of asserting oneself, one may overcome this fear and learn to stand up to the other person, but this is not possible in cases where the partner is stronger, meaner, and better equipped to abuse. Second, people caught in controlling, abusive relationships have to resort to passive–aggressive behavior and seek outside help (usually the police, courts, or other authorities). The best time to counter abuse is the first time it happens, because after that it becomes more difficult to take action against it.

COMMUNICATION APPROACHES TO THE STUDY OF INTERPERSONAL VIOLENCE

More than one approach to the study of interpersonal violence appeals to communication researchers. These approaches lend further insight into the nature and management of interpersonal violence. The most common approaches are "communicator personality trait," "communication cognitions," and "communication interaction."

The Communicator Personality Trait Approach

What is the communicator personality trait approach to the study of interpersonal violence? According to this approach, members of the relationship are viewed as individual communicators, each endowed with personality traits. A **communicator personality trait** is tied to a particular set of beliefs (i.e., dogmatists are defined as closed minded persons who are unwilling to consider other sets of beliefs, or are unwilling to do so). The verbally abusive personality (high trait VA) desires or intends to dominate and is thought to be a type of hostility. They do the following:

- They insult the other person and make strong personal attacks.
- They lose their temper and say rather strong things to others.
- When individuals insult them, they get a lot of pleasure out of really telling them off.
- They like poking fun at people.

- When nothing seems to work in trying to influence others, they yell and scream in order to get some movement from them.
- When they are not able to refute others' positions, they try to make them feel defensive in order to weaken their positions.

In an interesting study of how high trait VA mothers differed from low trait VA mothers when playing games with their children, Roberts and her colleagues found that high trait VA mothers treated the game activities as tasks to be accomplished tending to control their child's choices and how she or he played the game. In contrast, low trait VA mothers tended to be more supportive of their child's choices and his or her way of playing the games.[29]

With few exceptions such as the study by Roberts and her colleagues, the communicator personality trait approach is not as popular as it was over 10 years ago. Furthermore, none of the researchers developed a training program or manual for trait VA abusers who want to improve their conflict and communication skills. Trait VA researches are credited with calling attention to the value of argumentation, such as recognizing controversial issues, advocating positions, and verbally refuting positions of others. Thus, advocates of this communication approach argued that people would benefit from taking academic courses that taught them how to reason and argue effectively.

The Communication Cognition Approach

In more recent years, researchers have focused on **communication cognition**, which consists of beliefs, perceptions, attributions, and other predispositions that promote violent conflict communication behavior. This communication cognition approach has identified factors such as beliefs and attitudes, identified abusers' violence prone predispositions, and described the mental beliefs and attributions needed to enable one to enact or avoid verbal and physical aggressiveness in conflict situations.

In the interpersonal violence communication research literature, many researchers are using **qualitative methods** to study the beliefs and perceptions of abusers and their victims. Qualitative research is useful as a means for explaining the sense-making processes conflicting parties use to legitimize verbal and non-verbal aggressive communication behaviors.[30] Qualitative researchers focus on each conflicting party's subjective perception or assessment of the quality (or the impression) of their own and the other's conflict communication behavior. They attempt to answer the question: How do conflicting parties perceive their own and the other's communication behavior in a conflict situation? This includes how abusers and their victimized partners rationalize the interpersonal violence.

Researchers who utilize qualitative methods in communication typically either observe as participants in the conflict situation or interview one or both parties in conflict. **Participant observation** occurs when a researcher observes social behavior while taking an active role as one of the social actors. Perhaps a researcher is a member of an abusive relationship or family, and is in a good position to report violent acts. **Unstructured interviews** allow abusers or their victims to respond to open-ended questions, such as "What were the events that led up to the abusive encounter?" They may also describe in their own words an abusive relationship. In their search for multiple interpretations, qualitative researchers are known for considering "alternative voices," such as the victims of abuse, who are often ignored or have no way to publicize their situation in American society (such as abused children, elderly, people with disabilities). To increase real world relevance, qualitative researchers seek to make the research experience a part of the subjects' natural habitat, such as conducting interviews in their homes. In cases of potentially violent conflict communication, parties may be interviewed separately; whereas in less threatening situations, the parties may be interviewed together. In some studies, people may watch video tapes of their conflicts and explain why they did, what they did, how they felt, and what their goals were. The parties involved may be in a premarital, marital, or parent–child (including elderly parent–adult and parent–adolescent) relationship. When given permission by the conflicting parties, video or audio recording the partners in conflict appears to be useful for interpretation later. It is argued that understanding the conflicting parties can assist the practitioners, social workers, family, and psychotherapists working with the conflicting parties, especially in violence prone dating, marital, and parent–child relationships.

Qualitative researchers have theories to explain conflict communication. **Social construction theory** attempts to identify and explain the ways people perceive and interpret their violent or potentially violent experiences with an eye toward values and stereotypes that people learn from the society and the times in which they live. For example, violence as portrayed in the media may create expectations that violence is common or even legitimate at home, school, or work. If the media portrays a male physically attacking a friend who shows interest in his girlfriend, young men may think that is an appropriate response to that social situation.

Ethnography is a related theory that provides descriptions of behavior in cultural groups and identifies the pressures toward conformity in the form of rules, roles, rites, and rituals. This type of study might take the form of a field study or a case report. As participant observers, ethnographers usually live with the people of interest and try to determine their reasons for acting as they do. They may apply their methods to couples or entire families. Ethnographers focus on relationships and social structure, verbal and nonverbal language codes, practices, rites, and rituals. *Ethnography is useful in identifying the rules that govern conflict communication.* In college classes, students sometimes write essays on their participation in a sport, theater, university student senate, or club, identifying the unique set of rules that govern their participation in that "subculture." For example, rules for males touching other males may vary greatly depending on the subculture.

Being from a lower class blue color working family, I could never have afforded attending a wealthy private school without a scholarship. While there, I made friends with Richard, whom I did not know was from one of the wealthiest families there, although he never flaunted his wealth. He seemed like a regular guy to me. However, he invited me to his home one weekend, only a few miles from campus. Now that I look back on it, I have to laugh because I was the one who drove, my old car. His parents lived in a huge estate with an electric gate, long drive, and a mansion on a hill. When we arrived up front of the house, his father popped out the door, ran down the steps, yelling "Dicky, Dicky," hugged his son and kissed him smack on the face. Now my father would have never done this: We would have shaken hands and not even hugged. A hired hand drove my car away to park it.

As Richard was showing me to one of the many guest rooms, I said to him, "Dicky, Dicky?" He was a little embarrassed.

There is no violence here, but we include this scenario to illustrate how different groups or subgroups live according to their own rules. The rules governing how upper class fathers greet their sons may differ from those of the lower classes. Ethnographers look for these rules as explanations for these different behaviors.

Narratives are personal stories that reveal people's perception of events. By collecting individual stories from particular couples/families, researchers can learn which events generate stories and which ones do not, and gain access to a deeper understanding of the abuser's or victim's perceived realities. For example, the narratives of people in dysfunctional relationships may be compared with those in more "normal" relationships.

Qualitative researchers who conducted interviews of abusive men found that they denied having a problem and blamed their women for violent incidents. Researchers interviewed 15 abusive male spouses to better understand how they perceived themselves, thought about their spouses, and rationalized their abusive behavior. The men provided accounts for their abuse in the form of justifications, excuses, denials or efforts to minimize the significance of their acts, and blamed their wives for their abusive behavior.[31] In other qualitative research, when confronted with evidence of an assault, abusive men made light of it, describing it as a "light slap" or a "little push" or "holding her to keep her from hurting herself." Abusers often cited their "loss of control" as an excuse to explain their violent behavior.[32] They claimed this didn't happen often. When pushed to explain their violent tendencies, the men became defensive. Finally, they didn't take seriously the woman's thoughts, feelings, and motivations. Meanwhile, qualitative researchers also found that abused women provided accounts for their abusive men's behavior to dissociate the "real him" from his abusive acts, such as "he wasn't being himself." In most accounts, abusers and their victims perceived the abusive acts differently but both in ways that attempted to excuse the abuser.[33]

Another researcher attempted to better understand the sense-making process couples used to legitimize the use of aggression by interviewing 31 people. She found that many of the abusive partners denounced the use of aggressive behavior but also said their use of verbal abuse and physical violence was appropriate and effective given the circumstances of their particular relationship. These findings suggest a unique relational culture where verbal abuse and physical aggression are perceived as appropriate, even though abusive couples admitted that such acts deviated from the social norm.

Subjective interviews also revealed what researchers call dialectical tensions that differed between abusive and non-abusive partners. A **dialectical tension** occurs when people experience competing but equally important demands. The most relevant tensions existed between autonomy versus connection (cohesion) and stability versus change (adaptability) in partners' everyday lives. That is, people want to be able to make their own decisions about their lives, but also want to be in relationship with others. Cohesion is the result of balancing these two demands. And while people want some amount of predictability in their lives, things should not be so rigid that change is impossible. Abusive partners experienced greater difficulty managing their dialectical tensions more than did non-abusive partners, who got more help from friends and family or had good communication skills. In a study of couples with and without a history of abuse, qualitative researchers found that abusive partners were less connected to one another and less effective in adapting to changes in their lives, while the non-abusive couples were more interdependent, collaborative, and more effective at managing changes in their lives.[34]

Qualitative researchers have also studied parent–child violence. Wilson and Whipple found patterns of attributions about a child's behavior that result in dysfunctional child rearing beliefs, which in turn automatically produce abusive responses to a child's (mis)behavior.[35] Later, Wilson and his colleagues studied the way mothers and children interacted during play periods. Mothers who were prone to physical abuse used fewer affirming messages with their children (e.g., "That's a good idea") and also asked fewer questions of their children (e.g., "Would you like to try this?" "How do you feel about that?" "What is the name of that toy?") than mothers who were not prone to physical abuse. In addition, children of high risk (prone to abuse) mothers played differently than children of low risk mothers. Children of high risk mothers were more involved in the play (for example, engaging in conversation with the mother) but less cooperative than children of low risk mothers, suggesting that the children maintained alertness to the situation while not following the mother's lead completely. The children's lack of cooperation wasn't exhibited through tantrums or throwing toys, but by not complying immediately with the mother's lead or acting in ways contrary to it.[36]

In sum, the cognitive approach with its qualitative methods has identified factors such as beliefs and attributions and other violence prone predispositions. Advocates of this approach recommend learning how to adopt particular mental beliefs and attributions that enable one to avoid verbal abuse and physical aggressiveness in communication.

The Communication Interaction Approach

Communication interaction is said to be "the sine qua non of relationships; it is through communicative action that persons initiate, define, maintain, and terminate their social bonds."[37] This explains why many communication scholars view the interaction between communicators as joint ventures where meaning is mutually created. Presumably, humans construct their reality and coordinate their actions by intentionally using verbal and nonverbal symbols whose meanings are shared by one another.

What constitutes a "communication interaction approach" to the study of interpersonal violence? The **communication interaction approach** identifies the sequence of behaviors within communication patterns that differentiate violent from nonviolent interpersonal relationships. Thus, violent conflict communication is viewed as a process of "escalating antagonism" between person A and person B: A's action upsets B; B orders A to cease the action; A fails to comply; B and A verbally abuse each other, which may result in physical violence.[38] The interesting point about this sequence of antagonistic acts is that they increase in intensity until physical aggression is seen as justified.

However, while there may exist an understanding among many Americans that violence ends the escalating antagonistic episode for both parties, this is not the same as saying that physically violent behavior is the best way to resolve an escalating conflict. Recall back in Chapter 1, we introduced the concept of communication competence as including the appropriate use of conflict communication skills. More specifically, **communication competence** refers to the ability to appropriately and effectively use verbal and nonverbal symbols within a given "speech community" (e.g., culture, family, or relationship). Stepping into the shoes of an ethnographic communication researcher, we would believe that symbols arouse meanings according to commonly shared conventions (e.g., rules, rituals, norms, and customs). Verbal and nonverbal communication are regulated by these social conventions that vary from one culture to another and that govern what is appropriate, expected, permissible, or prohibited in specific social contexts. Appropriate communication avoids the violation of valued social conventions, whereas effective communication obtains valued goals or effects.[39] Advocates of this communication approach focus on sensitizing individuals to the social situation and teaching them behavior that is appropriate to the situation. Because verbal abuse and physical violence in interpersonal relationships are considered inappropriate responses to most conflict situations, communication researchers view abusive and violent acts as the dark side of communication and the abusers and violators as communicatively incompetent.

CONFLICT MAY BE INEVITABLE BUT VIOLENCE IS NOT

We do not believe that a conflict needs to turn violent because we have options when handling our differences with others. Back in Chapter 1, we pointed out that we always have choices (or options) in conflict situations, and we are all responsible for our own actions. The notion of choice applies to interpersonal violence in two ways. First, when we turn violent or others use violence against us, people are using force to prevent others' freedom of choice. Second, the notion of choice should help us realize that we need not turn violent in the first place. By exercising choice we can make a difference in our lives and others. Although we learned in Chapter 1 that conflict is inevitable, it need not, and should not, physically or psychologically harm others or our relationships with others.

Unfortunately, partners involved in interpersonal violence are all too quick to forget that choice is or should be present. We doubt that you would say that you would physically or psychologically hurt a good friend or colleague, romantic partner, or family member. Yet some people do. Violators often claim that they lost control or forgot themselves, and some of the violated, who function as enablers, say "he wasn't himself," or "she just got carried away."

By teaching nonviolent solutions to problems, setting an example in our daily lives, and raising our children to resolve interpersonal conflicts peacefully, we are helping to reduce a serious social problem. Thus, learning to avoid escalation (i.e., learning de-escalation) is an important goal of this chapter as well as this entire book.

Dealing with Patriarchal Violence

> My husband's abuse got worse and worse. It finally reached a point where I decided to leave him, but I was afraid of what he might do to me. So, when he was at work, I left our home and went to our cottage on a lake up north. No sooner did I get there than I realized that this was the first place he would come looking for me, so I left for a motel in town. A couple of days later, I decided to go back to the cottage to pick up some things, but when I got there I saw the back door was left open, and everything inside was trashed. Even a large bookcase was turned over and dishes were broken all over the dining area. I believed that if he had found me there, I would have died of fright.

Patriarchal violence refers to a male–female dating or marital relationship in which the man severely and regularly beats the woman, who is left feeling frightened and isolated. This type of violence is an example of patriarchal violence that relies on **relational control-motivated aggression**. Relational control-motivated aggression refers to the use of power tactics such as intimidation, coercion and threats, emotional abuse, minimization and denial, using the children, isolation, and economic deprivation. The term **intimate terrorism** also comes to mind. As Johnson says, men's violence against women "is a product of patriarchal traditions of men's right to control their women . . . that involves the systematic use of not only violence, but economic subordination, threats, isolation, and other control tactics."[40]

Similarly, hypermasculinity or machoism is among the values shared by these abusers. Shelters for Battered Women and Restraint Orders enable some women to escape or maintain distance from their abusers. In cases like these, batterers need more than simple training in anger management or conflict communication skills to overcome their violent tendencies. An example of a more intensive type of program is the state operated **Batterer Intervention Program (BIP)**, which is usually court mandated for men accused of battering the women they live with. A popular approach in the administration of a BIP is known as the Duluth model which attempts to resocialize men by getting them to change their oppressive behaviors toward women by changing how they view their role as a male. The program teaches men to hold themselves accountable for their behavior, challenge their gender based beliefs, as well as teach them how to facilitate changes in their behavior.[41]

Dealing with Parental Violence

Parent-to-child violence may also fall into a patriarchal violence pattern, especially in the case of parents who are verbally abusive to their children. Examples of parental verbal abuse include making the child the brunt of jokes and teasing, using sarcasm to ridicule, mocking or scorning, blaming, belittling, criticizing, insulting, name-calling, cursing, threatening, and making cruel statements to the child.[42] What is not commonly recognized is the fact that verbal abuse may be as damaging as physical aggression, especially in cases where it has injurious effects on a child's psychosocial development.[43]

Parental violence can also rely on relational control-motivation. While not all authoritarian parents necessarily abuse their children, this parenting style could create the conditions for it to occur. Authoritarian parents rely heavily on power and control. They expect compliance, demand loyalty, and push for perfection from their child and resort to whatever is needed to ensure compliance, including all degrees or levels of physical punishment. Authoritarian parents may place unrealistic and inappropriate demands on their children and are unresponsive to their needs. They express low levels of support, affection, and empathy for the child.[44]

However, not all violence is based on relational control-motivation, as illustrated in the next story.

> My wife and I received a call from our minister, asking if we would shelter a woman who was trying to leave her husband but feared for her life. After she arrived, she told us about the guns he collected and that he told her that he was not afraid to shoot people if they deserved it, whatever that meant. Anyway, one day he arrived at our house and knocked on the door. He wanted to know if we had any knowledge of his wife's whereabouts, which we denied. He seemed friendly and jovial, which surprised us. He said he meant her no harm and to tell her it was OK to come home now, if we should see her. After he left, his wife told us that now she felt safe returning home. We tried to talk her out of it, but she went back to him. The next year they moved from the area, and we lost track of them.

Sometimes there is a blowup and everyone runs for their lives, but it is not an everyday event. This occurs more frequently because it is a temporary or one-time loss of control. Researchers have identified this as **common couple violence,** where men and women both engage in occasional violent acts that do not become more frequent or more severe over time. This pattern portrays a less systematic and pervasive pattern of control than the patriarchal type. The temporary loss of control was such a common type of violent conflict among prison inmates and cell mates in New York state that Quakers developed the **Alternatives to Violence Project (AVP)** especially for the prison system.

What is AVP? Based on Quaker traditions of peaceful demonstrations, civil disobedience, conscientious objection to wars, mediation, and negotiation, AVP conflict communication principles are taught through experiential exercises, brainstorming, negotiation techniques, and group discussions of case studies. Trainers promote the learning and use of effective conflict communication skills. Because one of the authors volunteered to assist the Quakers on their mission to the prisons, he incorporated many of the ideas and techniques in this book. For example, AVP trainers taught inmates how to make I-statements and then try to use them in simulated interpersonal conflicts with other inmates during training sessions. At the same time, individuals learned effective listening techniques and practiced them during confrontation exercises. Many problem solving exercises were also presented. The communication style emphasized by AVP instructors is facilitative (discussion, sitting in circles or small groups, group decisions, relaxed atmosphere) rather than more dominant and controlling alternatives.[45]

Dealing with Alcohol and Jealousy

Whereas deep-seated social values regarding men's domination and control over their women explain *patriarchal violence,* jealousy and alcohol/substance abuse are viewed as contributing factors to common couple violence.

I used to own and operate a bar that was popular with the town's people. Even though I was making pretty good money off the place, I closed it down because of an increase in violent incidents. Men and sometimes women would follow their partners to the bar and watch them meet or dance with other guys or gals and then they would start a fight inside the place or outside in the parking lot. We not only had fist fights, but stabbings, and then a guy was shot in the parking lot. We never felt safe especially late at night on weekends. Who wants to work in a place with bullets flying around? It wasn't worth it.

While the above story combines jealousy in an alcohol setting, each can be examined as a contributor with or without the other. Alcohol/substance use refers to cases in which the violent incident was precipitated by alcohol or drug consumption on the part of the man or woman. As teachers, your authors have discovered that our students readily admitted that fights were frequent at local "college bars" and that alcohol or drugs contributed to these violent incidents. How much alcohol consumption are we talking about here? Violent abusers report experiencing any of the following along with their drinking:

- Fuzzy or unclear thinking
- Alcohol-related physical sickness
- Family and friends upset over one's drinking
- Impaired speech, regret for what one said to others
- Regret for own behaviors
- Hangovers[46]

Because many people experience one or more of the above after drinking too much, the potential for violence from alcohol consumption is probably quite high. There is substantial research literature that found that alcohol and other substances are associated with conflicts getting out of hand and turning violent. Studies have found on average 24–45 percent of interpersonal violence involved alcohol or drugs.[47] This may begin in the dating stage. Late adolescents who use alcohol or marijuana are more likely to perpetrate dating violence.[48] A common complaint sounds like this:

We were having an argument, when he went out to a local club and had several alcoholic drinks. He returned home and resumed the argument. That is when he started throwing things, pushing me around, and hitting me.

Of course the violence may not be directed at one's partner but rather at the competition. This happens when jealousy is involved (e.g., "I didn't trust her with other guys," "I was suspicious of my partner's friends.").

I read in the local paper about a young woman who had a flat tire on her way into town. A nice guy stopped and offered to change her tire. However, her boyfriend also happened on the scene and shot the Good Samaritan. The paper reported that she had never seen the nice guy before and had welcomed his help. It went on to report that the trigger happy boyfriend claimed he didn't need some other guy helping her. He said that he didn't want to see some other guy with her, so he shot him.

Some individuals cannot control their jealousy. It is usually associated with perceived infidelity.[49] Jealousy is also an intense emotion, which can be overwhelming for some people similar to escalating anger, frustration, tensions, or embarrassment. As a wife said:

> At Christmas she joined her husband who was on leave for ten days from U.S. Army stationed in the Middle East. During their few days together, she admitted to two short affairs while he was overseas. Over the next few days, his emotions intensified and their conflicts escalated until he threatened to kill her.

What Can be Done about Alcohol/Drug Abuse and Jealousy? Obviously, just as people should not drink and drive, the best way to avoid complicating a conflict is not to drink alcohol or take drugs. Similarly, avoid getting into disagreements at bars. Since avoiding heavy drinkers may be difficult to do, it would be best then to avoid getting into a disagreement with them until they are sober. It would also make good sense not to get involved with people who have a drinking problem.

What about having a jealousy problem or partner who gets overly jealous? Jealousy may have its roots in the psychodynamic theory as discussed in Chapter 3, which means that it is related to the one's temporary loss of control due to a transient psychological state. Still, one can learn to curb one's jealous emotional states, avoid talking about problems when feeling overwhelmed by jealousy, and avoid others who are too jealous. Abusers need to learn how to manage their emotions (see Chapter 8 on Anger and Stress Management) as well as techniques for dealing with conflict as presented in Chapters 4, 9, and 10.

Dealing with Violence in the Workplace

Workplace violence refers to both intimate partner violence that spills over into the workplace and sexual harassment that occurs between employees. Both types of incidents may be due to paternal violence, based on coercion and control, or common couple violence, based more on temporary situations where one drank too much or became severely jealous. For example, emotional upset or physical injuries caused by intimate partners can make working difficult. Instances of abuse have been known to occur at or near a woman's work site, including a male partner following his girlfriend to and from a job interview to deter her from gaining employment because he didn't want her to get a job. Other instances include seizing a woman's driver license or car keys to prevent her from getting to work. Sexual assault may result in psychological, emotional, and physical health problems that can affect a woman's performance in the workplace. Recent studies have demonstrated that women's ability to work effectively is impacted by stalking. To what extent are supervisors trained to work with victimized employees or taught how to react when abuse occurs at or near her work site? Do they have policies and resources that are responsive to the array of victimizations that women may experience?

Sexual Harassment in the Workplace Since its naming in the late 1970s, a growing body of work has documented and explored the prevalence and effects of sexual harassment in the workplace.[50] In this day and age, one would think that sexual harassment would be a thing of the past, but news reports and research show otherwise. Sexual harassment consists of unwelcome sexual advances, requests for sex, as well as other physical or verbal conduct of a sexual nature. There are two types: (1) a superior demands sexual favors from a subordinate in exchange for promotions, reviews, or continued retention (which is called quid pro quo sexual harassment) and (2) an organization creates or tolerates a hostile environment where nonverbal, verbal, or physical conduct of a sexual nature interferes with a woman's work performance and creates an intimidating, offensive, or hostile work environment.[51]

While instances of violence may break out anywhere, there are some workplaces that have an organizational culture that makes life difficult for women attempting to work there. **Organizational culture** includes the values, beliefs, and assumptions held by the employees.

Several high risk factors for sexual harassment have been identified. One factor is if men greatly outnumber women at a workplace. For instance, women with aspirations to get ahead have ignored, tolerated, and not reported sexual harassment in order to be thought of as "part of the team." So institutionalized are some offensive behaviors that they are not even seen as harassment. Another risk factor is job status, where women may occupy roles deemed lower in the company hierarchy, while men serve at higher levels. This may increase the likelihood of men expecting sexual favors for promotion or even for teaching women how to do their jobs more effectively. Unprofessional work environment has also been cited as a factor in some organizational cultures. Women report workplace incivility (see Chapter 1) such as disrespect, rudeness, or condescending comments and bullying in addition to sexual harassment. A final part of organizational culture is the supervisors' and colleagues' response to sexual harassment. Women may tolerate and not report incidents due to a lack of confidence that their concerns would be taken seriously and the abuser would be punished, or due to fear of retribution and concerns about future employment within the organization.[52]

What Can be Done about Violence in the Workplace?

- First, organizations both large and small must put in writing their definition of sexual harassment and their policy against it.
- Where possible, they should have gated parking lots, guards on duty, or a locked entry system to prevent intimate partners from having direct access to the women when at work.
- All employees should be encouraged to be on the lookout for lurking offenders when outdoors or in the parking lot. While taking a smoking break, one female employee saw a man force another employee into his car and drive away with her. So, she went back inside and reported the incident.
- Individuals must be encouraged to report instances of sexual harassment or actions that contribute to a hostile work environment. A convenient system must be made available for reporting incidents in a way that does not embarrass the person making the complaint.
- Employees should receive training on "violence in the workplace" and "sexual harassment" to help victims of intimate partner abuse, to deal with potentially violent situations that may arise at work, and sexual harassment. Workshops could be offered on workplace violence, diversity, conflict

resolution, and sexual harassment. As part of these workshops, employees should learn what constitutes inappropriate and offensive behavior as well as how to deal with situations that may arise.

- Supervisors should act on complaints of employee misconduct and abusers should learn that their offensive behavior has consequences to possibly include police arrest and loss of job.
- Employees can watch for offensive behavior, encourage colleagues to report it, and inform supervisors of observed instances. They should be supportive of victims. These would help create a culture that does not tolerate sexual harassment. It takes a lot of courage for a man or woman to report a rape when the violator is a popular athlete, politician, supervisor, teacher, minister/priest, or community figure. However, the only way to stop these abuses may be by reporting them.
- Employees who are victims of abuse should recognize that the responsibility for the behavior rests with the offender and not with the victim.

MANAGE IT

This chapter is about interpersonal violence. After theorizing about why people are violent, the authors argue that interpersonal violence occurs when a person imposes his or her will (i.e., wants, needs, or desires) on a friend, romantic partner, family member, or colleague at work through verbal or physical intimidation. Interpersonal violence involves harming another person physically, emotionally, or mentally. While conflict may be inevitable, we do not believe that a conflict needs to turn violent because we have options when handling our differences with others.

Violent communicators interrupt, dominate, and control others. They make threatening gestures (fist, finger), push/shove/poke with finger/hitting, make verbal threats, and damage the other's possessions. They engage in verbal abuse, defined as attacking the self-concept of another person in order to cause psychological pain for the other, and physical aggression, which is often linked to initial verbal abuse, and consists of physical harm to others. Intimate partner violence, particularly physical assault, rape, and stalking, are gender based. Researchers report that interpersonal violence is more likely when there is verbally aggressive conflict communication. The authors describe two cycles of violence: the interpersonal violence cycle and the chilling effect cycle.

There are three communication approaches to the study of interpersonal violence. For the communicator personality trait approach, violence is tied to a personality trait, which refers to a particular set of beliefs (i.e., dogmatists are defined as closed minded persons who are unwilling to consider other sets of beliefs, or are unwilling to do so). The verbally abusive personality (trait VA) desires or intends to dominate and is thought to be a subset of hostility.

The communication cognitive approach has identified factors such as beliefs and attitudes, identified abusers' violence prone predispositions, and described the mental beliefs and attributions needed to enable one to enact or avoid verbal and physical aggressiveness in communication situations. Many researchers use qualitative methods, such as participant observation and unstructured interviews and theories based on social construction, ethnography, and narratives to gain access to people's subjective interpretations of their perceptions and experiences.

The communication interaction approach has been helpful in identifying the steps in "escalating antagonism" between person A and person B: A's action upsets B; B orders A to cease the action; A fails to comply; B and A verbally abuse each other, which may result in physical violence. The interesting point about this sequence of antagonistic acts is that they increase in intensity until physical aggression is seen as justified.

The authors take the position that while conflict is inevitable in close personal relationships, violence is not. Two types of violent conflict communication are patriarchal violence, which refers to a male–female dating or marital relationship in which the man severely and regularly beats the woman, who is left feeling frightened and isolated, and common couple violence, which occurs when men and women engage in "occasional" violent acts that do not become more frequent or more severe over time. For both types of abuse, victims need to learn how to assert themselves, use the ideas in this book, and seek outside help when abused.

Jealousy and alcohol/substance abuse are viewed as contributing factors to common couple violence. The best way to avoid complicating an argument is not to drink alcohol or take drugs. Again it might be best to avoid those who can't control their jealous feelings. Abusers need to learn how to manage their emotions as well as techniques for dealing with conflict as presented in this textbook.

Workplace violence refers to both intimate partner violence that spills over into the workplace and sexual harassment that occurs between employees. Both types of incidents may be due to paternal violence, based on coercion and control, or common couple violence, based more on temporary situations where one drank too much or became severely jealous. We listed a number of steps that organizations can take to play a more responsible role in protecting their employees and helping them deal with violent situations.

EXERCISES

THINK ABOUT IT

1. At what point does a behavior change from nonviolent to violent?
2. Is it possible that one sex may view a behavior as violent and the other not? What might be some examples where the sexes may differ in their interpretation of a behavior?
3. What is the best way to make a member of the opposite sex aware of how her or his behavior affects you? What is the best way of handling a person who becomes offensive, threatening, or sexually harassing?
4. How should someone respond when a member of the opposite sex accuses him or her of being offensive, threatening, or sexually harassing?

APPLY IT

Identify whether the following behaviors are physically violent, sexually offensive, or verbally abusive.

1. Your boss suggests that you go out with him to dinner.
2. A colleague stands up, glares at you, raises his voice, and jabs a finger in your chest.
3. Someone you consider as just a friend suddenly tries to kiss you when you two are alone together.

4. Your employer calls you at home and asks to stop over on his/her way home from work.
5. A teacher takes every opportunity to touch you on the arm and shoulders, when talking to you.
6. A male supervisor occasionally bumps or brushes against a female worker.
7. At a local bar, men pat women on the backside.

WORK WITH IT

Form several small groups of about five persons in each group (if possible make them mixed, male and female). Assign the groups to discuss the following questions, one at a time with one person designated to report the group census to the class. After achieving a consensus on how to deal with the problem, ask the designated person to summarize the group's view. Compare and contrast the different solutions posed by each group to see if there is a class consensus on how best to deal with the situation before moving on to the next question.

1. How should you deal with violent acts by a family member?
2. How should you prepare for possible violent acts in the workplace?
3. How should you deal with road rage?
4. How should you deal with jealousy by a romantic partner?
5. How should you deal with sexual harassment in the workplace?

DISCUSS IT

Read the following conflict narrative and discuss the answers to the questions that follow it.

"Because I was the commander of a U.S. Army infantry company in an Asian country, I was also responsible for all aspects of the company mess hall. One day, when eating in the mess hall, I noticed the male cooks all smiling and in good humor. It was then that I saw the centerfold pictures of naked women on the walls where we all eat. My unit had a number of women, so I immediately was concerned that this was a serious problem, because I did not want the women in my company to feel uncomfortable. I wandered over to a table where several of the women were eating and asked them if they were upset by the pictures on the walls and wanted them removed. One of them said, 'My only objection is that there are no pictures of naked men.' The other women agreed, so I said, it is only fair that if one sex can display pictures of the opposite sex, the other sex should have the same right. They said they would be happy to take care of that. So I told the mess sergeant that there could only be pictures of women if there were also centerfolds of men, which the women would provide.

The next day, when I came into the mess hall, I saw as many centerfold pictures of naked men as there were of women. The women were again seated together, displayed a lot of good humor, and were pointing at some of the male centerfolds while talking in low voices.

However, on the third day, when I walked in, all the pictures were gone. I asked the mess sergeant what happened to all the pictures, and he said, 'We don't need no pictures of naked men when we are sitting around eating meals.' So when the shoe was on the other foot, the men objected. That was the end of the centerfolds."

1. What issues existed between the men and the women in this military unit as implied in this narrative? Was there a potential for offensive and even violent behavior?
2. Why would the women object to the men's choice of pictures to display on the walls?
3. Was the women's choice of pictures a good way to deal with the mess hall problem?
4. Why did the men fail to see the humor in the women's choice of pictures and respond as they did?
5. How should the commander have handled the situation? Did he make the best decisions?

NOTES

1. Monica H. Swahn, Thomas R. Simon, and Robert M. Bossarte, "Measuring Sex-differences in Violence Victimization and Perpetration within Data and Same-Sex Peer Relationships," *Journal of Interpersonal Violence* 23 (2008), 1120–1138.

2. World Health Organization, "The Economic Dimensions of Interpersonal Violence," retrieved on November 12, 2011 from http://www.who.int/violence_injury_prevention/publications/violence/economic_dimensions/en/

3. Loreen N. Olson and Dawn O. Braithwaite, " 'If You Hit Me Again, I'll Hit You Back': Conflict Management Strategies of Individuals Experiencing Aggression during Conflicts," *Communication Studies* 55 (2004), 271–286.

4. Marvin Wolfgang, Marvin and Franco Ferracuti, Franco.. *The Subculture of Violence: Toward an Integrated Theory of Criminology* (London: Tavistock, 1967).

5. C. Nathan DeWall and Craig A. Anderson, "The General Aggression Model: Theoretical Extensions to Violence," *Psychology of Violence* 1 (2011) 245–258.

6. Dudley D. Cahn, "An Evolving Communication Perspective," in Dudley D. Cahn (Ed.), *Family Violence: Communication Processes* (Albany, NY: SUNY, 2009), p. 16.

7. Loreen N. Olson, "Exploring 'Common Couple Violence' in Heterosexual Romantic Relationships," *Western Journal of Communication* 66 (2002), 104–125.

8. William R. Cupach and Brian H. Spitzberg (Eds.), *The Dark Side of Interpersonal Communication* (Hillsdale, NJ: Erlbaum, 1994).

9. Dominic A. Infante and C. J. Wigley, "Verbal Aggressiveness: An Interpersonal Model and Measure," *Communication Monographs* 53 (1986), 61–69.

10. Kelly A. Rocca, "College Student Attendance: Impact of Instructor Immediacy and Verbal Aggression," *Communication Education* 53 (2004), 185–195.

11. Belinda R. Walsh and Emma Clarke, "Post-Trauma Symptoms in Health Workers Following Physical and Verbal Aggression," *Work & Stress* 17 (2003), 170–181.

12. Carolee Rada Verdeur, "Parental Verbal Aggression: Attachment and Dissociation in Adolescents," *Dissertation Abstracts International*: Section B: The Sciences & Engineering, 63(3-B) (Sep 2002), 1571.

13. Angea B. Swanson and Dudley D. Cahn, "A Communication Perspective on Physical Child Abuse," in Dudley D. Cahn (Ed.), *Family Violence: Communication Processes* (Albany, NY: SUNY, 2009), p. 142.

14. Kathy Skuja and W. Kim Halford, "Repeating the Errors of Our Parents? Parental Violence in Men's Family of Origin and Conflict Management in Dating Couples," *Journal of Interpersonal Violence* 19 (2004), 623–638. See also Kerstin E. Edin, Ann Lalos, Ulf Högberg, and Lars Dahlgren, "Violent Men: Ordinary and Deviant," *Journal of Interpersonal Violence* 23 (2008), 225–244.

15. Sonia Miner Salari and Bret M. Baldwin, "Verbal, Physical, and Injurious Aggression among Intimate Couples over Time," *Journal of Family Issues* 23 (2002), 523–550; Clyde M. Feldman and Carl A. Ridley, "The Role of Conflict-Based Communication Responses and Outcomes in Male Domestic Violence toward Female Partners," *Journal of Social and Personal Relationships* 17 (2000), 552–573; see also George Ronan, Laura E. Dreer, Katherine Dollard, and Donna W. Ronan, "Violent Couples: Coping and Communication Skills," *Journal of Family Violence* 19 (2004), 131–137.

16. Brenda Geiger and Michael Fisher, "Will Words Ever Harm Me? Escalation from Verbal to Physical Abuse in Sixth-Grade Classrooms," *Journal of Interpersonal Violence* 21(2006), 337–357.

17. Dominic A. Infante, Teresa A. Chandler, and Jill E. Rudd, "Test of an Argumentative Skill Deficiency Model of Interspousal Violence," *Communication Monographs* 56 (1989), 163–177.

18. Nancy J. Brule, "Adolescent-to-parent Abuse," in Dudley D. Cahn (Ed.), *Family Violence: Communication Processes* (Albany, NY: SUNY, 2009), p. 179.

19. Loreen N. Olson, "'As Ugly and Painful as It Was, It Was Effective': Individuals' Unique Assessment of Communication Competence during Aggressive Conflict Episodes," *Communication Studies* 53 (2002), 171–188; Loreen N. Olson and Tamara D. Golish, "Topics of Conflict and Patterns of Aggression in Romantic Relationships," *Southern Communication Journal* 67 (2002), 180–200.

20. Scott L. Feld and Dawn T. Robinson, "Secondary Bystander Effects on Intimate Violence: When Norms of Restraint Reduce Deterrence," *Journal of Social and Personal Relationships* 15 (1998), 277–285.

21. Linda L. Marshall, "Physical and Psychological Abuse," in William R. Cupach and Brian H. Spitzberg (Eds.), *The Dark Side of Interpersonal Communication* (Hillsdale, NJ: Erlbaum, 1994), pp. 281–311.

22. Ibid.

23. Sarah McMahon and Alexandria Dick. "'Being in a Room with Like-Minded Men': An Exploratory Study of Men's Participation in a Bystander Intervention Program to Prevent Intimate Partner Violence," *Journal of Men's Studies* 19 (2011) 3–4.

24. Christine M. Englebrecht and Bradford W. Reyns, "Gender Differences in Acknowledgment of Stalking Victimization: Results from the NCVS Stalking Supplement," *Violence and Victims* 26 (2011), 574.

25. Jessica J. Eckstein, "Communication of Men Revealing Abuse," in Dudley D. Cahn (Ed.), *Family Violence: Communication Processes* (Albany, NY: SUNY, 2009), pp. 89–111.

26. Sandra Petronio, *Boundaries of Privacy: Dialectics of Disclosure* (Albany, NY: SUNY, 2002).

27. Emma Hettrich and K. Daniel O'Leary, "Females' Reasons for Their Physical Aggression in Dating Relationships," *Journal of Interpersonal Violence* 22 (2007), 1131–1143.

28. Michael E. Roloff and Denise H. Cloven, "The Chilling Effect in Interpersonal Relationships: The Reluctance to Speak One's Mind," in Dudley D. Cahn (Ed.), *Inmates in Conflict: A Communication Perspective* (Hillside, NJ: Lawrence Erlbaum Associates, 1990), pp. 49–76.

29. Felicia Roberts, Steven R. Wilson, Julie E. Delaney, and Jessica J. Rack, "Distinguishing Communication Behaviors of Mothers High and Low in Trait Verbal Aggression: A Qualitative Analysis of Mother-Child Playtime Interactions," in Dudley D. Cahn (Ed.), *Family Violence: Communication Processes* (Albany, NY: SUNY, 2009), pp. 155–177.

30. Dudley D. Cahn, "Conflict Communication," in V. S. Ramachandran (Ed.), *Encyclopedia of Human Behavior,* 2nd Edition (San Diego, CA: Academic, 2012), pp. 571–579.

31. Glen H. Stamp and Teresa C. Sabourin, "Accounting for Violence: An Analysis of Male Spousal Narratives." *Journal of Applied Communication Research* 23 (1995), 284–307.

32. Teresa Sabourin, "Making Sense of Abuse," in Dudley D. Cahn (Ed.), *Family Violence: Communication Processes* (Albany, NY: SUNY, 2009), pp. 49–72.

33. Julia Wood, "That Wasn't the Real Him: Women's Dissociation of Violence from the Men Who Enact It." *Qualitative Research Reports in Communication* 1 (2000), 1–7.

34. Teresa C. Sabourin and Glen H. Stamp, "Communication and the Experience of Dialectical Tensions in Family Life: An Examination of Abusive and Nonabusive Families" *Communication Monographs* 62 (1995), 213–242.

35. Steven R. Wilson and Ellen E. Whipple, "Attributions and Regulative Communication by Parents Participating in a Community-Based Child Physical Abuse Prevention

Program," in Valerie Manusov and J. H. Harvey (Eds.), *Attribution, Communication Behavior, and Close Relationships* (New York: Cambridge University Press, 2001), pp. 227–247.

36. Steven R. Wilson, Wendy M. Morgan, Javette Hayes, Carma Bylund, and Andrew Herman, "Mothers' Child Abuse Potential as a Predictor of Maternal and Child Behaviors during Play-Time Interactions," *Communication Monographs* 71 (2004), 395–421.

37. Leslie Baxter. "Accomplishing Relationship Disengagement," in S. Duck and D. Perlman (Eds.), *Understanding Personal Relationships: An Interdisciplinary Approach* (London: Sage, 1985), p. 245.

38. Linda Harris, Kenneth J. Gergen, and John W. Lannamann, "Aggression Rituals," *Communication Monographs* 53 (1986), 252–265.

39. Brian H. Spitzberg, Daniel Canary, and William R. Cupach, "A Competence-Based Approach to the Study of Interpersonal Conflict," in Dudley D. Cahn (Ed.), *Conflict in Personal Relationships* (Hillsdale, NJ: Erlbaum, 1994), pp. 183–202.

40. Michael P. Johnson, "Patriarchal Terrorism and Common Couple Violence: Two Forms of Violence against Women," *Journal of Marriage and the Family* 57 (1995), 284.

41. Maria Villar, Victoria Orrego-Dunleavy, and Joan Farr, "Measuring Change in Attitudes Targeted by Batterer Intervention Programs," in Dudley D. Cahn (Ed.), *Family Violence: Communication Processes* (Albany, NY: SUNY, 2009), pp. 73–87.

42. Yvonne Vissing and Walter Baily, "Parent-to-Child Verbal Aggression," in Dudley D. Cahn and Sally A. Lloyd (Eds.), *Family Violence from a Communication Perspective* (Thousand Oaks, CA: Sage, 1996), pp. 97–99.

43. Linda Ade-Ridder and Allen R. Jones, "Home Is Where the Hell Is," in Dudley D. Cahn and Sally A. Lloyd (Eds.), *Family Violence from a Communication Perspective* (Thousand Oaks, CA: Sage, 1996), pp. 59–84.

44. Swanson and Cahn, "*Family Violence*" p. 142.

45. Dudley D. Cahn, "Incorporating Training in Alternatives to Violence in the Interpersonal Communication Course," *Speech Communication Teacher* (Spring, 1995), p. 12.

46. Heather M. Foran and K. Daniel O'Leary, "Problem Drinking, Jealousy and Anger Control: Variables Predicting Physical Aggression Against a Partner," *Journal of Family Violence* 223 (2008), 141.

47. Ibid., 142.

48. Melissa P. Schnurr, Brenda J. Lohman, and Shelby A. Kaura, "Variation in Late Adolescents' Reports of Dating Violence Perpetration: A Dyadic Analysis," *Violence and Victims* 25 (2010), 86.

49. Becky Fenton and Jill H. Rathus, "Men's Self-Reported Descriptions and Precipitants of Domestic Violence Perpetration as Reported in Intake Evaluations," *Journal of Family Violence,* 25 (2010), 150–152; Schnurr, Lohman, and Kaura, *Violence and Victims,* 86–87.

50. Sharyn J. Potter and Victorial L. Banyard, "The Victimization Experiences of Women in the Workforce: Moving Beyond Single Categories of Work or Violence," *Violence and Victims* 26 (2011), 515–517.

51. Jodie L. Hertzog, David Wright, and Debra Beat, "There's a Policy for That: A Comparison of the Organizational Culture of Workplaces Reporting Incidents of Sexual Harassment," *Behavior and Social Issues* 17 (2008), 169–182.

52. Ibid.

Managing the Conflict Climate

OBJECTIVES

At the end of this chapter, you should be able to:

- Describe the role that climate plays in general in conflict situations.

- Describe the role played by an imbalance of power in a conflict situation and explain how to equalize power.

- Describe the role played by competition in a conflict situation and explain how to encourage cooperation.

- Describe the role played by distrust in a conflict situation and explain how to create trust.

- Describe the role played by defensive behaviors in a conflict situation and explain how to engage and encourage supportive behaviors.

- Explain how the concept of defensive behavior differs from that of power imbalance.

- Explain how groupthink leads to mismanaged conflict.

KEY TERMS

Abilene Paradox
competition
conflict climate
cooperation
defensive behaviors
distrust
groupthink
harmful conflict climate
healthy trust
imbalance of power

Lucifer Effect
mixed motive situation
neutral speech
nurturing conflict climate
power
power abuse
powerful speech
powerless speech
Prisoner's Dilemma (PD)
supportive behaviors

threats
thromise
trust
unhealthy trust
win–lose outcomes
win–win outcomes

As you move from one location to another, you are aware of changes in the emotional tone of voices, the looks on people's faces, their body movements, dress code, and room décor, which can reveal expectations for behavior. If you enter a location where a party is held, you are likely to encounter noise, a crowd of young people, loud music, a lot of social interaction, and a dress code that fits the occasion. You might smell cigarette smoke and alcohol. Many partygoers view a party as a positive experience and conducive to socializing or else they would leave. Conversely, at another location such as a hospital's patient ward, you probably encounter a quiet place with restricted visiting hours and frequent visits by hospital staff. There is no drinking of alcohol, smoking, or using cell phones, and you'll see many people in a variety of medical uniforms. Perhaps you smell a sterile environment that you associate with hospitals. If you were not visiting a patient, you would probably want to leave the hospital as soon as possible. Depending on the event or place, there is a climate, environment, or an atmosphere that makes you feel comfortable or uncomfortable in a psychological as well as physical sense. Whether or not we are aware of it, the climate surrounding us affects the way we manage conflict. Competent conflict managers do what they can to create a climate that facilitates constructive conflict management.

CONFLICT CLIMATE

What is meant by climate in a conflict communication situation? We know that physical processes, such as plant growth, depend on their physical environments to nurture them. Similarly, social processes like conflict management depend on a nurturing social climate or environment. Although the concept of social climate is difficult to describe in concrete terms, we are still aware of it and its effects on our interactions. Of the many factors or properties that are part of the climate, we limit our scope of a **conflict climate**, or the psychological atmosphere impacting a conflict, to these opposing concepts: imbalance of power versus equity, competition versus cooperation, distrust versus trust, defensive versus supportive behavior, and groupthink verses individual decision making.

Harmful Conflict Climate

Conflict management produces destructive and negative results when it suffers from a **harmful conflict climate**, consisting of the threats of power abuse, competition, distrust, and defensiveness. Such threats foster avoidance and accommodation (possibly resulting in avoidance and chilling effect cycles) or competition (meeting force with force, which may foster a competitive escalation cycle that eventually becomes violent).

Nurturing Conflict Climate

Conversely, conflict management is more productive and positive in other situations because it benefits from a **nurturing conflict climate**, consisting of equal power, cooperation, trust, and supportive behavior that encourage openness, assertiveness, collaboration, and mutually satisfying outcomes.

   The purpose of this chapter is to provide you with skills for managing conflict by creating a nurturing conflict climate, avoiding creating a harmful conflict climate, or converting a harmful climate into a nurturing one.

Converting Power Differences in Conflicts

> Recently my parents and I argued about my job. My parents don't want me to work while in school because they think it could interfere with my studies. But in reality they don't give me enough money to do what I want to do. While talking to my parents they believe that only their opinions are legitimate. They do not even consider what I have to say and rarely even give me a chance to speak.

In general, **power** is the ability to influence or control events. People have power over us to the extent that we depend on them, they can affect our goal achievement, and they have the resources we need to accomplish our goals. In our daily routine, we encounter people who are more or less powerful than we are, and these are often cases of legitimate power differences, such as the boss–employee, commander–troops, parents–children, and teacher–student. In the case above, the young man is still living at home, letting his parents pay his bills, and resents the fact that he is a dependent, powerless teen.

Legitimate power recognizes that a situation often exists in which someone must take control to accomplish a task or to protect the welfare or interests of the group. In such cases, we should hold that person responsible for performing certain leadership tasks, and we should grant him or her authority over us and work with that person to successfully accomplish the tasks. Because we all vary in our capabilities and resources, power often shifts from one situation to another, creating opportunities for different people to have power over others at different times.

People often respond with anger when they feel as though they are being forced to do something.

Power contributes to a harmful conflict climate when it is perceived as threatening. When this occurs, we call it **power abuse**.

> As a Captain, I once taught counseling to a group of high-ranking U.S. Army officers. When I finished a list of dos and don'ts for officers counseling enlisted personnel who had personal problems that might affect the performance of their duties, my list included hanging one's military jacket and hat (both covered with rank insignia) on a coat stand before meeting with the individual. As soon as I said that, Colonel Johnson suddenly stood up, turned to face the class, and said, "I am a Colonel in the United States Army and when someone comes into my office to see me, that person is going to know I am a Colonel." There was a moment of silence. I then asked the class, "How many of you would go to Colonel Johnson, if you had a personal problem?" Everyone laughed, and someone even said "No way." Not receiving the support for his position that he expected, the Colonel suddenly grew embarrassed, said he got the point, and sat down. He told me later that he hadn't really thought about the problems he created by "pulling rank" on people.

Obviously we tread on hallowed ground here. The idea of sharing power may seem radical or even shocking to some people like the colonel above. After years of graduate study and passing extremely demanding exams, they have attained a Ph.D., M.D., D.D.S., or law degree, so the last thought they may have in mind is to sacrifice the status and power that comes with such extraordinary achievement. We could say the same for those who worked their way up from the lowest to the highest levels of any organization and worked hard to attain a position of influence. Because they made great sacrifices, overcame difficult barriers, and demonstrated high abilities to earn their rank or position in an organization, they believe that they have paid their dues.

Now we come along and ask them to share their hard-earned respect, power, and status with others. We recognize that we are asking a lot for privileged people to set aside their perceptions of themselves as outranking the rest of us, to treat us with mutual respect, and to work with us as their equals. We can hear their response: *Forget it!*

However, those who abuse their power create worry, anger, and resentment in the less powerful. In such cases the abuse of power has a stifling effect. *Powerful people may be seen as intimidating or threatening.* Powerless people respond by avoiding, accommodating, or not asserting themselves. When power is abused, we do not expect to resolve conflicts in a mutually satisfactory way.

Some power differences are institutionalized, formal, and official. The police, judges, teachers, parents, university officials, hospital administrators, and bosses at work are given some powers over the rest of us in limited contexts, such as the courtroom, classroom, public office, hospital, or other workplace. However, in other relationships we are more equal, but one person may still assume power over another. In these cases power is not a finite quantity but something produced by human transactions. For example, a friend or romantic partner may try to take control of a relationship and dominate the other but only succeeds to the extent that the other permits. Recall from Chapter 1 that we now consider effective communication to be transactional rather than linear. If we extend this idea to dominant–submissive interpersonal relationships, we realize dominant people do not have authority over another unless the other person grants this power to him or her, even though it may often seem to both the submissive person and observers as though the submissive person has no choice. People do have choices in how they respond to others, although frequently they must be taught how to exercise those choices. We are, of course, talking about situations in which people are communicating verbally, and not using the threat of physical violence or weapons to create their dominance over the other, who now has no choice but to do as demanded.

As in the situation where power is institutionalized, dominant people abuse their power when they rely on threats to intimidate others and stifle input. Flagg noted that there are distinct differences in patterns of language use between people who are perceived as power abusers and people who are perceived as power sharers.[1] **Threats** are statements that link the other person's noncompliance with negative outcomes. In addition, the dominant individual may use a **thromise**—a message that sounds like a promise (i.e., if you do x you will receive y) but operates like a threat because there is a penalty associated with noncompliance that may hurt the recipient. The recipient doesn't simply fail to receive a benefit.[2] You have probably experienced a thromise in your educational experiences. An instructor may have told you that you could do some extra work to raise your grade, but may also have indicated that failing to do so would result in being graded more harshly at the end of the semester as it would indicate a lack of motivation and interest in the class.

Like subordinates in more formal situations, submissive friends and partners respond to the more powerful or dominate people by avoiding dealing with issues, accommodating to the dominant others, and failing to assert themselves. Many conflicts do not get resolved in a mutually satisfactory way.

Besides avoiding the use of threats and thromises, how does one dominate others less? One way is to avoid using either powerful or powerless speech. **Powerful speech** refers to verbal and nonverbal messages used to dominate and control others. Powerful speech can occur in different degrees. At one level it includes interrupting others, speaking loudly, controlling the topic of conversation, and sounding like one knows he or she is right (implying that the other is wrong). Such a manner of speaking may also take the form of leaving no choice for the listener to respond in any other way than the speaker demands (e.g., "I expect this to be done immediately.") At another level such speech also includes talking down to people, put downs, efforts to belittle others, interrupting the other, talking through the other, and talking louder than the other. At the extreme it includes very aggressive and abusive behaviors (see Chapter 5).[3] These could include verbal threats, swearing, name calling while shouting, standing up to the other, or standing over that person accompanied with menacing facial expressions.

Erickson and his colleagues identified some differences between powerful and powerless speech. Powerful speakers used more intensifiers (e.g., very), fewer hedges (e.g., I guess), especially formal grammar, fewer hesitation forms (e.g., uh, you know), more controlled gestures, fewer questioning forms (e.g., rising in intonation at the end of a declarative sentence), and fewer polite forms when addressing others.[4] Some examples of how people gain and maintain their power in interpersonal relationships are also found in gender studies. According to

Van Dijk, men typically do less work in conversations than women, because they tend to show less interest in the conversation and provide less support for topics that women introduce. Women tend to interrupt less often than men do.[5]

Powerless speech is talking up to others, making requests or asking questions (showing that one is in need or is uninformed), speaking softly, and sounding tentative, uncertain, or unsure of oneself. Powerless speech includes hedges (It could be that...), disclaimers (I've only thought a little about this), and tag questions (I don't know, what do you think?). More speech devices are included in Chapter 7 on the topic of "Face Management." When people are avoiding/accommodating, as we discussed in Chapter 2, they also engage in powerless speech. Like the avoiding/accommodating individuals, powerless and submissive people fail to effectively stand up for themselves, while aggressive people do it in a way that violates the rights of others (see Chapter 5).

How does one avoid using either powerful or powerless speech? One may employ **neutral speech,** where she or he does not talk down or talk up to the others but talks to them as equals and relies on objective language. People in authority may go by their first names and ask others to treat them as a colleague or an equal rather than as a superior. A person using neutral speech both seeks out and values input from others ("Here's an idea I have. I'd like your input."). He or she doesn't make decisions and simply announce them, but engages others in the decision-making process. (For example, "We need to figure out a way to provide coverage on the front desk so that everyone gets a full lunch break.") There is a true sense of equality when listening to neutral speech.

Civil and assertive people treat others as they want the others to treat them by striving for outcomes that benefit all conflicting parties and not just one of them at the other's expense. A civil communicator who demonstrates respect, restraint, and responsibility helps to set a conflict climate that is conducive to the creation of mutually beneficial outcomes. The assertive behavior serves as a goal for the powerful or dominant people (who should take the other into consideration) and for the powerless or submissive speakers (who should stand up more for themselves).

Sharing Power To improve the conflict climate, change in the power dimension needs to come from the powerful people, such as bosses, parents and older family members, and teachers. If the change is demanded by the people who don't have the power, their actions may be considered a mutiny, disobedient act, disrespectful, or not following orders. The powerful people must value the input of others and seek to focus on resolving problems. Those of us who have participated when powerful people have solicited our input may have experienced these outcomes:

a. Our ideas are utilized, which makes us feel good.
b. Our ideas are not used, but we are provided with an explanation as to why not, which makes us realize that the situation was more complicated than we realized.
c. Our ideas are not used because power sharing was a pretense on the part of the more powerful person.

We have all heard of the expression, "two heads are better than one"—generally speaking, decisions made after seeking input from others are more effective than decisions made without input from others. In addition to making the best decision because of input from others, people are more satisfied in situations where they have some say or influence.

However, in conflict situations where one person outranks the other, there is a high likelihood that only "one head" prevails, and the powerful or dominant party fails to seek the input from others for better ideas. Why surround yourself with advisors who are simply "yes men" or "yes women"? You could just as easily disband the group and make the decisions by yourself. Moreover, people are less likely to speak up if they fear the consequences or believe that the powerful person may not listen to them. The bottom line is that you should welcome input from people who disagree with you.

Those who do not wish to abuse their power should initiate and employ solution oriented behavior rather than abusive power perpetuating behavior.[6] People in powerful positions or dominant roles should consider the idea that "we are all in this boat together" in that we share a sense of purpose and the primary goals of the college class, athletic team, family, military unit, or work organization. Because there is a job to do, a task to accomplish, we should focus on the task and not on the preservation of status or power. The powerful and powerless all benefit by the success of the class, team, unit, or organization, so stop worrying about sharing power and actively seek ways to share it.

There are ways conflicting parties can avoid abusing their power. One way is to give up some of the more obvious power resources and symbols of authority. By removing his hat and jacket, loaded with rank insignia, Colonel Johnson in our previous narrative gives up power resources and status symbols that intimidate subordinates. By abandoning a podium or large desk to sit with the students, a teacher does the same. Bosses who leave the secure confines of their offices to walk among their employees to see firsthand how they are doing and what they need are also giving up power resources.

Another way to avoid abusing power is to make power resources accessible to everyone in the group. With regard to some responsibilities in a relationship, there are times when person A is the more powerful person, and other times person B is the more powerful. When leaders or authorities turn over responsibility and control to subordinates even temporarily, they raise the subordinates' status and equalize the playing field. The aforementioned colonel may appoint a subordinate to take command in his absence. When people in authority delegate tasks to subordinates, they need to delegate some of their power for them to do the job. The teacher may let students give reports or conduct discussions in class rather than lecture, thus giving them more responsibility for the learning that takes place in the classroom.

In a class I took last semester, we were assigned to work in groups, with one person designated as a group leader. In my group, a woman named Lynn made it known that she had worked in a marketing company over the summer and "knew more than we did." She started ordering us around and made all the decisions by herself. As we lost interest in the project and started not showing up to group meetings, she began to do all the work by herself.

We figured we might as well let her since she knew everything anyway. Finally, it became apparent that the project was taking too much time, and she could not do a good job without our help. She asked us if we could meet, and for the first time she listened to everyone's complaints about her role as leader. Lynn agreed to let the group have more say and help define her role along with everyone else's.

In the narrative above, Lynn was able to see how she had abused her power. She was able to pull the group back together by pointing out that everyone's grade depended on the quality of the group project, and that quality would not be as high if she did all the work herself. Everyone's knowledge, ideas, and thoughts then made the group stronger as a whole. By combining the power in the group, no one person was overwhelmed by the project and the final result showed the efforts of everyone.

We've talked about the more overt kinds of power, such as the kind people have due to their roles or the kind people assume when they dominate others. Another kind of power is more subtle. In relationships, the person with the least amount of interest in maintaining the relationship typically has more power in it. If you work for an employer that makes it clear that you could be replaced tomorrow, and you really need the job, the employer has more power (even beyond the legitimate power derived from the employment relationship). If you do all the work in getting together with a friend, that friend is demonstrating less power interest in the relationship, and has more power. So another way to share power is for the one with the least interest in a relationship to increase his or her level of interest. Perhaps the person demonstrating more interest has a terrific personality or brings certain advantages to the relationship. Better yet, the one with the least interest might better appreciate the commitment and attention received from the other, and he or she should see that as a fair exchange for his or her own assets. After all, teachers need students to teach, leaders need followers, and bosses or supervisors need workers to do their jobs. In any case, the more powerful person may change his or her perception of the other and increase her or his own level of interest or investment in the other person, which may distribute power more equally.

Finally, the more powerful person can give power to the relationship that exists between the friends, romantic partners, or workplace members by acknowledging their relationship, making commitments to it, and taking it into consideration as they behave. For example, when two people marry, they change their perspectives on themselves and each other, because they now have their marriage to consider. This also happens if romantic couples have children. They may change their perspectives on themselves because they are part of a family, which now must be taken into consideration. From this day forward, they engage in actions *because they are married or because they have a family*. Whatever the relationship, it can become a third entity that can exercise power over the partners. As married persons, fraternity brothers or sorority sisters, roommates, friends, romantic partners, or workers, we don't engage in some behaviors and do engage in others for the sake of relationships with others. This change in perspective of who we are and of our relationship to one another results in our delegating some of our power to the relationship itself.

As powerful people create conditions for equalizing power in a conflict situation, previously powerless, submissive, or nonassertive persons need to be responsible and respond by asserting themselves more. Does this surprise you? The suggestion that you challenge someone you perceive as the authority or dominant person may strike you as unnatural, disrespectful, or even mutinous. However, when the powerful offer to work with you in a more equitable manner, it is our position that you should take advantage of this opportunity. All too often, subordinates fail to adequately step into a position of authority and do not exercise responsible leadership. For example, when the students are asked to discuss the subject, they sometimes fail to adequately prepare themselves for their participation and fail to seize the opportunity to act responsible for their learning and exercise some authority and control in the classroom.

While we have discussed many ways in which the powerful may, at least temporarily, set aside their power resources and symbols, stop using threats and thromises, and rely more on neutral speech, we now ask what the powerless can do to equalize the conflict situation. Like all perceptions, we need to consider alternate views of situations. Maybe you have more power than you think, or the stronger person may relinquish more power to you if you ask for it, but you are choosing to remain powerless.

As a subordinate, you can test the water to see how your teacher, boss, or dominant partner responds but not in a demanding way or appear to refuse following orders. Try the following:

- Be assertive, stand up for yourself, and offer your opinion.
- Ask for reconsideration or appeal but use a different rationale.
- Offer suggestions, solutions, and your rationale behind them.
- Ask for more responsibility and show that you deserve it.
- Let your feelings, wants, needs, and interests be known but let it be known that you are willing to be a team player
- Ask for another chance but next time try harder to produce results.

Notice the shift in perspective required here: It isn't a question of who is superior but rather what is the best way to resolve the conflict. We should realize that asserting ourselves doesn't mean that our opinions necessarily effect the change we intended. Perhaps our idea is not a good one or impossible to implement or problematic in some way. Also, our ideas can threaten others, who may make us regret our suggestions. We have all met or worked for someone who couldn't handle our being forthcoming, so we learned quickly to guard our opinions and switch to a different place that was less threatened by our assertiveness. This brings up the factor of competition, which is another property of a conflict climate.

Converting Competition to Cooperation

Another dimension that affects how we relate and interact with others ranges from competition to cooperation. In Chapter 2, we discussed competitive communication behavior, such as competitive arguments, and how such behavior can contribute to a competitive escalation cycle. In Chapter 10, we describe competitive and cooperative negotiation techniques for resolving conflicts. In this chapter, we describe the role of competition and cooperation as dimensions of the conflict climate.

In **competition**, the parties are positioned against each other, emphasis is placed on winning, and outcomes are framed as win–lose. Americans often watch or participate in competitive events. Perhaps this is because they view competition as a challenge and a way to grow stronger or more skilled. Sometimes competition is healthy and fun. Competition contributes to a harmful conflict climate because the parties perceive the resolution of the conflict in terms of **win–lose outcomes**, where the gain or loss is significant to those involved. The problem occurs when they take their losses in competition as reflections of their personal competence. *Then the situation is seen as threatening.* Competitive attitudes and desires have their impact on the atmosphere surrounding a conflict.

Cooperation is a situation in which we place greater emphasis on the quality of an interpersonal relationship than on the outcome. Cooperation means working together rather than against one another. A cooperative climate is characterized by the open and honest communication of relevant information between those involved. When communication processes lead to perceived cooperation rather than competition, participants have an increased sensitivity to similarities and common interests rather than a focus on differences or threats, and conflict becomes a matter of mutuality, a problem to be solved rather than a win–lose situation. Cooperation generally increases levels of trust, openness, and collaboration, which leads to win–win outcomes. In **win–win outcomes**, the parties are mutually satisfied with the resolution of the conflict.

How does one create a cooperative climate within conflicts situations? Applying the skills you have learned so far can help. Choose a collaborative communication option so that the other person knows you are committed to finding a solution that both people can embrace. Use S-TLC (Stop, Think, Listen, Communicate, see Chapter 4) so that the other person doesn't feel attacked. And keep the focus on the issue at hand to prevent the conflict from escalating out of control. When we think that the other party is competing with us in ways that result in his or her winning at our expense, the conflict climate is more harmful than nurturing. We need instead to emphasize cooperation. This brings up the factor of interpersonal trust, which is another property of a conflict climate.

Converting Distrust to Trust and Avoiding Unhealthy Trust

> My best friend, Marilyn, and I knew each other for about a year. I was interested in another guy who also was friend with my best friend. Meanwhile, my ex-boyfriend was trying to come back into the picture. I didn't think Marilyn would tell my new love interest about my ex, but I was wrong because she did. You would think she would have had my interests at heart, and she would have been concerned about how the situation would affect me, her friend, in the end. After that situation I felt plenty of distrust toward her.

Just as an imbalance of power and competition produce a harmful conflict climate, so does a violation of trust. **Trust** is the belief that another is benevolent or honest toward the trusting individual, and that the other person's caring transcends any direct benefits the other receives as a result of caring.[7] In other words, we trust others when we think they have our best interests at heart and do not wish to hurt us.

Distrust means we lack confidence in another person, we do not rely on that person, and/or we are suspicious or wary of her or him. In the above case study, the young woman trusted her friend, Marilyn, who didn't behave as a friend she can confide in. In cases like this, breaches of trust are seemingly unforgiveable, a topic we treat in Chapter 9 on "emotional residues and forgiveness."

In addition, **unhealthy trust** means gullible. It is typically inflexible, rigid, and consistent in actions toward others, without regard for the situation. Those who trust pathologically have a tendency to confuse risk-taking and trusting situations, overestimating the probability of getting what they want or underestimating the negative consequences of not getting what they want. Pathologically trusting persons may also overestimate the benevolence of the trusted person or overestimate their power to affect the trusted person's behavior. An example of unhealthy trust is illustrated by the following conflict between two roommates.

> I own a great deal of expensive photography equipment, which I keep at my apartment because I often do my studio work there. My roommate has this weird idea that the world is safe—he leaves doors and windows unlocked all the time. He comes from the Midwest, where "people are decent" and he never locked a door in his life. I believe that he is just too trusting.
>
> This conflict used to arise when I would come home in the afternoon and find the apartment door wide open. Sometimes, if he went next door he would leave the door standing open, but most of the time he would go to work and leave everything unlocked and the windows wide open. If I confronted him, he would fall back on the fact that if God wanted us to have our material possessions then He would make sure that they were not stolen (since everything is God's and He lets us keep them or takes them away).
>
> Then an incident happened. Without telling my roommate, I loaned my television to a friend. When my roommate came home early to an unlocked apartment, he found the set missing. Well, he panicked and called the police and had them looking our apartment over until I came home and straightened everything out. This taught him just how he would react in a real robbery situation and that he should exercise more caution in securing the apartment. After that incident, he did decide to lock the doors.

Both distrust and unhealthy trust are threatening to an interpersonal relationship when they contribute to a harmful conflict climate. To a great extent, **healthy trust** is earned. If our actions warrant it, we gain the trust of others over time. Although trust depends on the previous actions of those involved, it still requires a leap of faith. Most people go ahead and act as though a sense of security about the other is justified, because evidence for trustworthiness is seldom conclusive. Our initial trust is often rewarded. Research seems to indicate that, to begin with, trusting individuals are more likely to assume positive implications of behaviors than are distrusting individuals. Although they do not deny the negative elements in their relationships, they limit the implications negative events have for the relationship;

distrusting individuals overemphasize the importance of negative events. Trusting individuals tend to see negative events in a larger time frame, stabilizing perceptions and making conflict less threatening.[8] In another study, couples who trusted one another were more optimistic, and they tended to report that their partner's motives were positive, even to the extent of saying that the other person's motives were more positive than their own. People who had high trust for their partners usually did not change their opinions of the other person's behavior.[9] In the case of this narrative, it sounds as though the husband didn't have much trust for his wife before she told him about her pre-marital affair.

> A few years ago, I told my husband about a brief affair I had with a friend before we got married. I vowed it would never ever happen again and I meant it. Now I should be happy that I am pregnant. The problem is that my husband wants me to have a paternity test. He wants proof that the child is his. I have been true to my husband, but I am upset that he does not trust me. This tells me that there is something wrong with our relationship.

How does one engender trust? People gain the trust of others when they:

- begin by trusting others,
- perform cooperative actions,
- avoid suspicious activity, and
- reciprocate in trusting ways.

We can see how trust or distrust develops in an exercise called the **Prisoner's Dilemma (PD)**. PD is a classroom exercise played like a game based on a familiar situation: Supposedly, two people are caught burglarizing a building and are brought separately to different interrogation rooms at the police station. These are their options: If both of them remain silent, they both go free, but an incentive to speak the truth exists—if only one confesses, the one confessing receives a reward and goes free and the other goes to jail. However, if both take the bait and confess, they both go to jail. In order to both benefit the most, then, they must trust each other to act in each other's best interest and not just one's own and remain silent. This is called a **mixed motive situation**, because those involved have incentives to both cooperate and compete, but they can choose to stick with just one.

The notion that you can choose to maximize your gains and expect others to choose to lose is unrealistic and unsupported by research.[10] If we think that you are trying to maximize your gains at our expense, we distrust you and choose to compete. When PD is played in class, some students become angry when they find that they can't trust those they play the game against. They often accuse the others of ruining the game. Emotionally intense and lively discussion usually follows the PD exercise.

One interesting issue connected with trust is the illusion of self-interest. Often, if a person sacrifices his or her own goals for the group, the group gains, but the person making the sacrifice loses. In some cases, though, the person making the sacrifice sees making a moral choice (i.e., sacrificing on behalf of the group) as serving his or her own interest. The altruistic choice is reframed as self-serving because it is in line with the person's moral outlook.[11]

Criticisms of the PD paradigm are widespread. Perhaps the most serious concerns the artificial and limited conditions under which communication can take place in PD simulations. However, the exercise has increased our understanding of trust and suspicion in conflict situations. In a similar game situation called "the sequential dictator," researchers found that participants usually reciprocated altruistic moves made by the other.[12]

A harmful climate includes distrust, whereas a nurturing climate manifests trust that is earned. We cannot say enough about the importance of trust in conflict situations. The next section examines the role of defensive and supportive behavior in the conflict climate.

Converting Defensiveness to Supportive Behavior

It was time for the annual review where I work, and my supervisor asked me to come into his office to administer my review. When I entered, to my surprise not only was my boss present but so was a friend of his who is a supervising manager from another department. My boss zipped through a lot of points. When he was finished, without asking for any input from me, he asked me to sign it. I told him that I did not have enough time to digest all that he said and I was not sure I agreed with some of it. I wanted to take time and go over it point by point and defend the inaccuracies. I was also uncomfortable discussing some of the points in front of the other supervisor. It was at that moment that he said, "I am your supervisor and this is your review." It was like he was ordering me to sign it.[13]

In the above case study, the young woman saw the situation as threatening because her boss engaged in a series of behaviors that created defensiveness in her—judgment of her behavior, an air of superiority, and an impatience with her feelings about the situation. Such behaviors help create a harmful conflict climate. When interacting in your own relationships, you should make an effort to establish a nurturing conflict climate by being supportive and avoiding behaviors that generate defensiveness in others, as well as avoiding being defensive yourself.

In a seminal article, Gibb identified communication behaviors that are defensive or supportive (see Table 6.1). These behaviors play a role in their respective conflict climates because they either encourage people to become closed and hostile toward one another or encourage them toward greater openness and cooperation.

According to Gibb, **defensive behaviors** consist of evaluation, control, strategy, neutrality, superiority, and certainty, while **supportive behaviors** involve nonjudgmental description, problem orientation, spontaneity, empathy, equality, and provisionalism.[14] It helps to consider these behaviors as opposites in pairs:

- An *evaluation* consists of praise and blame, while a *nonjudgmental description* is worded in a way that does not threaten the other's self-esteem.
- *Control* refers to attempts to dominate another's behavior, whereas a *problem orientation* is a focus on the issue rather than on preserving ones' power over another.

> **TABLE 6.1**
>
> **Defensive versus Supportive Climates**
>
> | Defensiveness Arises From | Supportiveness Arises From |
> | --- | --- |
> | Evaluation | Description |
> | Control | Problem orientation |
> | Strategy | Spontaneity |
> | Neutrality | Empathy |
> | Superiority | Equality |
> | Certainty | Provisionalism |

- While *strategy* suggests motives and agendas, *spontaneity* is straightforward, unplanned, and captures the spirit of the moment.
- *Neutrality* refers to a lack of concern for the welfare of others (i.e., "that is not my problem"), while *empathy* involves taking an interest in others.
- *Superiority* means "pulling rank" on others, versus *equality,* which expresses a desire to cooperate and invites participation.
- *Certainty* appears dogmatic because it refers to statements that consist of "all" or "every," such as "you always do that to me" or "everybody does it," while *provisionalism* suggests tentativeness, a desire to withhold one's judgment until all the facts are in.

What is the relationship of defensive behavior to the concept of power discussed earlier in this chapter? You may notice that a few of these behaviors are sometimes associated with people in positions of power, such as evaluation (critical), control (domination), neutrality (uninterested in subordinate's problems), and superiority ("pulling rank"). We do not want to confuse the subject of defensiveness by associating it with power. Defensive behaviors are associated with anyone, whether in positions of authority or not. They are more consistently associated with the feelings of inadequacy, insecurity, fear, or uncertainty that make one turn defensive in a threatening situation. To the extent that powerful people manifest defensive behaviors, they probably also experience feelings of insecurity about their roles as supervisors, leaders, or parents, but their underlings may also give off defensiveness because of feelings of insecurity about their roles as subordinates, followers, or children. In romantic couples, defensive behavior is triggered when partners don't express support for one another through listening, a supportive tone or comments that overtly indicate support.[15]

In the following narrative, we added Gibb's key terms in parentheses to connect this example with his description of a defensive climate. How would you feel if you were the husband or wife in this marriage? What impact does this husband have on the management of conflicts between him and his wife? Do you see where the husband may be failing to communicate warmth and acceptance to his wife?

As a husband, I intentionally exercise a lot of influence over my wife (control). I want to monitor everything she does (strategy). So when I gave my wife a new cell phone for her birthday, I got her the best deal for phoning, texting, and working the Internet (evaluation). I set her up on *Facebook,* so I can see what she posts there and who her friends are. I told her that I am always concerned about her safety, so I got an app that enables me to track her whereabouts on my cell phone. She doesn't know that I receive copies of all texts she sends. I set up her email account, so I can monitor it, too. She has complained about losing phone connectivity frequently, but I don't do anything about that because it is not my problem (neutrality). I want her to think of me as the boss (superiority) and that I know what is best for us (certainty).

As you read this narrative, how do you think the husband and wife feel? He appears to be insecure and afraid of losing control of their marriage. Do you feel sympathy for the wife? One would not expect that his forceful hand would result in any mutually satisfying outcomes.

Now consider this next narrative. We again added Gibb's key terms in parentheses to connect this example with his description of a supportive climate. How would you feel if you were the husband or wife in this marriage? What impact does this husband have on the management of conflicts between him and his wife?

I don't criticize my wife (nonjudgmental description). We tackle problems together regardless of what the problem is. I don't think that either of us is better at solving problems than the other, but together we can come up with the best way to spend and save money (equality). I believe that what is important is that we come up with the best solution to a problem (problem orientation) rather than think I have to make all the decisions for us. I value her input. I don't first attempt to solve the problem and then try to convince her of the solution (provisionalism), but rather wait until we can discuss it together, because I value her input (spontaneity). I care about her feelings, wants, and needs, so I want to take her into account (empathy).

One would expect that by working together in a supportive rather than a defensive manner, the couple would develop more mutually satisfying outcomes when in conflicts.

Although the above listing of defensive and supportive behaviors that make up harmful and nurturing conflict climates may appear in an "either-or" format, typically climates exist somewhere in between such extremes. This means that every conflict climate has some degree of defensiveness and supportiveness. However, the nurturing conflict climate has more supportive than defensive behaviors, while the harmful conflict climate has vice versa.

Mutually satisfying outcomes are more likely to occur when communicators participate in the decisions, agreements, solutions to problems, and resolution of conflicts that affect them. When we confront another, we need to express our needs and feelings, which is sometimes difficult to do, because we may feel vulnerable. To the extent that we feel safe enough to assert our interests, needs, and goals, listen to the expression of others, and cooperate in the process of achieving an understanding, the more likely we are encouraged to cooperate and collaborate.

Overcoming Groupthink by Asserting Individual Responsibility

Recently newspapers carried an account about a prominent college athletic program. After coaching a highly successful university football program for over years, the coach was abruptly fired just a couple of days before an important football game. According to newspaper accounts, he was quoted as knowing about a subordinate's alleged child-sexual abuse several years earlier, and although he claimed to have reported it at the time to his superiors, nothing came of the incident. The problem was that too many people looked the other way. No one stepped in to stop the incident when it occurred or informed the police. A few days after the cover up dominated the news, the coach admitted publically that he wished he had done more years ago. He also announced his decision to resign at the end of the season, but the university's Board of Trustees decided to fire him effective immediately. How does an organization, group, family, or couple look the other way and not take action when serious offenses occur?

Groupthink occurs when people are so committed to the people, goals, and/or ideals of a group that they fail to engage in conflict when they should. This may affect how people view matters, how they view their understanding or misunderstanding of issues, and how they view their work or academic life in relation to their lives outside of "the office." When a group is too cohesive and wants to maintain an image of being cohesive, members of the group censure themselves and do not speak up even when they believe the group is headed toward a bad decision. When people are "overly concerned with reaching agreement, avoiding conflict, and preserving friendly relations in the group,"[16] the result is often groupthink. Other examples of groupthink at a national level include the political groups responsible for the "surprise" bombing of Pearl Harbor, where warnings were ignored, the Bay of Pigs fiasco during John F. Kennedy's administration, Watergate during Richard Nixon's administration, and the invasion of Iraq during George W. Bush's administration. Groupthink also occurs at the smaller group level, where members may decide on a course of action that doesn't work out for the group, as this student relates:

> We had this giant group project assigned by a pretty demanding teacher. He had given us clear instructions, but we had this person in our group who had taken a class from this instructor before and claimed that he knew what we needed to do to get a good grade. We weren't really convinced, but we went along with him and didn't say anything. As it turned out, we didn't do what the teacher expected and wound up doing terribly on the assignment.

The "Abilene Paradox" Jerry Harvey believes that the "Abilene Paradox" results from mismanaged agreement.[17] That is, while people disagree with the decision being made (along with others), they do not voice their opinion and just go along with the decision. This idea is related to "uncertainty theory" and false conflicts as presented in Chapter 3. One has to wonder, if the coach described above had made a bigger scene years ago when he first learned of his subordinate's child abuse, perhaps others would have joined in with him. An example of effectively dealing with the Abilene Paradox in an interpersonal situation was relayed by this student:

> My friends and I had a great time at the beach and were trying to decide what to do next. The group of us settled on a movie, a new slasher flick. I wasn't all that interested but wanted to continue having fun with the group, so I took off with two others in my car following those who had chosen the movie. On the way, I thought I would ask one of my passengers what they thought of going to that particular movie. He wasn't interested like I thought he was, and then I had the courage to say I didn't want to see it either. The other passenger then chimed in that she didn't want to see it. We realized that none of us wanted to see it, so we called the others and told them we were going to go to the mall instead.

While the above student altered the plans, not everyone would speak up in a situation like that. The Abilene Paradox occurs because people experience anxiety over choosing a particular course of action, fear being separated from the group, have negative fantasies about what might happen if they do speak up, and are unwilling to take the consequences of what might happen if they do. In the above example, once one was brave enough to speak his mind, the others quickly decided against the idea, breaking the Abilene Paradox. The paradox can be recognized from these conditions:

1. Those involved agree privately about the nature of the problem but don't actually say anything. In the example above, the three who went to a mall agreed that seeing the new slasher flick was a bad idea but didn't say anything.
2. Those involved also agree privately on what the solution would be, but don't realize they are in agreement. Apparently some of the friends were thinking that they didn't really want to see that movie.
3. With nothing said, the group goes along with what they think the consensus is and generally wind up doing something they don't want to do. Only when someone like the above student speaks out, then others may openly voice their opinions.

Similar to the conflict avoidance/accommodation cycle described in Chapter 2, the Abilene Paradox reminds us that good conflict management is necessary for groups to function well. Lencioni argues that a fear of conflict is one of the five major dysfunctions of a team;[18] the Abilene Paradox is evidence of that dysfunction. As suggested in Chapter 3 on uncertainty theory and false conflicts, communication is needed to clear up misunderstandings of this sort.

The "Lucifer Effect" The "Lucifer Effect" is a term coined by Philip Zimbardo, who conducted the now-famous Stanford Prison studies, where students randomly assigned to roles of prisoner or guard took their roles so seriously that negative consequences occurred and the experiment had to be shut down prematurely. The **Lucifer Effect** is applied to circumstances where individuals get so caught up in the situation they are experiencing that they begin to act in ways that are harmful or even illegal.[19] We include it here as an example of destructive climate because, largely, the Lucifer Effect occurs where people fail to resolve issues by avoiding conflict. They are so caught up in the events surrounding them that they do not question what is happening or observe conflict between their private beliefs and their public actions.

Keep in mind that the students in the Stanford Prison study, who just happened to to be assigned either to the role of "guard" the role of "prisoner," knew that the study was an experiment, their participation was voluntary, and they were not really guards and prisoners in real life. However, they ignored the reality and got too caught up in the role play fantasy. "Guards" harmed "prisoners." "Prisoners" didn't request that they see the head experimenter and ask to be released from their voluntary participation in the experiment. Someone needed to remind the role players that "the Emperor isn't wearing any clothes." They needed a reality check. The study illustrated how all too often members of a group or organization forget that there is a real world out there that can hold them responsible for their actions as part of a group. The Nuremburg trials are a case in point where previous Nazi leaders were later tried for their crimes against humanity and some were sentenced to death. In the news account described above, the football coach's dismissal would not have occurred if he (and others) had come forward at the appropriate time and taken more action against the child abuser.

What leads to the Lucifer Effect and how can it be combated? The effect occurs when the right combination of circumstances in a group cause group members to act in ways contrary to their personal beliefs and values. In essence, the circumstances of the situation become more powerful than the people within it. These circumstances include the rules that govern the situation, the roles that people play, and the ways in which roles relate to one another. Let's look at each of these factors.

Rules are important because they tell people what to expect and how to act in particular situations. When people are in a group or organization for a long period of time, rules may come to have "an arbitrary life of their own and the force of legal authority even when they are no longer relevant, are vague, or change with the whims of the enforcers."[20] For example, you may be in a group or organization that, when you question why something is done a particular way, you are told that is just the way it is or that is the way we always do it. When rules are unquestioned, and people obey them without thinking, the Lucifer Effect begins to appear.

A second aspect of the situation that leads to the Lucifer Effect is the role that a person enacts in the situation. When a person cannot separate himself or herself from the role that is expected, there can be negative outcomes. For example, if you are in a subordinate role in a group or organization, you may not think it is your place to bring up negative aspects of a decision being made. Your decision not to engage in a conflict in this case may lead to serious consequences.

The final aspect of the situation that leads to the Lucifer Effect is the way in which roles relate to one another. You can't be a subordinate unless someone is over you and vice versa. When the roles that people play become entwined to the point that they no longer think about what they are doing or what others expect of them, the Lucifer Effect becomes possible.

Essentially, the Lucifer Effect is a condition that occurs when people are not encouraged to stop and think about what is happening and engage in conflict when they realize they are veering off into dangerous territory. The Lucifer Effect is a reminder of the importance of engaging in a moderate amount of task conflict and a sufficient amount of process conflict to ensure that we know what we are doing and where we are going as a group. Groups should create an environment where individuals are free to raise questions such as: Why are we doing this? Is this the best way to do it, why do we always do it this way, and what would happen if we...? Many individuals who have been held responsible for the dire outcomes of a group's or organization's immoral, illegal, or uncivil "way of doing things" probably wish their group had been more open to "whistle blowers" and taken actions that were called for rather than continue to cover them up.

MANAGE IT

Our purpose of this chapter is to describe the role played by climate in conflict situations. An abuse of power, competition, distrust, defensive behavior, and group-think create a harmful conflict environment that produces unsatisfactory outcomes for one or both parties. Un-abusive power or equity, cooperation, trust, supportive behavior, and individual responsibility create a nurturing conflict environment that is more likely to produce mutually satisfactory outcomes.

Abusive power contributes to a harmful conflict climate because it is perceived as threatening. It results in displaced and misplaced conflict because the powerless person wishes to avoid threats and abuse. Although it is difficult to embrace the idea of giving up power, sometimes doing so is one's best option in resolving conflict. At least de-emphasizing power differences leads to a more nurturing conflict climate. Those with less power in the situation should also seek opportunities to be more assertive, use power-neutral language, and take personal responsibility for the outcomes in the conflict situation.

Competition becomes part of a harmful conflict climate when the parties view the conflict situation only in terms of win–lose outcomes. This perception results in the conflicting parties seeing themselves as individuals who must win at all costs. By shifting to a conflict in terms of win–win outcomes, the conflicting parties can view themselves as partners, where maintaining and preserving the relationship is as important as, if not more than, winning an argument or forcing one's decision on another.

Both distrust and unhealthy trust are threatening to an interpersonal relationship when they contribute to a harmful conflict climate. Some people distrust others too much and some are too trusting. Earned trust contributes to a nurturing conflict climate. People maintain the trust of others when they continue to act in cooperative ways, avoid suspicious activity, and reciprocate in trusting ways to the actions of the other.

Critical to our success in conflict situations is the use of communicative behavior that is supportive and nonthreatening. Conflicting parties should try to establish a nurturing conflict climate by being supportive and avoid being defensive. The most significant steps toward creating a supportive climate are found in communication that describes behavior rather than judges it, that is oriented toward solving problems rather than assigning blame, that focuses on description and problem-solution, rather than a "you-orientation," that manifests an attitude of empathy rather than an attitude that is neutral and unconcerned, and that conveys a sense of equality with the other rather than a position of superiority. Finally, a supportive climate is created spontaneously rather than through behavior perceived as strategic, and through talk that suggests the conversation is still in process rather than certain and final.

The concept of defensive behavior differs from that of power imbalance. While a few defensive behaviors are sometimes associated with people in positions of power, such as evaluation (criticizing), control (being dominating), neutrality (lacking interest in subordinate's problems), and superiority ("pulling rank"), defensive behaviors may appear irrespective of power. They are more consistently associated with feelings of inadequacy, insecurity, fear, or uncertainty that make one turn defensive in a threatening situation. When powerful people manifest defensive behaviors, it is an indication of feelings of insecurity about their role as supervisor, leader, or parent.

In this chapter, we looked at conflict that arises from "groupthink" and its related paradoxes and effects. Groupthink occurs when people are so committed to the people, goals, and or ideals of a group that they fail to engage in conflict when they should. This may affect how people view matters, how they view their understanding or misunderstanding of issues (the "Abilene Paradox"), and how they view their work or academic life in relation to their lives outside of "the office" (the "Lucifer Effect"). Groups should encourage individual responsibility and create an environment where individuals are free to challenge "the way things are done around here." Many individuals who have been held responsible for the dire outcomes of a group's or organization's immoral, illegal, or uncivil "way of doing things" probably wish their group had been more open to whistle blowers and taken actions that were called for rather than continue to cover them up.

Communicators who create nurturing climates are more likely to create mutually satisfying outcomes. If we feel safe enough to assert our interests, needs, and goals, listen to others, and collaborate in interpersonal conflicts, we are more likely to successfully manage conflicts.

EXERCISES

THINK ABOUT IT

1. How does it feel when you are in an unbalanced power relationship? What is it like to have more power? Less power?
2. How do you make amends after you have engaged in a displaced conflict with someone close to you? What can you do to avoid such displaced conflicts in the future?
3. Under what conditions are you likely to use powerful speech? Powerless speech? Neutral speech? Why?
4. When have you ever lost your trust in someone? How did you react to the loss of trust? How was the trust restored?
5. When have you seen groupthink, the "Abilene Paradox," or the "Lucifer Effect" take place in a group? What conditions gave rise to them?

APPLY IT

1. Think of a particular relationship where there is an imbalance of power. List the power resources and power symbols associated with that relationship and the powerful speech cues of the person in authority. Are there any power resources or power symbols that the stronger person has overlooked or not utilized? How might the person's use of power affect the situation if a conflict should arise? How might the situation change if he or she shares power with you?

2. Arrange to play the Prisoner's Dilemma game with other members of your class, some as individual contestants, others as pairs, and some with three members on each team. At the conclusion of the game, describe the role of both trust/distrust and competitive/cooperative behavior in interpersonal behavior, conflict, and outcomes. Discuss feelings about the opposition.

3. Take a piece of paper and draw two columns on it. Compare two past or present conflict situations, one in which the other engaged in supportive behavior and another in which the other resorted to defensive behavior. What role does the supportive or defensive behavior play in each conflict situation? How do you feel about the other person in these relationships?

4. Using the example you identified in Think about It, #4, or a new example, analyze a situation in which groupthink, the "Abilene Paradox," or the "Lucifer Effect" took place. Who was involved? What roles did each person play? What was the situation? How did it come to be dysfunctional?

WORK WITH IT

1. Read the case study and answer the questions that follow it.

I had just bought a new computer, and was in the process of getting it all set up. Space is a precious commodity in university housing. My roommate has had a laptop computer for over a year that obviously requires less space to operate than does a full-sized computer like mine. He also has a printer that is about half the space of mine. Prior to my computer being shipped, we realized we would need another desk in the room. We were able to find one that barely fit in our room, and we moved it in. The new desk was half again as big as the one already in the room, and he started using it first.

Once I got my computer partially set up, I realized that it was going to be a tight fit to squeeze all the equipment into the available space, and I asked my roommate if we could switch desks. He quickly and firmly replied "No." I asked why not, since my computer took up so much more space, and it was already cramped in the corner where my desk is, without even having all the equipment set up. He replied that he simply liked the bigger desk so that he could spread out more. I half jokingly said

I would pay him to switch, and he said, "This isn't a barter system, and you can't bid on this desk." I reminded him that he has used the smaller desk for a year and a half without any problems whatsoever.

My roommate then reminded me that he was in this room a year before I moved in. He also felt he was a better judge of arranging the place than I was. "You always have such stupid ideas," he said.

   a. What are the issues in this conflict?
   b. Define power and describe the role played by an imbalance of power in this situation. How might the parties equalize power?
   c. Define competition and describe the role it played (could have played) in this situation. How might the parties convert the situation from a competitive one to a cooperative one?
   d. Define trust and describe the role played by distrust in this situation. How might the parties regain one another's trust?
   e. Define defensive behavior and describe the role played by defensive behaviors in this situation. How might the parties engage in more supportive behavior?
   f. Define groupthink and describe the role played by groupthink in a situation. How might the parties have engaged in constructive conflict management?

2. Think of two different conflict situations with individuals you know well and see often.
    *   In the first situation, the other person is subordinate to you (you have some authority over her or him at home, work, or school).
    *   In the second situation, the other person is superordinate to you (has authority over you at home, work, or school).

Your purpose is to describe the communication and conflict patterns that exist in the two types of interpersonal relationships where you are superior or subordinate. Although you are to write about both relationships, divide each relationship into two parts. In the first part, describe how the powerful person (you in one case; the other in the next case) might try to retain all the power and use it against the other. Also, try to describe the likely outcome of the conflict as a result of holding most of the power. In the second part, describe how the parties might redistribute the power in a way that would benefit the relationship, group, or organization. Again, try to describe the likely outcome of the conflict as a result of trying to create a balance of power.

When you discuss your two relationships, describe the verbal and nonverbal communication patterns. Do you find that you use the same communication behaviors for both persons, or do you find that you tend to use some with one person but not the other? Also, thinking of each person one at a time, go through the list of examples of powerful, powerless, and neutral speech and determine which ones you tend to do with each person and which they use with you.

As you analyze the imbalance of power and its effects on your relationships, also consider the role of trust, competition, and defensiveness. Do you trust each person equally well? Do they trust you equally well? Is there a sense of competition in the air? Are you more defensive or supportive with one another?

NOTES

1. Murray Flagg, "An Exploratory Study of the Use of Language in the Abuse of Power," unpublished doctoral dissertation, Trinity University, 2005.
2. John Waite Bowers, "Guest Editor's Introduction: Beyond Threats and Promises," *Speech Monographs* 41 (1974), ix–xi.
3. Loreen N. Olson, "Compliance Gaining Strategies of Individuals Experiencing 'Common Couple Violence,'" *Qualitative Research Reports in Communication* 3 (2002), 7–14.
4. Stephen K. Erickson and Marilyn S. McKnight, *The Practitioner's Guide to Mediation: A Client-Centered Approach* (NY: John Wiley, 2001).
5. Teun A. van Dijk, "Structures of Discourse and Structures of Power," in James A. Anderson (Ed.), *Communication Yearbook 12* (Newbury Park, CA: Sage, 1989), p. 33.
6. Larry Powell and Mark Hickson, III, "Power Imbalance and Anticipation of Conflict Resolution: Positive and Negative Attributes of Perceptual Recall," *Communication Research Reports* 17 (2000), 181–190.
7. Robert E. Larzelere and Ted L. Huston, "The Dyadic Trust Scale: Toward Understanding Interpersonal Trust in Close Relationships," *Journal of Marriage and the Family* 42 (1980), 595–604; John G. Holmes and John K. Rempel, "Trust in Close Relationships," in Clyde Hendrick (Ed.), *Close Relationships* (Newbury Park, CA: Sage, 1989), pp. 187–220.
8. John Holmes, "The Exchange Process in Close Relationships: Microbehavior and Macromotives," in Melvin J. Lerner and Sally C. Lerner (Eds.), *The Justice Motive in Social Behavior* (New York: Plenum, 1981), pp. 261–284; John K. Rempel, "Trust and Attributions in Close Relationships," unpublished doctoral dissertation, University of Waterloo, Ontario, 1987.

9. Holmes and Rempel, "Trust in Close Relationships," p. 205.

10. Gary Bornstein and Zohar Gilula, "Between-Group Communication and Conflict Resolution in Assurance and Chicken Games," *Journal of Conflict Resolution* 47 (2003), 326–339.

11. Jonathan Baron, "Confusion of Group Interest and Self-Interest in Parochial Cooperation on Behalf of a Group," *Journal of Conflict Resolution* 45 (2001), 283–295.

12. Andreas Diekmann, "The Power of Reciprocity: Fairness, Reciprocity, and Stakes in Variants of the Dictator Game," *Journal of Conflict Resolution* 48 (2004), 487–505.

13. In using this particular story, we'd like to point out that the supervisor violated basic human resource practices. An evaluation should never be given in the presence of another unless that person is also evaluating the subordinate. Further, you have the right to have time to reflect on your evaluation and respond to it before signing.

14. Jack Gibb, "Defensive Communication," *Journal of Communication* 11 (1961), 141–168.

15. Jennifer A. H. Becker, Barbara Ellevold, and Glen H. Stamp, "The Creation of Defensiveness in Social Interaction II: A Model of Defensive Communication among Romantic Couples," *Communication Monographs* 75 (2008), 97.

16. J. Dan Rothwell, *In Mixed Company*, 7th Edition (Boston: Wadsworth, 2010), p. 231.

17. Jerry B. Harvey, *The Abilene Paradox and Other Meditations on Management* (San Francisco, CA: Jossey-Bass, 1988).

18. Patrick Lencioni, *The Five Dysfunctions of a Team* (San Francisco, CA: Jossey Bass, 2002).

19. Philip Zimbardo, *The Lucifer Effect* (New York: Random House, 2007).

20. Ibid., p. 212.

Managing Face

OBJECTIVES

At the end of this chapter, you should be able to:

- Explain the role of face and face saving in conflict.
- Explain the difference between positive face and autonomous face.
- Identify at least three preventative strategies you can use to avoid threatening the other person's face in a conflict situation.
- List three general ways and three specific techniques you can use to support another's face during interaction in a conflict situation.

- Compare and contrast three conflict situations using the repair sequence: one where you offer an account, one where you make a concession, and another where you offer an apology.

KEY TERMS

account	disclaimers	positive face management
acknowledgment	excuses	preventive face
apologies	explaining	management
autonomous face	face	remedy
autonomous face	face (impression)	repair sequence
management	management	reproach
concessions	justifications	scanning
corrective face	offending situations	supportive face
management	positive face	management

The impressions that people have of themselves and each other may be the central issue in a conflict or arise out of one as a secondary issue. The study of the role of these impressions or what we call managing face is a rather challenging topic.

A fundamental assumption that underlies our approach to interpersonal conflict is that people are motivated to create and maintain impressions of themselves. This requires that we distinguish between face and face management. The sociologist Goffman termed **face**, as the image people have of themselves.[1] The concept of face is basic to who we think we are.

We do more than have an image of ourselves or face; we actively work to get others to accept us as the person we think we are. This face work behavior we call **face (impression) management**, which is what one does during interaction with others who may support, alter, or challenge one's face. Domenici and Littlejohn claim that "Face is an accomplishment of interaction as communicators work together over time to negotiate face issues."[2] According to Goffman, we all have images of ourselves, and we project that image (our face) in interactions with others.[3] As we interact, we also look for confirmation of the face we present.

The projection of face is cooperative—as long as the image we project seems consistent and believable, others usually accept it and respond to it as presented. For example, we authors attempt to appear as competent teachers (or present our "face") and trust our students to support us in our roles (i.e., manage our "face" in the classroom, hallway, or faculty office). Similarly, the students act like prepared and motivated individuals and expect the faculty to respect their image of themselves. Of course, the situation is made more complicated by the many factors that affect our perceptions, understandings, and actions, but this teacher–student example can give you an idea of how we present and manage face in everyday interaction.

In this chapter, we want to address an important skill in developing competent conflict management behavior: The ability to maintain one's own impression and that of others to avoid escalating the conflict and to restore a relationship if face is lost. We help you identify people's face, identify techniques to prevent the loss of face, describe general and specific ways to support the other's face in conflict situations, and describe steps you can take to correct a situation after it has occurred.

UNDERSTANDING THE DEMANDS OF FACE

The mutual cooperation involved in projecting face is a principle of interaction that is taken for granted. Being able to create and sustain an identity for oneself, as well as helping the other person to create and maintain an identity for himself or herself, is a fundamental component of communication competence. In the past, intercultural communication researchers claimed that everyone has face concerns during conflict, but members of different cultures present, protect, lose, and save face in different ways because of different levels of face concerns. However, recent research suggests that these cultural differences are not as great as we think.[4]

The idea that face is the result of negotiation between self and others who may or may not accept the image one projects implies that face management frequently includes the management of interpersonal conflict. A person may think he is smart, funny, and lovable, but when challenged is likely to be offended. In fact, the remark may so anger the person that he or she walks out of the room and has nothing more to do with the other person. Because people tend to accept others for the image they project (unless they see a reason to object), face is something that lurks behind the scenes and may or may not make a difference in a conflict situation. However, when aroused, it may make all the difference in the world. Consider the role of face in this conflict:

On the way into a restaurant in a hotel, I slipped on the slick marble floor and fell down. My husband, instead of being concerned, began to yell at me for being so clumsy. He even refused to help me up off the floor, even though I was having trouble getting up. After we were seated, he could see that I was crying, and he began to yell at me again, telling me I shouldn't cry, that if I'd been paying attention I wouldn't have fallen, and if I weren't so fat, I wouldn't need his help getting up anyway. When he left for the restroom, the waitress came up to me and asked if she could do anything for me. I couldn't talk because I was just so embarrassed. All I could do was sit there and wonder how I had become a person who would take that abuse from someone who said he loved me.

The lengths to which people may go to maintain and repair face are wonderfully summarized in a recent book called *Mistakes Were Made (But Not by Me)*, which examines years of research on how we justify our actions when faced with the possibility that they are wrong. The authors note:

> If . . . admitting mistakes is so beneficial to the mind and relationships, why aren't more of us doing it . . . even when people are aware of having made a mistake, they are often reluctant to admit it, even to themselves, because they take it as evidence that they are a blithering idiot.[5]

If this sounds familiar, it is because the act may be explained by attribution theory and attribution error as described in Chapter 3. You may recall that we tend to take more credit than is due when the outcomes are good, and assume less responsibility than we should when the outcomes are bad (it is his or her fault, not mine).

Another reason people don't want to lose face is that they may also experience shame more than guilt. While both emotions are reactions to untoward behavior, shame is more self-focused (e.g., I am such an idiot), and guilt is more behavior focused (e.g., What a dumb thing I did!). Of the two, guilt is the more productive emotion. While guilt "causes us to stop and re-think—and it offers a way out, pressing us to confess, apologize, and make amends,"[6] shame does not lead to those outcomes. When we feel shame, we are more likely to think less of ourselves, withdraw and avoid others, deny our responsibility for the situation, and to shift the blame to others. Guilt tends to lead to a felt need for restoration; shame leads to defensiveness. In the narrative above, the woman who fell may feel guilty about her weight or lack of dieting, but it is her husband who attempted to lower her self-respect by shaming her (verbal abuse). Because of how shame affects others, we should avoid shaming them in conflict situations.

In addition to creating conflict situations, threats to face can also make them worse. Negative comments about the state of a romantic couple's relationship have been found to be more face-threatening than those concerning either partner's personality, physical appearance, or specific behaviors.[7] However, something as simple as answering cell phone calls and the length of the phone conversation with others when on a date with a romantic partner can produce negative face threats and negative feelings.[8] In fact, romantic partners have to deal with potential face threats when initiating, intensifying, or ending romantic relationships.[9]

Any interaction is potentially face-threatening; but in conflict situations, face threats can escalate a conflict and cause it to get out of hand.

As discussed in Chapter 2 on functional and dysfunctional conflict communication cycles, one source of a competitive conflict escalation cycle is the introduction of face issues, which add an extra issue to the initial conflict problems. The disagreement may be over "X" but by calling the other person "stupid" you have now introduced another issue "Y." Because face is so important to people, they try to repair their damaged image before the initial conflict issue is settled (e.g., "So let's argue over whether or not I am stupid before we even think about getting back to the main issue"). Threatening the other person's face is a good way to guarantee that the conflict does not enter the resolution phase.

When people lose face they may also seek retaliation. You now see the other as mean, divisive, uncooperative, problematic, a barrier to achieving a goal. As we said in Chapter 3, you are making internal attributions to explain the other person's behavior, which you see as an attack on your face. Aggressive or violent responses to face-losing situations are more likely when people believe that the other person in the situation has caused it. Such situations are as mild as someone criticizing you or teasing you. It is sometimes more serious, such as one embarrassing another in public (e.g., a teacher criticizing a student in class or a supervisor reprimanding a worker in front of the other workers).

TWO TYPES OF FACE: POSITIVE AND AUTONOMOUS FACE

In a seminal work, Brown and Levinson concluded that people experience two kinds of face needs.[10] **Positive face** is our belief that we are likable and worthy of other's respect. **Positive face management** occurs when we work to get other people to like and respect us. We manage our positive face when we get others to support us, value what we value, express admiration for our unique qualities, and show acceptance of us as competent individuals. **Autonomous face** is that part of us that wants some independence, privacy, recognition for our contributions, or time alone.[11]

> [Autonomous] face is the desire to maintain one's own autonomy. Individuals in any culture want to be shown proper deference and respect and not have their privacy and space invaded, their resources spent, and their actions restricted without just cause.[12]

While each of us enjoys the company of our loved ones, family, and friends, there are times when we respond to autonomous face needs and want to engage in a creative activity (writing, painting), spend some time in reflection (walking or sitting and thinking), prepare for a big event (get our act together), contribute to some large project, or simply rest after a lot of socializing. We engage in **autonomous face management** when we try to get other people to recognize, encourage, support, and approve our autonomous face needs. We also want to put some of ourselves into the products and services we provide for others, which is another way to look at our autonomous face. When others recognized the personal contribution we made as well as the time and effort we put into the activity, our autonomous face is again supported. Sometimes others respond as we would like, but other times we have to remind them of our role in a project and the contributions we made. When we try to get others to appreciate what we did, sometimes they do not accept our autonomous face or reward us for our efforts.

> My roommate, Sarah, only gets paid if the woman she works for, Anna Marie, actually uses her designs. Keep in mind that Anna Marie constantly calls Sarah and takes up a lot of her time. The designs take many hours and even days to do, but there is no guarantee that Sarah will benefit from all her time and effort in the end. She has a lot of school work and not enough time to stay on top of it all. Anna Marie should pay Sarah for her time and effort, not just if she occasionally uses one of her designs.

Interestingly, one person's positive face management may produce autonomous face conflict in another. One may want others to communicate support of her or his positive face by expressing admiration for that person, spending time with that person, and so on, but by doing so, one can encroach on the person's autonomy. Constantly calling each other on cell phones and texting may be taken as positive face support between romantic partners but also leave them with little time alone (an autonomous face need).

On a recent television show, an elderly but wealthy woman took an interest in a family struggling to make ends meet. At first the parents were delighted to be invited to the wealthy woman's home and enjoy her many luxuries. The problem occurred when the woman started spending a great deal of time with the children and took over the parents' roles, buying the children whatever they wanted, giving them a room of their own in her house, letting them do whatever they wanted such as painting on the walls of the children's room. She even crawled into bed with the parents one night when they were watching TV in her guest bedroom. The parents enjoyed her hospitality up to a point but that ended when they felt that their privacy and independence was threatened along with the challenge to their parenthood.

Supporting a person's positive and autonomous face requires a balance under the best of circumstances. Consider how these competing needs are threatened in a conflict situation.

> I would say that the biggest conflict in my life arises when my girlfriend gets emotional. Of all the girlfriends I have had, I have never dated one as emotional as my current girlfriend. The conflict usually comes when I have had a hard day and still have work to do in the evening. My girlfriend comes over and yells at me for ignoring her and not really loving her, because I have been gone all day without giving her any attention. When I try to tell her I have been busy and still have much to do, the conflict gets worse. She starts to cry and becomes crazy. At this point, I cannot deal with the situation and want to hide under a rock. The conflict usually has to defuse itself by me leaving and not speaking to her until later that evening or the next day. If she follows me out the door, I have to stop and order her back inside and not answer her calls for a few days. When she becomes calm, the situation gets resolved, but sometimes it can last for a week or so.

While the man's positive face is supported by his partner's desire to spend time with him, his autonomous face is threatened by her need for too much of his limited time. According to O'Sullivan, it is unlikely that people would perceive a particular encounter as strictly positive or negative.[13] So, in the above example, the couple's conflicts arise out of the need to support both positive and autonomous face. Sometimes our individual needs smother another's need for autonomy. Take this case with Aron for example.

> Last semester, my friend, Aron, started seriously dating Vicky. In the beginning of their relationship, he hung out with me and our mutual friends. But, as things progressed, he seemed to cling to the girlfriend, and completely ignore the rest of us. We know he enjoys our company and likes spending time with us, but as his relationship with Vicky progressed, he simply disappeared. She demanded his total time and attention and completely shut out his other friends and interests. He needs to gain a balance between her demands for his time and attention and his own personal needs (i.e., independence from the girlfriend).

Sometimes face threats occur unexpectedly. A study of 911 calls, for example, claims that the required questions for information asked by the operators "can threaten callers' desire to be treated as trustworthy, intelligent, and of good character, as well as threaten their need to feel unimpeded in their requests for timely police service."[14] And while most of us would agree that being told we are cared for is good, a directly affectionate message, while supporting our positive face, might threaten our autonomous face.[15]

To help solve the dilemma posed by competing desires for positive and autonomous face, we offer a before, during, and after set of recommendations. Before committing loss of face, people may take steps to prevent it. During interaction, they can go a step farther by supporting the other's face in general or specific ways. Finally, if a threat to face is made, they can use corrective face management, using constructive responses to loss of face in a conflict situation.

FACE MANAGEMENT

There are four factors in face management: the act (what is or should be said or done?), the conversation (what do I think is happening right now?), the episode (how does this fit into a larger pattern of interaction with the other?), and the lifescript (who am I?). All four factors are interconnected—as changes occur in one they also occur in others. That is, your choice of different conversational strategies as you perceive and interpret different conflict situations affects your lifescript and vice versa. Face management is generally one of three kinds: preventative, supportive, or corrective.

Preventive Face Management

By avoiding or minimizing threats to face, **preventive face management** forestalls becoming embroiled in face-saving issues during conflict situations. The means of doing this include the following:

- Trying to see the situation from the other's perspective—how the issue affects the other and the other's self-image.

- Accepting what the other person says at face value (no pun intended). Unless there is a good reason to the contrary, it is best to accept what the other person says as an accurate reflection of his or her feelings.
- Accepting the other person's right to change his or her mind. No one can predict the future with any degree of accuracy. The fact is that goals change, people change, and life changes. To treat a change in goals as a sign of the other person's insincerity or instability threatens the other person and sets up future conflicts concerning that very issue.
- Avoiding face-threatening topics (which is almost impossible in a conflict situation) or employing communication practices that minimize threats to face.

The last approach of avoiding threats to face consists of communication practices such as politeness and **disclaimers** (additions to the message that soften the forcefulness of the message) that help to minimize threats to face before they happen.[16]

This narrative illustrates how to maximize a face threat. We hope you notice as well that the evaluation, control, and certainty with which the dissatisfaction was expressed also created a defensive climate (see Chapter 6).

> Just recently, my mother was expressing her dissatisfaction to me about the host in the dining room at the retirement home where she lives. She had come a little late to lunch and found that "her" table had dishes all over it. Instead of moving to a different table or asking someone to take away the dishes, she turned to the host and said, "When are you going to start doing your job?" As she told me the story, she was amazed that the host had subsequently been rude to her. I tried explaining conflict management skills to her, but someone with as much practice at engaging in nasty behavior as my mother is not likely to change.

In the above conflict situation, for example, the person making the complaint could have used either of the following disclaimers to soften the effect of the complaint:

- *Hedging:* indicating uncertainty and receptivity to suggestions. "Is this my table? No one has cleared it yet."
- *Cognitive disclaimer:* asserting that the behavior is reasonable and under control, despite appearances. "I don't want to sound demanding, but I'd really like to sit down now and the dirty table is bothering me."

Other disclaimers available in a conflict situation include the following:

- *Credentialing:* indicating you have good reasons and appropriate qualifications for the statement you intend to make. "I am your friend and I care about you, so I want to say . . ."
- *Sin license:* indicating that this is an appropriate occasion to violate the rule and one should not take the violation as a character defect. "Well, this is a special occasion and . . .")
- *Appeal for suspended judgment:* asking the other to withhold judgment for a possibly offensive action until it is explained. "Hear me out before you get upset . . ."[17]

The above prevention techniques are illustrated in this person's situation:

A conflict situation in which face-saving was an issue is when I had to address my fellow sorority members about a bad situation. We had a fund-raising event on an upcoming Friday night, and with 30 women in the sorority, only five were planning to help out. The problem is, we could not do the fund-raiser with only five people there to help out. It looked like we might have to cancel the event. I was upset by this and decided I needed to say something about it at our next meeting. I was worried about my "face" because the girls are important and I would like them to like and respect me, and the problem was pretty touchy. Some preventative strategies I employed to avoid threatening their faces were seeing the situation from their point of view, avoiding face-threatening topics, being polite, and using disclaimers. In this specific conflict situation, I decided to assume that those who were unable to make the event had legitimate reasons they could not attend, and I did not question anyone's absence, to avoid threatening others' faces. I also understood that the fund-raiser was not their priority. I used the cognitive disclaimer when I started off by saying "I don't want to sound like your mother, but we really need people to be there on Friday, and because not everyone could come together, we stand to lose out on raising any money." I used another disclaimer when I said "I don't want anyone to take personal offense by this, but . . ." By using the disclaimers I was able to minimize threats to face.

Supportive Face Management

When in a conflict with someone, use **supportive face management** to help reinforce the way the other is presenting himself or herself. In a general way, people want others to like them, respect them, encourage them, consult them, include them, appreciate them, reward them, make references to them, ask them for their opinion or input, smile at them, greet them warmly, help when needed, and make them feel safe. Ask yourself if you do the following when in a conflict:

Do I try to make the other feel important?
Do I try to make the other look good to other people?
Do I try to make the other think that they are winning?
Do I try to make the other feel secure?
Do I try to make the other believe that I am honest and trustworthy?

We can support others in a general way by what we do and what we say. If we don't include, consult, ask, reward, or help others, they may feel put down by our actions. It is also possible to put people down verbally by insulting them or showing disrespect. We can also support others in a more specific way. To do this, you need to determine what traits or characteristics the other perceives in himself or herself and point out the ones you have in common or are capable of supporting.

You like to fish? Well, so do I.
I like people with red hair.
You're a jogger, so let's jog together next time.

You have taken three classes from Professor Hamad. I hope to take a class from her soon.

We both want to lose weight.

One of our students illustrates this more specific type of support for the other in the following situation:

I wasn't close with one of my housemates when we first moved in. One day it was just the two of us at home, and she was watching TV in our common living room. I didn't know her well but wanted to put in the effort. So I came in and sat down, and we started talking about our mutual love of the particular show she was watching. By having that in common with her we both started to open up and get along much better.

When people say they don't like others with a particular color hair, and you have that hair color, you may feel put down. Because they say they don't exercise regularly, you may see that as some kind of disapproval for your doing it. If their goal in a conflict is to inflict serious mental harm on you, they can resort to verbal abuse and put you down. If their goal is to solve a problem, then they want to avoid abuse and support your face.

In the earlier example of a sorority member trying to get her sisters to participate in a Friday fund-raising event, she goes on to describe how she supported their faces in the ongoing interaction.

First, I tried to make the others feel important, secure, honest, and trustworthy. Second, I specifically recognized their individual needs and interests by saying "We all want money for the dance festival that is coming up . . ." and "We are sisters. We feel the need to come together . . ." and "I know that everyone is really busy right now . . ."

Corrective Face Management

When a threat to face has been made, you should use **corrective face management,** or statements meant to ameliorate the effect of face-threatening messages. When you are the one whose face has been threatened, one means of corrective action is simply to act as though no threat to face has been made, ignoring the action that caused a face threat. This is a good strategy for minor issues, but ignoring a major face threat may result in a larger conflict later on. Other forms of corrective action have been generated by Thomas and Pondy, who viewed impression management (ensuring that the image one projects is the one that others perceive) as critical in moving a conflict to its resolution phase.[18] People's beliefs about the other's intent affect the conflict strategies they choose and how they interpret the other's strategies. Thomas and Pondy found that when people were asked to recall what conflict resolution mode they had used, the majority (74 percent) were most likely to recall using "cooperative" modes: collaboration, compromise, and accommodation. However, the majority (73 percent) also recalled that the other person in the conflict had been competitive rather than cooperative. Thus, people are not being perceived as cooperative even when they think they are being cooperative.

The authors identified a number of ways in which people can work to manage the impression they make in a conflict to help ensure that the image they project is the one the other person perceives. Two of their suggestions include scanning and explaining.

Scanning is the process of checking out the perceptions being created. We can question the other to confirm that we are "on the same page." We use **explaining** to clarify when we perceive that the other has not taken our message in the way we meant it. Both of these techniques are illustrated in the narrative below:

> I went to talk to my boss about my job. I started off by saying that I was getting to the point where I couldn't meet the deadlines he set. It just seemed like there was no end to them, and no down time. I asked him if he had been able to get the second person to take half of the work as he had promised over a year earlier. He started to get defensive about his budget and his hands being tied, so I said I understood all that, but I was there to talk to him about whether I could continue to work at this job. Part of being able to do so was whether he anticipated providing the help that had been promised. Of course, this was pretty threatening because he thought I was talking about broken promises or his inability to get what he said he would. I kept telling him that I knew the system was making life difficult for him but that I was at the end of my rope. I finally said that I couldn't continue to work at this pace. It had nothing to do with him, or the organization, it was just that I didn't have the stamina to do it anymore. I informed him that I had decided to accept an offer from one of our competitors, and I gave him my resignation.

Repair Rituals

What should we do if we realize that we have offended the other person? We have available to us a ritual known as a repair sequence, which has these four steps:

Offending situation: the other's behavior is seen as intentionally hurtful, whether or not that person did intend it
Reproach: request for an explanation of an offense from the one offended
Remedy: an account, concession, or apology supplied by an offender
Acknowledgment: evaluation of the account supplied by the one offended

The **repair sequence** is a specialized version of the conflict process where a triggering event is followed by initiation, differentiation, and perhaps resolution. The difference is mainly in the relationship of the issue to the episode. Whereas in conflict both people perceive that the other is interfering with their goals or engaging in incompatible activities, in a repair sequence there is a clear distinction between the offender and the offended party. The offender has created a problem (i.e., the offender has not acted in accordance with the face she or he has created for the other person) and must explain his or her actions. Let us consider each of the phases or steps in the repair sequence.

Offending Situation. **Offending situations** are those in which a person believes that the other has acted in an intentionally hurtful way. Usually, the offense is face-threatening in nature. Nothing is more awkward that having to continue interacting with a person who has offended you and refuses to acknowledge it or appears unaware of it.

Reproach. People are unlikely to walk away from an offense without saying anything at all, although that can happen on occasion, especially when the consequences are minimal. In more significant cases, one can call attention to an offense by simply commenting on it or confronting the offender and asking him or her for an explanation (e.g., "What do you have to say about the broken window?"). In some cases, one can make an offender aware of an offense even by remaining silent. The other may perceive this as "the silent treatment," realize what caused it, and come forward with an explanation. Finally, the offended party may also use nonverbal cues (e.g., slamming doors, dirty looks) to let the offender know an offense has occurred, which assumes that the offender knows what he or she did to upset the other.

Remedy. Reproaches create a need for us to take an action that rectifies matters. However, it is possible that an offender may respond to a reproach by refusing to act, the most aggravating response. Refusals include denying that one was even involved in the offending event or that the event took place (which may mean lying). A person can also refuse to act by turning the reproach around and questioning the right of the offended person to make a reproach. In cases where one cannot deny the event or one's role in it, there are three broad types of actions an offender can take to restore a relationship: offer an account (through excuses or justifications), make a concession, or offer an apology; one can also act in a way that combines any of these. (See Table 7.1 for a complete listing of actions.)

TABLE 7.1

Image Restoration Strategies

Less Restorative

Excuses

I didn't do it, someone else did.
I was forced to do it; you made me do it.
I lost my head; I didn't know what I was doing.
I didn't mean to do it.

Justifications
I meant well.
It was a one-time thing: it's not characteristic of me. You know me better than that.
It looks a lot worse than it really is.
It actually was a good thing to do given the circumstances.

Concessions
Let me give you something for your pain.
I will make the offense right; I will change my ways.

Apology
I am so ashamed and so sorry this happened. Please forgive me.

More Restorative

An **account** is an explanation for behavior when questioned. Accounts are also part of the conflict interaction (when a person is challenged on an issue and must respond) or its aftermath (when a person tries to explain what was done and said in a conflict situation). Accounts serve an important function in that they explain how people interpret the situation at hand.

Accounts may take the form of excuses or justifications. **Excuses** admit that the offense occurred but deny responsibility for it. The offender can claim

- impairment (e.g., "I was drunk"),
- diminished responsibility (e.g., "I didn't know"), scapegoat status (e.g., "they made me do it"), or
- that she or he is a "victim of a sad tale," in which the offender recounts a series of misfortunes that have resulted in the way the offender is today. Sad tales are often the staple of courtroom drama, in which defense attorneys try to prove their client incapable of responsibility in a crime.

In contrast to offering an excuse, the offender may choose to offer a justification, which diminishes the meaning of the offense rather than diffusing responsibility for it. **Justifications** may acknowledge that an act was committed while claiming that

- it hurt no one (e.g., "it was just a practical joke"),
- the victim deserved it (e.g., "he hit me first"), other people who have committed similar offenses were not punished, he or she had good intentions when choosing to commit the offense, or
- the offense was needed because of loyalty to others (e.g., the reasons used by various political subordinates when explaining why they broke various laws).

Because not all excuses or justifications are acceptable or sufficient in themselves, the offender may need to make some sort of concession. **Concessions** admit the offender's guilt and offer restitution. For example, a husband brings his wife flowers, she does something with him that he enjoys doing (play golf, sail, or watch a football game), one gives a gift to the other, and a relative buys the other tickets to an athletic event. Concessions are often done in combination with excuses or apologies.

Apologies are admissions of blameworthiness and *regret* on the part of the offender. Apologies allow a person to admit to accepting blame for an action, but they also attempt to obtain a pardon for the action by convincing the offended person that the incident is not representative of what the offender is really like.

Schlenker and Darby have identified several levels of apology, which are used progressively by actors as the offense committed becomes more serious and as the actor's responsibility for the offense increases. An apology can include a simple "pardon me" or something more complicated, including statements of remorse (e.g., "I'm sorry"), offering to help the injured party, self-castigation ("how clumsy of me"), or direct attempts to obtain forgiveness.

In one study, respondents were asked to imagine that they had bumped into another person in a public place, either in a crowded shopping mall or in a hallway at school between classes. The degree of felt responsibility was manipulated by explaining that the actor was either knocked from behind, thus bumping into the victim, or had not been paying attention and bumped into the victim without noticing. Offenses of varying degrees were that the victim had been bumped on the arm (low), knocked to the ground but was unhurt (medium), or knocked to the ground and was moaning in pain (high). Respondents were asked whether they would use one of the levels of apology, respond with no oral apology (e.g., saying or doing nothing, or responding nonverbally), or respond in justification ("I'm glad to see you're not hurt"), or excuses ("I didn't see you"). According to Schlenker and Darby, when apologies appear to be sincere and the offender does not seem likely to repeat the offense, acceptance is a socially expected result of the apology. Under these circumstances, it would be unusual for social interaction not to return to normal.[19] Effective apologies have these components:

- an explicit expression of remorse (e.g., "I'm sorry.")
- a *specific* statement of why one feels remorse (e.g., "I'm sorry *for stepping on your toe*," as opposed to, "I'm sorry for *what happened*.") and being sorry for the right thing (e.g., "I'm sorry *I called you a liar*," as opposed to, "I'm sorry *you feel that way*.")
- a comment that accepts responsibility for your actions (e.g., "It's my fault.")
- a truthful explanation for the offensive behavior without trying to excuse the offence and shirk responsibility (e.g., "I'm sorry. *I wasn't looking where I was going*," vs. "I'm sorry I bumped into you *but I had to answer my cell phone quickly*.")
- a promise of future good behavior. This is a statement to say that the offensive behavior is not reflective of the offender's true character, therefore the victim can trust the behavior will not recur (e.g., "I'll be more careful in the future.")
- an offer of restitution (e.g., "I'll pay to have it cleaned.")[20]

Apologies are particularly important when one is faced with the reality of having offended a high trait hostility person. When a person is faced with an offending situation, his or her blood pressure and pulse rises. Those who rate high on trait hostility or anger have much higher increases in blood pressure and pulse when subjected to verbal harassment. But, if after the experience they are given a sincere apology, their blood pressure and pulse returns to normal much faster than if they receive an insincere apology.[21]

Acknowledgment. After an account has been rendered, the offended party responds with an acknowledgment in one of several ways. The most mitigating way is to honor the account, accepting its content and signaling, verbally or nonverbally, that the "score is even." The offended party may retreat from the reproach, dropping his or her right to make it (e.g., "I didn't know that you were forced into action"). The offended party may also simply drop or switch the topic, moving away from the reproach without resolving the issue. More aggravating is *rejection* of the account, either by taking issue with it (e.g., "I can't believe you expect me to believe you") or by simply restating the reproach as though no account was given.

In an effort to apply the repair ritual in his own life, a student writes:

Some of my old high school buddies visited during Homecoming at the college. One night after too many beers, I started getting a little rowdy with one of them, and friendly child play turned into drunken wrestle-mania right there in the bar. After taking the rest of the night to sober up and cool off, I felt I needed to say something to break the ice due to the fact that my buddy wasn't speaking to me. I decided that I should be the one to explain and apologize for my actions because I realized that I instigated the whole mess. So instead of ignoring the situation and pretending like nothing happened, I admitted to my friend (the person I offended) that my behavior was unacceptable, but I also explained that it was unintentional. I had one too many drinks that night. After I explained myself to him, he was completely understanding and forgiving. I offered to treat him to breakfast, so we went out. If I hadn't tried to excuse my behavior, apologized, and bought him breakfast, we would still not be talking to each other. However, I realized that taking responsibility for what I did was my best way to get out of the dog-house.

Let us authors hasten to add, that we do not condone using the excuse of alcohol or drugs for inappropriate, immature, or offensive behavior. Some excuses are more acceptable than others; however, the above scenario illustrates the repair ritual in a way that some students can identify with and understand.

Reactions to Face Management

In a recent study, Benoit and Drew examined the ways in which people respond to impression management strategies. They had people rate how appropriate and effective various strategies are when someone has damaged one's impression. The scenario was one in which person A bumps into person B, spilling something on B's favorite coat. B accuses A of ruining B's clothes, and A replies with denial ("I didn't do it"), evasion of responsibility for the event ("it was an accident; it wasn't my fault"), reducing the offensiveness of the event ("it's not that bad"), corrective action ("I'll have the clothing cleaned"), or apology ("I'm so sorry"). The results indicated, not surprisingly, that apologies and offering some corrective action were seen as the most appropriate and effective ways to restore one's image in this kind of circumstance.[22] Unfortunately, Elana didn't do all she should have done.

I do not think I used the right remedy after offending my boyfriend. I just said I didn't mean to upset him and that I thought what I said was no big deal. I never said that I was sorry for upsetting him, and I never showed regret.

Conflict and Impression Management in Cyberspace

A newly developing area of communication study is online conflict that occurs in real time chat rooms or asynchronous discussion forums. In their study of online conflict, Smith, McLaughlin, and Osborne found that few people replied to reproaches and seldom completed the traditional repair sequence.[23] How can you explain this difference between online and face-to-face (FTF) conflicts? We suggest that it is much easier to "walk away" from an offending situation online than it is FTF, especially where there is a relationship between the parties involved. In many of these online offending situations, there is no (previously established) relationship to repair. When FTF, if you call me on the carpet for something I said or did, I may feel obligated to respond and seek your acceptance of my excuse, apology, or concession, but in an online discussion group, I might find it easier and less awkward to simply exit the discussion. The research is corroborated by others examining the difference between FTF conflict and conflict in computer-mediated communication (CMC). Zornoza and colleagues, for example, found that negative conflict behaviors were more frequent in CMC than FTF, and the number of positive conflict management behaviors actually decreased over time.[24] In addition, Dorado and colleagues found that there were higher levels of avoidance and lower levels of forcing in computer-mediated negotiation, while FTF negotiation displayed more forcing and compromise.[25] Finally, Hobman and colleagues' research indicated that CMC groups displayed more process and relationship conflict than FTF when first starting, but those differences disappeared after the first day.[26]

Another line of research in cyber communication involves the creation of impressions and their management by users of Social Network Sites (SNSs) such as My Space and Facebook. Teachers who use *Facebook,* for example, and allow students access may be perceived as more accessible and similar to students, which may result in higher student participation and affective learning.[27] Among students, the number of friends one has, the descriptions that one makes about oneself, and the comments made by others are related to the impressions people make on others in SNSs. Specifically, the number of friends one has on *Facebook* is related to perceptions of popularity but only up to a certain point. People having fewer than 100 friends or more than 300 friends are viewed as less popular than those in the middle, but for different reasons. People with more than 300 friends may be perceived as too *Facebook* dependent. They are viewed as substituting the computer environment for FTF interactions. Too many friends may be seen as an act of desperation rather than a sign of popularity.[28]

While the number of friends is related to positive impressions of the person being rated, the number of friends one has does not have any particular relationship to ratings of physical attractiveness.[29] However, the attractiveness of the friends who leave messages on a person's "wall" in *Facebook* affects impressions of that person's attractiveness.[30] Further, the comments made by others about a person on his or her profile are more influential in creating impressions than statements one makes about oneself.[31] While it has been commonly expected that people seek out online relationships because of their inability to handle FTF ones, research does not bear that conclusion out. While people who are anxious about FTF communication do use *Facebook* to pass the time and assuage feelings of loneliness, they have fewer friends. The author concludes: "Such results seem to justify the rich-get-richer hypothesis, which states that the internet primarily benefits extraverted individuals. Our results are in contrast to findings that socially anxious individuals are more likely to form relationships online."[32] Still another study demonstrated the utility of *Facebook* for solidifying relationships that might otherwise be weak, and for creating social ties linked to a sense of community.[33] Sometimes, though, those ties can be complicated, as in the narrative below.

> My boss is my "friend" on Facebook, largely because I didn't want to deal with the consequences of not accepting the request. One day I was really bored in a meeting. They were going on and on about something that could

have been decided in minutes. I posted an update on *Facebook* about being in the worst meeting in the world. The next day my boss called me into his office and chewed me out for making that remark.

Facebook and other SNSs are the new age in face and face management. Comments made by students in class and local newspaper accounts raise many issues regarding face. What happens when prospective employers look at your profile picture as well as other photos you make available on *Facebook* or *MySpace*? What happens when romantic partners find that they differ on how they designate their relationship status? Should it matter if a partner includes ex-romantic partners among his or her friends? Can you tell when a *Facebook* entry is using the site like one might use an online dating service? Of course we could raise other face management issues for other social media as well as other sites like the work related *LinkedIn* as well as online dating services. You probably have a presence on the web. What do these sites say about you? Have you effectively managed your face online?

MANAGE IT

Some other cultures more openly discuss and emphasize the importance of face and face saving techniques than many Americans do. However, the concept is no less important for Americans. One of the primary reasons conflicts escalate or get out of hand is due to face threats. In this chapter, we distinguish between face and face management. Face is the image people have of themselves—who we think we are. We do more than have an image of ourselves or face; we actively work to get others to accept us as the person we think we are. This face work behavior we call face (impression) management, which is what one does during interaction with others who may support, alter, or challenge one's face.

There are two types of face and face management, positive and autonomous face. Positive face is our belief that we are likable and worthy of other's respect. Positive face management occurs when we work to get other people to like and respect us. We manage our positive face when we get others to support us, value what we value, express admiration for our unique qualities, and show acceptance of us as competent individuals. Autonomous face is that part of us that wants some independence, privacy, recognition for our contributions, or time alone. We engage in autonomous face management when we try to get other people to recognize, encourage, support, and approve our autonomous face needs. We also want to put some of ourselves into the products and services we provide for others, which is another way to look at our autonomous face. When others recognized the personal contribution we made as well as the time and effort we put into the activity, our autonomous face is again supported. The desires for positive and autonomous face, under the best of circumstances, can create a dilemma because it requires balance.

Conflict managers can prevent threatening another's face before, during, and after interaction. An effective conflict manager may precede a face-threatening message with a disclaimer such as hedging, cognitive disclaimer, credentialing, sin license, or appeal for suspended judgment.

Once engaged in conversation with another, an effective conflict manager can employ general ways and specific techniques to support another's face in conflict situations. In a general way, people want others to like, respect, encourage, consult, include, appreciate, and reward them. They want others to ask them questions, greet them warmly, help them when needed, and make them feel safe. We can also support others in a more specific way. To do this, we need to determine what traits or characteristics the other perceives in himself or herself and point out the ones we have in common or are capable of supporting.

In a conflict situation in which we lose face, we can employ a repair sequence to regain it. A repair sequence has these phases or steps: the offending situation, a reproach (request from the offended person for an explanation of the other's offense), a remedy (an account from the offender such as an excuse or justification, a concession, or an apology), and an acknowledgment (evaluation of the account).

Some offenses are worse than others. When the violation creates more than an offending situation, a relational transgression occurs, which we examine in Chapter 9. When relational transgressions occur, forgiveness and perhaps reconciliation are necessary to restore the relationship. Threats to face can also cause stress and anger, which are the subjects of the next chapter.

EXERCISES

THINK ABOUT IT

1. Under what conditions in the past have other people commented on your face management? Were these positive or negative experiences? How did you react?
2. How have you seen issues of autonomous and positive face create conflicts in your experience? What have you done to resolve issues of autonomous and positive face? Are the strategies you use for each issue different?
3. What are your general and specific face needs? In general, what actions could others take that would show support for your face needs? What specific actions could they take?
4. Can you remember a time that you used preventative face work to avoid making the other person feel defensive? What was the nature of the situation? How did you use it?
5. Can you remember a time that you needed to use corrective face work in order to repair a relationship? What was the nature of the situation? How did you use it?
6. If you are a member of *Facebook, My Space,* or another Social Network Site (SNS), or work related sites like *LinkedIn,* think about the way you use it. How do you present yourself? What impression do you hope people will get from reading your profile? Have there been times people have posted something on your profile that you wished they hadn't?

APPLY IT

1. Imagine that you have to say something potentially face-threatening to a friend. Explain how you could use each of these disclaimers to soften the complaint:
   a. hedging
   b. cognitive disclaimer
   c. credentialing
   d. sin license
   e. appeal for suspended judgment

2. Visit a number of different SNS sites. How does the site itself describe its purpose? How do you see the profiles of people within the site exemplifying that purpose? What are the differences between the various sites?

WORK WITH IT

Read the following case study and answer the questions that follow it.

A group of us live together in a sorority house. One of our sisters, Gina, is normally quiet and easygoing. However, one day she suddenly verbally attacked each one of us and accused us of plotting against her behind her back. I said to her, "What? Where is this coming from?" We were all shocked at her suddenly different behavior. She even threw a textbook at one of her sisters and stormed out of the room. That evening she rejoined the group but said nothing about the incident. At first, a couple of us raised the issue, but she just smiled and said, "I don't know what you are talking about."

1. Is this an offending situation?
2. Does a reproach occur?
3. Was a remedy offered? If not, what might it be? As for acknowledgment, what remedies would likely receive rejection from the narrator? What remedies might receive acceptance?

DISCUSS IT

Read the following case study and discuss in class your answers to the questions that follow it.

A long-lasting conflict centered on the amount of time and affection Frank's wife, Judy, was spending on their cat, Lucky. This conflict took place a number of times, usually whenever Frank was feeling neglected. Whenever Judy entered the house, she lavished the cat with affection. In fact every time she passed the cat in the hallway, she would stop and caress her, talk to her, and go out of her way to make the cat feel loved. From his perspective, Frank felt that Judy always had time to give the cat the affection she needed (and more) while never having time to provide the affection he felt that he needed. He inferred from her actions that she was never too busy for the cat but rarely had enough time for him. He was jealous of the cat.

From Judy's perspective, the cat was helpless and her lavishing attention was only because the cat was so "cute and defenseless." Judy didn't realize that Frank would really enjoy short, quick doses of affection throughout the day like she was giving the cat. Because of a few instances where Judy interrupted Frank while he was working intensely on something and he responded a bit negatively, she also felt that he might put a damper on her affectionate overtures toward him by not being responsive, or by failing to "purr."

1. What is the likely outcome of this conflict situation?
2. How could the characters have supported one another's face using general techniques? How could the characters have supported one another's face using specific techniques, and what would then have been the likely outcome?
3. Suppose you recommend corrective actions to the couple. Describe the steps in the repair sequence as they would apply to this conflict. Also, what role could accounts, concessions, and apologies play in this case study?

NOTES

1. Erving Goffman, *The Presentation of Self in Everyday Life* (New York: Overlook Press, 1959); *Interaction Ritual: Essays on Face-to-Face Behavior* (New York: Pantheon Books, 1967).

2. Kathy Domenici and Stephen W. Littlejohn, *Facework: Bridging Theory and Practice* (Thousand Oaks, CA: Sage Publications, 2006), p. 22.

3. Ibid.

4. John Oetzel, Stella Ting-Toomey, Tomoko Masumoto, Yukiko Yokochi, Xiaohui Pan, Jiro Takai, and Richard Wilcox, "Face and Facework in Conflict: A Cross-Cultural Comparison Of China, Germany, Japan, and the United States," *Communication Monographs* 68 (2001), 235–258; John Oetzel, Stella Ting-Toomey, Martha Idalia Chew-Sanchez, Richard Harris, Richard Wilcox, and Siegfried Stumpf, "Face and Facework in Conflicts with Parents and Siblings: A Cross-Cultural Comparison of Germans, Japanese, Mexicans, and U.S. Americans," *Journal of Family Communication* 3 (2003), 67–93.

5. Carol Tavris and Elliot Aronson, *Mistakes Were Made (But Not by Me)* (Orlando, FL: Harcourt, Inc., 2007), pp. 221–222.

6. June P. Tangney and Rhonda L. Dearing, *Shame and Guilt* (New York: The Guilford Press, 2002), p. 180.

7. Shuangyue Zhang and Laura Stafford, "Perceived Face Threat of Honest but Hurtful Evaluative Messages in Romantic Relationships," *Western Journal of Communication* 72(1) (2008), 19–39.

8. Amy E. Hubbard, Hae L. Han, Whitney Kim, and Leanne Nakamura, "Analysis of Mobile Phone Interruptions in Dating Relationships: A Face Threatening Act." Paper presented at the International Communication Association, San Francisco, CA, 2007.

9. Adrianne Kunkel, Steven Wilson, James Olufowote, and Scott Robson, "Identity Implications of Influence Goals: Initiating, Intensifying, and Ending Romantic Relationships," *Western Journal of Communication* 67(4) (2003), 382–412.

10. Penelope Brown and Stephen Levinson, *Politeness: Some Universals in Language Usage* (Cambridge: Cambridge University Press, 1987).

11. Originally the research literature referred to this concept as "negative face." Because the term seemed misleading, we chose to refer to the concept in a more descriptive way as "autonomous face."

12. Steven R. Wilson, Carlos G. Aleman, and Geoff B. Leatham, "Identity Implications of Influence Goals: A Revised Analysis of Face-Threatening Acts and Application to Seeking Compliance with Same-Sex Friends," *Human Communication Research* 25 (1998), 65.

13. Patrick B. O'Sullivan, "What You Don't Know Won't Hurt Me: Impression Management Functions of Communication Channels in Relationships," *Human Communication Research* 26 (2000), 403–431.

14. Sarah J. Tracy, "When Questioning Turns to Face Threat: An Interactional Sensitivity in 911 Call Taking," *Western Journal of Communication* 66 (2002), 152.

15. Larry A. Erbert and Kory Floyd, "Affectionate Expressions as Face-Threatening Acts: Receiver Assessments," *Communication Studies* 55 (2004), 254–270.

16. Renee Edwards and Richard Bello, "Interpretations of Messages: The Influence of Equivocation, Face Concerns, and Ego-Involvement," *Human Communication Research* 27 (2001), 598.

17. John Hewitt and Randall Stokes, "Disclaimers," *American Sociological Review* 40 (1975), 1–12.

18. Kenneth W. Thomas and Louis R. Pondy, "Toward an 'Intent' Model of Conflict Management among Principle Parties," *Human Relations* 30 (1997), 1089–1102.

19. Barry R. Schlenker and Bruce W. Darby, "The Use of Apologies in Social Predicaments," *Social Psychology Quarterly* 44 (1981), 271–278 .

20. Jeremy C. Anderson, Wolfgang Linden, and Martine E. Habra, "Influence of Apologies and Trait Hostility on Recovery from Anger," *Journal of Behavioral Medicine* 29 (2006), 348.

21. Ibid, p. 347–358.

22. William L. Benoit and Shirley Drew, "Appropriateness and Effectiveness of Image Repair Strategies," *Communication Reports* 10 (1997), 153–163.

23. Christine B. Smith, Margaret L. McLaughlin, and Kerry K. Osborne, "Conduct Control on Usenet," *Journal of Computer-Mediated Communication* 2 (1997), retrieved on November 19, 2011 from http://jcmc.indiana.edu/vol2/issue4/smith.html.

24. Ana Zornoza, Pilar Ripoll, and Jose M. Peiro, "Conflict Management in Groups that Work in Two Different Communication Contexts: Face-to-Face and Computer-Mediated Communication," *Small Group Research* 33 (2002), 481–508.

25. Miguel A. Dorado, Francisco J. Medina, Lourdes Munduate, Immaculada F. J. Cisneros, and Martin Euwema, "Computer Mediated Negotiation of an Escalated Conflict," *Small Group Research* 33 (2002), 509–524.

26. Elizabeth V. Hobman, Prashant Bordia, Bernd Irmer, and Artemis Chang, "The Expression of Conflict in Computer-Mediated and Face-to-Face Groups," *Small Group Research* 33 (2002), 439–465.

27. Joseph P. Mazer, Richard E. Murphy and Cheri J. Simonds, "I'll See You On 'Facebook': The Effects of Computer-Mediated Teacher Self-Disclosure on Student Motivation, Affective Learning, and Classroom Climate," *Communication Education* 56 (2007), 1–17

28. Stephanie T. Tong, Brandon Van Der Heide, Lindsey Langwell, and Joseph B. Walther, "Too Much of a Good Thing? The Relationship Between Number of Friends and Interpersonal Impressions on Facebook," *Journal of Computer-Mediated Communication* 13 (2008), 542, 531–549.

29. Ibid.

30. Joseph B. Walther, Brandon Van Der Heide, Sang-Yeon Kim, David Westerman, and Stephanie Tom Tong, "The Role of Friends' Appearance and Behavior on Evaluations of Individuals on Facebook: Are We Known by the Company We Keep?" *Human Communication Research* 34 (2008), 28–49.

31. Joseph B. Walther, Brandon Van Der Heide, Lauren M. Hamel, and Hillary C. Shulman, "Self-Generated Versus Other-Generated Statements and Impressions in Computer-Mediated Communication: A Test of Warranting Theory Using Facebook," *Communication Research* 36 (2009), 229–253.

32. Pavica Sheldon, "The Relationship between Unwillingness to Communicate and Students' Facebook Use," *Journal of Media Psychology* 20 (2008), 67.

33. Nichole B. Ellison, Charles Steinfield, and Cliff Lampe, "The Benefits of Facebook 'Friends:' Social Capital and College Students' Use of Online Social Network Sites," *Journal of Computer-Mediated Communication* 12(4), retrieved November 19, 2011 from http://jcmc.indiana.edu/vol12/issue4/ellison.html

Managing Stress and Anger

OBJECTIVES

At the end of this chapter, you should be able to:

- Identify four types of stress.
- Distinguish between hyperstress and distress.
- Identify the sources of hyperstress in your life.
- List some of the likely sources of distress in people's lives.
- Explain how hyperstress and distress affect your communication behavior in a conflict situation.
- List the three solutions for developing a more playful attitude.
- List some specific techniques for dealing constructively with hyperstress and distress.

- Explain the ABC model, differentiate between positive and negative beliefs, and apply the model to a conflict situation.
- Determine whether you are anger-in, anger-out, or anger-controlling.
- Explain how anger can negatively affect a conflict situation.
- Identify the "primary emotion" that is being interpreted as anger.
- List ways to effectively control your anger and express it in constructive ways.

KEY TERMS

ABC model
anger
anger controllers
anger-ins
anger-outs

conflict proneness
distress
eustress
hyperstress
hypostress

playful spirit
secondary emotion
stressor
ventilation approach

As teachers, we have found that this chapter really resonates with students. Stress and anger are so much a part of student life that it is often taken for granted, as though you can do nothing about it but suffer. Moreover, when asked to list the stresses in their lives and situations that make them angry, students (as well as single mothers, newly married couples who have moved and started jobs, couples with children, recently promoted men and women to much higher levels of responsibility, etc.) open up and swamp us with the many pressures they are under and frustrations they experience at home, at work, or at school.

In the first half of this chapter, we define the common types of stress, describe many common sources of stress, and suggest ways to constructively deal with stress. To the extent that you accept our philosophy and welcome the techniques and suggestions offered in this chapter, you should find that stress management goes hand in hand with the next section on anger management. Together they can help you deal with difficult situations and make your life more enjoyable.

STRESS MANAGEMENT

Stress is experienced as a biochemical reaction within the body due to the way in which we interpret and respond to external pressures, which may be positive or negative. Contrary to popular belief, stress does not cause this reaction; it *is* the reaction.

Some interpersonal conflict textbooks highlight the idea that stress is a reaction to conflict. Of course, when we are focused on a problematic situation affecting an interpersonal relationship, dreading a confrontation with someone important to us, and looking at conflict negatively, we are likely to experience stress as a reaction to the conflict situation. Researchers have found that, in particular, competing, avoiding, and accommodating produce stress.[1] In Chapter 2, we introduced the topic of stress by distinguishing personal stress from relationship stress and by taking the position that collaboration produced less stress of both types when compared to the other options in a conflict situation.

While conflict situations can produce stress, we also believe the opposite is true: conflict is itself a reaction to stress. One of your authors has witnessed such an eruption all too often.

> I learned early on in teaching that when a student would see me during my office hours upset over a particular grade on a quiz, test, or paper, I found that if I asked the student questions about what else was going on in the student's life, I would find that she or he had other more serious problems, such as withheld grades, a problem with graduating that semester, problems with parents, a relationship or marital breakup, loss of employment, eviction from an apartment, or death in the family. The combination of grade and a negative life event was upsetting the student. I would then shift to my advisor role, and let the student elaborate on his or her other problems. I would offer suggestions about ways to manage coursework while dealing with these outside pressures. All this seemed to have a comforting effect on the student, who often apologized for how he or she behaved initially.

Because stress leads to interpersonal conflict, the first half of this chapter focuses on how to reduce stress in our lives.

Types of Stress: Eustress, Hypostress, Hyperstress, and Distress

Interestingly, while some stresses upset us, not all stress is bad for us. Selye has identified four kinds of stress.[2]

1. A good kind of stress, **eustress** is a short-term stress that encourages us to take more seriously and expend more energy on important activities.

For example, hitters stepping up to the plate in a baseball game may experience eustress, if they are psyched up to perform.

2. **Hypostress** is underload. This happens when we start feeling anxious because we're bored or unchallenged by our situation. This problem is easily resolved when you switch to "being productive and doing something worthwhile."

3. **Hyperstress** occurs when too many tasks and responsibilities pile up on us and we are unable to adapt to the changes or cope with all that is happening at once. This is the kind of stress frequently experienced by students and teachers.

4. **Distress** arises when we lose control over a situation and the source of stress is unclear to the individual. It is related to anxiety as introduced in Chapter 3, which may cause us to suppress the real issues. There are those who may tell you that everything is OK but they aren't happy and find that they are having trouble getting along with other people. It may take the help of others to determine exactly what the problem is. One person recalls a time of stress in college that seemed to have no apparent reason:

> For a period of several months during my last year in college, whenever I went out on a date, my stomach became so upset that I felt like throwing up. I then had to "call it a night" and go home early. Needless to say that embarrassed me and disappointed and confused the young lady who was with me. I had no idea what was the matter at the time. Meanwhile, over the next several months, I was accepted to graduate school, graduated from college, and started taking graduate classes. My stomach problem "magically" disappeared. Without realizing it, I must have been worried about graduation, acceptance to graduate school, and succeeding in graduate study. These hurdles must have been looming somewhere in the back of my mind and affecting me by upsetting my stomach.

Distress is more encompassing than the other forms of stress. It relates more to our world view, personality (Type A, too controlling, workaholic, etc.), and self-fulfilling prophecy (or expectations). Because distress can make us appear difficult or act in ways that appear unpleasant to others, it can contribute to conflict proneness.

Conflict proneness due to distress occurs when people take themselves too seriously, don't enjoy what they are doing, or fail to see the humor in their everyday affairs. Distress makes people unhappy. Fearing that they are falling behind or not succeeding in achieving their goals, they have lost sight of the fact that they are not playing for fun. Instead, they are concentrating entirely on the end result. Athletes do this when they focus only on winning or outperforming others. Many of these people are not happy, having fun, or enjoying life.

Hyperstress and distress as well as frustration and anger are among the reasons people explode in overblown conflict. Recall from Chapter 3, we defined overblown conflicts as occurring when people get carried away and exaggerate a conflict, generally using a relatively unimportant issue as a focal point. *Overblown conflicts* are often resolved when the person who has done the ranting and raving apologizes, usually making some excuse for the untoward behavior (e.g., "I was stressed out") that the target of the conflict accepts as a reasonable excuse. However, it is preferable to avoid overblown conflicts in the first place. This is

One source of stress is competing demands on our lives,
as NiniLii Paxton has depicted in her conflict art.

done through more effective stress management. We begin with the easiest to perform, the activities approach.

The Activities Approach

Walker and Brokaw suggest a number of different activities that a person can do to manage stress.[3] These entail eating sensibly, getting enough sleep and rest, living a balanced life, engaging in relaxing activities, spending time with good friends, saying "no" to requests you really can't take on, and accepting what you can't change. In addition, avoiding self-medication through the use of nicotine, alcohol, or drugs helps us keep stress at a minimum.

One of the most effective stress reliever activities is regular exercise. It doesn't necessarily have to be strenuous; even a stroll around the block can lower your blood pressure, regulate your breathing, and create a sense of relaxation. Yard work or other physical labor can also be effective. Making a piece of art or even coloring in a children's activity book can relieve stress. You can discuss a stressful event with a trusted friend. This doesn't mean you vent anger but that you seek advice from a more objective person, who can help you move toward resolution of the stressful situation. You can give in during a quarrel about something that isn't particularly important, heading off the stress before it starts.

Other activities that relieve stress involve your environment. Tackling your more difficult tasks first, and then finding a way to reward yourself with a pleasurable activity following it can be helpful. For example, you can tell yourself you'll watch a movie you've wanted to see when you finish a difficult task. If you anticipate a stressful event, you can rehearse it ahead of time to avoid overreacting while in it. You can also clean your living area or reorganize your work space, as this person does:

> One of my most effective ways of dealing with stress is to clean the house or my studio. I actually find it satisfying and relaxing because I can think about the problem that's bothering me and the symbolic aspect of having my place cleaner when I'm done really helps me focus. When I'm really stressed, I move the furniture around in my studio. If nothing else, it helps me look at things in a new way.

Finally, we suggest that you turn your attention to helping others as a means of reducing stress. Throwing a party or dinner for friends, volunteering at a charity, and finding ways to do something for another person can actually reduce your stress. Post and Neimark's remarkable research on the power of giving concludes that people who are generous have a lower risk of illness and lower rates of depression. In addition to having physical and mental benefits, their research suggests that people who are prone to giving to others have more empathy and are typically more competent socially than those who are not.[4] Students seem to welcome the idea of using activities to relieve their stress, and with a little work, they can also benefit from using the **ABC model**.

The ABC Model of Stress

This approach consists of:

A = Activating event or the **stressor**
B = Beliefs or our relevant thoughts
C = Consequences or effects and reaction to the stressor

"A" produces the stress. In hyperstress, we can easily point to the stressors, but in distress, we can't. We may be aware of some approaching calamity, or wrestling with an important decision but not connect it to physical and psychological symptoms of stress we are experiencing. "A" can include:

- anticipated life events (e.g., graduation, aging)
- unexpected life events (e.g., the death of a loved one, the loss of a job, or too much happening at once)
- the need to make tough decisions (e.g., should I go to grad school or marry or get a divorce?)
- struggle among the various roles we play and how much time and attention we should give to each one (e.g., perhaps you're all these roles: a student, a child, a friend, a part-time worker, and a romantic partner)

Of course, it is nice if we can eliminate the source of our stress from our lives. There are two ways to do that: change something in the environment (turn off the computer or don't check your email if it is stressing you at night before you go to bed) or change environments (pick up and leave, go somewhere else, get a new job, break up a stressful relationship). In the news recently, an airline pilot became so stressed over his next flight that he refused to get on the plane. Of course, he needed professional help, but at the same time, the passengers had to appreciate the fact that he decided to avoid a situation that was too stressful for him to handle that day. Unfortunately, each life event we encounter (courtship, weddings, childbirth, taxes, death, applying for jobs, promotions, etc.) produces stress to some extent. So, we can't always eliminate the stressor entirely even if we want to.

We make the observation that the same event "A" produces different reactions in people. Some interpret practically any event as good, others as indifferent, and still others as a disaster. Why is that? Some people are simply "hardier" than others. They see change as a challenge rather than as a threat. Can you become hardy? It is partly a matter of the way you think about stressors, and you can change your way of thinking about events.

Like our discussion of attribution theory, back in Chapter 3, we can change "B," or our beliefs about the stressor, and interpret, perceive, or label the activating event in a more constructive or positive way. When you cannot cope with your circumstances, we suggest that you try changing yourself (or at least the way you think or look at something).

To what extent should one change his or her beliefs to reduce stress? We should not overlook the fact that changing "B" may be much more difficult in some cases than in others. Where one can change her or his thoughts about an event, there is evidence it can reduce stress.[5]

> I expected to put in a lot of hours in teaching, low pay, and occasional encounters with difficult teaching colleagues and administrators. I know I am experiencing stress quite frequently, but I expected that. It comes with the territory. I choose not to let it get me down. I think instead about the advantages of having a job with a roof over my head, heat, electricity, dependable pay, and occasional days off as well as the entire summer. Maybe this comes from my time spent in the military overseas where I was sometimes subjected to unbearable living and working conditions. I have come to appreciate a job like teaching.
>
> I tell my students that if the classroom is too hot and uncomfortable, imagine themselves living or working under worse conditions like the workers outdoors who are right now digging a trench around the building as part of a new campus hot water line project. Our situation looks pretty inviting compared to those workers.

Consider two people's different reactions to the same activating event:

1. I am awful, no one accepts me, I am always rejected by others, I am a worthless person, I deserve this because I am unpopular, I wish someone could do some magic and change me into a better person.
2. I don't like this, I wish it hadn't happened, it was unfortunate, undesirable, we would have had a lot of fun together, I am good company, he or she doesn't know what he or she is missing, I'll go do something I know that I want to do.

Obviously, the first reaction is going to produce more stress in the individual than the second reaction. The key point here is that *if you choose to react as in option 1, you choose to be upset*. This is a self-fulfilling prophecy in that if you expect the worst, you are likely to receive it. Here is a list of thoughts that contribute to stress and the escalation of conflict: irrational thinking, ineffectual thinking, self-damaging thinking habits, self-damning, wishful thinking, intolerance, pessimism, expecting the worst, perfectionist thinking, expecting some magic, being superstitious, being dogmatic, blaming, or damning others for everything. In addition, being too other-directed (or accommodating) is a problem, as one thinks too much about what others think of her or him. If your self-acceptance depends on what others think, you lose control of who you are—which is a stressful event! On the other hand, being too self-directed (or competitive) is also a problem when you think you must win every argument, always come out on top, and have to show up the opposition. If your self-acceptance depends on being Number One, the fear of failure is a constant source of stress.

"C" stands for the consequences or outcomes. We experience stress internally and behaviorally. Biochemically, the **hyperstress cycle** occurs in three stages.[6] First, we experience alarm, where our hearts beat faster, blood gets redirected to skeletal muscles, and so on. Essentially, your body is preparing to fight or run away. Second, we experience resistance. Our temperature, blood pressure, and breathing are still high, and our body releases hormones that affect us both physically and emotionally.[7] Finally, if stress is not relieved, we experience exhaustion. We become more susceptible to illness or even collapse because we have few physical and emotional reserves left. While we suffer physically, behaviorally we may avoid people, attack those closest to us, lock ourselves in a bedroom, drink in excess, or do something productive/constructive, as we suggest later in this chapter.

Self-Talk

So, how can you control your thoughts so as to reduce your stress? The first step is to discover the ways in which your "self-talk" contributes to your stress. Back in Chapter 4, we introduced self-talk and defined it as verbalizing, either out loud or to ourselves, inner messages. Self-talk was offered as a way to talk yourself into avoiding or confronting a conflict and as a means for improving your self confidence. In this chapter, we use self-talk to improve the way we think about other potentially stressful events. Consider how these different ways of thinking about the same event, shown in Table 8.1, can increase or reduce stress.

TABLE 8.1

The Effect of Self-Talk on Stress

Situation	Self-Talk Increasing Stress	Self-Talk Decreasing Stress
Romantic	I'll never find someone like him or her again.	I enjoyed my time with him or her and I know there's someone else out there.
Failing a test	I'm so stupid. I won't pass.	I can take other actions to bring up my class grade. I can study differently next time.
Getting a speeding ticket	Everyone was speeding. Why me?	I was going over the speed limit. I intend to concentrate more on my driving.

We're not suggesting that you ignore the reality of the situation when you engage in supportive self-talk. What we are suggesting, however, is that if you can avoid "doom and gloom" thinking about situations and focus on the power and choices you do have within them, you can reduce your stress level. Ellis claims that it is not the events themselves that cause stress but how we talk to ourselves about the events that causes our stress.[8] Consider how this person handled a stressful situation.

> There's a co-worker who is really unpredictable. I never know if he's going to snarl at me or say hello. It really depressed me, and I'd slink around the hallways hoping I wouldn't run into him. But whose life was being ruined? Mine. So, I decided I'd cheer up and greet him. To heck with him if he wants to be nasty. At least I'll know I acted like a nice person.

Therefore, if your point of view or thoughts and beliefs are not producing positive results, then you should consider adopting a different way of looking at the world.

Helpful self-talk is rational. Three unhelpful kinds of statements are "shoulds," "awfuls," and "overgeneralizations." "Shoulds" have to do with the expectations we have for ourselves, for others close to us, and for the world in general. "Should" statements also contain words like "ought," "must," and "have to." Some of the shoulds are unreasonable, and create expectations that are impossible to meet. Consider how this person responds to "shoulds."

> Three of us meet regularly to gripe and complain to each other as well as encourage each other. All three of us came from rotten families and we have committed to letting go of the negative messages of our childhood. All three of us have lots of "shoulds" in our lives—I should parent better, I should spend more time with my spouse, I should work harder, I should this, I should that. When one of us starts to talk this way, we tell that person to stop "shoulding" on him or herself.

Recognizing when you are "shoulding on yourself" is one way to escape negative self-talk. Another kind of negative self-talk includes "awful" statements. When people talk about how horrible their circumstances are, or the fact that it is simply unbearable, it is pretty easy to start thinking that nothing can change. Continuing self-talk that makes change seem unlikely probably results in situations that do not change.

The final means of negative self-talk, "overgeneralizations," contains words like "always," "never," "everyone," and "no one." Overgeneralizations happen when people think one event is indicative of their entire life. You failed a test, so you're a complete failure. Someone didn't listen to you in this one instance, and that person never listens to you, and so on.

Negative self-talk is a poor means of controlling your thoughts in a situation. It leads to stress, and the need for more self-talk. When you are in a situation where you cannot control other people's responses, you still have control over your own. Recognizing that is a way of reducing the stress that you feel about the situation.

People can learn how to reduce the stress they experience.[9] Avoiding over-generalizations and learning more positive self-talk are constructive actions you can take.

Developing a Playful Spirit

People who take themselves too seriously often suffer a great deal of stress, making it difficult for them to manage conflicts effectively. They need to develop a "playful spirit."

How do we change our attitudes and adopt a playful spirit? Play theorists encourage us to develop a **playful spirit** by changing our attitude toward life in a way that enables us to lighten up. The following techniques may be of help to you:

- Don't blame yourself for everything that goes wrong or doesn't pan out.
- Look for situational factors that you may learn to accept rather than fight against.
- See irony in problematic situations.
- Visualize absurdities. Make a joke to yourself of something negative. An excellent example of this is the line of products promoted by Demotivators. Com. They sell "inspirational posters" that are a spoof of the high gloss photographs one often sees in offices.[10]
- Ask yourself: Am I happy right now? What can I do now to be happier?
- Learn to say "No," without feeling guilty.
- Take on a new role, which is more enjoyable than the present one.
- Do something you can succeed at, especially after failing something else.
- Hang a sign in your room or workplace: Success is happiness!

This list is aimed more at changing the way you look at the world and making lifestyle changes.

Men and women can learn from older people who avoid distress by grasping a playful attitude. Books have been written on the stress encountered by women over 50. The recent upsurge of "Red Hat Clubs," where women celebrate the fact that they're over 50 and deserve to be called "Queen Mother," is an example of how people may adopt this playful attitude.

We can also try to find the humor in stressful situations. Some research suggests that the "tendency to tell jokes and stories...predicted perceiving events and situations in one's life as more predictable and controllable."[11] This is especially important when stress levels are excessive. However, the use of humor in conflict situations is a double-edged sword. On one hand, used appropriately, it can alleviate some of the stress in the situation and help people express some of their negative emotions in a more positive way. Appropriate humor may also help maintain social order, channel hostility, or assist people in saving face. But if the humor is inappropriate, it can also make the conflict situation worse. The ability to use humor in a conflict situation, though, is an indicator of the level of trust in it—those who trust one another can laugh together.[12]

Note that we are not saying that you should act silly in the presence of others. Much of what we suggest may be accomplished covertly, that is mentally. We can see the world differently, talk to ourselves in a constructive matter, and make light of some matters as a mental state. We can feel less guilty and experience less anxiety. Meanwhile, we still continue to be productive, and do what is possible or what it takes to keep a job or earn good grades.

According to Sutton-Smith, a playful spirit contributes to well-being, and is associated with being an emotionally, socially, physically, and mentally healthier person.[13] Approaching our environment as a game to be played as well as taken seriously can convert an unhappy life into a happy one—or at least reduce one's conflict proneness.

Changing How We Look at Life's Challenges

We start our life as children with an obvious demand for joy. Even as adults, there is a child hidden in each of us, and this child would like to come out and play. However, later we learn to take everyday activities too seriously, such that they become obligations, which usually rob us of fun, joy, and merriment. Our preoccupation with achievement whether in winning or outperforming others makes us feel insecure. In his book *If Life Is a Game, How Come I'm not having Fun?*, Paul Brenner says that "Unfortunately, the traditional repression of play, humor, and wit deeply changed our ability to enjoy life and to be content. It has turned us into severe, aggressive, function-oriented rather than people-oriented creatures."[14] Brenner describes three ways to make life more fun.

The First Solution. We can make a distinction between work and play. We can view work as what we do for the sake of something else, while play is what we do for its own sake. So, we can add to our week a few mindless entertainment and fun activities in an effort to balance work. You certainly could give this solution a try. However, it may not work because a few fun events in the evenings or on weekends may not be enough to balance 40, 60, or 80 hours of a demanding job or academic program during the week. It helps, but is it enough? The type of mindless entertainment and fun activities may lose impact if they are passive rather than active. Watching a movie may be somewhat relaxing, but more benefit may be gained from taking a walk or playing a game with someone.

The Second Solution. The second way to lighten up is to take the view that "play is an attitude of mind that may pervade any human activity."[15] Sometimes we turn play and fun activities into work. Professional sports may be an example where some "players" no longer enjoy the "game." It has ceased to be fun for them. The same might be said of some entertainers and actors who have lost the joy of "playing" before others. Let's take an activity that should be fun like a vacation. Often people say they need a vacation to recover from their vacation! Why is that? Part of the reason is that they spend a great deal of time planning it, working overtime to pay for it, worrying that the experience might not live up to their expectations, and obsessing about how many tasks are piling up on their desks when they return to work.

If you can find some joy in your work, it is likely to reduce the stress associated with it. As Bakke points out:

> Many have heard the story of the visitor to a job site where workers were busy in a variety of construction activities. "What are you doing?" the visitor asked one of the workmen... "I'm helping to build a great cathedral," he replied, leaving no doubt about his passion for his work.[16]

Bakke's point is simple but important: the attitude with which we approach our tasks has an important impact on the level of stress we feel about them. So, it isn't our actual experiences, but what we make of them, which gives meaning to our existence. It has been said that life can be easier than we actually make it. It's as though we need to give ourselves permission to have fun. We can change the way we feel about our everyday activities at home, work, or school. We must find joy in the work we do. We should work as if at play, because that is what we are doing anyway—playing at work.[17]

We need to take ourselves less seriously, treat matters more gamefully, and designate all our activities as games that we play. We need to make the decision that if we must do our everyday activities, we might as well enjoy doing them. We need to catch ourselves every time we take ourselves too seriously. When we do that, we come alive—we lighten up.

The Third Solution. The third solution can be termed integration—one understands that joy and pain are often found in the same place, depend on one another, and that both are to be valued. Goldingay remarks:

> So many things we achieve are achieved only through struggle and conflict, not in easy ways....I have so longed to find somewhere in life some corner where joy is unmingled with pain. But I have never found it. Wherever I find joy, my own or other people's, it always seems to be mingled with pain.... The bad news is that there may be no corner of reality where joy is not related to pain. The good news is that there is no corner of reality where pain cannot be transformed into overflowing joy.[18]

There can be no joy if we have never known pain. You probably take your teeth for granted, but then getting rid of a painful tooth makes you appreciate its absence. Having discussed ways to better manage the stress in our lives, we turn now to the topic of anger and how to more effectively manage it.

ANGER MANAGEMENT

Few people feel nothing during a conflict. For most of us, a conflict situation is often associated with a number of emotional responses—excitement, sadness, resentment, and anger among others. Phillips and his colleagues claim that anger is the most important of all negative emotions because it can do so much damage to our social relationships.[19]

People think that behaving aggressively reduces their anger.[20] While some hostile individuals may need the help of therapists, we believe that reading about anger can enable many people to manage it more effectively. Many students take classes to make themselves more successful supervisors, managers, or leaders. When in charge you may feel the pressure to set a standard and bean example for others. Keeping your cool is important because you do not want those who look up to you thinking you are a hothead. In this chapter we do not teach you how to avoid getting angry, but rather how to manage it more effectively.

We begin by defining **anger** as a strong feeling of displeasure, a synonym for antagonism and rage. Generally, anger "can be seen as a means of trying to get something done by forcing a change in the target's behavior, especially when one feels that one has power or control over the target."[21] Anger is different from feeling hurt or irritated. We experience these other emotions when someone or something frustrates our desires, but anger carries with it the desire to get even or seek revenge. Later, when asked what they were fighting about or what started an argument, the conflicting parties may not even remember, which is a sure sign that the conflict itself is unimportant, but uncontrolled anger blew the conflict all out of proportion.

Many of us have experienced anger and the escalation of conflict to a point where we wanted to inflict pain on the other person, whether physically or emotionally by verbal abuse. Lee tells this story:

> Sometimes when teaching conflict management, I like to pair off students, ask them to hold hands, and then role play an interpersonal conflict. Even though the students were told to continue holding hands throughout the conflict, some simply couldn't do it and let go of each other because they felt they had to. Others, who continued to hold hands, leaned away from each other or squeezed the other's hand uncomfortably hard while arguing with each other. In the class discussion that followed, students reported that it seemed incongruous to argue and hold hands at the same time. They often admitted that when they got angry during a disagreement, they wanted to hurt the other person or at least not to welcome any warm and friendly contact.

We have all seen anger expressed in different ways. It can occur instantly like the eruption of a volcano in people who are not generally viewed as hostile or aggressive. Sometimes it festers away for days, months, or even years such as when one plans for revenge.

For some it is attached to people's personality, always lying just beneath the surface it would seem, but quickly manifesting itself in the form of hostility whenever these individuals feel pressured, defensive, or attacked. Research indicates that people may actually have trait-like anger, which "is conceptualized as an enduring disposition to experience anger more frequently, more intensely, and for a longer period of time."[22] People who have high-anger trait process events in a way different from those who do not have high-anger trait. Such people are especially attuned to anger-related words (e.g., "Why did you do that stupid thing?") and respond to them more quickly than they do to words reflecting other emotions (e.g., "You did a great job").[23] On the other hand, people who have low-anger trait tend to spontaneously reframe the circumstances in ways that deflect or inhibit their anger.[24] It may well be that anger lies along a continuum, ranging from a form that may be quickly brought under one's control to a form that requires a great deal of psychotherapy.

People often respond with anger when they feel as though they are being forced to do something.

Although we have a tendency to see anger in a negative light, feelings of anger may be positive if that anger serves to change a situation or relationship that is currently unsatisfactory into something more acceptable. Further, research suggests that if a person knows he or she has to engage in a confrontation, that person is "sometimes motivated to undertake activities likely to increase their anger, despite the fact that such activities are less pleasant than alternative ones....Angry participants performed better than excited participants in a confrontational task."[25] So, like stress, a little anger can motivate, but too much of it is a problem. So, anger can be used constructively when it motivates us to get off our seats and stand up for our interests, needs, and wants or what we think is right.

Experiencing Anger

How do you know anger when you feel it? Which of these do you experience when angry?

- headache, neck ache, shoulders ache
- tightness in the face or chest, unable to breath, rapid breathing
- butterflies in the stomach, rapid heart rate
- hands clenched, gritting teeth, rigidity, twitching
- stare angrily
- sweating, feeling hot, feeling cold/chills
- numbness
- crying

People feel anger in different ways as these narratives suggest.

I had invited my work group over to my house, but I really had hoped a particular person would not come. But he did and within a half-hour of his arrival I had a headache that wouldn't stop. I realized that my neck was really tense and my leg muscles hurt. For me it's the back of my neck that gets extremely hot. I feel hungry and nauseous at the same time. I always tense up my body, make a fist, and take quick breaths.

There are some interesting differences that occur when researchers examine gender and age differences in anger and aggression. First, men and women experience anger that results in aggression in different ways:

> ...the anger experience is different for women because of the power differential between women and men. For men, anger is empowering because they have more power, and being angry ensures the continuation of that power especially if it is accompanied by threats and/or violence. Women's anger, on the other hand, emerges out of feelings of frustration and powerlessness.[26]

Some researchers have found that as people grow older they are less likely to exhibit trait anger. Anger for older adults (over 50) is less frequent and less intense. In addition, older adults are less likely to engage in external anger displays, such as slamming doors or being verbally aggressive.[27]

Anger as a Secondary Emotion

As Rosenberg claims:

> At the core of all anger is a need that is not being fulfilled. Thus anger can be valuable if we use it as an alarm clock to wake us up—to realize that we have a need that isn't being met and that we are thinking in a way that makes it unlikely to be met. To fully express our anger requires full consciousness of our need. In addition, energy is required to get the need met. Anger, however, co-opts our energy by directing it toward punishing people rather than meeting our needs.[28]

An insightful and highly useful way of looking at anger is to view it as a **secondary emotion**, meaning that its origin is in other emotions such as fear. If we are angry at or with someone, we think we are justified in our emotions, and it is easier for us to lay the responsibility at the other person's feet, than if we say, "I fear . . ." or "I am disappointed." Anger protects us; admitting our fears or disappointments may make us feel vulnerable.

For example, a teacher may feel angry because not all members of her class pass an exam. She may not realize it but her fear is that she is not teaching as well as she could or should. So if she gets a lot of questions during a review session prior to the exam, the teacher may suddenly become defensive, turn angry and accuse her students of not studying enough. Her apparent anger is really a response to her fear that the students may fail and make her look bad as a teacher (see managing face in Chapter 7). Once the teacher realizes that, she is much less likely to act angry toward her students.

Regardless of the cause of anger, we usually know who or what made us angry. It is the person (or the person's behavior or lack of behavior) who upset you, the romantic partner who is late, the person who offended a member of your family, or someone who destroyed something of yours. In any of these situations, we may react with aggression, hostility, and revenge. These reactions may permanently harm an interpersonal relationship, such as a romantic partnership. For those who disrupt frequently or carry their resentments over a long period of time, they may suffer physiologically (i.e., cardiovascular problems and heart attacks).

Do you lose control of your anger? Or does it work as an impetus for change and make you more productive? While your ability to control your anger is likely to improve with age, it is possible to make improvements now if you understand the nature of anger and how to manage it.

Three Common Ways People Manage Their Anger

People tend to manage their anger in one of the following three different ways: anger-ins, anger-outs, or anger controllers. Keep in mind that these three avenues have to do with the expression of anger, and may not bear a direct relationship to trait anger.

A common feature of **anger-ins** is that they do **not** express their anger to the person who has upset them. They are avoiders and accommodators or people suffering from the chilling effect cycle who:

1. have a hard time even admitting that they are angry.
2. know they are angry with someone but do not want to tell the other person.
3. tell others about their anger but not the one who upsets them.
4. are passive aggressive.

Contrary to popular conceptions of the way men and women act, males are just as often "anger-ins" as women.[29] It is common knowledge that the suppression of anger can lead to stomach upset and ulcers, depression, and heart disease. In addition, it may be harmful to those experiencing chronic pain, as suppressing anger heightens perception of the pain and magnifies its impact.[30]

We would include as anger-ins people who vent their anger to others, like a friend, parent, colleague, or bartender, rather than the offensive person. This is called the **ventilation approach**. We often think of ventilating as letting off steam, erupting, venting our anger at someone or something, but here we are using the term differently as venting to someone who is not the problem. In some cases, ventilation may be beneficial, such as times where it is not a good idea to confront the offensive person directly—a boss who gets angry, an abusive partner, a defensive, insecure person who cannot take criticism. In addition, venting sometimes elicits helpful advice from the other to help one get a better understanding of the problematic situation, devise constructive ways to handle it, and receive encouragement to confront the problem person. In this case, venting may be useful.

However, there are many other times when venting is problematic. Simply expressing anger, without directing it toward the person responsible or toward problem solving, actually increases it. Talking rehearses the anger and makes us feel it even more deeply. In addition, tantrums and rages increase it.

We would suggest, then, that these anger-in behaviors are ways of how not to respond to conflict. However, doing the direct opposite, like an anger-out, is no better.

Anger-outs are people who are quick to express their anger, vocally or physically, to the person who upsets them. Adam says:

> When growing up, I would lash out at my father and criticize him. I was always afraid that one of us would start punching the other. I often felt bad after the argument and sad that I had hurt my father. But I was upset and angry and just let him have it. We usually ended up with a strong sense of resentment for one another. It is hard to change after fighting this way all these years.

Anger-outs express their energy outward often aggressively rather than hold it in. They tend to engage in:

1. automatic reactions that are quick to criticize, blame, and accuse
2. minor aggressive acts such as bickering
3. verbal abuse
4. physical aggression, force, violence

Does one sex tend to have a greater number of "anger-outs?" Actually, "men and women are equally likely to keep quiet when they feel angry, or talk it out, or scream it out, or even get violent.... It does not depend on gender and it does not depend on personality."[31] As was discussed, previously, men and women experience and interpret anger and aggression in different ways, though there isn't much difference in the way they express it.

However, when expressed anger turns to aggression, men and women differ in the explanation they give for becoming aggressive. For most women, acts of aggression produce anxiety and unpleasant emotions, and "women believe that such [aggressive] acts reflect a loss of self-control."[32] On the other hand, men see aggression as a challenging behavior; it is their way of exerting control over others in order to gain important social rewards such as respect.[33] Campbell and Muncer conclude that gender differences in aggression are largely attributable to "women's greater ability to suppress or divert the expression of aggressive behavior,"[34] most likely because they do find the expression of aggression to be unacceptable on a number of levels.

One should not overlook the social context and the consequences of anger. You don't want your expressed rage to result in another person physically attacking you. Likewise, these anger-out behaviors are ways of how not to respond to conflict:

- When the other person says what is bothering him or her, come back with a "Well, you..." response and attack, accuse, or deny.
- Listen closely so that you can pick apart what the other person is saying.
- Argue over the way something is stated rather than what is being said.
- Call the other person names.
- Remind the other person of every stupid behavior he or she has ever done with respect to the issue at hand.

- Disregard the other person's feelings. Tell the person, "You shouldn't feel that way."
- Tell people that you know their situation better than they do (i.e., "I know exactly how you feel").
- Make threats.
- Fail to cooperate if it isn't your idea (i.e., "If I can't have my way, I won't do anything at all").
- Indicate that nothing can change and you're both doomed to failure anyway.
- Ask the impossible of the other person.

While many people are either anger-outs or anger-ins (that is why we have text-books on conflict and anger management), people can choose to become **anger controllers**, who practice S-TLC (Stop, Think, Listen, Communicate—see Chapter 4).

When a problem arises, let's say noise during quiet hours, we resident hall staff must enforce the rules. Rather than running out of the office yelling and screaming that the residents are being too loud and they need to quiet down, I sit in the office, take a deep breath, think about how I am going to approach them, take another deep breath and remain calm, but stern, and tell them that it is quiet hours and they need to lower their voices. Most of the time if I say it seriously with no smile and raise my eye brows (some nonverbal communication!) they get the idea that I am to be taken seriously.

Anger controllers are assertive individuals who do not let their feelings control how they respond in conflict situations. They still "get it off their chests," but they do it in more constructive ways than do the anger-ins and anger-outs. They put into practice what is recommended in the previous chapters. Anger controllers tend to:

1. think positively about conflict and try techniques to better manage it (Chapter 1)
2. collaborate and work together toward mutually satisfactory solutions (Chapter 2)
3. apply theories to better understand conflict management (Chapter 3)
4. use assertive communication behavior; employ the steps of the interpersonal confrontation ritual (Chapter 4)
5. use the S-TLC system (Chapter 4)
6. compromise (Chapter 2) where a collaborative resolution is not possible and negotiate (Chapter 10)
7. manage the conflict climate (Chapter 6) and stress levels (see the first half of this chapter)
8. manage their anger by expressing it effectively and heeding the dos and don'ts before, during, and after interacting with others as discussed in the second half of this chapter.

Controlling anger is a matter of (1) practicing new habits so that we don't lash out during our flight-or-fight anger episodes and (2) learning to express the underlying emotion when we experience the slow-building kind. How we learn to control anger depends on the more general habits we have about it. Some of these habits occur before we express our anger, and others later.

Before Expressing Anger: Dos and Don'ts

In a way similar to the ABC model of stress management, we should realize that when someone does something that upsets us "A," how we think about a situation "B" determines whether we experience anger or not "C." This sounds a lot like the ABC model we applied to stress. When someone is late, when someone has disappointed you, when someone has said something hurtful, how do you frame or think about the event? (Another use for self-talk.) Your interpretation of the event is probably the best indicator of how angry you feel and how you choose to express it. Do you assume that the other person has hurt you on purpose? Do you look past the person's behavior for external causes that are beyond the other person's control? We are not suggesting that you consistently make excuses for another person. But the kinds of inferences, assumptions, or conclusions you make about another in a conflict situation affect the way you respond to the other. We learned about attribution theory in Chapter 3 that when you believe the other has acted in a way that constrains your behavior, that such action was intended to harm you (internally motivated), and that such action is uncalled for, you respond with anger. Further, making attribution errors, we tend to draw different conclusions about others' behavior than we do about our own—we make excuses for our failures but attribute the failures of others to their shortcomings. So, what assumptions are you making about the other? Is it possible that the other is innocent of intent to harm you, as this person suggests?

> It may make me sound like Pollyanna to say this, but I do find that if I say to myself, "Thanks for not running into me," rather than accusing another driver of "not having the brains God gave an amoeba," my blood pressure generally doesn't rise and my anger is momentary rather than lasting. In addition, if I try to assume that a person cutting me off simply didn't see me rather than assuming he or she is an idiot, I also contain the amount of anger I feel while driving. It takes practice, and quite honestly, it's harder on a day when I'm tired or upset about something.

In general, when you find yourself in a situation where you are becoming angry, there are specific techniques you can undertake before expressing your anger:

1. Take time out: Exit temporarily if you can.
2. Do relaxation exercises: Shut your eyes, tighten muscles (clench your fist, tense your body), and fantasize your anger—imagine it, feel it all over your body, and then suddenly release the tension and picture something serene and relaxing. Monitor your body as you release the different muscles. Breathe slowly and regularly. Concentrate on relaxing your muscles—tense them up and then release them again.
3. Engage in positive and helpful self-talk.
4. Seek alternative ways to release your anger: Physical exertion, like running or other exercise. Would you believe that something like housework, particularly cleaning toilets, is helpful? (And quite symbolic!) So is gardening and pulling weeds, viewing art, and listening to music.
5. Uncover the primary emotion that is disguised as anger

Overall, dealing with anger requires first that we build habits of positive rather than negative and destructive responses to anger-provoking situations.

While Interacting: Dos and Don'ts

We are now interacting and feeling angry, and we know that anger can escalate a conflict and help cause it to get out of hand. If one chooses to do so, how is it best to express one's anger to the offender? Unfortunately, many of us have learned destructive ways to deal with anger from our families and peers.

We believe that the best verbal response to anger is contained in the skills we discussed in Chapter 4. We also offer a list of dos and don'ts. Let's begin with the actions we must avoid doing: "The Don'ts."

- Speaking more loudly or yelling.
- Standing over another person or invading their personal space.
- Making threatening gestures.
- Poking or pushing or shoving another person.
- Swearing and cursing.
- Engaging in threats or using a "thromise" which we said in Chapter 6 is a promise of reward if the other cooperates and a threat of punishment if they do not can heighten anger and escalate conflict.
- Bring in unrelated issues sensitive to the other.
- Mocking the other.
- Working to increase a competitive atmosphere or encouraging rivalry.
- Not listening to the person at whom you are angry, or allowing yourself to be egged on by bystanders
- Expressing anger under the influence of alcohol or drugs. *In vino veritas* aside, we are likely to regret what is said under such circumstances. When people introduce drugs or alcohol into the picture all bets are off. Those times are not good ones to get into an argument/disagreement. Alcohol has a way of bringing out the worst in some people. Someone you know is normally calm and can effectively manage stress and anger, but then becomes a different person when drunk. You cannot expect a reasonable discussion if engaging in a conflict with someone who is drunk or on drugs. Leave them be until they sober up.

The actions we suggest using when expressing your anger are these (the "Do" list):

- Use your S-TLC skills
- Use "I" messages
- Try to avoid raising your voice
- Keep your body language as open as you can by leaning forward and using nonverbal indicators to show you are listening
- Keep your conflict focused on one issue. You're less likely to make yourself angrier if you don't add additional issues to the conflict.

In addition to calming our emotional reaction in a conflict situation, we can choose how we respond to anger expressed by others.

Responding to Another's Anger

One of the more difficult challenges we must face in a conflict is the anger and possible rage an anger-out person is feeling. Often, our fear about the way another may react affects our ability to solve a problem, as this narrative suggests.

Over the years, my husband has become calmer, but he still can lose his temper over unimportant issues pretty easily. When he loses his temper, he scares me. He's a big guy, and seeing all that muscle tense up makes me want to hide. I kept trying to hide a credit card bill from him, because I was afraid to tell him what a mess I had made. I was afraid he might even hit me when he found out. He finally picked up the mail before I did, and I prepared myself for the worst.

When you are dealing with someone who is extremely angry, it is important to do what you can to stay calm and not feed his or her anger. Often, people are loudly angry because they fear no one listens to them unless they yell and scream. Listening and reflecting are important skills in responding to another person's anger.

Equally important is acknowledging the importance of the source of anger. If you say something to the effect of "I can't believe you are reacting this way" or "I think you are being childish," you fuel that person's anger rather than subdue it.

When a person is on the verge of rage, it is not the time to express your anger about the situation. You need to focus on calming that person down before raising any issue of your own. If your attempts to acknowledge the other person's source of anger and the legitimacy of her or his feelings fail, and the person continues to rage and fume, it is often a good idea to exit the situation. Saying something such as "I can see you're really angry, and I think I'd like to give you some time to cool off before we talk about it" acknowledges that you sympathize with the other and have a commitment to work out whatever problem is there, but postpones the conflict until both people are calm and ready to talk about it. As Brian discovered:

I am reminded of my boss, the dean, at work, who had to make some tough decisions, sometimes not to everyone's liking. I can still see one of my colleagues, who stopped our dean on his way out his office. He stood right in front of him and started yelling at him. Interestingly, our dean did not respond in kind. He lowered his voice to almost a whisper, and looked like he was concerned about the issue. My colleague stopped ranting and raving when he realized that we were all staring at him and he was the only one making a scene, which embarrassed him. When he stopped yelling, the dean invited him to go in to his office, where they continued the "discussion" without all of us watching.

We not only need to know how to respond to anger-outs, but we also need to adapt to anger-ins.

As one fellow says:

Being an anger-in type of person I chose to hold my anger inside and vent to my wife or my friends. This would in fact re-enforce my thoughts that were at the root of my feelings of anger and frustration and make me want even more to retaliate and get even.

Anger-ins probably have the hardest time figuring out what the underlying issue is. An effective conflict manager creates a safe space where anger-ins can express their thoughts. They need help to figure out why they're really angry.

MANAGE IT

We began our discussion of stress by identifying it as a contributor to conflict. Stressed people may more easily fly off the handle and perhaps even turn violent. We also identified four types of stress. Eustress is a short-term stress that encourages us to take more seriously and expend more energy on important activities. Hypostress, or underload, occurs when we're bored or unchallenged by our situations. Because the eustress and hypostress are only temporary or do not lead to significant conflicts, we focused on hyperstress and distress, which offer greater challenges to the conflict manager. Hyperstress occurs when too many tasks and responsibilities pile up on us, and we are unable to adapt to the changes or cope with all that is happening at once. One distinguishing feature of hyperstress is that the activator (source) is usually clearly identifiable and clears up quickly if we eliminate the activator. Some specific techniques for dealing with hyperstress are listed in the chapter.

Distress arises when we don't think we have control over the situation and when the source of stress is unclear. Distress is more encompassing than the other forms of stress. It relates more to our world view, personality (Type A, too controlling, workaholic, etc.), and self-fulfilling prophecy (or expectations). Because distress can make us appear difficult or act in ways that appear unpleasant to others, it can contribute to conflict proneness. Both hyperstress and distress set the scene for overblown conflicts.

Conflict proneness due to distress occurs when we take ourselves too seriously, don't enjoy what we are doing, or fail to see the humor in our everyday affairs. Stress makes people unhappy and difficult to work or live with.

Some specific stress reduction techniques are listed in the chapter for dealing with hyperstress and distress along with learning to use the ABC model. A more encompassing way to manage distress is to develop a playful spirit, by learning to make a distinction between work and play, striving for balance between them, turn work into play so that you enjoy what you do, and learn how to appreciate the bad with the good because some suffering makes us better appreciate the good times.

Stress can lead to anger, which is a strong feeling of displeasure, a synonym for antagonism and rage. Anger is different from feeling hurt or irritated. We experience these other emotions when someone or something frustrates our desires. While we recognize that sometimes anger can be used constructively by motivating us to get off our seats and stand up for our interests, needs, and wants or what we think is right, destructive anger carries with it the desire to get even or seek revenge.

People tend to manage their anger in one of the following three different ways: anger-ins, anger-outs, or anger controllers. Anger-ins have in common that they do not express their anger to the person who has upset them. Anger-outs are the direct opposite of anger-ins. They are people who are quick to express their anger, vocally or physically to the person who upsets them. Anger controllers are those who practice S-TLC, the confrontation ritual (including assertiveness and I-statements), and compromise/collaboration. The chapter also includes some useful dos and don'ts for when responding to angry people.

While there may be people who are clearly one type of anger manager, many people are more likely to engage in all three types over a period. In a situation where you fear the reaction of another person or know you have no effect on that person, you may chose to be an anger-in. In another case, you find that the only way to motivate a person is to show some emotion and reveal some anger. Lastly, you may know individuals who listen and cooperate, control their anger following the S-TLC model, and express anger effectively through the use of I-statements. In all cases, the skillful manager is sensitive to the way she or he is feeling, thinking, and behaving in a conflict situation. Knowing which type one currently manifests and how to correctly and effectively manage one's anger in a conflict situation results in more mutually satisfying interpersonal relationships.

Experts differ on the cause of anger as some underlying emotional factor. Some say it is caused by a perceived loss of control. Others say that the primary emotion is the fear that occurs when our personal security is threatened. Still others say it is a cover-up for loss of self-esteem and sadness. In all these cases, anger protects us; admitting our fear or disappointment may make us feel vulnerable. We must find the underlying fear and deal with it.

EXERCISES

THINK ABOUT IT

1. When have you recently (or ever) blown up over something that was not such a big deal really? Can you think of times you got really upset but now can't remember why? Think back on these occasions and try to determine if there were other problems going on in your life. Did they put you on edge so that you felt overwhelmed and exploded?
2. Have you tried any of the techniques listed for reducing hyperstress? Which worked best? Do you know someone who should try some of these techniques?
3. Have you ever experienced distress as defined and explained in this chapter? If not, do you know someone who has? Were you or this other person able (at some point) to identify reasons for this distress? Did you or the other person try any of the techniques listed for reducing distress? Do you know someone who should try some of these techniques? Look at your work and school commitments. How might you apply each of the "three solutions" to improve how you feel about your job and school?
4. Are you a person who tends to blow up, do you express your anger calmly, or do you simply not express it at all? What are the outcomes of expressing anger in this way?
5. Under what conditions have you found yourself expressing your anger appropriately? How was the situation different from a time that you felt your anger was out of control? What do you think you could do to duplicate the situation under which you expressed your anger constructively?
6. What are some ways you use to work off your anger before talking to another person?

APPLY IT

1. Take a piece of paper and draw three columns on it. In the first column, identify the various sources of stress you have in your life. In the second, indicate whether the stress factor is positive (leading to eustress) or negative (leading to distress, hyperstress, or hypostress). In the third column, list the ways you can reduce the negative stress factors.
2. Take a piece of paper and draw three columns on it. In the first, list two or three stressors you are facing right now. In the second, list the kind of negative self-talk you are engaging in about that stressor. In the third, write a different self-talk message that can help reduce your stress level.

3. What makes you really angry? For one day, keep a journal of the way you are reacting to problems around you. You can do this by keeping track of your data in three columns. In the first, list the situation to which you reacted angrily. In the second column, rate how angry you were, with 1 = mildly irritated, 5 = extremely angry. In the third column, write down why you thought you were angry. How might you have reacted differently?

4. Go to a public space, such as a shopping mall. As unobtrusively as possible, observe when people are angry. What do they seem to be angry about? How long does their expression of anger last? How do they seem to resolve their anger? Are there differences in anger expression because of the gender, age, and/or ethnicity of the people you observe?

WORK WITH IT

1. Apply the ABC model to the major stresses in your life by listing the following in a four-column table.
   a. List activating events or stressors (triggering events, people, places, situations) in your life. Indicate which are temporary or short-lived stressors and which are longer term. Identify each as annoying or anger producing and disappointing or depression producing.
   b. List consequences (physiological effects/body reactions, behavioral effects, psychological effects–negative coping and defense mechanisms).
   c. List your internal pressures (irrational beliefs, self-damnations, thoughts, assumptions, wishful thoughts, intolerances). These are to include "should statements," "awfulizing statements," "overgeneralizations," and self-talk (or irrational beliefs).
   d. List the positive coping mechanisms that you would like to use.

2. Read the case study below and answer the questions that follow it.
   With my roommate Elena, I've been unhappy and stressed out over the fact that my roommate may or may not be coming back next year to room with me. We have been the best of friends since our first days in elementary school, and I can't imagine anyone else as my roommate. (Note that the roommate does not seem to realize that this uncertainty is making her edgy and irritable.) Everything she does right now is getting to me. I don't like it when she comes in late and wakes me, doesn't study when I do, and is too busy with her other friends to eat with me. We don't see each other any more and here we are roommates!

   Anyway, yesterday she left the room and took my laptop computer without asking me. I really erupted. I went hunting for her and found her in the library lobby typing notes with a couple of her classmates. I went right up to her and grabbed my laptop. I really told her off and left with it. She and her friends just stared at me.
   a. Which type of stress is the roommate experiencing?
   b. What specific techniques might she use to counter her stress?
   c. How might she develop a more playful spirit?
   d. How might the ABC model be applied in her situation?

3. Read each of the case studies below and answer the following questions.
   a. Which cases below illustrate an anger-in, an anger-in who is venting anger, an anger-out, or anger controller?
   b. In each case, was the anger managed effectively? If not, identify the "primary emotion" that is being interpreted as anger and explain how anger affected the communication behavior.
   c. List suggestions for better managing the anger in those situations that were not handled well.

Cases

1. When in conflict, one of my housemates always avoids everyone when she is upset, so we never know if she is upset at someone, or simply in a bad mood. It is hard to read her and we never know how to react, but yet she always expects us to understand how she is feeling. Those of us who live in the house are incessantly conflicted on what to do because we do not know how to respond to her avoidance.

2. My partner and I don't let our feelings get overwhelming. We express how we feel. We do not keep things bundled up inside and we definitely do not like to explode and let a conflict get out of hand. We take a time out, do relaxation exercises, or engage in self-talk. To take a time out, we can either exit temporarily or count to 100 backwards. My partner always stops and goes for a walk when he gets angry to blow some steam off. Relaxation exercises help to control our physical responses. I like to exercise or go to the gym when I feel overwhelmed or angry. Sometimes I do yoga-like exercises and breathing techniques and it really seems to help. Then, after our time out and we have calmed down, we can talk and listen to each other without losing our cool.

3. My roommate is really messy. She constantly throws her things around the room, leaving her items in the middle of the room. Then, she had the nerve to tell me that I do not clean the apartment enough. Why should I have to clean up her things that she leaves around? In fact, I do not even know where she would want me to put her things away. Instead of me confronting her about my anger, I went behind her back and talked to my best friend about the situation. I was just complaining about my roommate, and one complaint would lead to another, and eventually I was making myself more mad than I was in the beginning of the situation.

4. This weekend, my boyfriend and I got into an argument. I wanted to resolve the conflict right away but my boyfriend got so angry, he walked to his car and sat in it for 10 minutes while I waited outside his house. I had handled the matter badly, by shouting when I didn't get my way, and being impatient and demanding an immediate resolution to the problem, and in this case that wasn't happening as speedily as I wanted it to. I yelled at him and interrupted him a lot, told him he was ruining my night, and stated everything I wanted him to do not asking him what he wanted to do to resolve this conflict.

DISCUSS IT

Read the following conflict narrative and the instructions that follow it.

My wife has been unemployed for several months. She's had a couple of leads on jobs, but they haven't gone anywhere. She doesn't seem to be trying hard enough. In the meantime, I've been working overtime to try to keep us from going into debt. My wife expects me to carry out her "honey-dos" list around the house on the weekends. If we were both working, I wouldn't mind as much, but it hardly seems as though she does anything all day while I am gone, except play on her laptop computer. The house is not clean, and when I ask her what she did all day, she just shrugs and says she doesn't know. I got so frustrated that I grabbed her computer and slammed it down on the table and threw it the length of the house. She ran into the bedroom and locked the door. I don't know what came over me. I walked straight out of the house, got in the car, and drove to The Silver Dollar Bar.

As a way to apply the concepts you learned from this chapter, read the above case study and participate in a class discussion by posting an answer to one of the questions below.

1. Explain one of the following concepts: anger-in, anger-out, or anger-controlling. Which of these would best apply to the case study above and why?

2. Based upon what you have read, what specific technique might the husband use to counter his anger? Explain why you chose this specific technique.

3. Distinguish what principles might pertain to this case study to understand the role of anger better. Explain how they can be applied to the conflict above.

4. If you wish, you can demonstrate your knowledge of the key concepts by telling us about a conflict situation involving anger that you or someone you know experienced.

NOTES

1. W. A. Reich, B. J. Wagner-Westbrook, and K. Kressel, "Actual and Ideal Conflict Styles and Job Distress in a Health Care Organization," *The Journal of Psychology* 141(1) (2007), 5–15.

2. Hans Selye, *Stress without Distress* (New York: J. B. Lippincott, 1974).

3. Velma Walker and Lynn Brokaw, *Becoming Aware,* 6th Edition (Dubuque, IA: Kendall Hunt, 1995).

4. Stephen Post and Jill Neimark, *Why Good Things Happen to Good People* (New York: Broadway Books, 2007), p. 2.

5. Shevaun D. Neupert, David M. Almeida, and Susan T. Charles. "Age Differences in Reactivity to Daily Stressors: The Role of Personal Control," *The Journals of Gerontology: Series B: Psychological Sciences and Social Sciences* 62B(4) (2007), P216–P226.

6. Thomas Berstene, "The Inexorable Link between Conflict and Change," *The Journal for Quality and Participation* 27 (2004), 4–9.

7. These hormones are often tied to the perceived power a person has in the relationship; see Timothy J. Loving, Kathi L. Hefner, Janice K. Kiecolt-Glaser, Ronald Glaser, and William B. Malarkey, "Stress Hormone Changes and Marital Conflict: Spouses' Relative Power Makes a Difference," *Journal of Marriage and the Family* 66 (2004), 595–612.

8. Albert Ellis, "Overview of the Clinical Theory of Rational-Emotive Therapy," in Russell Grieger and John Boyd (Eds.), *Rational-Emotive Therapy: A Skills-Based Approach* (New York: Van Nostrand Reinhold, 1980), pp. 1–31.

9. Anthony D. Lamontagne, Tessa Keegel, Amber M. Louie, Aleck Ostry, and Paul A. Landbergis "A Systematic Review of the Job-stress Intervention Evaluation Literature, 1990–2005," *International Journal of Occupational and Environmental Health* 13(3) (2007), 268–341; Hieu M. Ngo and Thao N. Le. "Stressful Life Events, Culture, and Violence," *Journal of Immigrant Health* 9 (2007), 75–84.

10. www.demotivators.com

11. Nathan Miczo, "Humor Ability, Unwillingness to Communicate, Loneliness, and Perceived Stress: Testing a Security Theory," *Communication Studies* 55 (2004), 222.

12. Wanda J. Smith, K. Vernard Harrington, and Christopher P. Neck, "Resolving Conflict with Humor in a Diversity Context," *Journal of Managerial Psychology* 15 (2000), 606–625.

13. Anthony D. Pellegrini (Ed.), *The Future of Play Theory: A Multidisciplinary Inquiry into the Contributions of Brian Sutton-Smith* (Albany, NY: SUNY, 1995).

14. Paul Brenner, *If Life Is a Game, How Come I'm Not Having Fun?* (Albany, NY: SUNY Press, 2001), p. 90.

15. Ibid., p. 73.

16. Dennis W. Bakke, *Joy at Work* (Seattle, WA: PVG, 2005), pp. 240–241.

17. David L. Miller, *Gods and Games: Toward a Theology of Play* (New York: Harper Colophon Books, 1973).

18. John Goldingay, *Walk On: Life, Loss, Trust, and Other Realities* (Grand Rapids, MI: Baker, 2002), p. 100.
19. L.H. Phillips, J.D. Henry, J.A. Hosie, and A.B. Milne, "Age, Anger Regulation and Well Being," *Aging and Mental Health* 10 (2006), 250, 250–256.
20. Hermina Van Coillie and Iven Van Mechelen, "Expected Consequences of Anger-Related Behaviours," *European Journal of Personality* 20 (2006), 138.
21. Agneta H. Fischer and Ira J. Roseman, "Beat Them or Ban Them: The Characteristics and Social Functions of Anger and Contempt," *Journal of Personality and Social Psychology* 93 (2007), 104, 103–115.
22. Dominic J. Parrott, Amos Zeichner, and Mark Evces, "Effect of Trait Anger on Cognitive Processing of Emotional Stimuli," *The Journal of General Psychology* 132 (2005), 69, 67–80.
23. Ibid., p. 75
24. Benjamin M. Wilkowski and Michael D. Robinson, "Guarding Against Hostile Thoughts: Trait Anger and the Recruitment of Cognitive Control," *Emotion* 8 (2008), 582, 578–583.
25. Maya Tamir, Christopher Mitchell, and James J. Gross, "Hedonic and Instrumental Motives in Anger Regulation," *Psychological Science* 19 (2008), 328, 324–328.
26. Virginia Eatough, Jonathan A. Smith, and Rachel Shaw, "Women, Anger and Aggression: An Interpretive Phenomenological Analysis," *Journal of Interpersonal Violence* 23 (2008), 1771, 1767–1799.
27. Phillips, Henry, Hosie, and Milne, *Aging and Mental Health*, 254.
28. Marshall B. Rosenberg, *Nonviolent Communication: A Language of Life* (Encinitas, CA: PuddleDancer Press, 2005), p. 144.
29. Carol Tavris, *Anger: The Misunderstood Emotion* (New York: Touchstone, through Simon and Schuster, 1989), p. 203.
30. Phillip J. Quartana and John W. Burns, "Painful Consequences of Anger Suppression," *Emotion* 7 (2007), 400–414.
31. Tavris, *Anger*, p. 203.
32. Anne Campbell and Steven Muncer, "Intent to Harm or Injure? Gender and the Expression of Anger," *Aggressive Behavior* 34 (2008), 285.
33. Eatough, Smith, and Shaw, *Journal of Interpersonal Violence,* 1770.
34. Anne Campbell and Steven Muncer, "Intent to Harm or Injure? Gender and the Expression of Anger," *Aggressive Behavior* 34 (2008), 282.

Managing Conflict through Forgiveness

OBJECTIVES

At the end of this chapter, you should be able to:

- Distinguish relational transgressions from other types of problematic situations.
- Explain the advantages of forgiveness and reconciliation following relational transgressions.
- Distinguish forgiveness from forgetting and reconciliation.
- Explain which relational transgressions are hardest to forgive.
- Describe the steps one must take to forgive.

KEY TERMS

core relational rules
emotional residues
forgiveness
helping orientation

reconciliation
relational transgressions
revenge
self-fulfilling prophecies

transforming the meaning
truth bias
unforgiveness
victimization

Have you experienced something so upsetting that you have not forgiven the person? In previous classes, students have anonymously revealed the following instances:

- A friend needed me to co-sign for a car because she had credit issues. She failed to make her payments and caused me to have a low credit rating as a result. I will never forgive her.
- My mother said nasty things to me, like "I'm the mistake that she regrets in her life." I can't forgive her for that.
- After his graduation from high school, my son had serious financial problems that caused him to be indebted to me for thousands of dollars, which he will never pay back. I can't let him get away with that. We haven't spoken for years.
- My uncle shot and killed my father when I was a kid. He served a few years in prison for that. I can never forgive my uncle.

- Laying me off put us in a severe financial bind. I have hated my boss ever since.
- My boss was really harsh to me during the time my father was sick in the hospital and later passed away, telling me I was blowing the situation out of proportion and that he wasn't really that sick.
- My sister kicked our mother out of her house, so she came to live with us, but mother was quite ill. Then, my sister spread the word that she got ill on liquid cleaners we keep around our house, as though we caused her illness. I don't speak to her anymore.
- My ex and I had a lot of problems. For one thing, he was verbally abusive. He would always put me down and call me names. Finally, he punched me in the face. I could never forgive him for what he put me through.
- My ex had affair after affair with various men. She hurt me deeply.

In Chapter 7, we introduced the idea of an offending situation that exists when people have acted in ways that threaten the face of another person or that seem intentionally hurtful. Accounts, concessions, and apologies are ways of rectifying problematic situations. But when "offending situations" take on crisis proportions and become more intense than a simple face-management problem as in the above examples, we call them relational transgressions.

Some hurtful actions may not need forgiving, such as annoyances, slights, or disappointments. Smedes notes, "It is wise not to turn all hurts into crises of forgiving . . . . We put everyone we love on guard when we turn personal misdemeanors into major felonies."[1] However, when others do commit relational transgressions against us, we shouldn't down play them either. How do we manage conflicts that involve relational transgressions? In this chapter, we discuss conflict situations that involve central relational issues, the nature of forgiveness, its effects, the means people use to forgive one another, and the ways in which we may reconcile our differences. You are expected to learn how to distinguish forgiveness from forgetting, distinguish forgiveness from reconciliation, explain the advantages of forgiveness and reconciliation following relational transgressions, and identify the steps you can take to forgive others and, if you choose to do so, to reconcile with them.

THE NEED FOR FORGIVENESS AND RECONCILIATION
Relational Transgressions Defined

Relational transgressions are extremely problematic situations in which core rules of a relationship are violated, leaving high emotional residues. We'll explain each of these elements—rules and residues—in turn.

Core relational rules define our expectations about the way we should behave toward others as well as the way they should behave toward us. We treat strangers one way, friends another way, and our romantic partners still another. We relate to our parents differently from our more distant relatives. Part of the socialization process has taught us the rules that govern each type of social relationship such as romantic pairings, friendship, and being roommates. Relational transgressions occur when those rules we take for granted as "sacred" are broken by someone important to us.

Relationship rules exist when people are interdependent. Some of these rules cannot be violated without calling the relationship into question, so we call them core rules. Among friends, for example, a core relational rule becomes an issue when a person who claims to be your friend fails to help in your time of need. "Imagine that a person runs out of gas outside of town and calls someone she considers a good friend to come and give her a ride. Suppose the other responds with 'Why call me? Why don't you call a taxi?' If one fails to help in time of need, the friendship is in trouble."[2]

Another relationship rule is that you should not lie to your best friends. In American culture, committed romantic partners and spouses are supposed to also be among one's "best friends." Lying to an acquaintance about why you do not want to go to the beach is different from lying to your best friend, because best friends are supposed to trust each other. This is particularly true because as we develop friendship with others, we also develop a **truth bias** toward them: We assume that they tell us the truth. This truth bias makes us more vulnerable and less accurate in detecting deception when it occurs.

A lie is generally classified as deliberately altering information to change a person's perceptions about an issue. Certainly, "social lies," used to avoid sticky situations (e.g., "I really can't go with you to the beach because I have to study"), are part of our social fabric, whether or not we approve of them. They become a relational transgression, however, when another learns that a partner lied in a way that breaks core relational rules.

In addition to the cognitive effects, research indicates that the more involved people are with another person, the more intense their negative emotions when they discover that the person has lied to them. In addition, the more important the information lied about, the more intense negative emotions are on discovering the deception and the more likely it is that the future of the relationship is in jeopardy because being caught lying to one's best friend is a relational transgression.

Rules govern our romantic relationships as well. In a committed romantic relationship, a core relational rule is that you should not cheat on your partner. Metts asked respondents to rate relational transgressions in order of their difficulty in resolution and found that sexual infidelity was identified as the most difficult to deal with.[3] But sexual infidelity in romantic relationships is not the only relational transgression.

Clearly, interpersonal violence in a romantic or parent–child relationship constitutes a relational transgression, a violation of a core relationship rule. One expects his or her partner to love and protect. This occurs because as we develop romantic relationships with others, we tend to take a **helping orientation** toward them: We assume that they love us and desire to help rather than hurt us, as we do them. Verbal abuse and physical violence run contrary to a helping orientation. The same is true in parent–child relationships. Therefore, interpersonal violence, when it occurs, is a violation of another core relationship rule that motivates breakups and leaving home.[4]

In addition to violating core relationship rules, relational transgressions produce highly **emotional residues**; that is, people experience lingering emotional responses to the memory of the transgression. If a good friend or romantic partner has lied to you, you may experience shock, disbelief, hurt, anger, and/or betrayal.

You may wonder whether you can trust what that person says in the future. It may even cause you to check up on the person continuously, who is likely to add problems rather than solve them. People in long-term relationships face a need to forgive and perhaps reconcile the transgression in some way.

The need to study forgiveness and reconciliation is based on the assumption that conflicts are cyclical and repetitive (see schismogenesis, URP, and competitive and escalation cycle in Chapter 2), affected by what has come previously and affecting what comes after. Our ability to break out of dysfunctional conflict cycles and respond appropriately to conflicts in the present is in no small way dependent on our ability to forgive those close to us.

While once the province of religious discourse, forgiveness is an established part of the communication and psychology research literature. How then are we to understand this gift and bestow it appropriately?

Defining Forgiveness and Reconciliation

Forgiveness and reconciliation are related but separate processes with the former generally preceding the latter. **Forgiveness** is a cognitive process that consists of letting go of feelings of revenge and desires to retaliate. In his seminal work on forgiveness, Smedes lists the key stages that the process goes through, namely:

1. Hurt
2. Hate
3. Healing
4. Coming together[5] (We now know that "coming together" need not be taken in a physical sense but rather in a psychological, mental, and emotional sense, where you might cognitively forgive another without behaviorally reconciling.)

Overall, forgiveness occurs when a person lets go of his or her feelings of revenge and need for retaliation, and changes his or her thoughts about the transgression and the transgressor. It starts with anger over a transgression and moves toward **transforming the meaning** of the event, or changing the way we view the event in light of other events in our lives. Forgiveness is something that happens over time as "negative unforgiving emotions [are replaced] with positive other-oriented emotions . . . [and] negative emotions are repeatedly whittled away."[6] Forgiveness is "reframing of how one views the world . . . . [It is] in reality a case of acting in one's own enlightened self-interest."[7]

Writers in the field of forgiveness focus largely on the "victim's development of empathy toward the perpetrator as a necessary step in forgiveness;"[8] lasting forgiveness results from the ability to see the perpetrator as a human being rather than as a stereotyped victimizer. It is a necessary step in growing as a person; the choice not to forgive is essentially an unhealthy one. However, healthy a choice it may be, forgiveness cannot be rushed. "Premature forgiveness that takes place before self-affirmation and empowering are under way is deleterious. Frequently, it does not even seem to be forgiveness at all, but is instead a cover for passivity and anxiety."[9]

We can distinguish forgiveness from both unforgiveness and revenge. **Unforgiveness** is a cognitive process in which one doesn't let go of feelings of revenge and maintains a desire to retaliate. **Revenge** is a behavior based on the notion of "an eye for an eye." One wants to follow evil with more evil. Revenge characterizes the cycle of violence in which each aggressive act is followed by more aggressive behavior. The best way to stop the cycle is to switch to forgiveness and perhaps initiate reconciliation. **Reconciliation** is a behavioral process in which we take actions to restore a relationship or create a new one following forgiveness. It is a process distinct from forgiveness. As Freedman et al. argue, "Forgiveness . . . is one person's response toward another in a hurtful situation; reconciliation is the process of two people, together, negotiating and working out differences."[10] The evidence indicates that forgiveness is an important mental process that should follow traumatic conflict. Reconciliation, on the other hand, involves a series of actions we may choose to avoid, particularly if the offender is likely to violate us again.

Forgiveness does not obligate us to reconciliation. It is not simply forgetting that something happened. It does not release the other person from the consequences of his or her behavior. It does not deny anger. It does not put us in a position of superiority. It is not a declaration of the end of all conflict or of ever risking again with the other person (or anybody else). When forgiveness takes any of these forms, it feels demeaning, as though the other is simply waiting for a time to even up the score.

The widespread assumption by many people that forgiveness and reconciliation are virtually simultaneous is disturbing to us, because that assumption often moves people toward reconciliation before such action is actually warranted. One writer calls this reconciliation without true forgiveness as "compulsive, unconditional, unilateral attempt at peacemaking for which you ask nothing in return . . . when you forgive cheaply, you seek to preserve the relationship at any cost, including your own integrity and safety."[11] Reconciliation without true forgiveness is often driven by fear of the offender's anger, fear of the offender leaving, or fear of harming the offender. It is based on an unhealthy need to preserve a relationship that may not survive the cost of avoiding the conflict. In our experience, this usually only prolongs the painful period leading up to the eventual break up of the relationship. The desire for reconciliation must be tempered by recognition of the possible dangers involved within it. We do not forgive to become martyrs to the relationship. We forgive because it is better for us and better for the other person. We forgive because we want to act freely again, not react out of past pain.

ADVANTAGES OF FORGIVENESS
Forgiveness Benefits Our Mental Health

Most writers in the area of forgiveness have argued that holding onto grief and hurt is psychologically unhealthy. By placing blame on other people, we relinquish our control over our emotions and give that control to another.

Holding grudges constitutes an egocentric position wherein we view those who have hurt us only in terms of what we need, what we wish, or what we long for.[12] Those who not only do not forgive but additionally seek revenge do so ". . . based on the belief that . . . it is possible to measure the magnitude of an offense, to receive an equal amount of retribution somehow balances the account."[13]

Forgiveness is linked to both mental and physical benefits. For example, research examining social adjustment and the ability to forgive found a high correlation between the two: As a person's social adjustment score went up, so did the person's ability to forgive.[14] More recent research on the role of forgiveness in counseling and mental health has demonstrated that teaching people about forgiveness and training them in "forgiveness strategies" helped increase recovery from divorce (restoring positive feelings about oneself, etc.), decreased feelings of guilt, and decreased feelings of depression and anxiety.[15] Among other benefits, forgiveness intervention has been effective in reducing depression and anxiety,[16] raising self-esteem,[17] improving perceptions of self-efficacy,[18] and increasing self-esteem and feelings of hope while lowering depression and anxiety for incest survivors.[19]

Some people who forgive others cannot forgive themselves and vice versa. Researchers have found that the process of forgiving oneself is different than that of forgiving others, and being able and/or willing to do one does not mean a person is willing or able to do the other.[20] People who are unable to forgive themselves have higher levels of loneliness, although which causes what is not yet understood. It may be that people who are lonely overestimate the severity of their offenses and so do not forgive themselves. Or, it may be that people who do not forgive themselves for offenses cut themselves off from social contact. Whatever the direction of the relationship, learning forgiveness toward both others and self is an important skill.

Forgiveness Benefits Our Physical Health

Not only is forgiveness related to our psychological health, it is related to our physical health as well.[21] College students who report an ability to forgive others perceive their health to be better than those who do not.[22] Additionally, people who have high levels of trait-like unforgiveness tend to experience higher levels of pain than those who have lower levels.[23] In general, those who are able to forgive sleep better than those who don't.[24] And senior citizens who manifested greater abilities to forgive others reported better physical health than those who reported less ability to forgive others.[25]

Trait-like forgiveness or unforgiveness has some widely demonstrated links to cardiovascular health. People with higher trait-like forgiveness experience lower blood pressure and better recovery from incidents that raise blood pressure than those with low trait-like forgiveness.[26]

Harms resulting from the inability to forgive often involve anger and stress. We experience physical damage when this flight-or-fight mechanism, which was designed for short-term emergency responses to situations, becomes a long-term ongoing response. The desire for revenge may play a role in physical damage to our bodies making us more susceptible to physical illness.

So Why Don't People Forgive?

Given the number of mental and physical benefits to forgiveness, one would think that people would see the good in embracing it. We know this is not always the case. But why? There are several explanations for a lack of forgiveness in a relationship.

The most frequent reason people don't forgive is that the other has not admitted wrongdoing, apologized, or asked for forgiveness. In addition, people report refusal to forgive when the other continues in offensive behavior.[27]

Research has also demonstrated a link between a person's perception of an apology and whether or not it is accepted. When a person is offended, being offered an apology that is too elaborate for the offense or too simple may result in a lack of forgiveness.[28] Further, since people often refuse to forgive when the other has not offered an apology or explanation, they also might believe that by withholding forgiveness, they can prevent the transgressor from hurting them again.[29]

There are others who don't forgive because they prefer the role of victim. In a related manner, a few do not want to give up their right to hold a grudge; it gives them a sense of power to hold their hurt over the other person. Sometimes, being hurt has created a loss of face for the person who was offended, and forgiving the transgressor would cause an even greater loss of face. And fear of vulnerability and giving off what might be perceived as "signs of weakness" are often a barrier to forgiveness.

People who lack empathy find it harder to forgive others.[30] In addition, empathy has a stronger relationship for forgiveness in men than in women; while women are more empathic in general, it does not affect their levels of forgiveness. However, men with higher levels of empathy are more forgiving than those with lower levels.[31] Those who are able to see themselves as potential offenders are also more likely to forgive than those who cannot imagine themselves as offenders; again, this effect is more pronounced for men than women.[32]

Age is also a factor. One study found that college-aged students, who were hurt in previous dating relationships, found it more difficult to forgive than any other age group who had similar experiences.[33]

Perhaps most importantly, some people don't forgive because they don't know how and no one offers support for doing so; in fact, some people think a forgiving person is stupid or naive.[34] People may learn to forgive while in short-term therapeutic intervention but will revert back to a place of unforgiveness over time when there is no continued support for their forgiveness processes.[35]

WORKING THROUGH FORGIVENESS AND RECONCILIATION

Learning to Forgive

Recall that we differentiated reconciliation from forgiveness. Whereas forgiveness is a cognitive process that consists of letting go of feelings of revenge and desires to retaliate, reconciliation is a behavior process in which we take actions to restore a relationship or create a new one. Because they are different processes, forgiving the other cognitively does not necessarily lead to reconciliation behavior. Many people forgive, but at a distance. They let go of their need for revenge but do not choose to put themselves in a position where the other can hurt them again.

> ## TABLE 9.1
>
> **Learning to Forgive**
>
> - Understand that forgiveness is a process.
> - Start by acknowledging how the other hurts you.
> - Allow yourself to experience anger.
> - Don't adhere to the "victim" stage.
> - Find people to support your forgiveness process.
> - Recognize that the other person may not treat you any differently than in the past. Focus, then, on your responsibility in the situation and your responses to it.
> - Try to see the other person as someone like yourself—human, having flaws, and making mistakes. This helps you escape from the villain or victim mentality.
> - Try to see yourself as a person like the other—capable of hurting people, capable of doing something wrong (not necessarily that you are capable of the same offense). This helps you escape from a position of superiority with respect to the other.
> - Think about what you have learned from the situation, and how you have grown as a result of it. Events usually have a positive and negative side to them. So you may often switch from a negative view to a positive view of the same event.

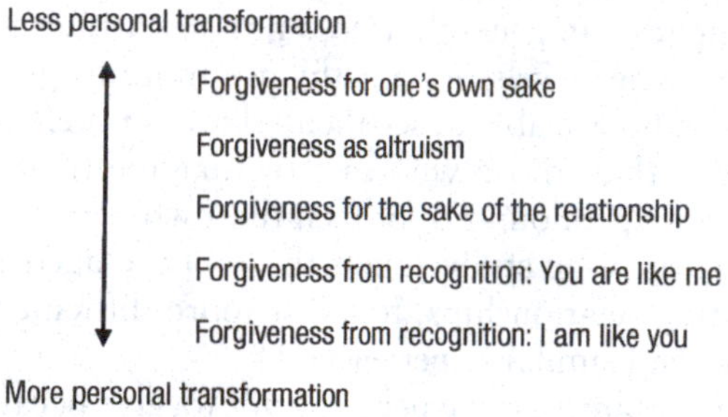

Less personal transformation

↑ Forgiveness for one's own sake

Forgiveness as altruism

Forgiveness for the sake of the relationship

Forgiveness from recognition: You are like me

↓ Forgiveness from recognition: I am like you

More personal transformation

FIGURE 9.1
Levels of Forgiveness.

Can people be taught to forgive? The answer is yes. While "unforgiveness tends to fade Naturally . . . specific training tends to speed and deepen the process."[36] The steps people need to learn in order to facilitate forgiveness are listed in Table 9.1. Further, the type of training in forgiveness that people receive affects their levels of forgiveness in the future.

Levels of Forgiveness

In addition to the practical steps listed in Table 9.1, we may also view different levels of forgiveness. Figure 9.1 illustrates the various levels a person may go through in seeking to forgive another. Each successive level, we would argue, results in greater personal transformation for the person who forgives. At higher levels, a person feels greater levels of empathy and greater awareness of his or her own limitations. At any of these levels, a person may simply forgive and not move into reconciliation, but reconciliation without forgiveness creates a dangerous emotional position for the one who has been hurt.

At the first level, a person may forgive because it is healthy to do so; forgiving makes us feel better. This is the most common understanding of forgiveness in one study of college students and community laypersons.[37] Forgiveness at this level is accomplished because the victim realizes that not forgiving hurts the victim rather than the offender. In some cases, such forgiving does enable reconciliation.

At the second level of forgiveness, a person might forgive because of empathy for the other, understanding that the other needs the person's forgiveness. Worthington observes that "this is a difficult sell . . . . Yet most people . . . come to see that anger, resentment, hostility, rate, and hatred destroy . . . . lasting satisfaction comes more often with creating."[38] While this type of forgiveness may not necessarily lead into processes of reconciliation, it does make reconciliation more probable.

The third level of forgiveness moves a person from forgiving for the sake of the other to forgiving for the sake of the relationship. Moskal describes this type of forgiveness as something that "lies at the place where three roads meet: the ethics of obligation, in the matter of forgiving what was done; the ethics of virtue, in the matter of the motive of love and the virtue of creativity; and the ethics of [authenticity], in implying a deep and abiding concern for the other who has disclosed."[39] This kind of forgiveness is generally precipitated by expressions of remorse and regret by the offender as well as promises of change in the future and lays a basis for possible reconciliation.

The fourth and fifth levels of forgiveness are unlikely to occur except in the instance of a relationship that is in the process of reconciliation and recreation. These two levels of forgiveness require high levels of empathy on the part of the forgiver and generally can occur only in close contact with the offender.

In the fourth level, the person begins to see the offender as "like me." Feelings of estrangement and separation, as well as feelings that the offender is unlike the other begin to diminish. Empathy increases. This results in a lessening of the victim–villain characterization of those in the relationship.

When forgiveness deepens, the victim is not only able to see the offender as "like me," but the victim is able to say, "I am like the offender." This is a difficult cognitive move. It requires that the victim sees himself or herself as a person capable of harming others. As the research discussed above showed, however, it is associated with higher levels of forgiveness. It does not require that the victim believes that he or she is capable of the same offense, but in this stage the victim is capable of seeing how he or she has inflicted pain on others and has received forgiveness for those offenses.

Levels of Reconciliation

As a person works through levels of forgiveness, he or she also considers how to move through the levels of reconciliation (see Figure 9.2). The first level involves no reconciliation at all, even if the other has been forgiven. This is not an uncommon outcome. Indeed, most of those reporting that they had forgiven others in Lulofs' study indicated that they had no desire to continue the relationship with the other person. They had forgiven for reasons of self-benefit or altruism but had

Less relational transformation

No reconciliation, even if forgiveness has taken place

Possible reconciliation, when offender admits culpability

Conditional reconciliation, when offender communicates regret for the offense and offers an apology

Processual reconciliation, offender attempts to remedy the harm done

Restoration, when trust is rebuilt and the relationship is recreated

More relational transformation

FIGURE 9.2

Levels of Reconciliation.

not expressed a desire to restore the relationship, even though in some cases the offender had attempted to remedy the situation in some way.[40]

If a person does decide to reconcile (possible reconciliation), it is usually because the transgressor admits guilt for the relational transgression, perhaps accompanying the admission with an explanation. Reconciliation may possibly move from conditional to processual. "Conditional reconciliation" may occur when the transgressor communicates some level of regret for the offense and offers an apology. "Processual reconciliation takes place as the offender attempts to remedy the harm done." Finally, restoration is achieved as trust is rebuilt and the relationship is recreated. If reconciliation is desired, the offended person may communicate her or his forgiveness to the transgressor. Sometimes, people do not state their forgiveness but simply behave in ways that communicate it. In doing so, the prior relationship is reestablished or converted into a different one. Trust rebuilds. And as trust rebuilds and the offender continues to act in trustworthy ways, the actions of each confirm that forgiveness and reconciliation have occurred; behavior constitutes the reality. The relationship between forgiveness and reconciliation is shown in Table 9.2. Where there is no forgiveness, reconciliation is, at best, a managed truce between people who try not to talk about the event. Where forgiveness is granted, reconciliation may not occur, but if it is, reconciliation can move through the levels discussed here.

For Those Who Seek Forgiveness

An unfortunate side effect of the recent surge of research on forgiveness is its tendency to focus on the person doing the forgiving instead of the person seeking forgiveness. Part of the reason for this is that we tend to overestimate how badly we have been hurt by others and underestimate how much we may have contributed to the relational transgression.

Ashby has suggested that seeking forgiveness mirrors some of the stages of forgiving. In the first stage, the person who has committed the offense against another experiences feelings of shame and guilt for the offense. Having experienced these feelings, in the second stage, the offender makes a decision to seek forgiveness. While we have a tendency to be judgmental about those who have hurt

TABLE 9.2

Interrelationship of Forgiveness and Reconciliation

Forgiveness Not Granted		Forgiveness Granted	
No Reconciliation	Pseudo-Reconciliation	No Reconciliation	Genuine Reconciliation
• Event may be repressed or alternatively used to establish victim status • Bitterness • Lack of trust with similar others	• People interact but maintain distance • Event generally not discussed: if discussed, may be used as means of maintaining power • Blaming cycles • Often sets stage for further conflict	• Victim forgives for own sake • Event is reframed over time • Distance kept from offender, or interaction only under limited circumstances	• Victim forgives for own sake as well as for the sake of the relationship • Victim forgives because the offender is in need of forgiveness • Over time, victim sees other like self • Over time, victim sees self like other • Relationship is recreated

us, the decision to seek forgiveness in a genuine way is a humbling experience to the offender and makes that person feel vulnerable. In the third stage, the offender expresses remorse and repentance. This includes confessing, taking responsibility for one's untoward behavior, apologizing, taking on the pain of the other, making amends, and changing one's behavior. It is important that the offender understands and acknowledges the extent of the impact that the offense had on the other. Sometimes it is impossible for the offender to adequately make up for the injury he or she has caused to the other, but the effort undertaken may be viewed as a move in the proper direction.

The final stage of seeking forgiveness is waiting, which in some cases may be the most difficult part. Just because a person has sought forgiveness in a sincere way, hoping to make amends, does not mean the other has to accept the apology and render forgiveness. When this is the case, the best people can do is remind themselves that they have done the right thing and then let it go.

STEPS TOWARD FORGIVENESS AND POSSIBLE RECONCILIATION

In this section, we describe a series of steps for effectively managing a conflict situation in which an offender and the offended party attempt to work through the issues necessary for forgiveness and reconciliation, if desired by both parties.

Step One: The Account and the Apology

The transgressor may explain her or his offensive behavior and offer an account and an apology. When people report to communication researchers that they have not forgiven the person who offended them, the primary reason for not forgiving is that they have not received an explanation and an apology from the other. Because the other has admitted no wrongdoing, they usually are not willing to forgive. In addition, people report refusal to forgive when the other continues the offensive behavior. Clearly, the process should begin with the transgressor understanding, recognizing, and admitting the offensive nature of his or her behavior; offering an account; following the explanation with an apology; and asking for forgiveness. We say that this step is optional because not all offenders explain and apologize; where it is to one's advantage, the offended person may choose to forgive without the transgressor taking the first step.

As indicated above, except in cases of sexual infidelity and emotional attachment or intimacy (to someone else), research shows that people tend to let the transgressor off the hook by accepting accounts and apologies. In explaining behavior to the offended party, research indicates that the transgressors tend to rely mostly on justification or apology.

Step Two: Acceptance of an Account and an Apology or Its Absence

Here the offended person may chose to not forgive or forgive the other if the transgressor has changed or is truly sorry for the transgression. The offended person makes a judgment call. Some people are willing to change, do in fact change, realize the errors of their ways, and are truly sorry for their transgressions, and others are clueless. The offended person needs to separate those who warrant forgiveness from those who do not. In deciding to forgive the other, the offended person must decide that it is a good idea to let go of any feelings of anger, resentment, and revenge. This person first needed to work through the steps of forgiveness as listed previously in Table 9.1.

An offended person may choose to forgive without any input from the offender. In the absence of an explanation and apology, the offended person may decide unilaterally that it is no longer in her or his best interests to continue feeling angry, resentful, and revengeful. Harboring such feelings is costly and drains one emotionally. Of course, when hurt by someone we trust and care for, it takes some time before we reach a point where we question the value of maintaining these feelings. If you are deciding to forgive without actually having discussed the transgression with the offender, it helps to keep these points in mind:

- With few exceptions, forgiveness is not equated with forgetting about the transgression.
- Forgiveness is generally conceived of as a process through which people move on with their lives after experiencing some hurt.
- Forgiveness involves reframing the event: One reframes the event so that it becomes less central in a person's life or in the life of a relationship.
- Forgiveness also includes reframing our perception of the other person: We see the person who hurt us in a different light. We may come to again value

the other person—that is, we see that person as having worth regardless of the hurt he or she has caused us. We may decide to trust again and take risks until it is seen by both people as authentic; however, forgiveness is not necessarily equated with the restoration of trust. We may love that person again.

- When we forgive, we recognize that we cannot change the past; we know that we can influence future events; and we accept the fact that the past is past.

Step Three: Forgiveness May or May Not Be Communicated

At this point, the offended person decides whether or not to explicitly communicate his or her forgiveness to the offender. If it is not communicated explicitly, the offended person behaves in ways that imply forgiveness has taken place. In some cases, we may choose to restore or alter the relationship when the other person convinces us that he or she has truly changed or no longer poses a threat to us emotionally or physically. If we decide to restore the relationship eventually, then it is important to risk telling the other about our hurt. It is a risk because, as research shows, the other person may tell us that our feelings are not justified or that we have no right to feel hurt. Such an action makes it more difficult to forgive the other.

It is easier to forgive when the other person admits guilt or offers an account and an apology. Even so, depending on the offense, we may have a problem in trusting again. A frequently asked question is this: "Does this mean I have to trust the other person like I did before?" We think the answer is no unless the person earns your trust over time.

Injuries heal and scars do remain. You neither ignore your scars nor focus on their ugliness. Injuries are not forgotten, but they do not always dictate the way you behave. We believe that forgiveness occurs when we no longer define our emotions, our desires, or our behaviors in terms of our injuries. Those scars become a part of us, not the whole of what we are.

Step Four: Transforming the Relationship, if Desired

If desired by the parties, reconciliation may result in a transformed relationship between the parties in the transgression—we may feel less enthusiasm than before, we may feel better than before, or we may create an entirely different type of relationship. For example, a relational transgression is often a reason for separation between spouses. Let us assume that two spouses are unable to forgive one another and seek revenge in the courts, where they spend most of their financial assets; expend considerable time, effort, and emotion seeking revenge against each other; and reaffirm their negative opinions of the other spouse. She blames him for his infidelity and he blames her for laziness and squandering. They fill the courtroom with anger and resentment. They may think they have no reason to communicate or relate to one another ever again, and they may not have to if the divorce occurs early in their marriage as they have no children. However, suppose they were married several years and do have children. Issues related to alimony and child support may make it unlikely that the spouses can avoid each other in the years to come.

Let us say that in another case, a couple with children suffer a relational transgression followed by a temporary separation but then decide to "kiss and make up." In addition to forgiving each other, let us say that they also restore their relationship and continue as husband and wife. All assets remain in place, and the spouses continue as parents to their children. In this case, forgiveness and reconciliation restored the relationship. Of course, the relationship may not be exactly the same because the spouses may have agreed to some changes to the issues that led to the conflict in the first place, but we would say that in most respects life is continuing as before the blowup. If the couple is willing, though, the relationship can become stronger than it was before the transgression, but this takes considerable time and effort at reframing the transgression.

In still another case, let us consider a family where the spouses suffer a relational transgression and decide to forgive one another, but they want to convert their relationship (i.e., they no longer want to remain husband and wife). However, due to the need to maintain alimony and child support, they want to continue to work together for the benefit of their children. They end up divorced but maintain open lines of communication and consult each other about the children. Perhaps the ex-husband continues to maintain the residence where his ex-wife and children live. Maybe they decide to share the same home (not present at the same time), with each living there for six months, so that the children can remain in one school. While the nature of this relationship may vary in its degree of warmth, former spouses may redefine their relationships as friends who help each other, especially in times of need and as parents as they continue to take care of their children while separated physically.

Step Five: Actions Confirm Forgiveness and Reconciliation

The role played by actions is found in research examining **self-fulfilling prophecies**, in which people act toward us in the way that we expect. If you act toward the other as though he or she is not trustworthy, the other may begin to act in untrustworthy ways. If you act toward the other as though the relationship is strained, he or she may come to believe it is strained and act in ways that reflect this belief.

As discussed in the previous section, reconciliation does not mean you simply forget what happened, but you do move forward in your relationship, perhaps rebuild trust, and possibly reestablish intimacy. Acting in ways that signal forgiveness creates expectations of a renewed relationship or a different relationship and the possibility of change. Reconciliation means acting in ways that do not lock the present situation into constant reexamination of the offense.

Social construction theory suggests that we make our social worlds by the way we talk about them, and we act within our social worlds based on the way we have made them through our talk. For example, a couple that is beginning to date might say, "We are just friends," and act accordingly. Later on, they may agree to move to a definition of "romantic partners." This change in the definition of their relationship occurs with a change in their behavior toward one another. In a circular way, their affectionate behaviors increase because they change the definition of the relationship, and as the affectionate behaviors increase they give labels to their relationship that define it as more serious. Thus, in the communication–reality loop, the way we communicate about our behavior helps to constitute the reality of it as does the behavior itself. As we describe our behavior, we affect the way we behave; as we behave, we affect the way we describe our behavior.

The process of forgiveness and reconciliation works in the same way.

1. After forgiving one another, we tell each other that the act is forgiven, which allows us to act without reference to the offense.
2. In turn, we feel better about our relationship with one another and can talk about our relationship without reference to the offense.
3. In turn, our actions confirm what we said so that our behavior constitutes the reality of our forgiveness.[41]

This approach highlights the role of communication in the aftermath of conflict and views forgiveness and reconciliation as social constructions: Those in a fractured or stressed relationship must create a meaning for the concept they term forgiveness and must create the actions necessary to make forgiveness seem real to them. Constructing reconciliation is the process of integrating what has become problematic into the realm of the unproblematic in relationships. Small conflicts may only cause people to temporarily pause and ask about the fit of the conflict into the total relationship. Transgressions interrupt their everyday reality, forcing them to reorganize vastly different pieces of the relationship. Accounts and apologies result in efforts to again reorganize the meaning of the relationship; reconciliation is the process of enacting that new definition so that it becomes permanent.

Thus, expressing forgiveness after conflict becomes a self-fulfilling prophecy when enacted correctly: We say forgiveness is possible; we act toward the other as though we have forgiven the person; the other, in turn, feels forgiven; and we are able to have a relationship that has moved beyond a relational transgression to where the transgression no longer defines the relationship. Here we have a communication process (involving verbal and nonverbal language, attributions, expectations, and confirmation) that is also a conflict resolution process. When any of these steps break down—if we say we forgive but do not act as though we have, or if we continue to refer to the offense as though it has not passed—forgiveness is almost impossible. Instead, we become victims of the relational transgression, and the transgression defines us and our relationship with the other. We can avoid the role of victim by forgiving and reconciling with the transgressor.

Although some therapists think that forgiveness is grasped quickly in some cases, most researchers in the field argue that the process of forgiveness takes time. The key in getting to the point of forgiveness is the ability to transform the meaning of the event that has occurred and to see it as an event among many in a relationship instead of the central event that defines the quality of the relationship. It is time consuming and cannot occur if people are not willing to explore and reconcile the different feelings that arise as a result of transgressions.

MOVING BEYOND VICTIMIZATION

If reconciliation is not advisable, the offended person may forgive without engaging in communication with the transgressor. This is why we say that the reconciliation step is optional. One may choose to forgive without reconciling. In some cases, it is appropriate to forgive at a distance, so to speak, when the other person has not changed, has shown no willingness to change, continues to engage in offensive behavior, or poses harm to us mentally or physically. Under these conditions, contacting the other and becoming vulnerable again by expressing our anger and our hurt may cause more harm than good, so we forgive for our own sake—to let go of the offense, to move on with our lives, and to approach new relationships freely.

We tend to look for others outside of ourselves to blame. But it is the ability to move beyond **victimization** or the feeling of being a victim that leads to a state of forgiveness:

> We had a family friend who lived with us throughout my childhood years. He molested me numerous times over the course of my childhood. I never told my parents until long after he had died. I thought I had worked through most of my forgiveness issues when I found out that my parents had let him live with us knowing that he had served time in jail for child molesting. What were they thinking? How could they let him spend time alone with me? How couldn't they know? I had forgiven my molester, and I had stopped thinking of myself as a child abuse victim, but in some ways it was harder to forgive my parents.

You may never experience a traumatic event like physical or sexual assault, or have someone lie to you about an important issue.[42] In the course of your everyday conflicts, however, you may at times think you are victimized (used, manipulated, or abused) by another. Perhaps the feeling results from having secrets you told to the other in trust used as weapons against you later in a conflict. It may arise from having your personal possessions taken or destroyed.

Remember that we view forgiveness as a process. A process view implies that forgiveness takes time, maybe years. But in the end, forgiveness allows us to act freely again. Without it, we are held captive by the event that victimized us; with it, we let go and move forward.

> I am unable to forget the time I took a trust and openness class in which the topic was "Someone in my life whom I want to forgive." As a group exercise, we discussed the steps to forgiveness and then we each had to contribute a personal experience of unresolved and unforgiving conflict with someone. You would not believe what happened. Adult men and women alike told shocking stories of wrongs done to them, and they talked about their anger and rage. The facilitator told us that we have suffered long enough. He asked us to picture our antagonists as children. Picture what was being done to us as being done to them as little children. He said we know that people do to others that which was done to them often as children. He asked us to free them from their wrongs and see them as the wronged, needy people they are. Instead of distancing us from those who had wronged us, he brought us together as mutual victims who are suffering together. I have difficulty believing what then happened. There were changes and healing like I have never seen before. We were all overwhelmed by what was happening. Some cried, some held hands, some hugged the facilitator and then one another. I couldn't help but wonder what would happen if everyone in the world went through a group experience like this.

If you cannot disengage some problematic people from your past, you enslave yourself to an ugly emotional affair. You may have unresolved conflicts with others, especially with family members. These unforgiving experiences are now serving as a barrier between you and that person, preventing you from having the positive relationship both of you need. Someday you may realize that these people are only doing the best they know how. They brought "past baggage" with them. Now you are in a good position to drop the baggage you are carrying in favor of new tools. You no longer have to act based on your past. As you move forward in your new ways, you can also let go of your feelings that "justified" your old ways. You can stop seeking revenge and choose to forgive. A new outlook, it is hoped, alters or reestablishes a much needed relationship. If the other doesn't respond, drop it. Forgiveness is your benefit alone to enjoy.

MANAGE IT

The conflicts in this chapter involve relational transgression. Relational transgressions are extremely problematic situations in which core rules of a relationship are violated, leaving high emotional residues. Core relational rules define our expectations about the way we should behave toward others as well as the way they should behave toward us. Every relationship has its core rules that cannot be violated without calling the relationship itself into question. This is why relational transgressions are so hard to forgive. The violator has abused loved ones or cheated on romantic partners and lied to them or to friends. They committed acts that produce highly emotional residues where people experience lingering emotional, cognitive, and behavioral responses to the memory of the transgression.

We believe that forgiveness is the most important part of conflict management. Following relational transgressions, conflicting partners may become consumed with unforgiveness and the desire to seek revenge. If we cannot forgive the hurt and perhaps reconcile with the other person, we let a relational transgression continue to define us and weigh us down rather than take control of our lives and move forward. To not forgive is to be forever bound to the desire for revenge, while forgiveness is linked to both mental and physical benefits and allows us to get on with our lives.

Forgiveness and reconciliation are related but separate processes with the former generally preceding the latter. Forgiveness is a cognitive process that consists of letting go of feelings of revenge and desires to retaliate. The key stages that the process goes through are hurt, hate, healing, and coming together. (We now know that "coming together" need not be taken in a physical sense but rather in a psychological, mental, and emotional sense, where you might cognitively forgive another without behaviorally reconciling.) Overall, forgiveness occurs when a person lets go of his or her feelings of revenge and need for retaliation, and changes his or her thoughts about the transgression and the transgressor. It starts with anger over a transgression and moves toward transforming the meaning of the event, or changing the way we view the event in light of other events in our lives.

We give up our right to change the future based on the past. While we may never forget a transgression, forgiveness begins with a decision to reduce our focus on the event as a defining characteristic of our relationship with the other person, or indeed, our entire lives. The ability to move beyond victimization leads to a state of forgiveness.

Reconciliation is a behavioral process in which we take actions to restore a relationship or create a new one following forgiveness. Once we forgive the other for the relational transgression, we do not have to reconcile unless we want to. We may wish to forgive at a distance and not communicate our forgiveness to the transgressor, or we may decide that we wish to reestablish a relationship or create a new one, so we choose to reconcile.

The steps toward forgiveness and reconciliation are as follows:

1. The account and the apology
2. Acceptance of account and apology or its absence
3. Forgiveness may or may not be communicated
4. Transforming the relationship, if desired
5. Actions that confirm forgiveness and reconciliation

Critical to our understanding of both forgiveness and reconciliation is the understanding that they are not one-time events. Often, we return to an event cognitively and emotionally, but we deal with different parts of it. Like the ability to analyze conflicts and the ability to effectively communicate feelings and desires, the effective use of forgiveness and reconciliation strategies to cope with difficult conflicts characterizes the competent conflict manager. The endnotes for this chapter point to further helpful readings for those of you in need. Through the processes of forgiveness and reconciliation, we can forge new relationships or repair former ones and move forward by letting go of the past. We must understand the kind of response necessitated by various transgressions and develop a repertoire of responses designed to remediate problematic situations. Of all the skills in conflict, we must learn how to put a conflict into perspective and move forward, otherwise our relationships become unstable; without forgiveness, our relationships eventually come to an end.

EXERCISES

THINK ABOUT IT

1. Was there a time when a "truth bias" worked against you in a relationship? What kind of relationship was it? How were you deceived? In retrospect, does it seem as though you should have known the other was lying to you?
2. Is there an event in your life that you find difficult to forgive? What is it? What makes it so difficult to forgive the other person? If you are not experiencing a difficult event now, describe a past event that you found difficult to forgive.
3. Seven years ago a thief broke into your home, went through your personal belongings, and stole many of your possessions. He was caught, much of your property was returned to you (but some was damaged), and he was sentenced to seven years in a state prison. Are you now in a position to forgive him for what he did to you? Should we forgive all convicted felons after they serve their time in prison? Do you feel differently if the crime was committed against you? Would you feel differently if you were the one convicted?

4. Return to the incident you described above in 2. What would it take for you to forgive the other person? What are the consequences of forgiving the other person? Of not forgiving the other person?
5. Anne Lamott wrote that "not forgiving is like drinking rat poison and waiting for the rat to die."[43] Are there times when we should not forgive? How does this affect us?

APPLY IT

1. What constitutes a transgression in your relationships? Compare two relationships you are in, one with a close friend and one with an acquaintance, and list three transgressions.
2. Do an Internet search using the terms forgiveness, reconciliation, and revenge. What kinds of sites do you find? Which term produces more sites? Why do you think that is?
3. Write out a description of a conflict involving a relational transgression that moved through the reconciliation process. Describe what happened at each step of the process. How long did it take? Was it worth it to you? Why?
4. Watch a movie that features a relational transgression that occurs between two or more people. How does it follow the model of forgiveness and reconciliation that was presented in this chapter? Some suggestions for viewing (in alphabetical order): *Atonement, Changeling, Notes on a Scandal, The Painted Veil,* and *There Will Be Blood.*

WORK WITH IT

Analyze the case study below in terms of the key ideas discussed in this chapter. You, personally, may not want to forgive anyone in this case study, but you are asked to take the necessary steps in forgiveness as an exercise to illustrate and apply the process. We selected a case study rather than have you describe an actual situation in your life so that you might analyze the conflict situation objectively and see ways to implement the suggestions in this chapter.

Write an essay on the case study below in which you answer the following questions. What did Jeanne do that upset Mark? Does his behavior constitute a problematic situation or a relational transgression, and why? What probably makes it difficult for Mark to forgive Jeanne? What would he and she have to do for him to forgive her? Why would forgiveness and reconciliation help Mark? Apply the steps of forgiveness to this situation and describe what Mark must do at each step if he is to truly forgive her. Explain how he might forgive her but not forget the incident and change the nature of their sibling relationship.

Everyone in my family is stupid about money. Some of us are more stupid than others. I've been trying to make things better and slowly but surely I'm working my way out of debt.

My sister came to me two years ago and asked to borrow some money. She was desperate. She thought I could just take a loan against a credit card. I refused. I knew my wife would be furious if she knew I had lent the money as my sister already owes us thousands of dollars.

She wouldn't let up. She actually came to my office to talk to me so my wife wouldn't know about it, and wouldn't leave. She finally convinced me to take out a loan through one of those pay-advance places that charges an enormous amount of interest. She promised me she would pay it back. Of course, she didn't. I had to take a loan from my retirement account to pay it back because the interest accumulated faster than I could pay it off. Naturally, my wife found out about it and she was furious, as I knew she would be.

I am like the comic character, Charlie Brown, when he listens to Lucy promise him that she'll hold the ball in place so he can kick it. She always pulls it away at the last moment and he winds up on the ground. I'm looking up at the sky wondering if I can ever trust her again, much less recover such a large amount of money. It really set my plans to retire debt back.

DISCUSS IT

Read the following conflict narrative and the instructions that follow it. "My name is Maria. Three months ago, David and I had tickets to see Harry Connick, Jr. in concert. We had just started seeing each other when we bought the tickets and planned to attend the concert together. A few days before the concert, David came to my house late at night to tell me he had a ton of studying to do on the day of the concert. He had a huge midterm on Thursday on which he had to receive an 'A'. He made me understand, after hours of continuous explanation, how he really felt it was best to give the tickets to his cousin because he couldn't afford not to study the night before the exam. I understood, but I was really bummed out. I sort of wished David would give me the tickets so I could still go to the concert, but he felt it was unfair that I go to the concert while he stayed home and studied. He said that he would make it up to me with something better.

I went over to his house the day after the concert so we could spend some time together and celebrate his test performance. David said, 'Maria, I lied, okay? I said it. I went to the concert. I didn't want to tell you. I didn't think I would feel this bad about it. I wasn't thinking, so I didn't tell you that I took Tina instead of you.'

My jaw dropped to the ground, and all I kept thinking was, 'Why? Why? Why? Tina? Why would you take your ex-girlfriend instead of me? You promised to take me. What about your test? Was that a lie too?' I didn't give him a chance to explain; I just told him I couldn't accept the fact that he lied to me, that it wasn't fair. Then, I stormed out of his place. I wanted so badly for him to realize that the person whom he loved had just walked out the door and was never coming back. I didn't want to listen to him. I was so angry that nothing could change the way I felt.

David finally called me and explained to me the real issue that he had avoided telling me all along. He explained that before we started going out, he and Tina had agreed to continue their relationship as friends. He said that he had originally bought the tickets so they could go to the concert together, but then we started dating, and he wasn't sure how I would feel about his friendship with Tina. David explained that he didn't know what to do. He avoided telling me, thinking I would never find out."

As a way to apply the concepts that you have learned from reading this chapter, read the above case study and participate in a class discussion by posting an answer to one of the questions below.

1. What are the issues in this conflict? For example, but not limited to tangible/intangible and behavioral, personality, relationship, and so on.
2. Does David's behavior constitute a problematic (embarrassing) situation or a relational transgression? Why?
3. Would forgiveness and reconciliation play a role in this case study? Explain your response.
4. Explain how Maria might forgive David but not forget the incident, and not continue the romantic relationship. Please use the steps of forgiveness in your answer.

You can participate in one or more discussions of the above questions.

NOTES

1. Louis Smedes, *Forgive and Forget: Healing the Hurt We Don't Deserve* (San Francisco, CA: Harper & Row, 1984), p. 15.

2. Dudley D. Cahn, "Friendship, Conflict and Dissolution," in Harry T. Reis and Susan K. Sprecher (Eds.), *Encyclopedia of Human Relationships* (Thousand Oaks, CA: Sage Publications, 2009), http://www.sage-ereference.com/humanrelationships/Article_n226.html.

3. Sandra Metts, "Relational Transgressions," in William R. Cupach and Brian H. Spitzberg (Eds.), *The Dark Side of Interpersonal Communication* (Hillsdale, NJ: Lawrence Erlbaum, 1994), p. 4.

4. For further reading on forgiveness after serious offenses, see Ruth Anna Abigail, "Forgiving the Unforgivable? Processes of Forgiveness and Reconciliation after Episodes of Family Violence," in Dudley D. Cahn (Ed.), *Family Violence: Communication Processes* (Albany, NY: SUNY, 2009), pp. 205–220.

5. Smedes, *Forgive and Forget*, p. 15.

6. Everett L. Worthington, Jr., Suzanne E. Mazzeo, and Wendy L. Kliewer, "Addicting and Eating Disorders, Unforgiveness, and Forgiveness," *Journal of Psychology and Christianity* 21 (2002), 259, 257–261.

7. Donald Hope, "The Healing Paradox of Forgiveness," *Psychotherapy* 24 (1987), 242; see also Albert Ellis and Robert A. Harper, *A New Guide to Rational Living* (North Hollywood, CA: Wilshire Book Co., 1975), who claim that forgiving leaves us sane and realistic.

8. Ann Macaskill, John Maltby, and Liza Day, "Forgiveness of Self and Others and Emotional Empathy," *The Journal of Social Psychology* 142 (2002), 663, 663–665.

9. Hope, "The Healing Paradox of Forgiveness," *Psychotherapy,* 242; see also Ellis and Harper, *A New Guide to Rational Living,* who claim that forgiving leaves us sane and realistic.

10. Human Development Study Group, "Five Points on the Construct of Forgiveness within Psychotherapy," *Psychotherapy* 28 (1991), 495, 493–496.

11. Janis A. Spring and Michael Spring, *How Can I Forgive You?* (New York: Harper Collins, 2004), p. 15.

12. Heinz Kohut, "Narcissism and Narcissistic Rage," *The Psychoanalytic Study of the Child* 27 (1972), 379–392; Jared P. Pingleton, "The Role and Function of Forgiveness in the Psychotherapeutic Process," *Journal of Psychology and Theology* 17 (1989), 27–35.

13. Hope, "The Healing Paradox of Forgiveness," 240.

14. James G. Emerson, *The Dynamics of Forgiveness* (Philadelphia, PA: The Westminster Press, 1964), used the Rogers and Dymond q-sort test of emotional adjustment, adding items concerning feelings about one's ability to forgive (Carl R. Rogers and Rosalind F. Dymond, *Psychotherapy and Personality Change* [Chicago, IL: University of Chicago Press, 1954]).

15. Mary F. Trainer, "Forgiveness: Intrinsic, Role-Expected, Expedient, in the Context of Divorce," Doctoral dissertation, Boston University, Boston, MA, 1984; Mellis I. Schmidt, "Forgiveness as the Focus Theme in Group Counseling," Doctoral dissertation, North Texas State University, Denton, TX, 1986; John H. Hebl, "Forgiveness as a Counseling Goal with Elderly Females," Doctoral dissertation, University of Wisconsin, Madison, WI, 1990.

16. John H. Hebl and Robert D. Enright, "Forgiveness as a Psychotherapeutic Goal with Elderly Females," *Psychotherapy* 30 (1993), 658–667.

17. Radhi H. Al-Mabuk, Robert D. Enright, and Paul A. Cardis, "Forgiveness Education with Parentally Love-Deprived Late Adolescents," *Journal of Moral Education* 24 (1995), 427–444.

18. F. M. Luskin, K. Ginzburg, and Carl E. Thoresen, "The Efficacy of Forgiveness Intervention in College Age Adults: Randomized Controlled Study," *Humboldt Journal of Social Relations* 29 (2005), 163–184.

19. Suzanne Freedman and Robert D. Enright, "Forgiveness as an Intervention Goal with Incest Survivors," *Journal of Consulting and Clinical Psychology* 64 (1996), 983–992.

20. Scott R. Ross, Matthew J. Hertenstein, and Thomas A. Wrobel, "Maladaptive Correlates of the Failure to Forgive Self and Others: Further Evidence for a Two-Component Model of Forgiveness," *Journal of Personality Assessment* 88 (2007), 158–167.

21. Everett L. Worthington, Jr., Charlotte Van Oyen Witvliet, Pietro Pietrini, and Andrea J. Miller, "Forgiveness, Health, and Well-Being: A Review of Evidence for Emotional Versus Decisional Forgiveness, Dispositional Forgivingness, and Reduced Unforgiveness," *Journal of Behavioral Medicine* 30 (2007), 291–302.

22. Tobi Wilson, Aleks Milosevic, Michelle Carroll, Kenneth Hart, and Stephen Hibbard, "Physical Health Status in Relation to Self-forgiveness and Other-forgiveness in Healthy College Students," *Journal of Health Psychology* 13 (2008), 798–803.

23. James W. Carson, F. J. Keefe, V. Goli, A. M. Fras, T. R. Lynch, S. R. Thorp, and J. L. Buechler, "Forgiveness and Chronic Low Back Pain: A Preliminary Study Examining the Relationship of Forgiveness to Pain, Anger, and Psychological Distress," *The Journal of Pain* 6 (2005), 84–91.

24. R. Stoia-Caraballo, M. S. Rye, W. Pan, K. J. Brown Kirschman, C. Lutz-Zois, and A. M. Lyons, "Negative Affect and Anger Rumination as Mediators between Forgiveness and Sleep Quality," *Journal of Behavioral Medicine* 31 (2008), 478–488.

25. Judith A. Strasser, "The Relation of General Forgiveness and Forgiveness Type to Reported Health in the Elderly," Doctoral dissertation, Catholic University of America, Washington, DC, 1984.

26. J. P. Friedberg, S. Suchday, and D. V. Shelov, "The Impact of Forgiveness on Cardiovascular Reactivity and Recovery," *International Journal of Psychophysiology* 65 (2007), 87–94; see also K. A. Lawler-Row, J. C. Karremans, C. Scott, M. Edlis-Matityahou, and L. Edwards, "Forgiveness, Physiological Reactivity and Health: The Role of Anger," *International Journal of Psychophysiology* 68 (2008), 51–58; Kathleen A. Lawler, Jarred W. Younger, Rachel L. Piferi, Eric Billington, Rebecca Jobe, Kim Edmondson, and Warren H. Jones, "A Change of Heart: Cardiovascular Correlates of Forgiveness in Response to Interpersonal Conflict," *Journal of Behavioral Medicine* 26 (2003), 373–393; Jeremy C. Anderson, Wolfgang Linden, and Martine E. Habra, "Influence of Apologies and Trait Hostility on Recovery from Anger," *Journal of Behavioral Medicine* 29 (2006), 347–358.

27. Roxane S. Lulofs, "Swimming Upstream: Creating Reasons for Unforgiveness in a Culture that Expects Otherwise," Paper presented to the Speech Communication Association Convention, San Antonio, TX, November 1995.

28. Alexander G. Santelli, C. Ward Struthers, and Judy Eaton, "Fit to Forgive: Exploring the Interaction between Regulatory Focus, Repentance, and Forgiveness," *Journal of Personality and Social Psychology* 96 (2009), 381–394.

29. Julie J. Exline and Ray F. Baumeister, "Expressing Forgiveness and Repentance: Benefits and Barriers," in Michael E. McCullough, Kenneth L. Pargament, and Carl E. Thorsen (Eds.), *Forgiveness: Theory, Research, and Practice* (New York: The Guilford Press, 2000), pp. 133–155.

30. Macaskill, Maltby, and Day, "Forgiveness of Self and Others and Emotional Empathy"; see also Varda Konstam, Miriam Chernoff, and Sara Deveney, "Toward Forgiveness: The Role of Shame, Guilt, Anger and Empathy," *Counseling and Values* 46 (2001), 26–39.

31. Loren Toussaint and Jon R. Webb, "Gender Differences in the Relationship between Empathy and Forgiveness," *The Journal of Social Psychology* 145 (2005), 673–685.

32. Julie J. Exline, Roy F. Baumeister, Anne L. Zell, Amy J. Kraft, and Charlotte V. O. Witvliet, "Not So Innocent: Does Seeing One's Own Capability for Wrongdoing Predict Forgiveness?" *Journal of Personality and Social Psychology* 94 (2008), 495–515.

33. Michael J. Subkoviak, Robert D. Enright, Ching-Ru Wu, Elizabeth A. Gassin, Suzanne Freedman, Leanne M. Olson, and Issidoros Sarinopolous, "Measuring Interpersonal Forgiveness," Paper presented at the American Educational Research Association Convention, San Francisco, April 1992.

34. Doris Donnelly, *Learning to Forgive* (Nashville, TN: Abingdon Press, 1979).

35. James N. Sells and Leslie King, "A Pilot Study in Marital Group Therapy: Process and Outcome," *Family Journal* 10 (2002), 156–166.

36. Alex H. S. Harris, Frederic Luskin, Sonya B. Norman, Sam Standard, Jennifer Bruning, Stephanie Evans, and Carl E. Thoresen, "Effects of a Group Forgiveness Intervention on Forgiveness, Perceived Stress, and Trait-Anger," *Journal of Clinical Psychology* 62 (2006), 729, 715–733.

37. Jarred W. Younger, Rachel L. Piferi, Rebecca Jobe, Kathleen A. Lawler, "Dimensions of Forgiveness: The Views of Laypersons," *Journal of Social and Personal Relationships* 21 (2004), 837–856.

38. Everett L. Worthington, Jr., *Forgiving and Reconciling* (Downer's Grove, IL: InterVarsity Press, 2003), p. 25.

39. Jeanne Moskal, *Blake, Ethics, and Forgiveness* (Tuscaloosa, AL: University of Alabama Press, 1994), p. 9.

40. Lulofs, "Swimming Upstream."

41. Roxane S. Lulofs, "The Social Construction of Forgiveness," *Human Systems* 3 (1992), 183–197.

42. For those who have experienced childhood trauma, two excellent resources are James E. Kepner, *Healing Tasks: Psychotherapy with Adult Survivors of Childhood Abuse* (San Francisco, CA: Jossey-Bass, 1995) and Gina O'Connell Higgins, *Resilient Adults: Overcoming a Cruel Past* (San Francisco, CA: Jossey-Bass, 1994).

43. Anne Lamott, *Traveling Mercies* (New York: Anchor Books, 1999), p. 134.

Managing Win–Lose Conflicts through Negotiation

OBJECTIVES

At the end of this chapter, you should be able to:

- Define tangible conflict issues and explain why negotiation is needed to resolve such issues.
- Explain the assumption behind negotiation in which people try to minimize their losses and maximize their gains.
- Distinguish between competitive and cooperative negotiation and

- explain when each approach is most appropriate.
- Describe six ways to generate more options.
- List several ways that conflicting parties can convert a potentially competitive negotiation into a cooperative one.
- Define BATNA and fractionation.

KEY TERMS

aspiration point
bargaining range
BATNA
brainstorming
commonalities
compensation
competition
competitive negotiation
concession
consulting

control the process
cooperative negotiation
cost cutting
equifinality
fractionation
interests
language of cooperation
minimax principle
negotiation
objective criteria

positions
prioritizing (logrolling)
resistance point
scarce resources
status quo point
tangible issues
thinking positively

We may do a lot more negotiating than we think, as this situation shows:

Recently, I was looking forward to a prime rib dinner at my favorite restaurant. However, when we got there and were seated, the waitress informed us that the restaurant was not offering prime rib on the menu that night. I expressed my disappointment and had to rethink the situation. I ruled out leaving the restaurant and considered other good meals I'd eaten before. I happened to mention that I liked the filet with blue cheese crusted top, but I had my heart set on the prime rib. The waitress said she would ask her boss if they could designate that the special that night in place of the prime rib, which meant I would get a lower price for the filet. That sounded good to me, so I ordered it. I'll get the prime rib next time.

This may seem so commonplace to you that you did not realize you were participating in a negotiation. The customer's expectation of ordering prime rib represented a goal or outcome, but she had to consider the fact that she liked eating at the restaurant, so other items on the menu could satisfy her even though she had "her heart set on prime rib." Interestingly, the waitress countered with a way to reduce the price for the filet, which helped seal the deal. Both the customer and restaurant were satisfied with the "agreement" to substitute the filet for the prime rib as that night's special.

Throughout our day, we probably engage in many more negotiations than we realize. Some encounters are resolved quickly (which movie shall we see tonight?), but others may take hours or even days and weeks (such as buying a new or used car). How well do we negotiate these situations? This chapter explains the basic principles behind effective negotiation and useful techniques. However, we first discuss conflict issues because negotiation is more useful for resolving some issues than others.

As discussed in Chapters 1 and 2, conflict issues are the focal point of the conflict, the "trigger" that people point to when they are asked what the conflict was about. There are two types of conflict issues, intangible and tangible. In Chapter 2, we explained intangible conflict issues and pointed out that we can often resolve such issues simply through interpersonal communication and by practicing S-TLC (see Chapter 4). In this chapter, we consider tangible issues because they often require negotiation. We also distinguish between competitive and cooperative negotiation in the hope that you use them when most appropriate. We conclude with specific suggestions on how to engage in cooperative bargaining, where we combine interpersonal communication skills with negotiation techniques. After reading this chapter, you can engage in effective negotiation for resolving conflicts over tangible issues.

THE NEED FOR NEGOTIATION
Defining Tangible Conflict Issues

In contrast to intangible issues, **tangible issues** are hard, physical, or observable assets that are often scarce, such that conflicting parties either get what they want or don't get it at all (win–lose). These conflicts are over one's personal property, money, land, grades, promotions, water/food/air supply, natural resources (oil, timber, and precious metals), awards/rewards, jobs, and so on. Some examples of conflicts involving **scarce resources** include the following:

- Another person asks to move in with you and your roommate in an apartment or room designed for only two occupants.
- You and another must share only one car.

- There is not enough money for both of you to buy what you each want.
- Both divorced parents want full custody of the children.
- An ex-spouse believes that she or he cannot maintain the current standard of living and at the same time pay alimony to the ex-partner.

Conflicts involving tangible issues require crafting a solution that is creative or perhaps ingenious. Of course this may take time and effort, as well as the many techniques we describe in this chapter to produce a win–win outcome. In the case of a married couple discussing how to spend their vacation, let us say that she likes the fact that they "always go to the East Coast to visit her parents," but this time her husband wants to go to Hawaii. They do not have enough money to do both. A solution that would seem like "winning" to both of them might consist of a vacation package in the Caribbean (with a warm climate, water, beaches, etc.) that would allow them a stop on the East Coast. This narrative describes a behavioral conflict based on tangible issues.

> My parents wanted me to come back and attend school near them next year.
> My mom said she missed me and wanted me to go to school nearby so that
> I could commute from my parents' house. They're having a hard time letting
> me go, so they tell me they can't afford this college. I work 30 hours a week
> and would pay for school on my own if I could take out more loans, but they
> are against that idea. There is so much tension in my family over this. I grew
> up in this state—my parents are the ones who moved. There's nothing that
> interests me where they are now living, so I don't want to leave here.

Table 10.1 lists the two types of conflict issues and gives examples of the way we might address them in a conflict situation.

Time issues may or may not be tangible. Is a conflict involving a person being late to an event a tangible or intangible issue? Conflicts over time management can be difficult to classify. If there is enough time available but your friend or romantic interest chooses to spend little with you, you might call this to the other's attention, and perhaps that person may try to spend more time with you. In this case,

---

TABLE 10.1

Issues in Conflicts

Tangible Issues	Intangible Issues		
Concern material resources that cannot be divided up equally. "We have only one car and on Wednesday I want to drive it to see my parents while you want to use it to get to work."	Involve immaterial resources that are we value, such as esteem, power, love, etc.		
	Personality Issues	**Relationship/ Normative Issues**	**Behavioral Issues**
	"You have always been lazy."	"Because we are part of a team you can count on me to get the job done."	"You cannot bring your dog into my house."

time is an intangible issue. However, if he or she has three jobs and school, the other person may be too busy to do anything else without cutting back on the time he or she needs to spend elsewhere. Here time is a tangible issue. In the first case, the person had time available and didn't know that the other person wanted to spend more time together, but in the second case, the person doesn't have enough time to do everything, so some choices must be made.

Can you learn how to negotiate conflicts over tangible issues? Research tells us that people who believe they can acquire negotiation skills through practice more often wind up with more integrative outcomes that are personally beneficial.[1] It helps, then, to take the attitude that these skills can be acquired and perfected.

Some courses in conflict management utilize role plays, classroom exercises, and game-like activities to provide an opportunity for students to actually practice negotiating a conflict situation over a tangible issue. At the end of this chapter is the description of an exercise that involves the class in a negotiation where role players are encouraged to use the principles and techniques taught in this chapter.

NEGOTIATION BASICS

Experienced negotiators do not see the conflict situation as either–or (win–lose), but rather view negotiation or bargaining as an opportunity to discuss a broad range of alternatives where anything is possible. Academically, **negotiation** is defined as "a particular type of conflict management—one characterized by an exchange of proposals and counter proposals as a means of reaching a satisfactory settlement."[2] Two people contemplating marriage might negotiate a prenuptial agreement, which usually involves tangible resources that the parties bring to the marriage. By agreeing to negotiate, people are agreeing (1) to engage in a conflict by confronting others rather than avoiding it and (2) to try to find an outcome that is mutually acceptable to all those involved in the conflict by exploring various options in the conflict. There is a lot we can learn from this chapter to apply to many of our everyday conflicts.

We can start by learning that in negotiation people try to minimize their losses and maximize their gains. We call this the **minimax principle**. Both parties start bargaining with an **aspiration point** (their most preferred option, which would maximize their gains) in mind. Both parties also have a **resistance point** (an identifiable amount that they are willing to concede to the other person with minimum loss or the lowest they would agree to). For both parties, between both points exists a **bargaining range** (also known as a "zone of possible agreement" or ZOPA in some research) between resistance points and aspiration levels. If an agreement is not reached, parties return to their **status quo point**, or the position they occupied before entering the negotiation situation.

In addition to learning about the minimax principle, you also need to learn about your BATNA (Best Alternative to a Negotiated Agreement), which is an acronym, Fisher and Ury have given to the idea of one's "Best Alternative to a Negotiated Agreement."[3] Initially, your BATNA is your status quo point. In other words, if you stopped negotiating, where would you be? Considering your BATNA forces you to deal with reality. Maybe the BATNA is undesirable or worse—a disaster. Recognizing this may convince you to return to the bargaining session with a more cooperative attitude (see Figure 10.1).

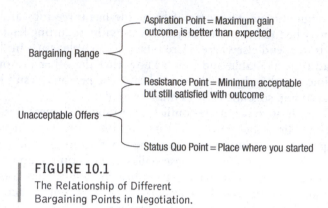

FIGURE 10.1
The Relationship of Different
Bargaining Points in Negotiation.

Your BATNA may change during a negotiation. The other party may make an early offer that is better than the status quo point, but you really want something better. At least now you have something to fall back on that is better than the initial status quo point, so your BATNA has improved some. Still you may be unsatisfied with this option and hope to achieve a better outcome by continuing to negotiate. When this happens, your personal beliefs and skills may make a difference in the negotiation process.[4]

We also need to learn to be more flexible because an important idea behind negotiation is that we should expect to make some concessions. *This is not the same idea as a compromise, where you settle for less than what you truly want to achieve in an agreement. Rather, you may need to set a higher goal than you think possible, knowing that you may need to settle for less in order to obtain what you truly want.* Say your aspiration point is a three-week vacation but your resistance point is one. You should ask for four weeks, so that by agreeing to a three-week vacation you are making a concession. If the other party agrees to three weeks, then you have made a concession but not compromised your aspiration point. Meanwhile, the other party may not offer any vacation at all, so that by agreeing to one week she or he appears to be making a concession. In this case, a compromise may be necessary for the parties to reach an agreement, but a creative or ingenious outcome may still produce an outcome that is better than a compromise. Research indicates that when people set their goals higher, they obtain better results than if they begin with goals closer to their resistance point.[5] Not only do people who set higher goals obtain better results, but those with specific goals do as well. Huber and Neale note:

> . . . if the aspirations of negotiators are too high, too easy, or nonspecific, the likelihood of an integrative win–win solution decreases dramatically. It seems that when goals are easy, negotiators acquiesce and compromise too soon; when goals are difficult, negotiators tenaciously seek high personal profit and subsequently fail to settle at a mutually beneficial level.[6]

You must understand the basic principles of minimax, BATNA, and concessions if you are to engage in successful negotiation. Research demonstrates that engaging in successful negotiation benefits you not only in the present situation but in the future: People who have failed to negotiate a good outcome in past situations are likely to repeat their poor performance in the future, regardless of whether they are dealing with the same person again.[7] Meanwhile, success begets success, so it is important for conflict managers to learn how to be effective negotiators. We take a step in this direction when we learn when to use competitive negotiation and when to be more cooperative.

Competitive Negotiation

Competition often involves tangible issues.

> Competition . . . involves striving for scarce objects (a prize or resource usually "awarded" by a third party) according to established rules which strictly limit what the competitors can do to each other in the course of striving; the chief objective is the scarce object, not the injury or destruction of an opponent per se.[8]

The two different approaches to negotiation are competitive versus cooperative. The **competitive negotiation** pattern is an exchange in which one starts high, concedes slowly, exaggerates the value of one's concessions, conceals information, argues forcefully, and outwaits the other.[9] The competitive negotiator learns as much as possible about the other person's position without giving away her or his own position. Such negotiators believe that they must not show weakness in their positions or offer concessions too soon.[10]

Competitive negotiation often proceeds from a "fixed-pie" outlook; that is, there is an assumption that the outcome is necessarily win–lose, leaving more for one person and less for the other. Going into a negotiation with this outlook frequently results in results that are not integrative or beneficial for all involved.[11] Frequently, those who negotiate from this position wind up underestimating the size of the pie while at the same time focusing on winning the larger slice in the end.[12]

If you decide to adopt this style of negotiation, you should base your decision on the demands of the situation. In cases that do not involve a significant interpersonal relationship, such as buying a car or home from a stranger, we might employ competitive negotiation to achieve the most value for our money. This is why negotiation is often taught in organizational communication courses. Because we sometimes are in situations that necessitate competitive bargaining, we should not simply reject it as a possibility, but choose it purposefully and sparingly as needed.

Cooperative Negotiation

Early in this book, we drew attention to the value we place on our significant interpersonal relationships—family members, romantic partners, close friends, neighbors, and colleagues at work. For these people, we need to shift our attention from competitive bargaining situations to cooperative ones. **Cooperative negotiation** is an integrative form that combines formal bargaining techniques with many skills taught earlier in this book based on basic interpersonal communication skills such as effective listening, assertiveness, supportive communication, and collaboration.

Cooperative negotiation works best when the parties trust each other and the situation is one where mutually satisfactory outcomes are possible, even though the parties may not know that at the outset. One implication is that negotiators should assume that win–win solutions are always possible and work to achieve them because they often do in fact discover mutually satisfying outcomes eventually.

Given the various ways in which bargaining is studied, what findings can help us understand how bargainers reach mutual agreement through integrative behaviors in negotiation situations? Pruitt argues that integrative solutions occur when people are rigid in the goals they are pursuing but flexible in means they adopt for those goals. In cooperative negotiation, the parties' goals are mutual gain, but they are open to a number of ways to achieve a win–win solution, known as **equifinality**. The formal definition of equifinality is that one cannot necessarily predict how something is going to turn out based on the way it started. In addition, Pruitt claims that information exchange leads to integrative agreements only when bargainers believe that the other is truly concerned with both their own needs and the other person's needs.[13]

According to Pruitt and Kimmel, when people think in terms of long-term rather than short-term results, they are likely to cooperate more. This is especially true if those involved understand that they depend on one another, that exploiting one another is not likely to achieve a good outcome, and that cooperating with the other probably generates more cooperation.[14] Further, people who feel good about a previous negotiation experience are more likely to be willing to engage in cooperative negotiations with the same person again.[15]

GENERATING MORE OPTIONS

One of the most important values negotiation brings to the conflict situation is the ability to generate more options, which open more doors for finding mutually satisfactory resolutions. Too often we only see our side of a conflict, while the other party sees only his or her side. Even then we are limiting the conflict situation to only two sides, maybe his and hers. When the issues are tangible, one wins at the other's expense. This either–or view of a conflict is another trained incapacity (see Chapter 4) that limits our options in a conflict. However, if we can introduce more "sides" or alternatives to his or hers, we increase the likelihood of finding a way to satisfy all concerned. In Chapter 4, we introduced you to the idea of creativity, which we defined as the process of making sense of some problem in a new way. We argued that we all have this potential to create something out of nothing. The skills we described are again useful in negotiation: vertical and lateral thinking, mind mapping, and visual journaling. Here are more skills that help generate more options in a conflict.

Brainstorming

Rachel and her husband, Rick, haven't gone to a vacation spot in years. The only place she could think of was a trip to Hawaii, but she knew they couldn't afford to do that. She is bothered by the fact that they aren't having more fun and opportunities to travel. What should she do?

You are probably aware that the first solution that occurs to you is not necessarily the best one. But how do you move beyond your first solution? **Brainstorming** is a process that requires you, the other party, and any one else you can involve in the process to list all possible solutions, irrespective of their initial feasibility. Perhaps you and other classmates engaged in brainstroming as a step toward resolving a problem at school. Not all the options are workable, but when you have examined all the possible solutions you can think of, it is easier to focus on one. Here is what happens to Rachel when she tried brainstorming with her husband.

> I wanted to go somewhere on a vacation but realized that financing it was a problem. I brought up the subject with my husband and said I thought we should just list a lot of places to go to for fun. I told him not to laugh or criticize any of the suggestions and he promised to do the same. I threw out Hawaii and he answered with Alaska. We both laughed, but then he said the Caribbean and I said the Florida Keys, which resulted in our adding other places in the mainland USA including Northern Arizona. We each came up with a number of possibilities when something affordable and fun suddenly occurred that neither of us would have never thought of on our own.

Brainstorming works best when everyone feels free to say whatever comes to mind, even if it sounds ridiculous at the time, because even a bad idea may cause some-one to think of a good one.

Focus on Interests Rather than Positions

Jamie wants to go out, but Ray says he doesn't want to. What should they do? Jamie could get so angry with Ray that she stomps out the door, slamming it behind her, and goes out alone to grab a bite to eat, but is that the best way to resolve this conflict? When conflicting parties focus only on their positions, they often blind themselves to other ways to resolve their conflicts. One way to increase their options is to shift their perspective from their positions to their interests. What is the difference between interests and positions? Think of **positions** as the final part of an I-statement (the goal part of the statement—what you want). Usually one can take only one position. Think of **interests** as needs that are satisfied by a number of different positions because they function at a more abstract or higher level. When a conflict is first identified, it is easier to identify the various positions people have taken than it is to determine the interests each party has in resolving the conflict. To determine the need or interest, we have to ask why the other person is taking a particular position. He says, "I want to buy a pick up truck" (which is his position), and she asks "why?" So he says, "I need it to carry the trash to the dump each week" (which is the need or interest).

It would appear that Jamie and Ray are at a standoff with her wanting to go out and him not wanting to. That is how it all looks if we only consider their positions or wants. However, what happens if we move to a higher level and examine their needs or interests? We may find that Jamie wants to go out to eat *because she is hungry*. Her position is "to go out," but the reason is "she wants to go someplace to eat." Meanwhile, Ray wants to stay home *because he wants to cook and try out a new recipe*. His position is "to not go out," but the reason he wants to stay home is "to try out a new recipe." Their reasons reveal their needs and interests. When their needs or interests become known, Jamie agrees to stay home so that they can eat a meal prepared by Ray (which, it is hoped, can be prepared quickly). She can satisfy her hunger need, and he gets to satisfy his need to try out his new recipe. Both win.

Here are more examples of focusing on interests rather than positions.

> My boyfriend and I are always trying to help each other out. Sometimes, when I need to use his car, he carpools with his friends on the way to work so that I can use his car. I also drop him off at his friend's house so that I can accomplish some tasks instead of the car sitting in a driveway. If I know that he is really busy with something, but still needs to get other tasks done, I take time out from my day to assist him. I do this also because I know he is not the best at multi-tasking.

> When one of my high school friends was planning to visit a mutual friend and me, we looked around for an empty bed he could sleep in, but it seemed as though everyone was staying in town for the weekend. We were about to schedule his visit for another weekend, but it turned out to be OK for him to stay with his cousin's friend. They talked to each other on the phone, the arrangements were made, and a weekend was not wasted.

> Yesterday my friend Kerry wanted to go to town and she needed someone to go with her, but I had to do laundry at my apartment complex. You might have thought that I couldn't go with Kerry. However, we decided that first I would go with her to town and then she would drop by my apartment so I could get my laundry, and I would do it in her dorm. By changing how we were looking at the situation, we both got to do what we wanted to do.

People may change their positions, if you show them other ways to meet their interests or needs. Thus, a good way to resolve win–lose conflicts is to shift from positions (where we want the same object) to interests (where different positions may satisfy both our needs).

Cost Cutting

Maria is planning a vacation with her husband and children, but the price of airline tickets is too much for all four of them to go right away (her kids are 17 and 18). Should she simply give up on the idea because it costs too much, or should she and her family just go, knowing that they cannot pay their bills? We must start by realizing that situations like these are not an either–or situation or win–lose. There are probably other ways to view the situation, and cost cutting can help. In **cost cutting**, one party to a conflict reduces the price of an item so that the other is more easily able to afford it. In the following negotiation example, you can see how one person reduces the price or cost to the other.

> I would like to not give up on the family vacation but I don't want to exceed our budget either. My husband and I decided to leave on Friday night and have the kids fly out on Sunday morning. This solution reduced the overall cost of the vacation. My husband and I also liked the idea that we can have some alone time together. We still got a family vacation, but at a cheaper cost!

In other examples of cost cutting,

> The family of my boyfriend, Scott, was planning a two-week vacation to St. Martin and wanted us both to go with them. I was busy with school and he was overloaded with work. We both really needed to take a vacation, but for financial reasons, Scott couldn't afford to take two weeks' vacation from work. After some discussion, we came up with the idea that I would leave a week early with his family and he would join us the second week. This worked great because I not only got the time to get away, which I really needed, and get to know his family more, but we also had a wonderful time together the second week. He really enjoyed the much-needed vacation, and he didn't have to take the full two weeks from work.

> I was hesitant about renting a particular apartment because I wanted to have a home office but no telephone jack exists in the second bedroom. The landlord settled the deal by installing a more convenient telephone jack, solving my need for the office setup.

Compensation

Andrew's girlfriend, Vannamarie, found a job after graduation and moved to a city 2 hours away. Andrew is still going to college full time for another year before he graduates and finds a full-time job, hopefully in the same city where she is now working and living. The problem is that she isn't getting enough time off to make the trip to his place, and he spends too much money trying to see Vannamarie. Should they see each other less? Should they consider breaking off the relationship because they are finding the distance between them too challenging? There are always options, but we are often blind to them. One option these two young lovers might want to consider is compensation. **Compensation** occurs when Party A provides something of value (often monetary) to Party B to make up for losses caused by A's behavior or that result from A's demands. Vannamarie goes on to say that:

> I would like to continue seeing Andrew, and I know he feels the same way about me. Since I am working and have a larger source of income than Andrew has, I offered to reimburse him for his trips. He can see me without it creating a financial problem back at his college. Of course Andrew liked the idea, too, and is continuing to come see me.

Prioritizing

Megan, Julie, and Bettina are sisters, but Bettina, the oldest, is engaged, getting married this weekend, and moving out of the home she grew up in. She told the family that she would no longer need her room and many toys, games, and stuffed animals now that she was moving on with her life. Megan and Julie, who share a room, immediately got into a fight over who would get what. Should the strongest get everything she wants? Should their mother sell all Bettina's possessions at their next yard sale and use her old bedroom for a guest bedroom?

Different items vary in value for conflicting parties. Some are more important to one person than to the other and vice versa. It is more difficult to bargain over items that are extremely important to one person, while other items may be more easily traded. A good system for working through the distribution of items that vary in value is called prioritizing. **Prioritizing** (sometimes referred to as logrolling) is a process in which each side grants to the other those issues or objects that the other gives top priority. "You can have items one and two on your list if I can have the top two items on my list." Conflicting parties have to want several items (not just one), but only insist on the top priority because of its importance and not insist on the others because they are less important. In the following example, Megan and Julie use prioritizing.

> Each of us made her own list of Bettina's items, ranking them from most wanted to least wanted. We agreed to let each other have the top items on their lists. After that exchange, both went to the next item, and so forth until we found we were both interested in the same items. At least we agreed on the top three items for each of us. After that we didn't care so much, so it was easier to divvy up what was left.

The following are other examples of prioritizing.

> I just wanted to watch a movie (top priority) while crocheting the other day and my housemate really wanted to play cards (top priority) and also liked to listen to music. You cannot listen to music (not his top priority) and watch a movie at the same time. Also, you cannot crochet (not my top priority) and play cards at the same time. Of course we argued about it first with neither of us giving in. We finally realized we were wasting time and getting nowhere so I agreed to play cards with him if we first watched the movie.

> I wanted to help with finishing an installation job on a van, but my fellow worker, Trish, wanted to go to lunch before I did that same day. We discussed the matter and decided that she could help me first with the van and then she could go to lunch early while I would cover for her. Each of us had our main concern dealt with. We gave into the other on something that was low priority for ourselves but high for the other.

Base Decisions on Objective Criteria

Getting back to our case study involving Megan and Julie, after swapping items highest on their list, they now find that there are some of Bettina's possessions they both want but not as much as they did the top three. Some of these may be decided along objective lines. One way is to try to base the decision on **objective criteria,** or guidelines we apply across a variety of situations to ensure fairness. Actually, we do this often in everyday situations when decisions are made on the basis of trade-offs, sharing, and turn-taking. For example:

- It's my turn this time to go first, and you can go first next time.
- Majority rules.
- Let's toss a coin or draw straws to see who gets it.
- He (or she) needs it more than I do.

Megan and Julie could decide to alternate who gets what on the remaining items on the list or flip a coin over some items. Take Bettina's room for example. Maybe Julie is older than Megan and they may agree that the oldest sibling should have first choice. Then Megan can have Julie's room now and probably will get Bettina's room later. Or maybe Julie is further along in her education and needs Bettina's room to better support her studying at home. Or they could simply draw straws, and the winner gets the room. These are common objective criteria we all use on occasion to settle everyday conflicts over scarce resources.

Converting Competitive Negotiation into Cooperation

Separating People from the Problem One of the most important actions we can take in a conflict is to keep our perceptions of the other person separated from our perceptions of the problem or issue. It is easy in a conflict to confuse how we feel about the issue with how we feel about the person involved with it. Because this can work in either positive or negative ways, our like or dislike of a person can cloud our decision-making processes.

An example of focusing on the problem rather than those involved is found in this narrative.

> As a driver of a school bus, I occasionally have conflicts with students, and sometimes these spill over to conflicts with their parents. That is usually when the principal, Mrs. Cummings, who is my boss, gets involved. Recently, parents complained that they felt I had falsely accused their son, Ariel, of misbehaving on the bus. They saw the "referral for misbehaving" as me attacking their child. When the meeting occurred in the principal's office, they immediately began by verbally lashing out at me and questioning my judgment as though I had something personal against their son. Mrs. Cummings really did a good job of separating their son and me (as people) from the problem, which was really Ariel's behavior, which led to conflicts with other children on the bus.

Offering Concessions As we said earlier, we need to offer concessions whenever we engage in negotiation. A person makes a **concession** when he or she grants something highly valued to the other person without asking anything in return, or when he or she drops a demand on the other. Researchers in social psychology suggest that, in general, bargainers who make concessions are more likely to elicit cooperative behavior from the other than are those who make demands or who make no concessions at all.[16]

Seeking Commonalities Your point of view makes a difference. We know, for example, that it is difficult to cooperate and collaborate with others if you start out focusing on what you and the other party most disagree on. That disagreement may produce distrust and competition. If instead you focus on areas of agreement, you are more likely to trust and cooperate, as this narrative demonstrates.

I once had a professor who divided my discussion class into two groups, which he assigned to different classrooms. He then gave each group different instructions, initially. He told one group of students that they would begin by listing their **commonalities**, which could range from physical (all men, all strong, all tall, etc.) to nonphysical items (all communication majors, all enrolled at the same college, all living in town). He told the other group of students to begin by listing their differences. These also could range from physical (mixed group of men and women, differences in eye color, sizes, height, etc.) to nonphysical items (where they were born and went to school, parent's occupations). He then assigned each group to accomplish a task. As it turned out, the group of students that started listing their similarities worked together in a more cooperative manner than did the group that began by discussing their differences.

Why should one group cooperate more than the other? By focusing on what they had in common, the first group saw their task as a cooperative venture. By focusing on how much they differed from one another, the second group was less inclined to cooperate.

Talking Cooperation   Unlike assertiveness that emphasizes one's personal feelings, beliefs, and interests, the **language of cooperation** is "we-based." We are not saying that you abandon your personal goals, but rather recognize that others often want the same as you do. The trick is to recognize those goals you both have in common and draw attention to them. "We both want this." "We both think that." "This is important to all of us." Often what we have in common is obvious: our sex, age, and occupation (dress code). Other commonalities we discover by engaging in discussion with the other person. A useful technique for identifying what we have in common is to proceed tentatively. "What would you say if . . . ." or "Do you think that's a good idea?" By determining what others want and think, you can discover what you have in common. Then draw attention to these commonalities initially and whenever you have an opportunity during the negotiation.

Consulting before Acting   This skill is of paramount importance. **Consulting** means to seek input before taking action. In line with discovering what you both have in common, don't assume that you know what the other wants. Don't assume that you know what is best for the other person. Instead, check your statements to make sure they are right, or even more conservatively, ask what the other person wants before tendering an offer.

Communicating Frequently   As conflicts escalate, you need to fight the desire to shut down communication. Conflicting parties can become entrenched in their positions, and conclude that since they are at an impasse, they should say nothing more. Although communication is not a magic cure-all for conflict, frequent and nonhostile communication keeps those in the conflict from making too many unchallenged assumptions about the other. Recall our definition of transactional communication, which suggests working with others rather than trying to always dominate, avoid, or give in to others.

Controlling the Process, Not the Outcome Viewed as a process, negotiation shares features with other processes. For example, by first agreeing to the ground rules in the election process, we can guarantee a fair outcome, but we still don't know who is going to be elected. We can have a similar approach in the negotiation process. By initially agreeing on procedures, steps, and goals, which are ways to **control the process**, the conflicting parties can create the conditions for a fair and honest problem-solving discussion, but they can't predict the outcome with certainty. They have to have *faith* that creating a cooperative negotiation process should produce a mutually satisfying outcome.

Thinking Positively People often resemble the characters in the children's book *Winnie the Pooh*. Some people are Rabbits, compulsive about everything, wanting to control all events. Others are like Piglet, worried that the sky might fall in. Some are happy-go-lucky Poohs. They are content to take life as it comes, which is a way to **think positively**.

In contrast, there are the Eeyores. They're pretty easy to recognize. They make comments like "I wasn't invited to the party, but I wouldn't have had fun anyway." Eeyores are not positive people, and their pessimism can really make it difficult for others to believe that they are making progress. Eeyores are the ones who shoot down all the solutions during a brainstorming session (dooming it to failure), who don't believe the parties can create any objective criteria to judge solutions to a problem, and who don't think any mutual interests exist when people are in conflict.

Moods indeed do have an effect on our bargaining and negotiation outcomes; people who have felt unsuccessful in the past tend to approach future tasks pessimistically, and subsequently do worse than those taking a positive approach.[17] A positive mood is related to higher levels of cooperation and less competition in negotiation situations. On the other hand, negative moods tended to trigger higher levels of competition and led to lower outcomes in negotiation situations.[18] Anger, in particular, may seem like a good negotiating tactic in movies or television shows, but studies indicate that it can backfire in real life negotiating situations, resulting in worse outcomes than if anger were not communicated.[19] You are rarely likely to benefit from communicating anger unless you clearly have more power than the other person in the negotiation.[20] Other emotions such as guilt and disappointment can affect bargaining outcomes as well—if you project guilt while bargaining, you will probably wind up with worse outcomes than if you project disappointment over the process.[21] So, beware of self-fulfilling prophecies! Don't become an Eeyore!

Engaging in Fractionation People in conflict may also engage in fractionation in order to work through the problem.[22] **Fractionation** is a matter of breaking the problem down into its smallest pieces, and then dealing with each piece one at a time. It is usually easier to get cooperation from others on small tasks than on much larger ones. Fractionation enables the conflicting parties to cooperate on something small and more manageable before moving on to other issues. This account shows how fractionation helped solve the problem of repairing a house.

We bought a lovely little house in a great location. Unfortunately, despite its great layout and look, it needed a lot of work. I would have rather done all the remodeling at once—preferably before we moved in! That simply wasn't possible. So, we finished out the garage so my son could use it as a bedroom and we fixed the fence to keep the dogs in. We repaired the roof before winter rains came, and painted the house because it made sense to do it at the same time. Inside issues have taken much longer. Inside we made replacing the windows the first priority. After that we moved to refinishing the wood floors and replacing the old linoleum with tile. It will take about five years to get it all done, but it's a lot easier to handle one task at a time.

In this chapter, we have focused on ways of addressing conflicts over tangible resources that appear to be win–lose. Successful resolution of these conflicts depends on our ability to assess the situation and decide how important it is to achieve our initial goal in the situation. Situations occur when we decide to back off the conflict, giving more importance to the relationship. At other times, we need to argue more forcefully. In most cases, though, finding a solution is a matter of learning how to "color outside the lines."

MANAGE IT

The type of conflict issue makes a difference in conflict management. Some conflicts are over intangible issues, which are emotional, mental, and psychological assets, and are not limited by nature. Consequently, such issues are often resolved through interpersonal communication. In contrast, tangible resources are physical and observable. Because tangible resources are often scarce, conflicts involving such issues take more than basic interpersonal communication skills to resolve; they must be negotiated. Negotiation is defined as a particular type of conflict management—one characterized by an exchange of proposals and counter proposals as a means of reaching a satisfactory settlement.

When confronted with a conflict over a tangible resource, skilled negotiators follow the minimax principle to minimize their losses and maximize their gains. They start bargaining at a point above their aspiration level but also have a resistance point in mind. While negotiating, a skilled conflict manager considers her or his BATNA (which initially is the status quo point) as a standard by which to measure the value of offers from others. One implication of this idea is that one should expect to make some concessions, so it pays to set a goal higher than one thinks possible to attain. Negotiators who make concessions are more likely to elicit cooperative behavior from the other party than are those who make no concessions at all.

Negotiators must distinguish competitive situations from cooperative ones. For example, when buying products from strangers, competitive negotiation is an exchange in which one starts high, concedes slowly, exaggerates the value of one's concessions, conceals information, argues forcefully, and outwaits the other. However, when negotiating with family, friends, romantic partners, and work colleagues, it is best to see the situation as cooperative. Cooperative negotiation is an integrative form that combines formal bargaining techniques with many skills taught earlier in this book based on basic interpersonal communication skills such as effective listening, assertiveness, supportive communication, and collaboration. In these cases, skilled conflict managers strive for a win–win outcome. Such outcomes are more likely to occur when the parties trust each other and the situation is one in which mutually satisfactory outcomes are possible, even though the parties may not know that at the outset.

Whether we approach a conflict from a minimax principle or a win–win orientation, it is important for the conflicting parties to expand the solutions (or generate more options) to the problem by brainstorming, focusing on the interests of the people involved rather than on their articulated positions, cutting costs for the other party, compensating, prioritizing, and trying to agree ahead of time on objective criteria.

How do effective conflict managers employ additional means to convert a potentially competitive conflict into a cooperative one? They do this by separating people from the problem, making concessions, seeking commonalities, talking cooperation, consulting before acting, communicating frequently, controlling the process (not the outcome), thinking positively, and engaging in fractionation. In the next chapter, we explain the mediation process to further our understanding of ways to convert potentially adversarial positions into more cooperative ventures that produce mutually satisfying outcomes.

EXERCISES

THINK ABOUT IT

1. When does the urge to compete affect your relationships? How do you make sure that both you and the other person understand that the competition is meant to be "friendly"?
2. In which common situations would you most likely resort to competitive negotiation? In which for cooperative negotiation?
3. Can you list some situations in which a different objective criterion is applicable? For example, list one that involves "majority rules" and others that involve other generally accepted standards.
4. Can you think of examples where people either focused on the other person or tried to deal with the problem or issue instead? Discuss the outcomes.

APPLY IT

1. Take a sheet of paper and make six columns on it. Label the columns mere disagreements, overblown conflicts, competition, verbally abusive conflicts, and physically abusive conflicts. In each column, identify a conflict you experienced or witnessed that took one of these forms. Your description should answer:

    What was the conflict about?
    Why did you think there was a conflict?
    How did you resolve the conflict?

2. Write out examples of times you have used cost cutting, compensation, and logrolling in scarce resource conflicts. What clearly distinguishes each example as one type or the other?

WORK WITH IT

1. Read the following case study and answer the questions that follow it.

   Last week I met with a colleague, the Division Chief for Right of Way (I am Division Chief of Planning), to discuss our mutual need to staff a receptionist position on the eighth floor of a new office building we will occupy beginning next month. She will have about 80 employees working on this floor, while my staff will total around 40.

   For security and customer service reasons we need to place a receptionist at a cubicle opposite the elevator where visitors can be greeted, screened, and directed as they enter the floor. We do not currently have this problem in our existing building as the organization has a guard hired to check visitors in and out of the only public entrance to the building.

   Since the Right of Way Division has twice the number of employees and many more visitors than we do in Planning, I attempted to convince her to agree to staff the position out of her budget. I have had some previous history negotiating with this Division Chief and have found her difficult to work with. This meeting was no exception. I tried to convince her that equity demanded she pay for the position or at least two-thirds of the costs. She refused, arguing that I should bear the entire cost because her budget had been reduced this fiscal year.

   After posturing for some time, it was clear that she was not going to budge in her negotiating position. I had more important issues on my plate that day and also I did not want to take this issue to our mutual boss, the District Director, to resolve. In light of this, I proposed that we split the costs 50–50, which she agreed to almost immediately. The problem I have is that this really is not a fair decision for my division and is another example of where I should have been more aggressive in sticking to my position, instead of looking for resolution through a compromise.

   a. To what extent did the parties apply the four principles of negotiation (people, interests, etc.)? If not, how could they?
   b. Did the parties use any of the four ways to generate more options (prioritizing, bridging, etc.)? If not, how could they?
   c. Did the parties incorporate any of the recommendations for converting competitive negotiation to cooperation (talking cooperation, fractionation, etc.)? If not, how could they?

2. Recall a recent conflict you observed or experienced that concerned a tangible issue or problem that is a scarce resource (not enough time together or money, a single object or place you can't share, etc.). The conflict should be one that you resolved or have managed for the time being. Write a short description of the conflict, and then analyze it by answering the following questions.

   a. How did you apply the four principles of negotiation (people, interests, etc.)?
   b. How did you use one or more of the four ways to generate more options (prioritizing, bridging, etc.)?
   c. How did you incorporate the recommendations for converting competitive negotiation to cooperation (talking cooperation, fractionation, etc.)?

DISCUSS IT

Read the following conflict narrative and the instructions that follow it.

My sister allows her 13-year-old daughter, Leanne, to publish a blog as an online journal. She did not know what Leanne was writing about online until she started receiving long distance telephone calls from older men asking for her by name. Both my sister and her daughter complain to me about the other. My sister tells me that she would like to start reading Leanne's blog daily and would like to delete any content that she finds inappropriate. Leanne tells me that her blog is like a diary, and she doesn't want her mother to read it. Both are upset with each other.

As a way to apply the concepts you learned from this chapter, read the above case study and participate in a class discussion by posting an answer to one of the questions below.

1. In your own words, explain the concept of mediation and demonstrate the role a mediator plays in conflict management. In the given scenario, evaluate and discuss whether a third party should intervene. Explain your response.

2. Would you need a mediator in a family situation, as described above? Please explain your answer in the context of what you read in the textbook.

3. List and describe each step in mediation. How would each of these steps apply to the above scenario?

4. When might you use mediation in a family conflict? Please explain your answer.

NEGOTIATION CLASS EXERCISE: "LET'S GET DOWN TO BUSINESS"

OBJECTIVE:

The objective of this exercise is to give students an opportunity to apply principles of cooperative negotiation over tangible issues. The following case involves a negotiation between a company's management team and representatives of the workers union over wages, benefits, and workload. Another negotiation such as buying/selling a house or a commercial negotiation game may be substituted for the following case.

TIME: 5 CLASS PERIODS

INSTRUCTIONS:

Step 1 (1st hour): If time permits, using brainstorming, the class creates a negotiation scenario (otherwise a prepared scenario may be provided for this part of the exercise). With one person agreeing to keep notes, members of the class make suggestions that lead to the description of a company in which the class is to be employed. What does it make? How much does a unit (of the product) sell for? How much does it cost to produce and what is the profit per unit? How many units are produced and sold (targets) per year? What are the different jobs needed for production? How many workers and how many managers (supervisors, bosses, and owners)? Where will the company be located? What is the company name? For the sake of discussion, assume that workers have been receiving minimum wage for a 48-hour-work week, while managers earn three times that (the status quo). Other relevant questions? Follow the suggestions for brainstorming presented in the chapter. (Note that brainstorming requires you to list all possible solutions without any negative comments because even a bad idea may cause someone to think of a good idea.)

Step 2: Divide the class into two groups: management and workers. Three students are selected as observers/judges, who are to complete Form 2 during and near the end of the negotiation. The observers/judges are not to be considered on one side or the other.

Step 3 (2nd hour): In an area where they cannot be overheard by the other group, each side discusses and agrees on answers to Form 1. (Each group should consider the issues listed below in step #5, which should be prioritized in order of importance.)

Step 4: If there are more than three persons in each group, have each group elect representatives so that there are three on each side: A management team of three and three representatives of the worker's union. Each team elects a leader and someone to take notes on areas of agreement and disparity. The rest of the workers and managers sit where they can observe the negotiation.

Step 5 (3rd and 4th hours): Each side negotiates the following issues, using principles and techniques discussed in the reading:

> *Work load* issues (i.e., the workers shifts, hours of operation).
> The workers and managers *pay, salary* issues (keeping in mind the company's annual revenue)
> *Benefits:* Medical care as percentage of pay/salary, breaks, lunch, holidays off.
> *Other relevant issues?*

Step 6: During the negotiation, breaks are scheduled so that the representatives can return to their side of the room to confer with the rest of their group before continuing the negotiation.

Step 7: The negotiation continues until a tentative agreement is reached, at which time it is voted on by the respective group members before it is finalized. If agreement is not reached, the negotiation may end because it has run out of time.

Step 8 (5th hour): The three observers/judges complete their Form 2 and report their observations and judgments to the class. The class discusses the negotiation. The class may discuss feelings they experienced at different times during the negotiation and point out specific behaviors that helped or hindered the negotiation.

Form 1: Negotiation Plan

Instructions: In separate rooms, each negotiation team prepares one form: Place your response next to or immediately below the question; single space responses and double space between questions.

Your Group's Name/Title (management/workers union) _____
1. List issues across a sheet of paper: 1. Wages, 2. Benefits, 3. Workload
2. Down the sheet under each issue, list your goals (pay, specific benefits, and number of hours/days/work schedule).
3. Under each goal, indicate your aspiration point and your opening/target/position on each issue.
4. Under each goal, indicate your resistance point.
5. List BATNA.
6. Indicate your interests/needs.
7. Prioritize the issues (see item #1) from most to least important.

Form 2: Observer's/Judges Negotiation Observation

Negotiation Title_____
Your Name _____
Date _____
1. On what issues did both sides agree? What issues did they disagree on?
2. What behaviors led to agreement on each issue? What strategies worked well?
3. What behaviors led to disagreements on some issues? What strategies did not work well?
4. Who/what side was in a more reactive or defensive position? Why?

NOTES

1. Laura J. Kray and Michael P. Haselhuhn, "Implicit Negotiation Beliefs and Performance: Experimental and Longitudinal Evidence," *Journal of Personality and Social Psychology* 93 (2007), 49–64.

2. Linda L. Putnam, "Bargaining as Organizational Communication," in Robert D. McPhee and Phillip K. Tompkins (Eds.), *Organizational Communication: Traditional Themes and New Directions* (Newbury Park, CA: Sage, 1985), p. 129.

3. Roger Fisher and William Ury, *Getting to Yes: Negotiating Agreement without Giving In* (Boston, MA: Houghton Mifflin, 1981), p. 104.

4. Peter H. Kim and Alison R. Fragale, "Choosing the Path to Bargaining Power: An Empirical Comparison of BATNAs and Contributions in Negotiation," *Journal of Applied Psychology* 90 (2005), 373–381.

5. William A. Cohen, "The Importance of Expectations on Negotiation Results," *European Business Review* 15 (2003), 87–93.

6. Vandra L. Huber and Margaret A. Neale, "Effects of Self-and Competitor Goals on Performance in an Interdependent Bargaining Task," *Journal of Applied Psychology* 72 (1987), 203, 197–203.

7. Kathleen M. O'Connor, Josh A. Arnold, and Ethan R. Burris, "Negotiators' Bargaining Histories and Their Effects on Future Negotiation Performance," *Journal of Applied Psychology* 90 (2005), 350–362.

8. Raymond W. Mack and Richard C. Snyder, "The Analysis of Social Conflict: Toward an Overview and Synthesis," in Fred E. Jandt (Ed.), *Conflict Resolution through Communication* (New York: Harper and Row, 1973), p. 34.

9. David A. Lax and James K. Sebenius, *The Manager as Negotiator* (New York: Free Press, 1986), p. 32.

10. James A. Wall, *Negotiation: Theory and Practice* (Glenview, IL: Scott Foresman, 1985).

11. Carsten K. W. de Dreu, Sander L. Koole, and Wolfgang Steinel, "Unfixing the Fixed Pie: A Motivated Information-Processing Approach to Integrative Negotiation," *Journal of Personality and Social Psychology* 79 (2000), 975–987.

12. Richard P. Larrick and George Wu, "Claiming a Large Slice of a Small Pie: Assymmetric Disconfirmation in Negotiation," *Journal of Personality and Social Psychology* 93 (2007), 212–233.

13. Dean G. Pruitt, *Negotiation Behavior* (New York: Academic Press, 1981).

14. Dean G. Pruitt and Melvin J. Kimmel, "Twenty Years of Experimental Gaming: Critique, Synthesis and Suggestions for the Future," *Annual Review of Psychology* 28 (1977), 363–392.

15. Jared R. Curhan, Hillary Anger Elfebein, and Heng Xu, "What Do People Value When They Negotiate? Mapping the Domain of Subjective Value in Negotiation," *Journal of Personality and Social Psychology* 91 (2006), 493–512.

16. Edwin Bixenstine and Kellogg V. Wilson, "Effects of Level of Cooperative Choice by the Other Player in a Prisoner's Dilemma Game," *Journal of Abnormal and Social Psychology* 67 (1963), 139–147; see also Marc Pilisuk and Paul Skolnick, "Inducing Trust: A Test of the Osgood Proposal," *Journal of Experimental Social Psychology* 11 (1968), 53–63; Gerald Marwell, David Schmitt, and Bjorn Boyesen, "Pacifist Strategy and Cooperation under Interpersonal Risk," *Journal of Personality and Social Psychology* 28 (1973), 12–20.

17. O'Connor, Arnold, and Burris, "Negotiators' Bargaining Histories and Their Effects on Future Negotiation Performance." *Journal of Applied Psychology* 90 (2005), 350–362.

18. Joseph P. Forgas, "On Feeling Good and Getting Your Way: Mood Effects on Negotiator Cognition and Bargaining Strategies," *Journal of Personality and Social Psychology* 74 (1998), 565–577.

19. Eric van Dijk, Gerben A. van Kleef, Wolfgang Steinel, and Ilja van Beest, "A Social Functional Approach to Emotions in Bargaining: When Communicating Anger Pays and When it Backfires," *Journal of Personality and Social Psychology* 94 (2008), 600–614.

20. Gerben A. Van Kleef, Carsten K. W. De Dreu, and Antony S. R. Manstead, "The Interpersonal Effects of Emotions in Negotiations: A Motivated Information Processing Approach," *Journal of Personality and Social Psychology* 87 (2004), 510–528.

21. Gerben A. Van Kleef, Carsten K. W. De Dreu, and Antony S. R. Manstead, "Supplication and Appeasement in Conflict and Negotiation: The Interpersonal Effects of Disappointment, Worry, Guilt, and Regret," *Journal of Personality and Social Psychology* 91 (2006), 124–142; Gerben A. Van Kleef, Carsten K. W. De Dreu, and Antony S. R. Manstead, "The Interpersonal Effects of Anger and Happiness in Negotiations," *Journal of Personality and Social Psychology* 86 (2004), 57–76.

22. Frank Tutzauer and Michael Roloff, "Communication Processes Leading to Integrative Agreements: Three Paths to Joint Benefits," *Communication Research* 15 (1988), 360–380.

Managing Others' Disputes through Mediation

OBJECTIVES

At the end of this chapter, you should be able to:

- Describe the difference between formal and informal mediation.
- Define mediation and contrast it with the other ADRs.

- Explain when a third party should intervene as a mediator.
- Describe the role of the mediator.
- List and describe the steps of mediation.

KEY TERMS

adjudication
ADRs
arbitration
behavioral commitments
caucus
co-mediating
common ground

conciliation
confidentiality
dispute
facilitate
framing
intake
mediation

mediator
neutral
ombudsperson
opening statement
open minded
reframing
rules

An older student, who is a father, wrote:

My oldest son is a person that never backs down from an argument. I am not saying he goes looking for a fight but, if he feels he is right, he never gives in. Unfortunately some of his friends are the same way so there have been many times that loud shouting matches have broken out between them. Once in a while it gets a little too heated and I want to get involved. I separate them on opposite sides of a table and ask them to tell me the story from all points of view without anyone interrupting until each side has had their say. Most often, they see how the other person is interpreting the problem, and they come to an agreement without any help from me.

The narrator says, "without any help from me," but is that true? He recognized an opportunity to act as a third party, stepped in, and caused the two conflicting parties to sit down and discuss the matter. He asked them to explain their points of view and stopped them from interrupting each other. The father probably engaged in other helpful third-party behaviors, more subtle or not reported here. However, he seems to have grasped some basic moves that facilitate mediation as a peaceful means for resolving a conflict.

Till now, we have concentrated on those concepts, principles, and skills that are most useful when you personally are involved in a conflict with someone you know. You can apply what you have learned so far to better manage or resolve the conflicts you yourself are having with others.

This chapter is different in that it focuses on what you need to know to help others who are having a conflict. Perhaps they invite you as a third party to intervene on their behalf. The nature of the conflict is different because it is one that the conflicting parties cannot handle by themselves. They need the help of a third party—a role you can perform after you study the topic of mediation.

In this chapter, we apply the principles taught in formal mediation training to the management of conflicts in informal or everyday settings. Basic information is provided on mediation concepts, skills, steps, and techniques, so that you can help your friends, family, and co-workers resolve their interpersonal conflicts. However, if you want to practice mediation on a more formal basis, you need certification, which means mediation training by an approved university program or state agency. For our purposes, you need to learn how to explain the alternatives to dispute resolution, define mediation and dispute, describe the role of the mediators, explain when it is useful to include mediators in conflict situations, explain the advantages and limitations of mediation, and effectively perform the steps you would take to mediate an informal dispute. At the end of this chapter, a mediation exercise is provided to practice the principles and techniques taught in this chapter. We begin first with an overview of the dispute resolution process in which mediation is one alternative.

THE NEED FOR MEDIATION

Dispute Defined

As will be shown shortly, mediation is one alternative to what is called dispute resolution. In fact, you cannot fully appreciate the idea of mediation without first understanding the concept of a dispute and the alternatives that exist for dealing with one. A **dispute** is defined as "a conflict that has reached a point where the parties are unable to resolve the issue by themselves due to a breakdown in communication, and normal relations are unlikely until the dispute is resolved."[1] Not all conflicts are alike. Conflicts become disputes when participants experience a communication barrier, preventing normal relations. The parties seek help from a third party because they cannot resolve the issues by themselves.

Alternatives to Dispute Resolution

When a dispute occurs, the conflicting parties sometimes resort to violent means to resolve it. Our prisons are full of people who took "justice" into their own hands by taking violent action against someone with whom they disagreed. For those who use their heads instead of their fists and guns, the following alternatives to dispute resolution (**ADRs**) exist:

- *Arbitration:* a neutral third party considers both sides of a dispute and makes a decision, which is more binding than that of a judge in the legal system if both parties have agreed in advance to abide by the decision (no appeal).
- *Adjudication:* a neutral judge and jury in the legal system hear attorneys who prosecute or defend people and decide a case, which either party may later appeal.
- *Ombudsperson:* one who cuts through the red tape on behalf of individuals who feel abused by the larger system (often governmental agencies) in which they work, study, or seek support.
- *Conciliation:* a neutral third-party practices "shuttle diplomacy" by traveling back and forth between conflicting parties who are unable to meet together for any one of a variety of reasons.
- *Mediation:* a neutral third party facilitates communication between the conflicting parties so that they may work out their own mutually acceptable agreement.

The Value of Mediation

While alternatives exist, we are focusing on mediation in this chapter because many studies have found that mediation produces superior results to adjudication.[2] It is less costly than other ADRs. Mediation conducted well reduces the likelihood that either of the disputants will seek legal remedy. Most importantly, it also has unique advantages that appeal to communication scholars:

1. Mediation restores communication and helps to normalize relations.
2. Mediation allows for full participation by the conflicting parties.
3. Mediation has a high success rate. It is estimated that "once the disputants have agreed to mediate, at least 80% of the time they are able to work out an agreement that is acceptable to both of them."[3]

FORMAL VERSUS INFORMAL MEDIATION

As it turns out there are cultural differences in mediation[4] and several different approaches to mediation, each with its own set of techniques, but the approach advocated here does not require the mediators to take sides, engage in psychotherapy, or play the role of advocate. Rather, mediators are viewed here as unbiased facilitators of communication between the parties in a private setting. In many formal settings where it is normally more satisfying, cheaper, and faster than litigation, this form of mediation has become a popular alternative. In such formal settings, one party typically calls a local mediation center for a mediation, and a first meeting between the parties and mediators usually occurs within the next few days or weeks. In any case, community and school mediations are often free or offered on a sliding scale that is cheaper than lawyers' fees.

In formal mediations, satisfactory agreements are often worked out at a single mediation session lasting one to three hours, although complex cases such as divorce settlements involving child custody may require weekly sessions until all the details are worked out. Disputing parties report that they are often more satisfied with mediated agreements than others who rely on the courtroom decisions of judges and juries and are more likely to comply with mediated agreements than they are to court orders because they have more control in the resolution of their dispute.

There are formal programs that train and certify mediators. Community and campus dispute resolution centers offer mediation for a wide range of conflicts including noisy neighbors, sexual and racial harassment, minor assault, breach of contract, landlord–tenant and buyer–seller disputes, small claims, bad checks, trespassing, and a variety of interpersonal issues such as gossip and rumors, misunderstandings, friendship issues, and post-breakup disputes. Although experience has shown that it is beneficial, mediation is still relatively unused in union labor disputes.[5] Mediation is a method of parental intervention in children's disputes.[6] Rapidly becoming a popular alternative to the courts,[7] divorce mediation is a branch of family mediation that deals with issues associated with child custody, visitation, child financial support, and the redistribution of marital property. Today, divorce mediation training is offered to workers from a wide variety of occupations, including family law attorneys[8] and family counselors and therapists.[9] However, communication among the mediator and disputants lies at the basis of all these mediation training programs. Before one can deal with child custody, emotional issues associated with divorce, the children's interests, or dispose of marital property, the mediator must create a communication climate that is conductive to a mutually satisfactory settlement. This can be particularly difficult with parents who use children as a bargaining chip in divorce proceedings.[10] Among experts in mediation, there is a concern with the growing number of lawyers involved in mediation processes. They note:

> . . . some lawyers are approaching mediation in the same way as litigation, by using adversarial techniques within the process. If the parties relinquish their autonomy in choosing the way mediation is conducted, then. . . . [m]ediation may in the long term not provide a "true" alternative to litigation . . . introduction of procedural conventions, increasing adversarial conduct and rising mediation costs are, perhaps, an inevitable downside of evaluative mediator practice as, parties select leading lawyer-mediators.[11]

For those who have gone through formal training, it is clear that mediation offers a practical application of many skills taught in undergraduate interpersonal communication and conflict management courses. In the following sections, we apply the formal mediation process to the management of everyday conflicts. First, we focus specifically on the role of the mediator.

THE ROLE OF THE MEDIATOR

The **mediator** is defined as a neutral third party who has no decision-making power regarding the outcome of the mediation. Some mediations have two people who serve as co-mediators. While the role of mediator may be performed by one person, there are advantages in **co-mediating** and sharing the duties with someone. A male might want a female co-mediator because one or both conflicting parties are female. A mediator might want a co-mediator of a different age, race, or religion because of the nature of the conflict and the fact that the parties differ greatly in age, race, or religion. A faculty member may want a co-mediator who is a student because one or both conflicting parties are students, and so on.

Although it may seem as though the mediator plays only a minor role, the mere introduction of a third person converts a private affair into a more public setting. Compared to private conflicts that tend to occur in the privacy of one's own home or involve only the partners themselves, mediation brings conflict to a social, public, and cultural level. The Chinese refer to this phenomenon as "the principle of three."[12] From the Chinese perspective, a culture of two is not a public affair and encourages a win–lose situation when two individuals engage in conflict. However, in a culture of three, the third party is there to remind the disputants that their behaviors are being viewed by others, thus bringing the behavior under social control and increasing the likelihood of social justice. The mere presence of mediators enables them to encourage cooperation rather than competition, strive for reasonable decisions that meet social concerns, and create and enforce rules to guide the interaction.

In informal situations, people can help others without formal training and certification. Thus, everyone can benefit from receiving training that is available to the general public and is similar to that required for certification. The focus on mediators' attitudes, skills, and knowledge can form a basis for orienting third parties to their role as mediator. Basically, mediators attempt to create a nonthreatening and constructive environment to encourage the disputants to communicate, cooperate, and work out their own mutually satisfying solution.

Mediator Skills

Who should take the role of the "third person" and function as the mediator? In the view that dominates mediation, mediators are expected to be **neutral**. This means that mediators are *unbiased, and there is no reason for them to take one party's side against the other*. In formal or informal cases, it is not a good idea to mediate if the prospective mediator is related to one of the disputants, is a friend, or knows one party better than the other. Mediators must also make every effort to demonstrate their neutrality by equalizing the speaking time, giving the same amount of time and attention to both parties, and not spending time alone with one of the parties without spending the same amount of time with the other during the mediation. Certainly, mediators are not to take sides in the dispute.

First, not only should the mediator not have a personal connection to either disputant, but she or he should also make an effort to suspend judgment during the negotiation. According to the Center for Mediation and Law at Harvard Law School, the mediator should develop a "subjective neutrality," in which he or she honors the validity and truth of each person's story without deciding who is right or wrong.[13] Letting go of one's personal biases is a challenge but essential for effective mediating.

Second, because mediation offers the disputants an opportunity to openly talk to each other about their feelings, needs, goals, and reasons for behaving as they do, mediators must maintain **confidentiality**. *They are not to make public*

the names of the conflicting parties, disclose the words spoken during the media-
tion, or retain notes after terminating mediation. In formal cases, trained mediators learn rules that cover a few legal exceptions that they include in their opening
remarks and make explicit on the mediation consent form, which is signed by both
parties before they make their opening statements. In informal settings, mediators
can simply state in their opening remarks that the mediation is considered confidential and ask the parties if they can agree to keep what is said "among us." It is
this guarantee of confidentiality that makes self-disclosure possible in mediation.

Third, the mediators are competent in communication. In your role as mediator, you must manifest these effective communication behaviors:

- Be descriptive rather than judgmental. For example, you might say, "It seems
  like you are raising your voice," rather than "It sounds like you are angry."
- Be specific. For example, "You have mentioned how bothered you are by
  your colleague's work habits. What specific habit bothers you the most?"
- Focus on behaviors that one can change.
- Give feedback when it is requested.
- Give timely feedback making it as close as possible to the behavior being
  discussed.
- Speak only for yourself. ("I understand you to say . . .", "I take it that
  you feel . . .", "I want you both to . . .", "I prefer to keep my opinions to
  myself.")
- Check what you see or hear with the other parties.[14]

Fourth, mediators are trained to **facilitate** communication by encouraging
cooperation and discouraging competition between the parties.[15] Essentially, a
mediator's objective is to create a safe and constructive environment for the parties
to discuss emotional and substantive issues and reach agreement. The process of
mediation is successful to the extent that it moves from a competitive to a cooperative orientation because competition creates a defensive communication climate
and cooperation creates a supportive atmosphere (see Chapter 6). Competitive
communication is self-promoting because it serves as a vehicle through which
individuals attempt to distort the other's perceptions of the situation in order to
obtain an advantage. A cooperative orientation consists of behaviors characteristic
of organized action (e.g., working together) and a thought process known as consensus (e.g., shared understanding, actual agreement). It also facilitates attempts to
discover areas of common interest regarding issues.

Fifth, mediators are **open minded**. They accept and support whatever resolution the parties agree to because mediators have no decision-making power with
respect to the outcome of the mediation. Initially, the conflicting parties often
expect mediators to solve their problems. Mediators must resist the temptation
to function like a judge or jury and need to inform the parties that they have
no authoritative decision-making power.[16] However, because many disputants
who enter mediation have found it difficult to communicate, relate, or work with
each other in the past, mediators instruct the conflicting parties in constructive
communication by announcing and enforcing communication rules. This topic is
described in detail in the next section.

We just described the role of the mediator. To understand how mediators gain
control over the mediation process to produce mutually satisfying outcomes, we

need to examine in detail a particular approach to mediation known as the rules or structural approach and the mediator's responsibility as a communication rules enforcer.

Mediators as Communication Rules Enforcers

To appreciate the idea that mediators primarily control the communication process to give them greater influence over the outcome of the interaction, one must understand how mediators create and enforce communication rules. Mediators are trained to create and enforce rules to give the conflicting parties greater control over the outcome of the interaction. **Rules** are obligations (they tell us what we must say, what we should say) and prohibitions (they tell us what we had better not say in certain situations). Many of the rules we abide by were learned through our families and other important people in our lives; for example, many of us learned that "If you can't say something nice, don't say anything at all" (which may be a reason so many people dislike conflict). At other times, we know that a rule exists because when we have broken it, we face some sort of sanction. For example, at a friend's wedding, it is customary to congratulate the groom and convey best wishes to the bride. Saying "congratulations" to the bride is considered in poor taste, and if you do so, others may give you a disapproving look. The rule is there, but it is not a strong one because so many people forget and can ignore the disapproving stares from others. On the other hand, laughing at a funeral is almost unheard of. It is prohibited, and anyone who breaks the rule is quickly escorted out of the room. This rule explains why there isn't more laughing at funerals.

Thus, a pattern of behavior is rule-governed when there exists mutual expectations or a consensus regarding what is appropriate behavior in a given situation. Although rules are social conventions, which are violated or changed by individuals or groups, it is argued that when people know the rules, they tend to conform to them. Mediation is viewed as a structured social activity guided and defined by rules designed to convert competitive orientations and actions into cooperative ones.

In their opening statements, mediators lay down the communication rules for the mediation. During the mediation process, the mediators are committed to the following:

- They enforce communication rules.
- They steer the disputants through the steps of mediation.
- They manage the tone of the discussion.
- They ask disputants to cease discussing some topics and stay focused on issues.

It is no accident that even early practice in formal divorce mediation was based on a rules approach.[17] As communication rules enforcers, mediators establish and enforce the rules by which participants interact. Some common rules that are useful for directing the communication process toward positive outcomes are as follows:

- taking turns to talk without interruptions
- talking without expressing hostility to one another
- creating a positive climate with no put-downs
- focusing on the future (what the parties will do) rather than the past (what was done)

- striving for a win–win solution with no one feeling dissatisfied or agreeing to something unacceptable
- striving to solve the problem rather than attacking or blaming the other person
- being honest and sharing your thoughts and feelings without fear of criticism or publicity
- adhering to time constraints set by mediator
- agreeing to abide by additional rules as announced by the mediators during the session

You have learned about the role of mediators. Anxious to delve into an actual mediation? You first need to study the steps mediators take from the beginning to the end of the mediation.

THE MEDIATION PROCESS: STEP BY STEP

In an effort to pull together much of the advice and principles of mediation, we have devised a list of steps that are common to mediating both (1) formal disputes conducted by certified mediators in divorce, community, or organizational settings and (2) informal disputes conducted by noncertified (but trained) third parties in family, friendship, or workplace settings. Once the conflicting parties realize that a dispute exists, the following steps are taken:

- One or both disputants seek mediation, or a mediator talks them into it (the intake process).
- The mediator brings the disputants together, provides a list of rules that govern the mediation, and makes an opening statement.
- Following the mediator's opening statement, each person is asked to take a few minutes to describe the dispute from his or her point of view without interruption.
- The mediator finds common ground on which to build agreement.
- The mediator writes up the final agreement.
- The mediator ends the mediation.

In the rest of this chapter, we explain and illustrate these steps in detail. Let us begin with the fact that the conflicting parties realize that a dispute exists. This is to say that they are at a point where they realize that they cannot manage the conflict without help. They initiate the mediation process by taking the first step, which means requesting that someone take the role of third party and mediate their conflict.

Intake

In formal mediation, the preliminary phase in which the parties seek help from a third person who decides to intervene is called **intake**. While informal mediations are often less methodical and sometimes seem quite chaotic initially, the parties eventually end up with someone who agrees to help them resolve the dispute. They may engage in "intake" without calling it that.

The decision to include a third party to mediate the conflict is an important one and involves the realization that such a person is necessary and that the parties must pick an appropriate person for the role. Both disputants may seek help from a third person, who becomes the mediator. If only one seeks help, the third person may contact the other disputant to see if she or he is agreeable to mediating the dispute. If neither disputant seeks help, a third person who is aware of the dispute may contact the disputants to see if they are agreeable to mediating the dispute. Asking to intervene in the conflict of others, however, should be done carefully. Uninvited mediation may seem like meddling rather than help.

Opening Statement

Obviously, if mediation is to take place, mediators must arrange for a first meeting with the disputants where they make an opening statement. After all, mediators are responsible for initiating, managing, and terminating the mediation sessions. Mediators must select a location free of interruptions and distractions. The conflicting parties should sit and face one another with the mediators at the end of the table.

At the first meeting, the mediator makes an **opening statement** explaining the purpose and process of mediation, including the mediator's role as facilitator of communication and lays out the communication rules that structure the mediation. Mediators also use the initial remarks as an opportunity to re-establish communication between the disputants and redirect it in a more positive direction. At the first session or meeting, mediators make the following clear to the disputants:

- That their participation in mediation is voluntary and the mediator or conflicting parties may terminate it at any time.
- That the mediator is unbiased (impartial toward either disputant) and will keep the mediation confidential.
- That the goal is a written agreement with which both parties are satisfied or at least comfortable.
- That the disputants are to try to work out a mutual agreement between them with the help of the mediator, who facilitates discussion, and does not make decisions for the disputants (not a judge or jury).

The mediators also inform the participants that they are to adhere to a few communication ground rules to include the following:

- The parties are encouraged to talk to and look at one another rather than at the mediator.
- The parties are asked to take turns talking without interruptions.
- The parties are required to adhere to time constraints set by the mediator.
- The parties are asked to strive to solve the problem rather than attack or blame the other person. Mediators have to help the parties learn to talk without expressing hostility to one another and to create a positive climate with no put-downs (focus on the problem, not the other person).
- The parties are encouraged to focus on the future (what they can do) rather than the past (what was done).

- The parties are told that they can openly share thoughts and feelings without fear of criticism or publicity.
- The parties are required to strive for a win–win solution with no one feeling dissatisfied or agreeing to something either party finds unacceptable.
- The parties are asked to agree to abide by additional rules as announced by the mediator during the session.

All this sounds like a lot for an opening statement, and it is. Sometimes not everything is included in the opening statement, but the mediators add to their opening statement as the mediation continues. As you gain experience mediating, you can keep the opening statement to essentials and then add the other rules and suggestions later as the need arises.

Note the essential items that the mediator chose to include in the following opening statement. Do you agree with his or her choice?

> I am glad that you both decided to try mediation and am pleased that you have asked me to help out here by serving as mediator. Let me start off by saying that your participation is entirely voluntary. I don't see any reason to say anything to others, so if you want to keep what we say just among us, that is fine with me. Is that what you want to do? OK, my role here is to help you work out your own agreement, one that you both feel comfortable with. In addition to not making your decisions for you, I must avoid siding with either of you or showing any favoritism. I may stop you to ask you questions, and I may make some notes, so that I can keep track of the issues and help you write up a mutually acceptable agreement. During the session, I may have to establish some ground rules. For example, let's agree right off not to engage in any name calling, and if the conflict escalates, I'll have to stop the session.
>
> I am going to ask each of you to tell us your side of the story, while I try to write down the key points, so I can insure that you address each of the issues. When one of you is talking, the other is not to interrupt. Are there any questions? If not, let's begin with Marisa. After hearing your side of the story, then Georgia can tell us hers.

The Conflicting Parties' Views of the Dispute

Mediators usually begin with the person who initiated the complaint against the other. For example, a neighbor who is upset about the other neighbor playing basketball in the driveway early in the morning, which annoys him, is probably the person who initiates the complaint (against the noisy neighbor). This person describes the problem from his or her point of view, explaining what happened and how she or he feels about it. The other person listening must not interrupt the speaker, but must hear out the speaker in his or her entirety. As soon as the first party finishes the opening statement, mediators ask the other party to explain what happened from her or his point of view, again without interruption. After each opening statement, mediators summarize back to the disputant the issues raised and how the mediators believe that the disputant feels about them. Mediators ask for confirmation of their summary from that disputant, and sometimes ask disputants to summarize what they heard from the other party. From these opening remarks, mediators identify the issues that are to comprise the agenda for discussion. At this early stage of the mediation, mediators may tolerate some venting of feelings for a short period to help get them out of one's system, but later they discourage the strong expression of feelings, which can escalate the conflict.

Sometimes it is useful for mediators to **caucus,** in which the mediator steps aside with one disputant for a private discussion. This may be done to overcome an impasse in the mediation or to call attention to something one of the parties does that is problematic or to request the disclosure of information that the disputant doesn't want to make in the presence of the other. In the private meeting, the mediator may help one of the parties to better understand how to contribute more positively to the discussion. To maintain an unbiased position, it is important that the mediator meets with both parties, separately of course, for about the same amount of time. Mediators should ask permission in private from each party before introducing into the discussion something disclosed in the caucus.

The following case might be a good place to caucus. The description of the dispute revealed the following:

> These two disputants are romantic partners, living in the same house and relying on only one car to drive to campus and town. Robert decided that he needed a "break" from his involvement with Cherene, which she initially agreed to. He wanted to stay in the same house (and move to another bedroom) and share the car. They had shared a bank account, but he withdrew half of the money and opened a new account of his own. Cherene had originally signed for the apartment, so she felt obligated to pay the rent, but she didn't have enough money now in her account to pay the bills unless he would give her his share of the expenses, and lately he became reluctant to do so. As time went on, she continued to act as his primary romantic interest even though he was looking to distance himself from her. That is why she told everyone she knew that "everything was fine between them." Consequently, he became more and more aggravated with her actions and his reactions hurt her a great deal. When he said that he might bring home other female friends of his, she told him that he better not do that, or she would do some serious damage to the car (which was originally his). Robert had met her parents, and they were visiting this next weekend. Because they liked him, she didn't want to tell them about Robert's recent behavior. There is a lot of miscommunication between the two since and the situation is progressively getting worse with many quarrels and screaming matches.

In this situation, the mediator might want to caucus with each person and ask him or her how one truly feels about the other person and the relationship. Do they love each other? Do they want out of the relationship entirely but don't know how to do it? Each person may not want to talk about these feelings in the presence of the other but may open up to the mediator. The mediator might help convince the other person to strive for more openness and honesty later when they resume the mediation.

Common Ground

Mediation sessions usually begin with a broad and confused discussion of issues seen from competitive orientations, but when mediators are successful, the mediation proceeds to a more organized and orderly discussion out of which cooperation and consensus (shared meanings) emerge. This idea of common ground is similar to "seeking commonalities" we presented in the chapter on negotiation (see Chapter 10). Mediators highlight **common ground**, which consists of attitudes, values, behaviors, expectations, and goals the parties share and can serve as a basis for an agreement. In addition, they may use fractionation, framing, and reframing.

The mediators begin with the easiest issues to resolve, leaving the most difficult for last. While thinking about the issues and discussing them, the mediators may rely on a useful technique for resolving conflict over an issue which we introduced in Chapter 10, called fractionation. You may recall that we said that this technique involves breaking down complex issues into smaller, more manageable ones. After separating issues into their smallest components, the mediators can ask the disputants to deal with each issue one at a time, which builds a feeling of success on small issues, until the larger issues are successfully resolved.

Another technique is known as **framing**, where mediators ask neutral or friendly questions that avoid blame or passing judgment and summarize issues. For example, if the dispute concerned car repairs that weren't completed to the car owner's satisfaction, the mediator might ask the repair person, "About how much would you say you have spent repairing the car?" One more technique is **reframing**, where mediators restate negatively loaded, biased, or accusatory statements made by one of the parties in more neutral terminology or restate positions in a way that makes the disputants look at the issues differently. In the car repair scenario, the mediator would rephrase the car owner's accusation ("This mechanic is an incompetent nincompoop who made the problem worse") to something like "You are saying that you believe that the car's problem was worse after you took it to the mechanic."

As soon as it seems appropriate, the mediators ask the parties what they want as an outcome of the dispute. Sometimes people do not know what they want and need time and encouragement to determine what they want. Once the wants are expressed, sometimes the opposing party discovers that the want is not what she or he expected to hear or as extreme as originally thought. Related to our discussion of uncertainly theory in Chapter 3, conflicting parties may not know what the problem is or what the other party wants. The clarification of wants may lead to a quick settlement, but oftentimes it does not. In any case, the mediators succeed in getting the conflicting parties' positions on the table as soon as possible.

Because the parties' interests and needs are broader than their specific positions or wants (see Chapter 10 for a discussion of interests versus positions), the mediators facilitate discussion of the interests that lie behind positions taken by the disputants. For example, the mediator discovers that the complaining neighbor wants the other neighbor to stop playing basketball, but what he really needs is to sleep in mornings without noise and interruption. However, the opposing neighbor says he wants to play basketball in the morning, but what he really needs is practice at shooting baskets sometime most days. As it turns out, he doesn't really need to shoot baskets in the early morning. By encouraging the conflicting parties to openingly discuss the problem and their interests, misunderstandings are identified and cleared up.

In addition to discovering interests and needs, the mediators also reframe the disputants' statements and positions. The mediators do this by helping the parties restate their comments in less offensive language and reword their utterances as proposals. For example, after neighbor accuses the other of "having no regard for others and purposely trying to keep people from getting enough sleep," the mediators might say, "Do you mean to say that your neighbor's basketball is keeping you awake in the early morning, but you would not object to his playing later in the day instead?"

As the discussion progresses, the mediators request proposals or solutions to the problem that would satisfy the interests and needs of both parties. The mediators also help the parties brainstorm alternative proposals. In many group communications, students of communication learned how to brainstorm solutions to problems. The idea is not to criticize or limit the proposals in any way, but simply to create as long a list as possible. Sometimes one suggestion, even if corny or ridiculous, triggers the parties to think of something better. Brainstorming plays an important role in expanding the range of options for reaching an agreement.

Throughout the discussion, mediators identify, highlight, and reinforce points of agreement, encourage positive contributions, and show attentiveness by responding verbally or nonverbally to comments by both parties. This positive feedback encourages the parties to continue the mediation and work toward agreement.

Try seeking common ground, perhaps as a member of a small group. Consider the list of issues you discovered from the above case study, involving a dispute between two romantic partners, Robert and Cherene. See if you can fractionate any of the issues into sub-issues. Then brainstorm solutions to the problem. Determine a list of points you think the two might agree on. It is important to keep this list of all the points the parties agree on because it forms a basis for the final agreement.

Final Agreement

Usually, the mediator keeps track of areas of agreement as the mediation progresses, so that eventually she or he has a rough draft of all points of consensus. Mediators learn early on in their training that wording of these commonalities is important. While it helps to list the different points of agreement, mediators need to employ the following format in the final agreement and say that "X agrees to this . . . Y agrees to that. . . ." Mediators attempt to keep the agreement simple. They use clear, specific details (spelling out who, what, where, when, how). It helps to think of the agreement as a list of **behavioral commitments** because it enumerates the specific observable actions each party needs to take to fulfill the agreement. When there are co-mediators, one usually takes the responsibility of keeping track of this list of behaviors, while the other encourages the conflicting parties to communicate effectively. In developing the agreement, mediators should strive for balance or "something for everyone." The agreement also needs to address questions of feasibility and practicality because the parties should find the agreement workable. Finally, the culminating step occurs when the mediators ask both parties to sign the agreement.

Because it is important that mediators take a neutral role and be open minded, they should not comment positively or negatively about areas of agreement. Mediators are not the ones agreeing to the behavioral commitments, so they should refrain from commenting one way or another. Mediators need to keep in mind that a mediation is not a negotiation in which both are trying to win the most they can from one another. Sometimes, one party settles for less than a mediator might expect simply because he or she knows that the other is more likely to live up to the agreement. By win–win, mediators are seeking a final agreement that both parties find satisfactory and can agree to. Although each may not end up with the most they can, the parties are happy with the outcome. Of course, the mediators can raise questions of feasibility. Is this idea doable? Can each of you actually do this?

In the following scenario, we offer an initial draft of the behavioral commitments as an example.

> Daria, who is a communication major and college senior living at home, often finds herself in the middle when her mother and her teenage sister engage in conflict. Both have come to rely on her to help them resolve their conflicts (or play the role of mediator). In this case, the sister wants more freedom and responsibility, which her mother is against before the mediation.

After facilitating the mediation, in which both parties explain their views, Daria, who has kept track of areas of consensus during the mediation, drafts an agreement as follows:

Agreement between Mother and Sister dated _____.

- Mother agrees to not wait up for the sister to return when out with friends or on a date on Friday and Saturday nights.
- Sister agrees to tell her mother whom she is with, the places they plan to go, and return home by 1 a.m.
- Mother agrees that sometimes plans change and sister may go places not originally intended.
- Sister agrees to not go to places that her mother is concerned about (namely, Mr. G's in town, Mathew's home when his parents aren't there, Linsey's home when her parents aren't there).
- Mother agrees to stop criticizing her boyfriend.
- Sister agrees to come home by 10 p.m. on school nights.
- Mother agrees to let her use her car in cases where she wants to meet her friends.
- Sister agrees to not drive and drink alcohol or use drugs.

Signed by _____ (Mother) and _____ (Sister)

Witnessed by _____ (Daria as mediator)

As you consider the above case, keep these points in mind. First, as mediator, Daria personally may not think this is a good agreement. She may think the mother is too strict or too lenient or the daughter is getting too much or too little, but as the mediator, she is not the one who is bound by this agreement. If this is what the mother and sister agree to, then Daria should keep her opinions to herself and encourage the two parties to live up to their agreement. Second, although the sister may have initiated the complaint, Daria tried to balance the agreement so that each party leaves the mediation with something she wants. Also, rather than say something vague or indefinite, such as "Mother doesn't want sister going out just any old time, staying out as late as she wants, or going to places that she doesn't approve of," Daria strove for specificity by clarifying the exact days, times, and places or people by name. Finally, Daria kept responsibilities clear by using the simple format, "X agrees to do . . . Y agrees to do . . . ." Note also that both parties gain something in the final agreement. Although mediators don't keep notes of the mediation after it is terminated, Daria may want to keep a copy of the agreement for future reference if the participants think that is a good idea or do not object.

Ending the Mediation

The mediators give each disputant a copy of the handwritten, signed agreement. The parties are more likely to live up the terms of an agreement if it exists in writing and has been signed by everyone. Whenever possible, the mediators set up a date for reviewing and evaluating the agreement. Knowing that the agreement won't be stuffed in a drawer somewhere and forgotten, the parties feel a stronger obligation to adhere to it. The mediator should thank the parties for using mediation and wish them well.

The agreement, whether written or sometimes not, culminates the process of mediation. The process as a whole works well in many everyday situations. Even young children can learn conflict mediation, making a difference in their lives and the lives of those around them.[18]

Following training in mediation in class, one of the author's students made comments such as these:

- I could relate to this subject because it reinforced my training as a Resident Assistant on campus. I've used mediation to solve conflicts among residents and staff members.
- I did not realize that I act as a mediator almost daily at work. I work with children. Children often find themselves in some sort of dispute or conflict with one another, it is my job to act as a mediator for them so that they can work out their own mutually satisfying outcomes.

Teachers, day care providers, and others who work with kids are mediators all day long. Mediating conflicts between children may seem simple or small, but they are important to the children involved.

- I think mediation happens almost every day on a more informal level. This can happen between roommates, families, coworkers, and so on. If there is a problem, a third party might intervene to help the resolution run more smoothly.
- I thought this subject helped me to see different ways of handling conflict situations and how important it is to sometimes have a third party involved. Many times I find myself in conflict with someone and we cannot come to a resolution, but with the help of someone else we come to a resolution that is fair to both of us. I see that having a neutral third party can be helpful when trying to deal with certain issues.

Like these students, we hope you may find mediation useful in your everyday life.

MANAGE IT

The study and practice of effective mediation is a natural fit for students of communication and conflict. For those who have gone through formal training, it is clear that it offers a practical application of many skills taught in undergraduate interpersonal communication and conflict management courses. However, we must shift our thinking from dealing with our own conflicts to helping others resolve theirs.

When should we intervene in other people's conflict? Help is needed when a dispute exists, meaning that the two parties are unable to resolve the conflict on their own. Unlike other alternatives to dispute resolution (ADRs) such as conciliation, ombudsperson, arbitration, and adjudication/litigation, mediators are unbiased third parties who facilitate communication between the conflicting parties so that the conflicting parties can work out their own agreement. Mediators keep confidential everything said in the mediation, maintain an open mind, demonstrate effective communication, encourage cooperation while discouraging competition, and encourage the parties to communicate with each other and create their own agreement. Mediators draw attention to a set of communication rules and enforce them throughout the mediation. While one person may serve as a mediator, there are often advantages and co-mediating by sharing the duties with another person.

A typical mediation usually proceeds through the following steps:

- One or both disputants seek mediation or a mediator may talk them into it.
- The mediator brings the disputants together and makes an opening statement.
- Following the mediator's opening statement, each person takes a few minutes to describe the dispute from his or her point of view without interruption.
- The mediator finds common ground on which to build agreement.
- The mediator writes up the final agreement.
- The mediator ends the mediation.

When drafting the agreement, mediators need to employ the following format: X agrees to this, and Y agrees to that. The mediators should attempt to keep the agreement simple. They use clear, specific details (spelling out who, what, where, when, how). It helps to think of the agreement as a list of behavioral commitments because it enumerates the specific observable actions each party needs to take to fulfill the agreement. In developing the agreement, the mediators should strive for balance or "something for everyone." The agreement also needs to address questions of feasibility and practicality—both parties should find the agreement workable. Finally, the culminating step occurs when the mediators ask both parties to sign the agreement.

EXERCISES

THINK ABOUT IT

1. Did you receive mediation training in elementary, middle, or high school? Did you find the training useful? What disputes did you mediate? If you did not receive such training, would you like to? Does your college or university offer mediation training?
2. What experience, training, and abilities do you possess that would make you a good mediator? Where are you weak? What could you do to become a better mediator?
3. Have you studied rules in other communication courses? What are communication rules? How do mediators enforce communication rules?

4. How might you use techniques such as fractionation, framing, reframing, and common ground for solving problems that don't involve interpersonal conflicts?
5. Why should communication majors make good mediators? Why might lawyers and psychotherapists find it difficult to effectively play the role of mediator?

APPLY IT

1. Now it is your turn. Imagine yourself as a mediator and write an opening statement for the following case.

   Two residence hall roommates, Mr. X and Mr. Y, have differences of opinion on what they like to listen to on the stereo, what they like to eat, when they have visitors, when they wake up or quiet down at night, and when they use their room for study.
2. Read the following case study, and identify the issues that the conflicting parties should discuss.

   Two employees, Brian and Jon, complain to you about the other's work habits. Both work in the same enclosed office and there are no other spaces available where either could be shifted. Brian likes to work with the door open, but Jon likes the door closed. Brian tends to shift tasks frequently, talking on his cell phone or speaking to people going by, while Jon prefers to do one task at a time. Jon tends to talk to himself as he is working. Jon also likes to put large post-it notes on the wall to visualize what he is working on, while Brian works primarily on his computer. Brian likes to spread a number of different items out to refer to as he is working, and tends to leave them on the ground and all around his desk until he is finished. Both are claiming that each other's work habits are preventing each other from working to full capacity.
3. For the above case, write out at least four statements that demonstrate fractionation, framing, reframing, and common ground.
4. Read over the following scenario and draft an agreement using the format, "X agrees to this and Y agrees to that." Strive for balance as much as possible.

   One roommate cares about the cleanliness of the shared apartment, but the other roommate has shown no interest in helping out. However, in the course of mediation between roommates over their messy apartment, they agree to divvy up the household chores and times/days to do them.

Imagining the typical chores and considering a reasonable schedule for the two roommates, draft an agreement that you intend to ask both roommates to sign. Use the appropriate format recommended in this chapter.

WORK WITH IT

1. Apply the chapter objectives to the following case study.

   My mother allows my 13-year-old sister, Leanne, to publish a blog [online journal]. She did not know what Leanne was writing about online until she started receiving long distance telephone calls from older men asking for her by name. Both my mother and sister complain to me about the other. My mother tells me that she would like to start reading her blog daily and would like to delete any content that she finds inappropriate. Leanne tells me that her blog is like a diary, and she doesn't want her mother to read it. Both are really upset with each other.

   - Define mediation and explain whether you think a third party should intervene as a mediator, and why.
   - Describe the role of mediator for whomever intervenes as a third party.
   - List and briefly describe the steps the third party should go through for this hypothetical mediation.

EXERCISE: MEDIATION ROLE PLAY

OBJECTIVE: To give everyone the opportunity to play the role of mediator or co-mediator and conflicting parties.

TIME

    10 minutes to select a scenario, participants discuss the roles to be played.
    30 minutes to discuss and resolve the dispute.
    10 minutes for the role players and observers to discuss the mediation.

INSTRUCTIONS:

1. Form groups of at least five persons, two conflicting parties, two co-mediators, and one or more observers. A class may have several mediations going on simultaneously in different areas of the classroom.
2. Conflicting parties should be separated temporarily from the co-mediators, to discuss how they will role play a mediation. They can pick a role play from the list below (or make up one of their own) and discuss how to proceed (one may decide to get a little emotional; one may be more stubborn at first and loosen up more later, etc.). Decide who will present his or her side of the story first to the co-mediators.
3. The two co-mediators should discuss their duties. Who will present the opening statement for the mediators and who will take notes on areas of agreement between the conflicting parties?
4. Now it is time for the two conflicting parties to meet with the co-mediators and make introductions. Observers do not sit with the role players but a short distance away where they can observe and hear the mediation. One conflicting party will let the mediators know that she or he would like to speak first when the parties are asked to tell their side of the story.
5. The co-mediators should present the opening statement for the mediators, announce ground rules, and ask one of the conflicting parties to "tell his (or her side) of the story." After that person finishes uninterrupted, the other party is asked to do the same.
6. The co-mediators ask the parties what they want from the mediation.
7. The co-mediators facilitate productive discussion of the issues, record areas of agreement, and help the parties find ways to resolve issues.
8. The co-mediators write up the final agreement and ask the parties to sign it. Everyone gets copies.
9. The observers use Form 1 to report on the mediation, discuss it with the parties and co-mediators, suggesting ways to improve it.

ROLE PLAYS

You may wish to devise your own role play. If not, then select one of the following situations to mediate and assign roles of two conflicting parties and one or two mediators. Role players are encouraged to embellish the case study and add details as desired. Others may serve as observers, but they cannot participate in the mediation. Co-mediators should start with their opening statements and follow the mediation steps as prescribed in the chapter.

a. Family members: Your father and his sister (your aunt) have asked you to mediate their dispute. Your father thinks that your aunt took an expensive piece of furniture from their father's house after he passed away without discussing it with him. Your aunt took care of their father in his final days and had a key to his house. Your aunt was also in control of their father's finances and your father thinks she took all his money during his final days. Now your father is angry at his sister.

b. Two romantic partners, Lacey and Henry, are living in a house with a third person, you. You treat them both equally. Recently, Lacy decided that she wants to watch some TV programs, even though they were on the same time as sports. Meanwhile, Henry wants to watch the sports on the weekend and some weekday nights. The negative atmosphere is so bad in the house that you asked each of them to let you mediate the conflict, and they both agreed to let you do it.

c. Two romantic partners are having a conflict over time management. Darren wants to spend time with his buddies and even invites one or two to join them when they go out together. Kristi doesn't approve of all of his friends and finds two to be offensive and a bad influence on him. She wants to go out more often as just the two of them. She also wants more time with him without his buddies hanging around.

d. Two roommates: Nicole spends too much money. She likes to buy a lot of clothes. She never has enough for meals or gas, so she is always asking her roommate, Erin, for food or gas money. Nicole wants money to help pay for her books and sometimes doesn't have enough to help pay their room expenses. Erin is fortunate to have enough money, but thinks it is unfair that her roommate isn't pulling her share and needs money from her so often. Nicole often doesn't pay back the money she owes her roommate.

e. Two roommates: Bryon comes home late and rowdy from the local bars on Thursday, Friday, and Saturday nights. Roommate Lee has Friday classes and needs to go to work early every weekend.

f. Two sisters: A borrows B's clothes without her permission. B occasionally snoops through A's room and tries to find her diary and other personal items.

g. Married seniors: Adam recently retired and now spends all his time in the house. He doesn't do any household chores and gets in his wife's (Angela) way.

h. Two neighbors: Pearson's (or Sara) dog barks, and when loose makes messes in his neighbor's yard. Recently, the dog ripped open the garbage container when the neighbor, Matthew (or Dorothy), placed it at the end of the drive for pickup.

Form 1: Observer's/Judges Mediation Observation

Mediation Title_____

Your Name _____

Date _____

1. Were the co-mediators' opening statements well prepared? (See suggestions under "opening statements.")

2. Did co-mediators enforce communication rules? (See suggestions under "opening statements.")

3. Did the co-mediators follow the mediation steps as prescribed in the chapter?

4. Did co-mediators point out areas of agreement and common ground? Did they engage in framing/reframing?

5. Did the final agreement (if there was one) consist of "behavioral commitments" for both parties?

6. How well did the co-mediators end the mediation?

NOTES

1. Nancy A. Burrell and Dudley D. Cahn, "Mediating Peer Conflicts in Educational Contexts: The Maintenance of School Relationships," in Dudley D. Cahn (Ed.), *Conflict in Personal Relationships* (Hillsdale, NJ: Erlbaum, 1994), p. 79.
2. See, for example, Robert E. Emery, David Sbarra, and Tara Grover, "Divorce Mediation: Research and Reflections," *Family Court Review* 43 (2005), 22–37; Frank E. A. Sander and Robert C. Bordone, "Early Intervention: How to Minimize the Cost of Conflict," *Negotiation* 21 (2005), 1–4; Lisa B. Bingham, "Employment Dispute Resolution: The Case for Mediation," *Conflict Resolution Quarterly* 22 (2004), 145–174.
3. Bruce C. McKinney, William Kimsey, and Rex Fuller, *Mediation: Dispute Resolution Through Communication,* 2nd Edition (Dubuque, IA: Kendall Hunt, 1990), p. 146.
4. Sook-Young Lee. "Mediation Techniques of an Informal Intermediary in Intercultural-Interpersonal Conflict," *Human Communication,* 11 (Winter 2008), 461–482.
5. Camille Monahan, "Faster, Cheaper, and Unused: The Paradox of Grievance Mediation in Unionized Environments," *Conflict Resolution Quarterly* 25(2008), 479–476.
6. Afshan Siddiqui and Hildy Ross, "Mediation as a Method of Parent Intervention in Children's Disputes," *Journal of Family Psychology* 18 (2004), 147–159.
7. James A. Wall, Jr., John B. Stark, and Rhetta L. Standifer, "Mediation: A Current Review and Theory Development," *Journal of Conflict Resolution* 45 (2001), 370–391.
8. Stephen K. Erickson and Marilyn S. McKnight, *The Practitioner's Guide to Mediation: A Client-Centered Approach* (New York: John Wiley, 2001).
9. Robert Coulson, *Family Mediation: Managing Conflict, Resolving Disputes* (San Francisco: Jossey-Bass, 1996); Stephen A. Giunta and Ellen S. Amatea, "Mediation or Litigation with Abusing or Neglectful Families: Emerging Roles for Mental Health Counselors," *Journal of Mental Health Counseling* 22 (2000), 240–252.
10. Robert B. Silver and Deborah C. Silver, "Practice Note: Divorce Mediation with Challenging Parents," *Conflict Resolution Quarterly* 25 (2008), 511–520.
11. Penny Brooker, "An Investigation of Evaluative and Facilitative Approaches to Construction Mediation," *Structural Survey* 25 (2007), 233. (220–238).
12. Wenshan Jia, "Chinese Mediation and Its Cultural Foundation," in Guo-ming Chen and Ringo Ma (Eds.), *Chinese Conflict Management and Resolution* (Stamford, CT: Ablex, 2001), p. 290.
13. Gary J. Friedman, Jack Himmelstein, and Robert H. Mnooking, *Saving the Last Dance: Mediation through Understanding* (Cambridge, MA: Harvard Law School, 2001). Video.
14. Joyce L. Hocker and William W. Wilmot, *Interpersonal Conflict,* 4th Ed. (Dubuque, IA: Wm C. Brown, 1995), p. 238.
15. Jean Poitras, "A Study of the Emergence of Cooperation in Mediation," *Negotiation Journal* 21 (2005), 281–300.
16. Jordi Agustí-Panareda, "Power Imbalances in Mediation: Questioning Some Common Assumptions," *Dispute Resolution Journal* 59 (2004), 24–31.
17. O. J. Coogler, *Structured Mediation in Divorce Settlement* (Lexington, MA: Lexington Books, 1978).
18. See, for example, Candice C. Carter, "Conflict Resolution at School: Building Compassionate Communities," *Social Alternatives* 21 (2002), 49–55; David W. Johnson and Roger T. Johnson, "Implementing the 'Teaching Students to Be Peacemakers Program,'" *Theory into Practice* 43 (2004), 68–79.

Managing Conflict in the Workplace

OBJECTIVES

At the end of this chapter, you should be able to:

- Describe the sources of conflict in the workplace.
- Describe diversity-based conflict.
- Describe work–life conflict.
- Describe workplace bullying.

- List strategies you can use to manage diversity-based conflict, deal with work–life conflict, and combat bullying in the workplace.

KEY TERMS

bullying
collective voice
cyberbullying
diversity-based conflict
exodus
forming
identity conflict
information processing
   perspective

instrumental/task conflict
mentor
norming
performing
process conflict
psychological detachment
relationship conflict
reverse discourse
roles

storming
subversive (dis)obedience
termination
work–life conflict
workplace conflict

What are your plans for after graduation? Tired of being asked? Some students have always known what career they want and are likely enrolled in engineering, nursing, pre-med., journalism, law, education, ROTC, law enforcement, or other major tied to a particular occupation. But many more are unable to predict what they want to do. One of the authors of this book remembers switching majors more than once in college and still being undecided at graduation.

Regardless what career you end up choosing, we can guess that you will in fact end up employed somewhere. This also means that you will have to deal with interpersonal conflicts in some organizational context.

It is also apparent to those of us who have been employed for a number of years that many types of interpersonal conflicts at work resemble those we had in college when we worked part-time, pursued an internship, played sports, partici-pated in a sorority/fraternity, or student organization, or were elected to office in the student government. Many students are already working fulltime while going to school. By applying our conflict management skills in your current organiza-tional environments as students, you can develop highly valued and much appreci-ated skills for resolving conflicts in the workplace. Your handling of these conflicts may make the difference between your success or failure in your chosen career. As De Dreu and his colleagues report,

> The effectiveness of individual employees, teams, and entire organizations depends on how they manage interpersonal conflict at work. . . . Managers spend an average of 20 per cent of their time managing conflict . . . , and evidence suggests that conflict and conflict management at work substantially influences individual, group and organizational effectiveness.[1]

It is really no surprise to discover that we encounter many conflicts when we par-ticipate in groups and organizations. Many working people spend more time with people at their jobs than they do with loved ones, so it shouldn't surprise them that conflicts are inevitable. Prolonged, unresolved conflict at work has negative conse-quences for team members' health[2] and for individual, group, and organizational effectiveness.[3]

There are many types of organizations. Basically, we can categorize them as workplace (small businesses, medium-sized companies, and large corporations), social (social fraternities/sororities, parents without partners, and other single organizations), and interest/entertainment (dance, hockey, and astronomy clubs). You go to a workplace to get a job done, or go to a social organization to socialize with others and perhaps "meet someone," or go to an interest/entertainment orga-nization to participate in an interesting, relaxing, and fun activity. Many organiza-tions combine all of these purposes, but one purpose stands out as primary—the *reason d'etre* for the organization's being. While we focus on workplace orga-nizations in this chapter, our principles and techniques cut across all of these types. Organizations consist of divisions or groups ranging from large to small. Sometimes these groups are referred to as teams.

In workplace organizations, coworkers are assigned to a group, often referred to as a team, staff, committee, subcommittee, department, or task force. The group becomes a close network of relationships to be managed. Group members are also part of larger units where there exists a network of relationships that are not as close.

At the outset, we want to distinguish the more common everyday workplace conflicts from the less common formal grievances and litigation. **Workplace con-flict** is defined the same as interpersonal conflict (see Chapter 1), but the inter-dependence among the parties involves workplace relationships (boss–employee, colleagues, department heads, employee–public, etc.). Workplace relationships are more or less mandatory relationships (if one wants a job and intends to keep it). Sometimes, these conflicts rise to the level of *formal grievances* in the organiza-tion that must be resolved by third parties such as human resources specialists. *Litigation* may include both lawsuits and issues involving regulatory agencies that oversee an organization. Sadly, many organizations ignore workplace conflicts until they become formal grievances or even litigation, when they are forced to address them.

How do we avoid unproductive conflict while allowing healthy dissension? In this chapter, we look at how different types of goals, roles, and people contribute to workplace conflict. We also examine the conflict between work and life and the topic of workplace bullying. Obviously, we cannot eliminate the problems created by these factors, but we can learn how to better manage the conflicts. At the end of this chapter, we provide a group conflict exercise to give you an opportunity to put into practice what you learn in this chapter. We hope that this chapter prepares you to be a more productive and less anxious employee.

CONFLICTS ARISING OUT OF DIFFERENCES IN GOAL SEEKING

> I had just started working for a Fortune 500 Company when I was told to plan and manage a weekend retreat for our department. When I asked my boss, colleagues, and Human Resources for more details on such retreats and what resources I had available to make the arrangements I was told that this was the first such recognition retreat, so there was no precedent.
>
> I was nervous the whole eventful weekend, running around and ensuring that all went as I hoped (I had to deal with a couple of unforeseen problems). While everyone appeared to have a good time and thanked me at the end of the retreat, I was still unsure of my success. However, a few days later I received a call from the same person in Human Resources who complemented me for the way I managed the event and asked me to write up a step-by-step description of how I planned and executed it. She said it would serve as a model for future years. I asked her if she would put that in writing and add it to my personnel file, which she agreed to do.

This woman's story serves to illustrate the main goals organizations tend to focus on. We learned about these types of goals back in Chapter 4, but now we must consider them in an organizational context. Recall that *instrumental goals* are those that focus on a task or problem or issue. If you want someone to do something, your instrumental goal is the actual behavior requested. While instrumental goals are set by the organization in the form of mission statements, policies, and handbooks, or SOPs (Standard Operating Procedures), workers may have their own ideas of how best to go about getting a job done. In the above scenario, the narrator's boss is representing the company, and he is trying to ensure the weekend retreat goes off as usual, every year. This is the company's and, therefore, the narrator's assigned instrumental goal.

Instrumental/Task Conflict

Instrumental/task conflict occurs when there is disagreement between supervisors and subordinates or among members of a team over how to get a job done—the instrumental goals. In the above scenario, the narrator engages her boss as well as others at work and received no help.

When others are involved such as in a team, their answers to her questions or offers to help may actually complicate matters. They may disagree with one another over how to best do a task. Under some conditions, task conflict does decrease worker satisfaction and feelings of well-being. In private, profit-structured organizations, conflict that persists over the best way to accomplish a task interferes with the feelings of its members. If conflicts persist even in the face of achieving goals, feelings of satisfaction and well-being are affected. Therefore, it helps when workers coalesce around a common understanding of the organization's task-oriented or instrumental goals.

Yet, a moderate amount of task-related conflict, while it may take precious time to resolve, may result in greater efficiencies and productivity in the long run.[4] From this point of view, task conflict "prevents moving to premature consensus, and thus should enhance decision-making quality, individual creativity, and work-team effectiveness in general."[5] Moderate levels of task conflict alone lead to the best productivity.[6]

Relationship Conflict

You may recall our discussion about relationship goals in Chapter 4. Relationship goals in organizations are formal and informal.[7] The organization chart or "chain of command" depicts the formal links, showing who reports to whom. The informal links include some of the formal relationships but others it takes to "get a job done" as well as people one meets in the lunch room or at the water cooler. **Relationship conflict** occurs when workers experience with one another issues of power, trust, supportiveness, competition, and differences over the rules that govern various types of workplace relationships. A team's capacity for effectively and efficiently processing information is impacted as "members spend their energy focusing on the personal antagonisms rather than on the task."[8] Some organizations go so far as to establish policies that forbid intimate relationships among workers or with clients. Still, platonic relationships are sources of conflict. Relationship conflict was found to negatively affect feelings of satisfaction and well-being in both private and public organizations.[9]

In the above scenario, the narrator reaches out to others, but no one responds to her call for assistance or even answers her questions. There were opportunities for the boss and colleagues to build a foundation for future cooperative projects, but they passed on them. The narrator opened the door for help but was forced to go it alone. She could have decided "to heck with it" and not planned the event, "because she did not know what to do." She could have quit her job because "they didn't like her or want to work with her." On the other hand, she may need the job and income and have no choice but to go it alone.

Identity Conflict

Because one's identity in the workplace is connected to that person's position in the organization, *identity goals* concern one's desires for status, prestige, and authority (see Chapter 4). Bosses or supervisors expect that their employees respect them. At the same time, each worker also wants to be treated with respect and appreciated for the work he or she does as prerequisites for promotion to higher levels and salary increases. We learned in Chapter 7 about autonomous face, where we need some time alone and hope for recognition for the work we do. "Worker of the month" is a coveted goal and its achievement is something an employee can be proud of. **Identity conflict** occurs when others treat a person contrary to the way that person sees himself or herself. This happens when workers go over their supervisors' head and challenge their authority (or identity). Higher level supervisors are unhappy if they are not given preferred parking spaces and larger, better furnished offices than their subordinates.

The narrator in the above scenario may feel some satisfaction in the fact that she was picked for the event and that her boss and colleagues must think she can handle the job. As the organizer of the event, she is now the "person in charge." She can contact people directly to secure support and make arrangements for the event. She has been delegated an important responsibility and hopes to pull off the event in a way that makes her look good. As it turned out, the narrator was complemented and asked to supply a write up of the event to serve as a model for future years, and a positive and permanent entry was made in her personnel file. She probably felt more confidence in her abilities as a result of doing an outstanding job—planning the event.

Process Conflict

Finally, as we learned in Chapter 4, process goals refer to alternative ways to manage communication and conflict. Some people prefer to manage others in a more open, consensual, and fair way, while others prefer to keep more to themselves, maintain control, and assert more authority. Still others seem more chaotic with no clear plan or set of expectations. Similarly, some organizations tolerate or advocate more autocratic styles, in which the supervisor makes the decisions with little or no input from employees. Other organizations encourage a more democratic style, where bosses consult with and utilize input from their workers. Such an organization may have a "suggestion/complaint box" and supervisors have an open door policy. Finally, some organizations seem much more unstructured and disorganized with unclear channels of communication and divisions of responsibility. **Process conflict** has to do with disagreements over the management style that is typical of a particular organization. Management might prefer more centralized authority and decision making, but employees may want a more decentralized system, so they can play a stronger role in making decisions that affect them.

In our vignette, the narrator appears to have no say in the way she was selected for the task. Her boss simply told her to do it. In a more democratic organization, she might have had an opportunity to volunteer for it. Her boss might have laid out some beneficial outcomes or inducements if she agreed to take on the responsibility. He might have laid out the company's expectations for the event and support resources. Perhaps he might have put together a team rather than expect one person to do it all. On the other hand, her boss and colleagues may have conspired to "test her." She was new to the department, and perhaps they did not want to associate with her until she had "proven herself." Perhaps others may now invite her to work with them on teams and give her more help on future tasks. So, in her case, her conflict management had positive outcomes.

Conflict is a natural part of workgroup development.

Conflicting Goals

Interestingly, moderate amounts of conflict can be helpful and therefore desirable in the workplace. To understand how this works, we need to take **information processing perspective** and apply some of what we learned about stress in Chapter 8. According to this view, at low levels of conflict, teams may not experience enough stress (eustress) to think actively, and in so doing may ignore important information. At high levels of conflict, teams may be overwhelmed (hyperstress), which could render them unable to process information well and so perform at low levels of productivity. Advocates of the information processing perspective state that "Compared to low levels of conflict, moderate levels arouse employees to consider and scrutinize the problem at hand, to generate ideas, and to select and implement adequate problem solutions."[10]

What does all this mean to the competent conflict manager? For one, it is important to stay focused and not let conflicts escalate beyond what is best for the organization and conflicting parties. It is apparent that if conflict in teams is to have any beneficial effect, it must be managed at its early stages using strategies appropriate to the type of conflict experienced. Conflict that is not managed quickly is a source of hyperstress that can also make employees feel helpless,[11] and may lead to emotional exhaustion, absenteeism, and turnover in organizations, particularly if employees think they have no one they can turn to for help in resolving the conflict.[12]

CONFLICTS AT DIFFERENT STAGES OF GROUP DEVELOPMENT

Development is a process view of changes that take place in groups and organizations. Looking at conflict from a developmental perspective helps us see conflict as a "natural part of workgroup development."[13] Effective and productive teams experience clearly identifiable phases of development that are largely defined by the kind of conflict that happens within them and the way in which that conflict is managed by workers. From this perspective, conflict is productive because its resolution can move a group toward a higher level of functioning. You have probably experienced these phases when working with groups in student organizations, jobs, or group projects in class.

The Forming Phase

When a young Ph.D. first joined the faculty at his university, he proposed to teach a section of an existing course he taught elsewhere on organizational communication. He was told that he was hired to develop the interpersonal communication area and not to teach courses offered by another colleague. At first there was a heated discussion of the faculty member's role, but after calming down, he simply accepted the situation and moved forward to develop the new area in the department.

In the **forming** phase, a tremendous amount of unfamiliarity with people who are in the work group and what they bring to it creates some conflicts over differing expectations. Some authors refer to this as the *dependency* and *inclusion* stage, as much of the focus is on how people are to be included in the group. This raises relationship issues. Do you belong in this group? How do you fit in? How are you supposed to work with the others? What role can you play? Because the group's structure is initially tentative, members need time to become acquainted with one another and prove themselves as worthy of the group. Conflict at this stage forces members to define and develop roles and check personal assumptions about both team goals and personal responsibility. Of course, not everyone always agrees about these roles, goals, and responsibilities, hence conflict is expected. If these differences are managed effectively, members become more attracted to the group, win acceptance, and develop a sense of loyalty to it; they also have a good idea of who does what and how the group is organized.[14]

The Storming Phase

Now that the new faculty member had proposed and created three new courses in interpersonal communication, he was asked to develop a fourth course in intercultural communication. After reflecting on his commitment to teach the three courses as well as other courses he was assigned to teach in the department, he requested to be released from the other courses. When his request was denied, he explained that he was unable to add more courses because he had reached his limit as far as teaching and research went. After a few days of discussions, the chair of the department agreed with the faculty member and decided to hire an additional scholar who had expertise in intercultural communication.

The next phase, **storming**, occurs as people begin to feel some identification with the group but don't really feel a sense of unity around its purpose. In many ways, group members are struggling with the idea of acceptance and the desire to be independent (autonomous face in Chapter 7); thus, this phase is also called *counterdependency* and *flight*. As group members prove themselves in the forming stage, they now may find that group expectations exceed their ability or desire to perform. In the storming phase, group members may use conflict quite purposefully to help create a clearer sense of their role in the group (i.e., identify goal) and to further influence how the group functions. Successful management of this stage increases trust among group members, greater interdependence, and a greater sense of their purpose.

The Norming Phase

> Now that faculty member had been teaching for a few years, he proposed at a department meeting that some guidelines be accepted that governed the number of courses new faculty were expected to teach, the diversity of those courses, and how often he or she would teach them. After considerable discussion, the department agreed to setting limits that would prevent new faculty from being spread too thin and overworked.

As a group works through the conflicts of the storming phase and begins to fall into regular patterns of behavior, the group evolves into the **norming** phase. Also called the trust and structure stage, this phase allows group members to plan how the group functions more effectively. This is a good time to clarify process goals. Spurred on by the need for quickly accomplishing a specific task or activity, the team members come to accept both their own individual roles and the responsibilities of fellow participants. A sense of unity emerges as members begin to repeat tasks and group norms become observable. In this phase, conflict serves to bring together different role expectations, reiterate and strengthen a participant's chosen action, and solidify his or her roles and responsibilities within the group. The norming phase allows a group to move into higher levels of productivity in the performing phase.

The Performing Phase

> Now that the department had guidelines that clearly laid out the expectations of new faculty and helped them specialize so they could be productive members of the department, the faculty successfully taught courses, were not spread too thin, and published articles and books in their specialized areas.

Finally, the group development process culminates in the team's awareness that they are focusing on the task, problem, or issue. In this **performing** phase (work stage), conflict serves to focus individuals on reaching consensus on expectations regarding problem-solving behaviors and accomplishing instrumental goals. Behaviors such as group interactions being focused on accomplishing the team's task, individuals consistently addressing potential solutions, and attainment of consensus confirm the team's arrival at becoming a highly productive and functional performing group.[15]

The Termination Phase

Unfortunately, sometimes good times must end. The college needed to reduce its expenses and had to reorganize by combining some departments. Journalism and communication were combined into a single department. Communication was told that Journalism was being added, but that the chair of journalism would continue as chair of the newly formed department because the chair of communication retired. Faculty members objected to all these changes but to no avail. Who would teach what courses? Who would work with whom? There was a lot of confusion over how individual faculty would fit into the newly formed department.

We are talking about the end of an era. The final phase of group development is **termination,** either of the group or of particular group members. The group itself may end, the particular task may end, or some members depart or are replaced by newcomers. At this stage, conflict arises from individuals not wanting to let go and move on and newcomers entering the forming stage of group development. Those senior group members may fight any effort to end the project or release workers, and the newcomers may encounter considerable ambiguity about what is expected of them.

Groups develop as workers successfully manage conflicts at each of these stages. To the extent that workers avoid these conflicts or unsuccessfully deal with them, groups become mired down at one stage with negative effects on productivity and morale. We all have had bad experiences working in one group or another probably due to the mismanagement of conflict at one stage of development. Should a group not be able to appropriately handle conflict, outside guidance or intervention, human relations training, or dispute mediation becomes necessary in an effort to move a group to the next stage of development.

CONFLICTS DUE TO DIFFERENCES IN ROLE EXPECTATIONS

Roles are associated with a set of expectations for the successful performance of a particular job or task. Workplace group members can take on one of three types of roles: task, maintenance, and disruptive. Conflicts over expectations can occur in any of these types of roles.

Task Roles

Task roles help the group or organization work toward expected outcomes. They are the means to achieving the instrumental goals we discussed earlier. If the goal is to answer questions from people in a home builder store, then the task is to be able to answer the questions in a way people understand and help them find the product they are looking for. Employees who do not help customers in an effective and efficient manner are in conflict with their supervisors expectations about their role. They should not respond with "that's not my department" or engage in prolonged conversations with the customer. Conflict over task roles may quickly lead to a counseling session, warning, and perhaps eventual termination of employment.

Maintenance Roles

Maintenance roles facilitate communication and resolve conflict in the pursuit of task roles. These roles include supporting and encouraging others, helping relieve tensions in the group, and monitoring the feelings of the group. Humor is actually beneficial here where used appropriately. Conflicts are likely to occur when maintenance roles are at odds with task roles. An employee may not be able to get a task done immediately and in an efficient manner for health, home and family, or vacation reasons. A supervisor may want employees to work the next weekend, but they may have made other arrangements or have home/family commitments. Here again, employees who turn down requests to work extra hours when their supervisors need to meet deadlines or goals run the risk of having their jobs in jeopardy as other employees agree to work the extra shifts.

Disruptive Roles

Some employees are problematic. Their attitudes, habits, or lack of training/education constantly interfere with the day-to-day operation in an organization. For these reasons, some employees engage in **disruptive roles** due to unmet personality needs. They may isolate themselves, demand the center of attention, clown around in situations where serious behavior is called for, or be cynical about all the tasks the group takes on. Supervisors find it challenging to get pessimists more on board and motivated to accomplish tasks, to get individuals who engage in offensive or immature behavior to change, or to encourage people to produce more than they think they can. People can change and sometimes do. Many of us who have worked many years can point to people who got the message, took up the challenge, and made an effort to change. The problem is that some don't.

People who engage in disruptive roles may do so for different reasons, and each type should be treated differently. In the above scenario, all of the staff members may have obsessions or unmet needs of their own that thwart their ability to work together.

Sometimes, disruptive roles can also arise when people take their roles too seriously. Again we refer to a topic we treated earlier, "trained incapacities," which included being too goal directed or too critical. People who are too goal directed and see themselves as high achievers, for example, may want to tackle tasks that aren't within their purview because they don't think that a problem is being solved quickly enough. The narrative below reflects one person's interaction with a high achiever and the problems that trained incapacity can create:

> We just switched to a new customer service delivery system and we are still ironing out all the bugs in it. My job is to manage the process—what gets done first, who does it, and where it goes from there. The first weekend we were up and running, when I thought I could finally relax, one of my coworkers (who I'm convinced never sleeps) sent me a series of emails on a part of the process, ultimately offering to address the issue on the following Monday. I finally wrote back and asked that she please let me deal with it. I didn't want to dampen her enthusiasm, but I needed to make sure that I was doing the job I'm responsible for.

Managers need to help employees identify their trained incapacities and help them learn how to be more effective. In a discussion about the problematic behavior, the manager needs to begin by recognizing the value such behavior may serve in certain situations, but then show how it is a problem in other situations. The goal is not to eliminate the behavior altogether but rather to help the individual recognize situations where such behavior is inappropriate or problematic. In the narrative above, care must be taken to value the employee's input while moving ahead to do what must be done.

There are times when supervisors or subordinates don't perform their roles well. Alert managers spot weaknesses in their lower level managers or employees and arrange for training to overcome these deficits. In the absence of such a training program, the manager may serve as a **mentor** who takes a personal interest in the subordinate and helps them adapt to the specific workplace and become more productive. It is common for many top-level managers to report that they owe their success to a person who taught them "the ropes" and how to learn what they needed to know. In some organizations, "mentors" are assigned to new employees to help them succeed at their jobs. However, the best situations are those where an employee is impressed by a successful person and makes the effort to work with or for that person. Then, a simple request for help often results in superior mentoring. Because some people are known for their effective role as mentors, it would behoove a person to seek them out and arrange to work for them.

Finally, disruptive roles occur when managers and employees cannot achieve the proper balance between the different hats they must wear to successfully perform their roles (role conflicts). These different hats may have conflicting expectations. For example, managers must often wear their supervisory hat and push employees to meet the company's instrumental goals. However, there are times they need to switch hats, take on their maintenance roles, and perhaps shift to a counseling or advising capacity to help their employees overcome some personal situations that may affect their job performance.

HOW TO MANAGE WORKPLACE CONFLICT
Adapting the S-TLC Model

As we said in the introduction, interpersonal conflicts are managed differently in groups. In the case of S-TLC (see Chapter 4), some adaptation is necessary. It is more difficult to STOP and take a time out when a group has only a designed time to meet each day or week or a deadline to make. In cases where it is possible, a member may suggest that "everyone take a break" and resume work in 20 minutes or that we adjourn for the day and hope that cooler heads prevail at the next meeting.

To THINK, groups may consult with others or ask "experts" to attend meetings and provide useful information. While thinking is considered a psychological activity in interpersonal conflicts, group members spend a lot of a meeting "thinking out loud." This is why groups are said to "deliberate." Because members are not always sure of answers to problems, this deliberation often influences the way group members view problems and their solutions. Therefore, this stage, viewed as deliberation, is key to group decision making.

To LISTEN, in addition to our suggestions in previous chapters, it is often permissible to take notes, designate a secretary to take minutes, or tape record a meeting. These aids are a useful record of what transpired, provide feedback to everyone, often encourage people to behave in a civil manner at the meeting, and permit people to "correct" or clarify comments made previously. Moreover, individuals should not "do all the talking." Time is limited. Talkative members need to get control of themselves and allow others an opportunity to contribute information and express their views.

To COMMUNICATE, it is useful to remember from previous chapters how to be assertive. As a member of a group, you have a right to be heard and an obligation to speak either in support or against what others say. People who avoid or accommodate add little, if any, value to a group meeting.

Adapting the Six Steps to Effective Confrontation

In the case of the six steps to effective confrontation (see Chapter 4), some adjustment is also necessary when managing group conflicts. The *preparation stage* is often taken for granted in the workplace. Members are commonly assigned to a group because they have an interest and knowledge that may be useful. They often come to meetings prepared, carrying reams of paper, books, and a laptop with them. Some use projection aids to show graphs and charts. Often, preparation for a group meeting exceeds what we encounter in our own personal conflicts.

The next stage, *setting aside a time and place,* is also taken for granted in the workplace. This is the time and location of the group meeting. Some places have a daily meeting in the morning, or at noon, or at the end of the workday. Others meet weekly or monthly or quarterly. Whereas it can be a challenge getting others to find time and motivation to meet in one's personal life, employees expect meetings and only need to be told when and where to meet.

The third stage, *the interpersonal confrontation,* is also common at group and organizational meetings. People even rehearse for the meeting during the preparation stage, because they know what resistance they are likely to encounter. Meetings are called for the purpose of making a decision—to approve or recommend some course of action for an organization to take. The decision usually has either beneficial or negative effects on other parts of the organization, so the outcome is important to the group members. Because they take the issues seriously, how they look and how they sound carry weight. Members who appear confident, authoritative, and articulate have impact on these decisions, whereas people who are not persuasive don't. While useful for personal conflicts, I-statements are more about one's position than group interests. By this we mean that the strongest basis for making group decisions rests on those who can tie together the common interests of others. What we share, how we can work together, and how we can all contribute define interests that form a basis for a group decision. Not everyone realizes this:

> A member of our group always talked about how everything would affect her personally. Every discussion and decision provoked her to talk about her interests. She never sensed the needs of the "group as a whole"—that there was something above and beyond what she would get personally. We grew tired of

hearing why she couldn't do this or couldn't do that when everyone else saw merit in an idea. The leader finally said we would vote on our decisions and that a simple majority would rule. At last we were able to make progress as a group by voting her down on one decision after another. The leader told me later that he wanted the group to be unanimous on its decisions, but realized that there was no way the group would make any decisions without voting and overriding her objections.

Continuing with the interpersonal confrontation step, we can include techniques we learned from previous chapters on mediation and negotiation. As we learned in Chapter 11 that the *caucus* is a useful tool for creating consensus. The group leader may ask to meet in private with a member of the group to find out why the person is taking a particular stand or acting in a problematic way. This may result in the resolution of some individual problem. Or, the group leader may find a way to have the individual replaced by someone else. Perhaps the leader of the above group could have met and talked about his concerns with the woman who could not let go of her personal life. Sometimes, two or more group members "have lunch together" to iron out some issues rather than take up valuable time to do that at a group meeting.

Other useful principles and skills were presented in Chapter 10. Because some problems are quite complicated, *fractionation* may be a useful way to identify components of an issue that may be tackled one by one. Group members should *separate people from the problem* and comment on ideas rather than verbally attack other group members. To *generate more options,* group members are encouraged to focus on *interests rather than positions* like the woman in the scenario above who insisted on focusing on her position or self-interests. In addition, the group can generate more options by *brainstorming, cost cutting, compensation,* and *prioritizing.* They are encouraged to *consult with others* before or outside meetings before presenting ideas at a meeting. As suggested in earlier stages, everyone should *strive for common ground* and *think positively.* With little adaptation, many of the principles and techniques presented Chapter 10 may be used to manage group conflicts.

The fourth step, *consider the other's view,* is important in workgroup conflicts. The suggestion to be empathetic, which we made earlier, applies here as well—up to a point that is. Sometimes it is necessary to lay off workers, to change their work schedule, which may cause personal problems for some, and to pressure some workers to be more productive to meet instrumental goals. While we should strive to make group decisions for the good of everyone, sometimes not everyone is happy with the outcome. The important goal is to be fair and open in the process. Remember, as a participant at group meetings, it is important that you and the group work hard on establishing and maintaining *the process than dictate or control the outcome.*

The fifth step is to *come to an agreement.* In the case of a task group, there is usually some problem requiring solution. The group's decision is then reported to management, which should take the group's deliberation and recommendation into consideration. In Chapter 10, we learned about establishing *objective criteria for making decisions.* Voting is a useful application of an objective criterion to the decision-making process. Some workgroups prefer to decide on the basis of consensus, which means that everyone agrees. In such cases, great efforts are undertaken to get everyone on board. Someone who holds out may be offered creative solutions that move the individual toward consensus. However, sometimes a "hung jury" occurs because at least one person refuses to go along with the rest of the group. This is why some groups prefer to vote, requiring two-thirds or a simple majority (51%) as a decision-making mechanism. Perhaps the group has formal bi-laws and follows *Roberts Rules of Order* (or a modified version of it) in the conduct of meetings. Still other groups that have a powerful manager may find that, after a serious discussion of a problem and its solutions, her or his decision is all that matters. At least the decision maker heard wanted input and was interested in what others thought before deciding. In any case, workgroups realize that they need a mechanism for resolving issues, so that the group reaches a decision in the time allotted and the organization can move ahead.

The sixth step is to *follow up on the solution*. Organizations may not always require a group to re-evaluate their decisions at a future date. However, a group may include an assessment in their recommendation. Managers are often interested in ways to measure outcomes and evaluate progress.

Adapting the Communication Options

In Chapter 2, we present the *communication options* in conflict situations. They are:

- avoiding/accommodating
- collaborating
- compromising
- passive–aggressive
- competitive conflict escalation

The strategy one should employ to effectively manage conflict depends on the type of conflict experienced. For reasons presented in Chapter 2, we would argue that *competitive conflict escalation* and *passive–aggressive communication* constitute inappropriate responses to conflict within a workplace group. However, a conflict manager may need to *avoid* some conflicts or *accommodate* when conflicts arise over relationship goals. One might think that it makes sense to openly confront all issues facing the team, but research says otherwise. Trying to deal with relationship issues may actually escalate their intensity rather than resolve them. In such cases, maintaining ambiguity through avoidance and accommodation may allow the issues to simply resolve themselves over time. De Dreu and Van argue that avoiding responses might be better for two reasons:

> . . . relationship conflict is difficult to settle to mutual satisfaction . . . (and directs) team members away from their tasks and instead focus them (even more) on their interpersonal relations. As a result, team members do not invest their time and energy in teamwork, and team functioning and effectiveness suffers . . . [16]

The preponderance of evidence suggests that task and process conflicts are productively confronted in their early stages through *collaborating* and *compromising* strategies. This is a logical conclusion: Since task and process conflicts have the potential to clarify issues and processes, a conflict manager should deal with those conflicts early in a direct way, so that information processing activities are activated, resulting in team creativity, innovation, and productivity.

Now that we've given you an overview of conflict in groups and organizations and the effect it has, we turn to three areas of research on group and organizational conflict that are especially problematic at this time: conflict arising from diversity, conflict arising from the clash of work and life demands, and conflict manifested in bullying.

CONFLICTS DUE TO DIFFERENCES IN PEOPLE: DIVERSITY IN THE WORKPLACE

Our culture, ethnic identification, and race have powerful influences on what we believe and how we behave. When people with different heritages find that these differences clash, we have **diversity-based conflict.** As the working world becomes more diverse, it is inevitable that different attitudes and practices come into conflict with one another. Whether or not the results of this kind of conflict are productive depends on a number of factors. The research in this area has produced contradictory findings. On the one hand, conflict from perceived differences between group members may result in negative effects; on the other hand, those differences may enhance the information and perspectives available to group members.[17]

Perhaps the greatest cause of conflicts in organizations arises from our perceptions of an in-group and an out-group, or us versus them.[18] Further, it is possible that, since it is one person's perception that indicates the presence of a conflict, that those who are members of minority groups are more likely to perceive a conflict than those in the dominant group. Dominant group members may be so accustomed to taking their view for granted that they "sometimes fail to realize their own prejudices. Modern racists, for example, do not recognize themselves as racist despite their capacity for holding subtly racist attitudes."[19] Two such conflicts about taken-for-granted assumptions are related below:

> Monday was my birthday and my supervisor invited me to have lunch. I was upset with her at first because she did not ask me but simply told me the time that I should meet her and where we would be eating. I felt that she was forcing me to do something and not taking my interest into consideration.

Of course, eating preferences are not the only way personal characteristics lead to diversity-based conflict in the organization. We subtly make judgments about the other person's gender, race, social standing, etc., whether or not we meet them face to face. And as we do so, our own gender, race, etc. become important in our interaction with others.

Informational characteristics also create conflict in ways we often are unable to see. While a group is more likely to be productive and have a variety of resources at its disposal where there is a high level of informational diversity, those invisible characteristics may lead to conflict that is difficult to manage. For example, a person who has studied communication might have different expectations about the way instructions are relayed than someone with a technical background.

While the principles and techniques taught in previous chapters are useful in managing conflicts that occur because the conflicting parties are from different cultural backgrounds, most important is showing respect by the way we communicate with one another. This often manifests itself when we *listen*. To begin with, we would caution you to be willing to accept that you may be wrong. Rather than engaging in conversation with the readiness to refute all the other has to say, be willing to listen to the other. Listening does not imply agreement, after all. It simply implies respect and regard for the other as a human being.

Second, we would ask you to remember that not only are your experiences unique, but so are the experiences of others. You cannot presume to understand what another person has lived, felt, or seen. You must hear them out to understand them. Honoring the stories of others, understanding that people carry a narrative important to them, is probably the most effective way to manage conflicts due to diversity.

We will return to the idea of diversity-based conflicts in Chapter 13, where we look at large-scale, intractable conflicts that arise from our fundamental differences in the way we see the world.

CONFLICTS DUE TO PRESSURES FROM OUTSIDE THE WORKPLACE: WORK–LIFE CONFLICTS

Defining Work–Life Conflict

While work comprises a major portion of our waking hours, it is not the only activity we engage in. For many of us, our home, family, and outside interests play an important role as sources of pleasure, physical health activities, and time away from pressures at work. Some of us are burdened by significant responsibilities due to the needs of our children, spouses, and relatives we care for because they cannot care for themselves. Problems occur. Unfortunately, there are times when these outside demands and interests overflow into the workplace. These **work–life conflicts** between one's personal life and the demands of work exist in two directions: The outside responsibility may interfere with one's job performance, or the job may interfere with one's adequately managing a responsibility outside of work. As more single parents have entered the workforce, questions of child and family care become more common. Should a single parent abruptly leave work because his or her child has been sent home from school? Should the workplace demand that an employee come to work on days that a person is confronted by a sick spouse or children? Some large companies provide "personal leave days" which are charged against sick leave to cover such cases, and some allow a person such time off without pay, but some businesses do not and may not continue to employ people who are "undependable."

Causes of Work–Life Conflict

Work–life conflict often takes the form of "a problem employee." This person may be late for work, frequently ask for time off, fall asleep on the job, or have recurring illnesses. While there may be problem employees, there are other times when circumstances make it difficult for an employee to do his or her job to the best of their abilities. We are reminded of our treatment of attribution theory in Chapter 3, because a supervisor may attribute internal causation (i.e., the employee is unmotivated, can't be trusted, and wants to take advantage of the system) while in reality the employee may be under severe external pressures, some of which we describe here. Especially for the working poor, work–life conflict reaches critical levels when attending to one's personal life may result in lost income, as the narrative below illustrates:

> For over three years, I've been trying to find a job I am trained for. I have a minimum wage retail job with unpredictable hours that helps me pay the bills. I went through a long process with one company and was one of the final candidates. Although they didn't hire me, they wanted me to come back the following week and interview again for a different position. On such short notice, I couldn't get the time off, and I had already lost so much money interviewing for them that I had to turn them down. I can't afford to lose the one job I do have.

This story illustrates one of the many ways a job interferes with other interests and activities or vice versa. Of course, we all realize that committing to a work schedule can prevent us from pursuing outside interests, but the schedule becomes problematic when it interferes with doctor appointments, children's important school events or days school is cancelled, and other pressures an employee may feel outside the workplace.

Work–life conflict isn't limited to one socioeconomic class. For example, technology such as Internet-connected phones typically carried by those in managerial positions has created an hourless workday (i.e., 24/7) and a sense of always being on call. In some workplaces, it is expected that people are immediately available and others get frustrated when they are unable to get a speedy answer to a question or request. We may find ourselves trying to do too many tasks at one time because of such devices—texting while in another meeting, checking email in the evening while watching television, and going over our upcoming schedule on a cell phone at home while getting ready for bed at night. However, receiving a cell phone call, text, or email at night that is upsetting interferes with one's sleep. In addition, in some cases the availability of such technology actually slows down decision making in an organization rather than speeding it up, because those at higher levels expect to be consulted since their availability can be taken for granted. Decisions that really don't require consultation wind up getting it anyway.

Work–life conflict is not necessarily limited to those with families, because single persons or couples without children would like to have a personal life outside of work.

Suggestions for Dealing with Work–Life Conflict

Throughout this book, we have argued that different types of conflict require different approaches for effective conflict management. There are three different kinds of conflict that can arise from the interference of work and life demands: conflicts due to time limitations, conflicts due to interference between roles at work and roles at home, and conflicts that arise when behaviors appropriate to one role carry over to another where they are not appropriate.[20] Because each type must be handled differently, we look at each of these in turn.

Clearly, the easiest conflict to identify and probably the hardest one to address is the limitation of time. When a person has multiple roles, the hours required by each may overwhelm that person. Because work–life conflict often contributes to hyperstress, which we discussed in Chapter 8, many of the suggestions listed in that chapter are helpful here. Among them, learning to say no, prioritizing one's schedule, and asking for more help or flexibility (being assertive) are ways to deal with such work–life conflicts. One of the authors is reminded of a colleague who made it clear to everyone at work, including her boss, that she would not read or reply to any emails or texts in evenings or on weekends.

A second contributing factor to work–life conflict concerns *inappropriate behaviors*. A special case of inappropriate behavior occurs when a work role interferes in some way with a role outside of work. For example, one role a person is playing (e.g., work) may create a great deal of pressure, which makes the person difficult to live with at home.

Recall from Chapter 2 that behaviors vary with the situation, occasion, or context. Behavior that is appropriate in one context may not be in another and vice versa. In Chapter 4 we called these *trained incapacities*. When a person is used to giving orders at work, it may be hard to turn that off when he or she comes home. Likewise, a person who is nurturing at home may be expected to be so at work as well, leading to compassion fatigue. Problems arise when a person is unable to adjust from one setting to the other.

Organizations and workers can lessen the impact of this type of work–life conflict. For example, "flex-account policies" and allowing "personal leave days" to count as sick days offer employees options for better balancing demands of work with those of home and family. Due to a unique situation at home, some workers need more flexibility in working hours, vacation times, child care, maternity leave, and elder care. What works well for a colleague might not work for you and vice versa. Such policies help reduce work–life conflict. Unfortunately, not everyone supports flex-account policies or allows "personal leave days." Some managers resort to the "fair but consistent" approach (deciding that everyone should be treated alike—claiming that consistency is the only "fair" way to make decisions—in effect, denying flexibility to everyone).

Supportive coworker relationships may also help reduce work–life conflict. "Talking with coworkers about family and personal life has been shown to lead to greater work satisfaction and higher work functioning as well as higher satisfaction with family activities."[21] Likewise, one can talk with family and friends about problems at work. However, you may recall, back in Chapter 8 we cautioned frustrated individuals from venting their anger on others rather than confronting the problem person. While we recommended using the constructive confrontation steps in Chapter 4 to work through conflicts with the person responsible for them, we also realize that not all people in the workplace or at home respond well to assertiveness. We recommend that you start out trying to be assertive, but if this backfires, then you can temporarily resort to accommodation and avoidance. In such cases, you may benefit by talking with coworkers about marital problems at home or venting to family and friends about problem people at work.

Overall, work–life conflict is a serious issue for organizations and the employees who work within them. Balancing demands, having sufficient rest and "down time," and setting reasonable boundaries on what organizations demand continue to be challenges for us. One of the authors makes every attempt not to read emails at bedtime to avoid losing a night's sleep.

CONFLICTS WITH BULLIES: WORKPLACE BULLYING

Defining Bullying and Cyberbullying

While workplace bullying is not a new phenomenon, the study of it is fairly recent. According to a recent study, "workplace bullying behavior is a noteworthy and prevalent issue in organizations around the world (e.g., Denmark, Sweden, Norway, Finland, Ireland, UK, Korea, Japan, Germany, Italy, Australia, New Zealand, Mexico, US, and other countries),"[22] and almost 80 percent of workers report having witnessed or experienced bullying.[23] State governments are passing anti-bullying laws and interest is growing in preventing cyberbullying.

Bullying is "a frequent, enduring abusive interaction *distinguished* by targets'—bullied workers'—inability to defend themselves."[24] In recent times, the introduction of the Internet has added a new dimension to such abuse. **Cyberbullying** occurs when people use the Internet to intentionally harm another person through instant messaging, chat rooms, or social media sites. Bullying is behavior far more serious than general unpleasantness or single-issue conflict. It is distinguished by "four specific features: intensity, repetition, duration, and power disparity."[25] It is meant to control or harm others through insults, gossip, criticism, ridicule, and other verbally aggressive behaviors. Bullying is a pattern of abuse that persists; it is estimated that ". . . the average duration for US workers is 18–20 months."[26] One of the difficulties organizations have in dealing with workplace bullying is that there are no legal remedies for it as there are for sexual harassment or racial discrimination in the workplace; there is simply no law against being a jerk.[27] We hope that this gets corrected eventually.

The effects of bullying on the target can range from mental stress through physical illness. How long a person is bullied affects the level of harm experienced; as it increases, so does the harm. Targets often report headaches, body aches, anxiety and panic attacks, sleeplessness, self-medication, overeating, or under eating (depending on one's typical stress-related patterns). Targets also often dread or fear going to work. They frequently are afraid their complaints about the bullying will not be heard or will make it worse. Targets often isolate themselves out of self-protection.[28] When people are bullied, they are ashamed of their vulnerability, and in turn create negative self-talk that essentially re-victimizes them.[29] "Victims of bullying may even show symptoms of post-traumatic stress disorder (PTSD) . . ."[30]

As tempted as one is to "bully back," unfortunately, this usually makes matters worse. Keep in mind schismogenesis from Chapter 2, where abusive behaviors escalate violence, which may worsen the bullying taking place.[31]

Bullying produces harmful effects that extend beyond victim suffering. Witnesses to bullying may also suffer by experiencing decreased creativity and mental performance.[32] Those who witness someone being bullied are more likely to perceive their organization in a negative manner than those who do not.[33] When a workgroup is aware that one of its members is being bullied, relationships among group members may be affected. Other group members may fear becoming the bully's target. Further, prolonged exposure to bullying behaviors may desensitize members to it and lead them to eventually engage in it themselves.[34]

Does a particular type of person engage in bullying? One mark of a bully is a person who wants to control, dominate, and abuse others. Early work in the area identified dispositional hostility, a lack of self-control, a history of enacting aggression, acceptability of seeking revenge, and substance and/or alcohol abuse as predictors of workplace aggression.[35] There is some evidence that a person likely to bully is also likely to act in a discriminatory manner toward cultural, ethnic, or racial groups other than his or her own. Additionally, trait anger, verbal aggressiveness, and the desire to have one's own ethnic or racial group be dominant have significant relationships with bullying. Further, a person less able to take the perspective of another is more likely to bully others as well.[36] Men appear to be more likely to bully than women, at least in those who have been studied, although typically people tend to bully members of their sex. In addition, large organizations that are male dominated tend to experience a greater degree of bullying than organizations that are not male dominated.[37]

If a particular type of person is likely to bully, is there a corresponding target profile? One study found that about a third of those who were bullied tended to be "more anxious and neurotic and less agreeable, conscientious and extravert than non-victims."[38] Generally, those who bully often believe they have power over their targets, although that power may be due to their superior strength or may be derived from a formal position of authority. Bullying by someone above the target's formal position is most frequent (superior to subordinate), followed by horizontal bullying (peer to peer), and lastly upward bullying. This student relates an example of superior-to-subordinate bullying:

> While serving in the Coast Guard, I had a supervisor who only knew one way to communicate with her coworkers—she was always "the boss." She demanded everything she wanted and most of her coworkers felt bullied in the workplace. Instead of using language that would encourage coworkers to work harder, she chose to demean people and challenge them with personal attacks. We later learned that she took the assignment in our office not because she wanted to but because she knew it would help her get promoted. She did not care about being fair to her colleagues.

As this narrative suggests, bullying is usually done by those in higher positions of authority or are physically dominating. However, upward bullying, while not common, may occur where employees see the supervisor as weak and ineffective. Upward bullying also often follows organizational change or a change in leadership.[39] The danger, of course, in even trying to determine whether there is a particular target profile is that it runs the risk of blaming the victim rather than preventing the negative behavior in the first place.

Managing Bullies

What is the most effective way to combat workplace bullying? In the absence of organizational systems that keep it in check, targets of bullying have several other ways of responding. The research discussed above indicates that counter attack is not effective. We believe that civility (see Chapter 1) may be an effective response to bullying, but it is difficult to employ in this case. Remember that how we treat others should be independent of what we think of them. Civility is a way of acknowledging others, thinking the best of others, listening, being inclusive, speaking kindly, accepting others, respecting their boundaries, accepting personal responsibility, and apologizing when appropriate. We listed five rules to help implement a civil response, which may be used here. In addition to civility, other strategies have been discovered.

Lutgen-Sandvik's research found that there were a variety of ways that people found to combat bullying.[40] First, a strategy that may be more empowering for the target is **reverse discourse**, which encompasses several tactics of responding to the bully through communicative means. One means is simply turning an insult around and treating it as though it is a compliment—"yes, I'm a troublemaker, but someone has to say something, and you should be glad that I am willing to speak up." Other communicative strategies, more passive-aggressive in nature, include avoiding the bully and going to lawyers, outside experts, or oversight agencies to help in bringing a halt to the bullying. This approach may include filing a grievance against the bully. The target may need to first document all interactions with the bully and make note of any witnesses, so that he or she can accumulate a body of evidence before engaging in a formal complaint. Often before filing a grievance, a person is required to speak to the bully first. If you run into this requirement, you could confront the problematic individual (i.e., a bully) by using the confrontation steps as presented in Chapter 2, which seems on the surface as a positive approach. As teachers and researchers of communication, we (the authors) believe in trying communication first, but unfortunately, we have found that it does not always work out as we hope. At least we can say we tried. Don't be surprised if bullies, unlike reasonable individuals, fail to respond productively to what you think, feel, or want. Now you can take further steps to file a grievance.

A second means of coping with bullying is **subversive (dis)obedience**, which is another form of passive–aggressive behavior we discussed in Chapter 2, where the target changes his or her work output or communication patterns in ways that disadvantage the bully. For example, the target of a bully may increase his or her work for a while and then let it drop off, making it difficult for the bully to predict workflow. The target may also work-to-the-rule, doing exactly what is required or the minimum required by the bully. A worker can insist that a job take a particular amount of time to process, even though it could be done more quickly. As this person writes in his narrative:

> I was in a meeting with my boss and tried to say something when he told me to shut up. Not only did he say it to me once, he actually said it to me three times, even though I was trying to explain something really important. I was pretty steamed at him. I thought it was degrading and parental. I decided that two could play that game. For nearly three weeks, I gave him no information and initiated no communication with him. He had to ask for everything. He never really apologized; he thinks it's his right to order us around. However, I felt better as a result.

A person may also engage in **retaliation,** which includes hostile gossip, which may result in others taking action against the abusive person. Using these options, a person uses the system in order to create problems for the bully. Subversive (dis) obedience also encompasses the creation of distance between oneself and the bully, physically if possible but also by limiting communication options.

Realize for your own protection that there can be a fine line between the aggressive behavior taken by a target of bullying and the person who is the bully. Deciding on your own that a supervisor is "out to get you" does not mean that your retaliatory behavior is justified. The abusive supervisor must in fact truly be a bully. Others must agree with you that the problem supervisor has a history of engaging in clearly inappropriate tactics, including picking on weaker people, and menacing, threatening, and offending them. Bullies cannot hide; they stand out clearly and are usually a problem for everyone including their own bosses.

Collective voice exists when most or at least many others have let others know that they have a problem with a particular supervisor or work colleague. The important aspect of collective voice is that it helps the bullied person realize that he or she is not alone and that the person is a real problem. Collective voice may also result in people agreeing to protect each other and even start keeping records or even reporting the bullying. However, some bullies may respond by increased harassment of individuals when they are not gathered as a group with the goal of reporting them. Moreover, some organizations go to great extremes to protect certain individuals, and you may not find it easy to take action against a bully. Knowing this, some workers find the workplace terrifying.

A third means of coping is through **psychological detachment,** or creating a sense of being away from work. Psychological detachment reduces the effect a bully has, as well as providing a healthy balance between work and life outside. Self-talk can play an important role here. You need to remind yourself to leave work and the bully at the office. In the office, it is the equivalent of taking a mental vacation. For instance, if you can imagine the bully in a ridiculous situation, or envision something funny happening, your stress level comes down. Be aware, though, that thoughts of revenge increase stress levels.[41]

Finally, one last way to deal with a bully is **exodus.** A person can quit, make a threat to quit, put in for a transfer, and aid others in finding new jobs. When we have recommended quitting, others often tell us that they can't for some financial reason. In such cases, we suggest that they view their work situation as temporary and plan ways to transfer or find a better place to work at some clearly defined time in the future, such as graduation, marriage, pregnancy, separation from a spouse, or repayment of a debt. We recognize that we all have to put up with bad work situations from time to time, but we do not want them to last longer than absolutely necessary.

MANAGE IT

It is really no surprise to discover that groups and organizations are sources of conflict in our lives. The effective management of such conflict may reduce its harmful effects, and at the same time, it may enhance worker productivity and job satisfaction.

You learned in this chapter that conflict in groups is a variation of interpersonal conflict. Workers may disagree over instrumental/task goals that concern the best way to accomplish the workgroup's assignment. They may differ over relationship goals that are related to what group members want in power, trust, supportiveness, competition, and rules that govern types of relationships in the workplace. There may be conflicts over someone's identity goal, which refers to the way that person wants to see himself or herself. Workers may disagree over process goals that concern the way they want to interact together. Research from the information-processing perspective indicates that focusing on process goals is most effective for a workgroup.

Conflicts may also occur at each of the developmental stages a workgroup moves through. In the forming phase, a tremendous amount of unfamiliarity with group members and what they bring to it creates some conflicts over expectations. The next phase, storming occurs as people begin to feel some identification with the group but don't really feel a sense of unity around its purpose. In the norming phases, a sense of unity emerges as members begin to replicate functions and group norms become observable. In the performing phase, conflict serves to focus individuals on accomplishing team goals and reaching consensus. At this point, there are clear expectations regarding problem-solving behaviors that are focused on goal attainment. The final phase of group development is termination, either of the group or of particular group members. Individuals may not agree over when a task ends, who may be let go, and when the group should stop meeting. Unless the team can effectively manage conflict in all phases, the sum of the conflicts may be greater than the team's capacity to be effective. Should the team not be able to appropriately handle conflict, outside intervention in the way of guidance, training, therapy, or mediation may become necessary.

As people act informally in groups and organizations, they can take on one of three types of informal roles: task roles that help the group or organization achieve instrumental goals, maintenance roles that facilitate relationship goals such as communication and resolution of conflict, or disruptive roles that keep the group from achieving its task.

Most of what was presented in previous chapters may be adapted to the workplace. We discussed the various communication options workers have to manage conflicts in workgroups. These include avoiding, accommodating, competing, compromising, and collaborating. For some issues, especially those involved in relationship and identity, avoidance and/or accommodation can be a good way to manage the conflict, as groups that develop over time also develop an understanding for those kinds of differences. However, we recommend a bias toward cooperation as we deal with conflicts in groups.

For conflicts resulting from diversity in the workplace, we need to be more in tune with cultural differences and how they may be accommodated in the workplace. As for work–life imbalances over the long run, we must strive for relieving hyperstress by balancing demands, having sufficient rest and "down time," and asserting ourselves when negotiating with our supervisors reasonable boundaries on what they can demand of our time and energy especially beyond the normal workday. For dealing with bullies in the workplace, a person may use a variety of communicative means described in this chapter. Remember our warning that one mark of a bully is a person who wants to control, dominate, and abuse others. The victim of bullying may engage in passive–aggressive behavior, may rally others at work in an effort to "gang up" on the bully, and quit the job or put in for a transfer.

Our approach in this chapter is to encourage you to carefully analyze a workplace conflict so that you can apply the appropriate response to it. All too often we respond to problematic situations by habit rather than make a more effective and appropriate response.

EXERCISES

THINK ABOUT IT

1. When have you seen task-related conflict contribute to productivity in a group or organization? When has it been unproductive?
2. Have you used an avoiding strategy in the past with a group and found that things did work out over time?
3. What kind of roles do you play in groups? Are you comfortable with those roles?
4. Where have you seen issues related to diverse members become a conflict in groups or organizations?
5. How do you try to balance your work and personal life? How do you avoid or minimize conflicts between them?
6. Have you ever been the victim of a workplace bully? How did you respond to it? Were your efforts effective?

APPLY IT

1. Think back to one of your experiences in a group. Describe the experience and show how your group went through the five stages of group development.
2. Give an example of a process conflict, a task conflict, and a relationship conflict in a group or organization.
3. Recall a group conflict in which you have been involved. Explain how you might apply any of the chapter's suggestions for managing that conflict.
4. Consider a situation in which you experienced a conflict based on diversity issues. What was it about? How did you manage the conflict? Explain how you might apply any of the chapter's suggestions for managing that conflict.
5. Have you encountered a bully? List the strategies you read about in this chapter that you could use to deal with a bully in that kind of situation.

WORK WITH IT

1. Read the following case study. Imagine that you are a human resources officer to whom this person is relaying the information. How would you advise this person to operate more effectively in his or her group given the information you have learned in this chapter?

> When I began working at my new job a little over 18 months ago I found that I always had to prove myself to my coworkers. Where I am employed, we often work as a team to get the job done. Perhaps it was my coworkers' way of "testing" me, but whatever the reason I found it frustrating. Even my good ideas would be brushed off simply because I was the "new guy." After a while I stopped arguing and took my ideas straight to our boss. The team got really upset over that. Now we aren't working together at all.

a. What kind of conflicts did this person encounter?
b. What stage of development is this group?
c. How have roles created conflict in this group?
d. What strategies from this chapter did he or she use to address the conflicts that arose?
e. What strategies from this chapter might have produced better outcomes?
2. Imagine you are in charge of creating a new program for employees at your place of business. Based on your reading of this chapter, create a list of principles for working together that you would teach to incoming employees.

DISCUSS IT

1. Read the following case and answer the questions following it.

A few years ago my position at work changed, and I suddenly became responsible for the nursing and ancillary staff on the unit. I had worked with some of these nurses as equals, but now I was playing a supervisory role; suddenly my friends were now my subordinates. Deciding how to deal with the various conflicts was quite challenging at first. One of my greatest challenges was trying to make the monthly staffing schedule. The problem was that everyone wanted specific time off, which would sometimes mean that most of the staff would request to be off on a particular day. I think that some of my former colleagues thought that they should be treated differently and get whatever they wanted because they were my friends. Since we were already short staffed, it was impossible to give everyone what they wanted and as such it was up to me to decide how it was going to be done in a way that would ensure we had enough staff to provide quality patient care, and at the same time not alienate the staff. I decided to set up a pattern of rotation in which everyone was treated equally and fairly, but that has resulted in a lot of complaints.

a. What kind of conflicts did the narrator encounter?
b. What stage of development is this group?
c. How have roles created conflict in this group?
d. What strategies from this chapter did he or she use to address the conflicts that arose?
e. What strategies from this chapter might have produced better outcomes?

GROUP CLASS EXERCISE: "MAKING A CHANGE IN POLICY"

OBJECTIVE:

The objective of this exercise is to give students an opportunity to apply principles of cooperative group conflict management. The following case involves small groups (4–6 members) discussing how to implement a policy change. It helps to provide the group with bare essentials but allow the members to embellish the situation as they see fit. Another group project or commercial group conflict exercise may be substituted for the following case.

TIME PERIOD:

2 class periods (1 for group discussion of policy change, followed by 1 evaluation session).

INSTRUCTIONS:

Step 1: The class is divided into small groups, ranging from 4 to 6 members each plus 1 or 2 observers for each group.

Step 2: Groups are assigned to discuss how they would implement one of the following policy changes (topic): academic calendar/holidays; teacher evaluation process/form; graduation requirements; parking regulations; college/university mission statement; student fees.

Step 3: Each group selects a discussion leader. Observers do not participate in the discussions, sit outside the group circle, but sit where they can hear and observe the group members.

Step 4: The group discusses how they would like to change the present policy regarding the selected or assigned topic. During and after the discussion, observers fill out Form 1.

Step 5: The group attempts to come up with a consensus regarding how to change and put into practice a new policy regarding the selected or assigned topic.

Step 6: At the conclusion of the discussion, group members fill out Form 2.

Step 7: Group members and observers discuss how the group communicated and resolved issues (this may be done by all groups simultaneously or as a presentation by each group to the class one at a time).

Form 1: Observer's/Judges Group Conflict Observation

Group's Topic_____

Your Name_____

Date_____

1. Was a discussion leader selected by the group? How well did that person function in his or her leadership role?

2. Were there conflicts over instrumental goals; how were they resolved?

3. Were there conflicts over relationship goals; how were they resolved?

4. Were there conflicts over identity goals; how were they resolved?

5. Were there conflicts over process goals; how were they resolved?

6. Draw the group (i.e., small circles for group members all in a circle) and show who talked to whom (draw lines/arrows from one person to others). Was there an equal amount of communication between the leader and other members of the group? Did group members interact with one another? Did cliques form in which a few interacted a lot more with one another than with other members of the group? (Show the diagram to the group for individuals' comments about the distribution of interaction, such as why it happened and how they felt about it.)

7. Which members seemed to most characterize the following roles:

   a. *Task roles* (that helped the group work toward expected outcomes)

   b. *Maintenance roles* (that facilitated communication and conflict resolution)

   c. *Disruptive roles* (that interfered with maintenance and task roles)

Form 2: Group Members Evaluation Form

1. What were the group's goals?

   a. What were the group's instrumental goals? Any conflicts over them?

   b. What were the group's relationship goals? Any conflicts over them?

   c. What were the group's identity goals? Any conflicts over them?

   d. What were the group's process goals? Any conflicts over them?

2. How effective was the leader?

3. Did anyone say anything to other members of the group that made anyone appear to feel uncomfortable? What did that person say? What efforts contributed to avoidance, accommodation, or competing?

4. Did anyone say anything to other members of the group that you thought helped facilitate the group's decision making or conflict management? What efforts contributed to compromise and collaboration?

5. What stages did your group progress through (forming, storming, norming, performing, termination)?

NOTES

1. Carsten K. W. De Dreu, Arne Evers, Bianca Beersma, Esther S. Kluwer, and Aukje Nauta, "A Theory-Based Measure of Conflict Management Strategies in the Workplace," *Journal of Organizational Behavior* 22 (2001), 645, 645–668.

2. Carsten K. W. De Dreu, Dirk van Dierendonck, and Maria T. M. Dijkstra, "Conflict at Work and Individual Well-Being," *International Journal of Conflict Management* 15 (2004), 6–26.; Maria T. M. Dijkstra, Dirk van Dierendonck, Arne Evers, and Carsten K. W. De Dreu, "Conflict and Well-Being at Work: The Moderating Role of Personality," *Journal of Managerial Psychology* 20 (2005), 87–104.

3. Dijkstra, et al. *Journal of Managerial Psychology,*

4. Carsten K. W. De Dreu, "When Too Little or Too Much Hurts: Evidence for a Curvilinear Relationship between Task Conflict and Innovation in Teams," *Journal of Management* 32 (2006), 83–107.

5. De Dreu et al., *Journal of Organizational Behavior,* p. 109.

6. Karen A. Jehn and E. Mannix, "The Dynamic Nature of Conflict: A Longitudinal Study of Intragroup Conflict and Group Performance," *Academy of Management Journal* 44 (2001), 238–251.

7. Ruth Anna Abigail and Dudley D. Cahn, "Working with You Is Killing Me: Learning How to Effectively Handle Workplace," in Jason Wrench (Ed.), *Workplace Communication for the 21st Century: Tools and Strategies that Impact the Bottom Line* (Westport, CT: Praeger, 2012), pp. 289–320.

8. Tracy L. Simons and Randall S. Peterson, "Task Conflict and Relationship Conflict in Top Management Teams: The Pivotal Role of Intragroup Trust," *Journal of Applied Psychology* 85 (2000), 102–111.

9. José M. Guerra, Inés Martinez, Lourdes Munduate, and Francisco J. Medina, "A Contingency Perspective on the Study of Consequences of Conflict Types: The Role of Organizational Culture," *European Journal of Work and Organizational Psychology* 14 (2005), 157–176.

10. Ibid.

11. Maria T. M. Dijkstra, Dirk van Dierendonck, and Arne Evers, "Responding to Conflict at Work and Individual Well-Being: The Mediating Role of Flight Behaviour and Feelings of Helplessness," *European Journal of Work and Organizational Psychology* 14 (2005), 119–135.

12. Ellen Giebels and Onne Janssen, "Conflict Stress and Reduced Well-Being at Work: The Buffering Effect of Third Party Help," *European Journal of Work and Organizational Psychology* 14 (2005), 137–155.

13. Marshall Scott Poole and Johny T. Garner, "Perspectives on Workgroup Conflict and Communication," in John G. Oetzel and Stella Ting-Toomey (Eds.), *The Sage Handbook of Conflict Communication: Integrating Theory, Research, and Practice* (Thousand Oaks, CA: Sage Publications, 2006), p. 269.

14. Ibid.

15. Ricky Griffin, *Management,* 8th Ed. (Boston, MA: Houghton Mifflin Company, 2005).

16. Lars Glasø, Stig Berge Matthiesen, Morten Birkeland Nielsen, and Ståle Einarsen, "Do Targets of Workplace Bullying Portray a General Victim Personality Profile?" *Scandinavian Journal of Psychology* 48 (2007), 317; 313–319.

17. Karen A. Jehn, Katerina Bezrukova, and Sherry Thatcher, "Conflict, Diversity, and Faultlines in Workgroups," in Carsten K. W. De Dreu and Michele J. Gelfand (Eds.), *The Psychology of Conflict and Conflict Management in Organizations* (New York: Lawrence Erlbaum Associates, 2008), pp. 179–210.

18. Kristin Smith-Crowe, Arthur P. Brief, and Elizabeth E. Umphress, "On the Outside Looking In: Window Shopping for Insights into Diversity-Driven Conflict," in Carsten K. W. De Dreu and Michele J. Gelfand (Eds.), *The Psychology of Conflict and Conflict Management in Organizations* (New York: Lawrence Erlbaum Associates, 2008), pp. 415–424.

19. Ibid., pp. 416–417.

20. Erika L. Kirby, Stacey M. Wieland, and M. Chad McBride, "Work Life Conflict," in John G. Oetzel and Stella Ting-Toomey (Eds.), *The Sage Handbook of Conflict Communication: Integrating Theory, Research, and Practice* (Thousand Oaks, CA: Sage Publications, 2006), pp. 327–358.

21. Ibid., p. 333.

22. Joyce Heames and Mike Harvey, "Workplace Bullying: A Cross-Level Assessment," *Management Decision,* 44 (2006), 1214, 1214–1230.

23. Pamela Lutgen-Sandvik, "Take this Job and . . . .: Quitting and Other Forms of Resistance to Workplace Bullying," *Communication Monographs* 73 (2006), 407, 406–433.

24. Ibid., p. 407 (italics in original).

25. Pamela Lutgen-Sandvik, Sarah J. Tracy and Jess K. Alberts, "Burned by Bullying in the American Workplace: Prevalence, Perception, Degree and Impact," *Journal of Management Studies* 44 (2007), 841, 837–863.

26. Lutgen-Sandvik, "Take this Job and . . . .: Quitting and Other Forms of Resistance to Workplace Bullying," p. 408.

27. Helen LaVan and Wm. Marty Martin, "Bullying in the U.S. Workplace: Normative and Process-Oriented Ethical Approaches," *Journal of Business Ethics* 83 (2008), 147–165.

28. Anni Townend, "Understanding and Addressing Bullying in the Workplace," *Industrial and Commercial Training,* 40 (2008), 270, 270–273; see also Lutgen-Sandvik, "Burned by Bullying in the American Workplace: Prevalence, Perception, Degree and Impact."

29. Dianne M. Felblinger, "Incivility and Bullying in the Workplace and Nurses' Shame Responses," *JOGNN* 37 (2008), 234–242.

30. Glasø, Matthiesen, Nielsen, and Einarsen, p. 317.

31. Raymond T. Lee and Céleste M. Brotheridge, "When Prey Turns Predatory: Workplace Bullying as a Predictor of Counteraggression/Bullying, Coping, and Well-Being," *European Journal of Work and Organizational Psychology,* 15 (2006), 371, 352–377.

32. C. Porath and A. Erez, "Overlooked but Not Untouched: How Rudeness Reduces Onlookers' Performance on Routine and Creative Tasks," *Organizational Behavior and Human Decision Process* 109 (2009), 29–44.

33. Lutgen-Sandvik, "Burned by Bullying in the American Workplace: Prevalence, Perception, Degree and Impact."

34. Heames and Harvey, *Management Decision.*

35. Jana L. Raver and Julian Barling, "Workplace Aggression and Conflict: Constructs, Commonalities, and Challenges for Future Inquiry," in Carsten K. W. De Dreu and Michele J. Gelfand (Eds.), *The Psychology of Conflict and Conflict Management in Organizations* (New York: Lawrence Erlbaum Associates, 2008), pp. 219, 211–244.

36. Irina Sumajin Parkins, Harold D. Fishbein, and P. Neal Ritchey, "The Influence of Personality on Workplace Bullying and Discrimination," *Journal of Applied Social Psychology,* 36 (2006), 2554–2577.

37. Margaretha Strandmark, and Lillemor R.-M. Hallberg, "The Origin of Workplace Bullying: Experiences from the Perspective of Bully Victims in the Public Service Sector," *Journal of Nursing Management,* 15 (2007), 332–341.

38. Glasø et al., *Scandinavian Journal of Psychology,* 317.

39. Sara Branch, Sheryl Ramsay, and Michelle Barker, "Managers in the Firing Line: Contributing Factors to Workplace Bullying by Staff – An Interview Study," *Journal of Management & Organization* 13 (2007), 264–281.

40. Lutgen-Sandvik, "Burned by Bullying in the American Workplace: Prevalence, Perception, Degree and Impact."

41. Bernardo Moreno-Jiménez, Alfredo Rodriguez-Muñoz, Juan Carlos Pastor, Ana Isabel Sanz-Vergel, and Eva Garrosa, "The Moderating Effects of Psychological Detachment and Thoughts of Revenge in Workplace Bullying," *Personality and Individual Differences* 46 (2009), 359–364.

Managing Social Conflict

OBJECTIVES

At the end of this chapter, you should be able to:

- Define intractable issue.
- Explain why social conflicts are often intractable.
- Define worldview and explain its importance.
- Explain the difference between nationalism and patriotism.

- Explain an intractable issue using critical theory.
- Explain an intractable issue using ripeness theory.
- Explain the concept of embrace.

KEY TERMS

beliefs	nationalism	ripeness theory
critical theory	nonviolent communication	rituals
embrace	other	values
ethics	patriotism	worldview
group-based hatred	pluralism	
intractable issue	praxis	
moral issue	ripeness	

In the fall of 2012, Congress appointed three Republican and three Democratic members to function as a bipartisan "supercommittee" charged with reducing the U.S. budget deficit by over a trillion dollars. The media gave a lot of attention to the importance of this group achieving consensus. Unfortunately, the issues in conflict were interpreted along party lines. Republicans would not support any tax increases or any new taxes or taxes even on the most wealthy Americans. Democrats would not agree to any cuts in the so-called entitlement programs (Social Security, Medicare, Medicaid). So, the supercommittee failed to meet the November deadline. Not only could they reach no agreement, but members of the group did not even show up to continue discussions as the deadline approached. There was too much of a divide between Republicans and Democrats.

Contrast this conflict with one that used to exist between cable firms (Comcast Corp. Time Warner Cable Inc. and Bright House Networks) and wireless companies (i.e., Verizon).

Many of us can well recall the huge divide that used to exist between cable and wireless companies who were known as mortal enemies. Yet, they recently announced an agreement in which the cable companies would receive over three billion dollars in exchange for rights to start up their own wireless network. In addition to the large payout, Verizon agreed to sell the other companies' cable services. Both sides declared the agreement a win–win!

So it is possible for representatives of both "mortal enemies" to sit down and come to a mutual agreement. Where the congressional supercommittee failed, the representatives of the media companies succeeded.

These conflicts involved a unique set of issues that are the focus of this chapter. As we have often pointed out in this book, different types of conflict issues require different ways of managing them. Now we take up in this chapter yet another type of issue, which we call *intractable*.

To understand the role of intractable issues in conflicts, we need to explain how each of us has a worldview and discuss ways of approaching others with a different worldview both theoretically and practically. We also end this chapter with a "Grand Society" exercise designed to introduce you to the notion of opposing worldviews that creates a number of difficult issues for you to discuss that are potentially intractable and problematic. It is important to do the exercises at the end of this chapter to make you aware of your own beliefs, values, and rituals that make up your worldview as a first step in understanding and embracing others who are different.

THE CLASH OF WORLDVIEWS: INTRACTABLE ISSUES

Intractable issues cannot be resolved by communication and negotiation techniques alone because they involve different and conflicting values, beliefs, and rituals. We left them to last because they are the most difficult to resolve. Also referred to as social conflicts, societal conflicts, and moral conflicts, intractable issues are *fueled by distrust and dislike of other groups*. Intractable issues are self-perpetuating and difficult to bring to any kind of resolution.

What makes the intractable issues different from other issues? An intractable issue is *central or lies at the core of our worldview* to be explained below. The conflicting parties become entrenched in the discussion of *who is right and who is wrong*.

Intractable issues exist because men and women see the world differently as do contemporary Republicans and Democrats, Arabs and Christians, younger and older citizens, rich and poor, East and West, and educated and uneducated. If anything, intractable issues have increased as more companies outsourced their manufacturing to other countries, as more companies became transnational (international in scope), and as more federal laws have forced companies to diversify their workforce. In the introductory example, Republicans could not give on taxes and Democrats would not agree to cuts in federal spending on certain social programs. While those involved may have started the conflict by trying to persuade each other to the other's point of view, the conflict began to repeat itself over and over as those involved failed to change the other and thus began to see the other as someone who was unable to understand reason. In a sense, an intractable issue transcends the people involved because it is a clash of their social/cultural, religious, political, and economic philosophies. In everyday encounters, these conflicts are represented by conflicting parties from different cultures, races, ethnic, religious, political, economic (classes), intellectual, social, and art appreciation groups.

What Is a Worldview?

Worldview, or what Germans call *Weltanschauung,* refers to the way one interprets the world based on how they were socialized at home, their place of worship, and school. Citizens in the United States can say that their worldview is what it means to be an American. Consider the world maps many Americans see in elementary school.

> Being an American visiting Bosnia, I was surprised to see a world map with Europe/Africa at the center, which put North/South America way over to the left and Japan/Australia on the right side of the map. What a different way to look at the world when I didn't see my country at the center of the map.

What is your worldview? Specifically, it is a composite of all the cultural values, beliefs, and rituals you hold, which assists you both in describing what you see and in prescribing what you should do. **Values** refer to what we hold dear, ranging from something of economic value, through sentimental value, to values we might die for (freedom, equal opportunity, and the love of someone dear to us). They may be personal, organizational, or cultural. Each professional organization articulates its own set of values like the American Medical Profession publicizes in its code of ethics. When asked to list values, we often think of loyalty, duty, selfless service, and integrity. In this chapter we are most interested in the *cultural values,* because they often serve as a foundation on which many of our organizational and personal values are based. They also make up our **ethics** or moral view, which defines what we believe and think is good and evil, right and wrong, virtue and vice, as well as just and unjust.

Our worldview is also made up of cultural beliefs. Because **beliefs** may or may not be true, they are related to knowledge. We say that a belief is knowledge if it is true. Beliefs that are not true, and therefore not knowledge, are false. The problem is that some beliefs are difficult to prove (who or what caused the "Big Bang" or the universe to expand?), so they are often taken as an act of faith, making beliefs broader than knowledge and implying that some of the unproven beliefs may in fact be false if there were means to test them. Thus, those who once believed that the earth was flat did not *know* it was flat but just *wanted to believe it* was. As Americans many of our beliefs are spelled out in the American *Declaration of Independence.* Americans are supposed to hold these truths to be self-evident that they are all created equal, that they are endowed by the Creator with certain unalienable Rights, and that among these are Life, Liberty, and the pursuit of Happiness. Even though these "truths" were laid out, the worldview of the time did not include women, children, or persons of color in the statement. Over time, those beliefs have undergone reinterpretation and clarification through additions to the constitution so their meaning is more inclusive today than when the declaration was first written. By reading the Declaration and the U.S. Constitution, Americans learn a great deal about their beliefs and their worldview. But it does not stop there. The songs citizens sing like "America the Beautiful" also add to that worldview.

Traditionally, Americans have embraced the following ideas without much reflection on their worthiness or helpfulness in creating a society that is truly a democratic one[1]:

1. achievement and success as major personal goals
2. activity and work favored above leisure and laziness, action/doing over reflection, controlling events and not just letting things happen
3. moral orientation, that is, absolute judgments of good/bad, right/wrong
4. humanitarian motives as shown in charity and crisis aid
5. efficiency and practicality as a preference for the quickest and shortest way to achieve a goal at the least cost
6. process and progress, a belief that technology can solve all problems and that the future will be better than the past
7. material comfort as the U.S. dream
8. equality as an abstract ideal OR equal opportunity (not equality of condition)
9. freedom as a person's right against the state
10. external conformity, the ideal of going along, joining, and not rocking the boat
11. science and rationality, as the means of masterminding the environment and securing more material comforts
12. nationalism, a belief that U.S. values and institutions represent the best on earth
13. democracy (free enterprise) based on personal quality and freedom
14. individualism emphasizing personal rights and responsibilities
15. racism and group superiority, themes that periodically lead to prejudice and discrimination against those who are racially, religiously, and culturally different from the northern Europeans who first settled in the continent

In addition to cultural values and beliefs, social rituals also make up our worldview. **Rituals** are symbolic actions that reinforce beliefs and values. Of course many of our behaviors have meaning, such as "thumbs up" and other hand gestures. However, social rituals play a broader role in defining our worldview because they are tied into our customs and traditions as a people. Christmas is celebrated by many people around the globe, and is a major holiday in the United States despite the diversity of the faiths and traditions celebrated in the United States. Many Western nations celebrate dates connected to important events that occurred during World War II. Saying the Pledge of Allegiance to the American flag, celebrating the 4th of July, and singing the National Anthem at national events are among the many cultural rituals that Americans take seriously. Imagine pledging allegiance to a different flag, or burning the American flag at a protest rather than saluting it, or singing another country's national anthem at a U.S. college football game. Sounds ridiculous doesn't it? Why? It seems absurd because Americans don't do that. It is not part of their worldview. We, authors, say this tongue in cheek because we realize that not every American understands or agrees with or practices all of the American values, beliefs, and rituals we have mentioned so far. We have witnessed Americans refusing to salute the flag, burning it, or protesting against some of the American values and beliefs. Because we value dissent and debate, Americans can embrace each other even if they don't completely agree on all facets of the American worldview.

While we have referred to American values, beliefs, and rituals, worldviews are broader than being a citizen of a country and provide such assumptions about people as "being basically good" as opposed to "being basically rotten," as well as helping us sort out our positions on large social issues involving same sex marriage, abortion, taxation, the role of the church in politics, and the appropriate response of a nation toward terrorism.

What Is Your Worldview?

What is *your* worldview? For some, this is a daunting question. You may feel defensive (what if my worldview is wrong?), so you may be hesitant to open up and be subjected to the criticism of others. You may feel ashamed (I have no worldview; I don't know what I believe in), and don't want to admit it.

The fact of the matter is, we all have a worldview but some have not reflected on it or articulated it. Moreover, we differ in the extent to which we have assimilated some of the teachings we were subject to in school, at home, and in a place of worship. We have our own comfort zone and resist pressure from others. So our worldview may be problematic for one of two reasons. First, we actually do have a worldview but don't know how to describe it. There are books that contain exercises and we provide some exercises at the end of this chapter to help you clarify your cultural values and worldview. Understanding your worldview can help you make many difficult decisions down the road.

The second problem is that one's worldview may be problematic in some respect. If all worldviews were equally valued, then Hitler's Nazi social engineering and way of managing his society would go uncontested. Only by articulating our worldview can we test some of our cultural values, beliefs, and rituals to determine if they are truly of value. Do your values encourage you to engage in immoral, criminal, and unjust acts or do you want to do good, virtuous, and just acts? We do not want to give you the impression that it is easy to determine what is right and what is wrong. We only invite you to begin the journey (if you have not already done so) by taking steps in a direction that is worthy of your efforts. The journey, itself, is lifelong. We encourage you to articulate your worldview as it presently stands and appraise it in an exercise at the end of this chapter.

One of the difficulties with identifying the cluster of beliefs, values, and rituals we hold as important is that we are rarely aware of them until they are challenged. Our worldview has a "taken for granted" aspect to it. We assume others believe as we do. But that is not the case. As Hollinger notes, we do take for granted the fact that we live side by side with other races, nationalities, ethnic groups, and cultures. But unlike a century ago when members of the dominant culture in the United States assumed that most others thought as they did (or agreed to live according to their rules because their group was dominant), this is not the case today.

> We not only rub elbows with people who are culturally and ethnically different from ourselves, but more significantly people (many of the same culture and ethnicity) who have varying perspectives regarding reality, moral frameworks, and the nature of a good society. They put their worlds together in significantly different ways from each other. In pluralistic societies humans live, work, and attempt civic responsibilities with people whose fundamental outlook on reality is at odds with their own.[2]

The Importance of Your Worldview

Worldviews drive our behavior. Because of their take-for-granted nature, they underlie intractable issues and drive them by blinding the participants to seeing the world in an alternative way. One author argues that it was the difference in worldviews, and the inability of the participants to understand those differences, that led to the deaths of nine people at Waco when the Branch Davidians engaged in a standoff with the FBI.[3]

You can see how differing worldviews can lead to conflicts between individuals who believe that they must convert others to their way of thinking, as though their worldview is the right one. Consider the two sets of abbreviated answers to some of the worldview questions in the example below:

Question	Person One	Person Two
What is a human being?	A human being is a divinely created organism reflecting the image of God.	A human being is a highly evolved animal.
What is the ultimate reality?	God is the holder of all time and purpose.	The universe is moving toward a state of disorder.
What happens to people at death?	They live eternally, either with or without God.	They die. Their bodies return to the earth.
What is the good?	Serving God's purpose.	Making a good living for oneself.
What is evil?	Failing to do God's will.	Treating oneself and others badly.

Now, consider all the ways in which difficult, worldview-based conflicts play out in American politics alone: Is the religious affiliation of the president relevant? Should we allow abortion and stem cell research? Is the death penalty an appropriate response to any crime? How should we deal with issues of addiction (or is drug addiction a crime)? Should homosexuals have the same marriage rights as heterosexuals? How should we respond to poverty and to the homeless? What role should the government play in the care and protection of its citizens? You can probably add many more significant questions to this list. To make a worldview more relevant to our lives, consider your views on patriotism and nationalism. We are hoping to challenge what you believe and value. Our goal is to get you to reflect on your worldview.

Patriotism and Nationalism

There is nothing wrong with having positive feelings for your country, but patriotism can become a trained incapacity (see Chapter 4) when those feelings overcome reason and turn to more extreme nationalism. **Patriotism** is "love for one's country as it is and a willingness to defend it against foreign aggression."[4] Citizens should be patriotic. **Nationalism,** on the other hand, is a "love of one's nation . . . once it has exterminated all its enemies, become totally unified, and achieved its grand purpose of world-historical destiny."[5] A nationalist not only wants world dominance, but believes that his or her nation is the only one suited to such dominance because the nationalist thinks it is to the benefit of everyone. Thus, nationalism fuels false beliefs and intractable issues.

Nine-eleven (9/11) had a profound effect on Americans. For the first time since WWII, the United States was attacked on its own ground by terrorists who hated the United States. The United States responded effectively to the terrorist threat; however, at the same time, Americans experienced a rising level of nationalism that characterized people questioning governmental and military actions as unpatriotic and unsupportive of our armed forces. Although one of the founding fathers, Thomas Jefferson, claimed that "Dissent is the highest form of patriotism," such an ideal was largely lost with the rise of neoconservatism during the next several years after 9/11. When a person is attacked for criticizing the decisions made by his or her government, it is a good sign that nationalism, rather than patriotism, is dominating the conversation.

Conversely, you might not be interested in including nationalism and patriotism in your worldview because you think that they fuel conflicts at a level where you don't want to operate. Think, however, of the way you talk to people who make different political choices from you, as the people in this narrative:

> I'm not sure how my sister and I grew up in the same family, because we are totally different politically. My sister is a Republican. I'm not always a Democrat; sometimes I register Independent or Green. She is completely a party-line person. There's no one in any other party worth her trouble, and she will vote for a Republican over a Democrat even if she doesn't like the candidate. All during the Bush administration she expressed her admiration for many of his decisions that I felt were wrong. When I told her I was supporting Barack Obama for president, she asked me how I could support a Black Muslim who hated America. In a knee jerk reaction, I asked her how she could support a fascist war monger. That was when I just said we ought to avoid talking about politics with one another.

When the level of debate stoops to name calling, unproven accusations, and intense feelings, we have shifted from a well thought out, reasoned point of view to one based on untruths and irrational beliefs.

In addition, we need to avoid saying and thinking "this is what the Republicans and conservatives think" or "what Democrats and liberals hold true" because not all members of either party are in total agreement. We should try to identify common ground shared by both or all political parties. Members of each political/economic group must also explain their views in a way that does not show disrespect to the other group.

We hope that you believe with us that our nation is best served by the presence of all the voices within it. Voices that suppress dissent, stereotype the opposition, and do not allow for the healthy exchange of ideas are those that create and perpetuate intractable issues. As one student wrote:

> It occurred to me that as we become a smaller world, we are "rubbing up against" people of many different cultures and backgrounds and the dissonance created has increased tremendously. The fallback reaction of self-justifying our own beliefs is not a solution. I think one of the reasons that I dread the upcoming political season is because we do not get to hear the underlying beliefs of either group. Instead, the name-calling rhetoric has taken center stage and no one winds up a winner. Ironically, it is the Christians who have gotten the worst reputation for being self-righteous, unwilling to hear other viewpoints, and in general, seen as ignorant fools. I do not have to accept others' beliefs as my own; however, I do have to accept their right to have those beliefs. By practicing the methods of civility and nonviolent communication, I would have the opportunity to gain a greater understanding of why other people believe what they believe, and also the opportunity to explain my own value system as well.

WHEN WORLDVIEWS CLASH: CONFLICTS BETWEEN YOU AND "THE OTHER"

Who Is the Other?

The **Other** is a generic term used to signify members of the out-group. In-groups do not have the same worldview as do out-groups. What happens when representatives of conflicting worldviews try to resolve their differences? Can they succeed in forging agreements like the media firms and wireless companies, or do they crash like the supercommittee described in the introduction to this chapter? In the field of communication, much of the early work on intractable issues was conducted using the term **moral issue**, referring to those conflicts that arose out of opposing views of right and wrong. Because of the inability of participants to agree on how to resolve their differences, intractable issues are persistent: They "fuel themselves and are therefore self-sustaining. Often the original issue becomes superfluous. . . . Participants in a moral conflict tend to treat each other as mad, bad, sick, or stupid, and they experience a crisis of rationality, feeling that they cannot reason with people 'like that.'"[6] An example of this inability to communicate is found in the abortion controversy. A person who believes that a woman has the right to control her body finds no common ground on that issue with a person who believes that a fetus is an unborn human being with rights independent of its mother.

Moral conflicts often take on a pattern that is something other than what any of the participants wanted or expected. Each side is hard-pressed to understand why its best efforts to communicate are not understood by the other side. What makes perfectly good sense to one person may be totally ridiculous to another when each is viewed within his or her values. As each party in the conflict is unable to understand, hear, or agree with what the other has to say, or disregards the arguments of the other, the conflict becomes more entrenched. The pattern of discourse in a conflict involving an intractable issue moves from persuasion to schism—from each side believing the other capable of understanding if it were only able to hear the arguments to each side treating the other as crazy and unworthy of communication. When moral conflicts become entrenched, participants on one side have nothing to say to those on the other side because they see them as subhuman, perverts, and infidels.[7]

As the conflict becomes more entrenched, the discourse in the conflict becomes more simplified and shallow. It no longer reflects the richness of reasoning that first characterized the conflict; instead, slogans and simple answers substitute for arguments and reasoning as each side despairs of winning the other to its way of thinking. When a person on one side in the moral conflict addresses those who think like him or her, discourse continues to be eloquent and elaborated; in addressing outsiders, discourse becomes simplified and defensive. As discourse fails, violence becomes more likely; "as a response to moral conflict, force becomes a self-sealing pattern. Each side views the other as aggressor or oppressor, and violence is viewed as necessary for self-protection."[8] An example of a conflict that is already entrenched is found in this narrative:

> I was listening to two family members argue about the topic of abortion. The first said she believed in the right to choose. The second got so mad that he said "that's what all liberal dogs believe." At this point I stepped in and said "Just because you do not agree with her views does not mean you should call her or liberals 'dogs.'" Next, he said "how about pigs, then, is that better? Whose side are you on? I thought you were against abortion!" I responded that I am against abortion, but I respect and understand her view. She has been a social worker for over 30 years and has seen a girl as young as 11 that was raped by a family member (father). As a result the girl became pregnant, so do you believe they should now force an 11 year old who did not make a choice to have sex in the first place, give birth to her own biological sibling? She strongly believes that this would further mentally and physically damage this young victim of domestic sexual abuse. I told him he was dehumanizing her and others whom he may not fully understand because of their views.

Intractable issues are fueled by many variables in the context surrounding them. The media may help inflame conflicts. Polarizing talk that asserts only two sides in the debate fuels intractable issues. Creation of an out-group, and dehumanization of the out-group, is especially provocative. Personal attacks rather than focus on issues, violence, and calls for sacrifice may also fuel intractable issues.

The characteristics of intractable issues are summarized thusly:

1. In terms of actors, intractable issues involve states or other actors with a long sense of historical grievance, and a strong desire to redress or avenge these.
2. In terms of duration, intractable issues take place over a long period of time.
3. Intractable issues involve intangibles such as identity, sovereignty, or values, rituals, and beliefs.
4. In terms of relationships, intractable issues involve polarized perceptions of hostility and enmity, and behavior that is violent and destructive.
5. In terms of geopolitics, intractable issues usually take place where buffer states exist between major power blocks or civilizations.
6. In terms of management, intractable issues resist many conflict management efforts and have a history of failed peacemaking efforts.[9]

Because of the nature of intractable issues, people often try to avoid topics that are likely to escalate, as this person notes:

> Participating in the discussions of morality is often not a first choice for most people, including me. I like to think/act respectful of everyone's opinion, and for this I have been told that I lack conviction. Our ability to think and express ourselves is a double edged sword; we have morals that differ based on our religion, culture, family and yet we are part of one world. What is most mind boggling for me is that if we live in a country where we have freedom of religion, why is it then that we do not have freedom of morality? Is it fair to say that what is right for some is not right for all?

Sometimes, those involved in intractable issues may have the opportunity to simply ignore one another, engaging in *silence* as a way of dealing with the conflict. Silence, however, cannot bring understanding or reconciliation to an intractable issue. Morgan and Olsen argue that "So long as dialogue in a community is perceived as dangerous, the community will forgo again and again the opportunity to learn from one another and to heal the differences and relational fractures that quietly separate them."[10]

In other cases we can agree to disagree. We can grant each other our views without them affecting us emotionally or intellectually. This approach works when we can accept the other but continue to think and believe as we do. This often happens in families or among friends. In fact one of the authors votes consistently for one party while his spouse votes for the other. He is one religion and she is another. Both agreed early on that they would not criticize the other for his or her political and religious beliefs or pressure the other to change. They frequently discuss their political and religious differences but understand that the other has a right to choose and believe as that person does. But what if the intractable issue is such that it presents a real problem for the parties? Some intractable issues cannot be ignored, accepted, or tolerated.

Problematic intractable issues that exist at the societal level are often driven by group-based hatred. Here the term group takes on a broader meaning than the type of workgroups and organizations discussed in the previous chapter. Group in this sense is more like a people, a society, a nation, or a culture. **Group-based** hatred is based on prejudice against the group and is orientated toward a particular goal; those who hold it want to hurt, relocate, or even eliminate the out-group.

> When I enlisted in the Army, I had no idea if I would be going to war for sure or put in a position where I might have to actually kill enemies. I wasn't sure I could kill anyone. Training changed all that. We were showed movies of the enemy and told about the atrocities they committed often against women and children. We chanted sayings, like "What is the spirit of the bayonet? To kill! To kill!" No one who has missed out on a systematic pattern of indoctrination can appreciate how a young GI from a nonviolent background can be honed into a killing machine, but it happens! After months of training, I was convinced that our enemies were ruthless, hated our guts, and would butcher us and our comrades if we did not get them first. The more damage we did to them, the less they could do to us.

Group-based hatred fuels the notion that an in-group is right, good, and holy and the out-group is wrong, bad, and evil. As Halparin notes:

> Hatred is a powerful, extreme, and persistent emotion that rejects the group toward which it is directed in a generalized and totalistic fashion. Group-based hatred is provoked in consequence to recurrent offenses committed against the individual or his or her group. These offenses are perceived as intentional, unjust, threatening the person or his or her group, and of a nature with which in practice the individual has difficulty coping.[11]

Intractable issues often revolve around these beliefs:[12]

- One person or group seeks to deny another person or group their sense of self, or denies the legitimacy of the other's group identity. For example, in most parts of the United States, a gay couple cannot marry. And even if they can marry, they still are not allowed spousal benefits such as tax benefits, health care proxy, and so on.
- One person or group seeks to deny another person or group such fundamental needs as security or the ability to pursue one's own goals. For example, the homeless are often told to leave public parks if they try to sleep during the day. At night, there are few places for them to sleep, and if they create places for themselves, authorities destroy them. Another example is when abortion protestors block the entrance of clinics, making it difficult for women, who believe differently on an intractable issue, try to seek treatment.
- One person or group seeks to put themselves ahead of others in the social, political, or economic structure. For example, commentators on both sides of the political spectrum often deride and denounce those holding political views different from themselves. They reflect no appreciation for others' desire and ability to hold different positions.
- One group seeks to control resources in a win–lose conflict where no expansion of the resources is possible. The ongoing conflict between Israel and Palestine over occupation of territory is an example of this intractable issue.

The narrative below gives an example of how intractable issues that are global in nature filter down to interpersonal relationships.

> For me, one of the most memorable experiences I had as a first year student at a large public university was developing friendships with people who were not likely welcome at my parents' home. While I was Protestant, my best friend was Catholic, and we sat up many nights discussing the nature of God, Heaven, and Hell, from our respective viewpoints. We both seemed open minded at the time, willing to hear each other out and learn from one another. Another of my classmates was from Switzerland and another from Jordan. My Swiss friend told me how his neutral nation shot down U.S. planes that flew over his country during WWII (to preserve their neutrality, he said that the Swiss defended their borders against everyone), while my friend from Jordan was critical of America's role in the Middle East. I learned from them that other views existed on the actions America has taken in the world at large. Somehow we were able to address issues and remain friends because we were open to each other's views.

This narrative suggests that common intractable issues, religious and political, may be managed in a way that does not do damage to people's relationships. What is the nature of these intractable issues and how can they be managed in conflict situations?

Ways of Approaching "the Other": Critical and Ripeness Theories

American society, and indeed most of the world today, faces problems created by pluralism. The **pluralism** we must learn to live with is "the socio-cultural reality of discrepant worldviews, ideologies, and moral frameworks, existing side by side."[13] This living side-by-side with people we characterize as **other,** or as strange and different from ourselves, has provided fertile ground for potential conflict over intractable issues. If we are to live in peace with others who are different from us, it is absolutely essential to learn how to manage conflicts over the intractable issues that arise from such deep differences.

Two recent theories have been proposed to account for the way conflict over intractable issues are managed by the parties. Critical theory focuses on the role of power as distributed between social groups in a culture, while ripeness theory emphasizes the role of timing as a means for resolving an intractable issue.

Critical Theory Critical theory is a complex approach to understanding situations, which analyzes power relations between the participants in an effort to uncover oppression, exploitation, and injustice.[14] Practitioners of critical theory are oriented toward social justice outcomes, changing situations that cause people to live in dehumanizing ways. As this definition is rather complex, let's take it apart and examine each of the terms.

At the core of critical theory is the assumption that the distribution of power in a society creates and perpetuates instances of oppression and injustice in societies. *Oppression* characterizes human relations where one group or set of groups are able to dominate and exploit another group or set of groups. *Exploitation* may be economic, physical, or psychological in nature. *Injustice* occurs where such patterns of exploitation are perpetuated and controlled through dominant social classes, and may include exploitative wage labor, poverty, homelessness, and lack of access to adequate education or health care.

In order to understand patterns of domination and oppression, critical theory analyzes power relationships between groups. This can be a difficult task, as power is not always expressed overtly. Dominant groups may use their power to restrict access to information or resources without making it seem as though they are the ones doing the restriction. Unlike a mediator, who tries to be as neutral as possible in helping others to manage a conflict, a critical theorist takes the approach that social actions cannot be neutral. In fact, if a practitioner attempts to support neither side (as the Swiss did in WWII), he or she might actually wind up supporting the status quo that continues in oppression. Critical theorists often align themselves with the less powerful party because they are the often suppressed and have no voice in actions that keep them subordinate.

> The primary method of critical theory is **praxis**, which . . . is the reciprocal, dynamic, and reflexive relationship that practitioners engage in when their theorizing about societal oppression informs their actions taken to challenge that oppression, and vice versa . . . . *Praxis* also puts the scholar or practitioner in a position of continuous reflection, questioning the theory–action relationship in order to continuously revise his or her approach. A *praxis* orientation is inherently future-oriented and hopeful, with scholar-practitioners creating new visions for societal relationships in overcoming societal domination, which in turn are an impetus for further societal analysis and action.[15]

Part of the critical theorists' worldview is a sensitivity to the mistreatment, oppression, and suffering of the less fortunate.

So, how might one approach an intractable issue from critical theory assumptions? To begin with, the conflict manager examines his or her own assumptions about the conflict. Where do his or her sympathies lie? How do his or her values impact the way the conflict is viewed?

Second, the conflict manager will look for ways in which people are allowed access to the expression of their ideas on the conflict. Is one group allowed better access than the other? Does one group have more resources than the other? Does one group have more right to define the conflict than the other group? One author argues that media coverage of crowds demonstrating with respect to a particular issue often can frame public reaction to them:

> . . . studies of press accounts likewise point to an association between the political position of the commentator and the type of language used to describe crowd events . . . those critical of crowd participants' motives are more likely to describe an event in negative terms (e.g., "riot") rather than neutrally (e.g., "demonstration") or positively (e.g., "people power"). The delegitimizing functions of such negative language and explanations are obvious. If the crowd is pathologized and criminalized, then its behaviour is not meaningful. There can therefore be no rational dialogue with it. Since the crowd is not part of the democratic process, it is legitimate and even necessary to suppress it with the full force of the state.[16]

Finally, the conflict manager needs to use many of the communication, mediation, and negotiation skills from our earlier chapters to analyze the problem; however, recognizing that a solution may be difficult and a long time in coming.

Ripeness Theory In addition to critical theory, **ripeness theory** is a means of accounting for and addressing intractable issues.[17] As reflects its name, this theory focuses on ripeness, which is a condition that is linked to one side's decision to negotiate with the other in a conflict. Proponents of this theory argue that, when conflict participants realize that the path they are following produces pain, they begin to seek ways to reduce that pain. If a less painful alternative is found for them, the parties want to seek out that alternative. **Ripeness** occurs when participants in a conflict realize that they are involved in a *mutually hurting stalemate* (neither can get the advantage and current actions hurt both self and other) and recognize a *mutually enticing opportunity* (both may gain without giving away something of value). "Thus, ripeness is based on two core motives: pain and opportunities to escape from pain."[18]

Some people have argued that a limitation of ripeness theory is that it assumes that people behave rationally. Some people may be so committed to their cause that pain, suffering, and sacrifice mean nothing as long as the cause is advanced. Further, the theory assumes that both parties have to be ripe at the same time, and that ripeness is an "either/or" means of orientation toward a conflict (either they are "ripe" or they are not) rather than varying degrees of ripeness. Despite these shortcomings in the theory, practitioners can work toward the management of conflict by doing the following:

1. Look for factors that might strengthen positive attitudes toward alternatives to the conflict. For example, look for alternatives that are less costly and painful.
2. Recognize the factors that create pain for the participants in the current situation. Realize that continuing with the status quo increases pain and suffering.
3. Look for factors that make destructive conflict less attractive and peace more so.

Applying Theory to Conflicts Both critical theory and ripeness theory suggest some methods for dealing with conflicts over intractable issues. We believe that at the heart of any success in ameliorating an intractable issue is the ability to approach someone who is *other*—different—in ways that are honoring to that person and in using communication that is nonviolent in nature.

Let's start with the ways of dealing with otherness that people sometimes engage in due to fear and misunderstanding of their differences. Each of these ways increases our separation from others.[19]

First, we sometimes *demonize* the other, by treating him, her, or the group as someone to be feared and eliminated if possible. Think, for a moment, of the way in which Americans talk about terrorists. Are terrorists people with ideas? With wants and desires? With any kind of agenda to be heard? It is unlikely that you will hear such sentiments. This does not mean that terrorists have a humanistic or legitimate worldview any more than Hitler had. We are simply drawing attention to the fact that Americans share a view of terrorists as the enemy, which creates a clear boundary between them and the other.

A second means of increasing separation is to *romanticize* the other by considering the other as far superior to ourselves. One student took issue with the romanticizing of former criminals:

> I am always amazed when people celebrate dirt bags like Stanley "Tookie" Wilson because they turned their life around and spoke out against those who still do the same horrific things they did. Or when they write a book like *Monster* or *Always Running* and are celebrated for these "masterpieces" and their support of community values.

The Western world has a long history of engaging in the next means of separation, colonization by the British Empire, France, Spain, and later, the United States. When we *colonize* others, we treat them as inferior, worthy of pity (perhaps) but more likely contempt. Proponents of slavery in the United States often argued that it was beneficial for African Americans because they couldn't take care of themselves. Entire native civilizations in Asia, Africa, and North and South America were subjugated by those who colonized them. Later revolting against colonial powers, indigenous people have tried to reassert their cultural beliefs and values calling attention to the way they were treated and subjugated under colonial rule.

The fourth means of separation is to *generalize* the other, treating people as nonindividuals. When we stereotype members of a society, nation, or ethnic group rather than knowledge members as individuals, we are generalizing.

Two ways of treating the other that enhances separation are at opposite ends of the spectrum. At the one end, we may *trivialize* the other—by ignoring what makes the other so different from ourselves; at the other, we may *homogenize* the other—claiming there really is no difference between them and ourselves. Both refuse to see the other as an individual.

Finally, perhaps the most disturbing way people create separation is to *vaporize* the other by making them disappear—refusing to acknowledge the presence of the other at all. Many of us do this a lot more than we think. We do that when we walk down a street and ignore those who might hand us a leaflet or ask us for money. Sometimes we do this because we're in a hurry. It still renders the other invisible. As Sutton notes, though, "The difference between how a person treats the powerless versus the powerful is as good a measure of human character as I know."[20] We are not saying that you have to take every leaflet or give money to all who ask for it, but you could look at the person, shake your head no or look sympathetic—rather than ignore them entirely. Interestingly, school newspapers have sometimes published an article on homeless individuals who many see on their way to school. Come to find out, the individual has a name and often reveals an interesting history. A recent publication described such a person by the name of Scotty as a college graduate who had a serious drinking problem and a history of failed romantic relationships. The drinking led to arrests resulting in his current unemployment status and homeless way of life. Learning about such an individual helps one better understand the phrase "but for the grace of God go I," opens the reader's eyes to problems of alcohol or substance abuse, and perhaps makes one realize how close the line is between those who are homeless and those who are not. In the future, students might at least say hi to this homeless person or even recognize him by name.

If we are to deal effectively with conflicts over intractable issues, we must find a way to diminish the separation between ourselves and others. We must see them as individuals, and much like the steps in forgiveness, we must not only see them as "like ourselves" but see ourselves as "like them" without denying the differences that do exist. Cameron argues that this may be accomplished through

> . . . curiosity about the other person and their perspective. Curiosity and a sense of commonality also characterize sympathy; what takes empathy beyond sympathy is a third factor—the "imagining and seeking to understand the perspective of another person" even when that perspective may be distasteful or lead to "emotional ambivalence."[21]

Embracing "the Other"

Miroslav Volf, a native of Bosnia intimately acquainted with the level of conflict there, takes this perspective-seeking even farther. Noting that so many conflicts have identity issues at the heart of them, he argues that we must be willing to embrace the other. He asks "What kind of self do I need to be to live in harmony with others?" where harmony is defined as more than simply getting along. To live in harmony with others is to live in an attitude of embrace. He defines **embrace** as

> *the will to give ourselves to others and "welcome" them, to readjust our identities to make space for them . . . prior to any judgment about others, except that of identifying them in their humanity.* The *will to embrace* precedes any "truth" about others and any construction of their "justice." This will is absolutely indiscriminate and strictly immutable; it transcends the moral mapping of the social world into "good" and "evil."[22]

You may find such an attitude toward others hard to adopt. Clearly, it is something to be worked toward rather than a change that can be employed overnight. But then, all of the skills involved in conflict are difficult. Even your authors, who have been teaching and writing on this subject for many years, sometimes slip up and mismanage a conflict. Part of the commitment we make to "process rather than outcomes" means that we don't always get the outcomes we desire, but over time we do far better than you might expect. So, to the extent that we can suspend our judgment of others and welcome them into our world, without denying the existence or legitimacy of theirs, we are able to better manage our conflicts over intractable issues more often than not.

Managing Conflict through Nonviolent Communication

In addition to the way in which we view the other, our language must reflect a desire to welcome the other and engage in communication. Nonviolent language extends the notion of civility we presented in Chapter 1, in that it takes seriously the notion that words shape our worlds, and to use violent language makes us think it is acceptable to commit physical violence against others, as in making good on our verbal threats to hurt others. According to Rosenberg, **nonviolent communication** makes observations, states needs, and makes requests, not demands. In that sense, it is akin to the S-TLC system we introduced you to in Chapter 4. But nonviolent communication is driven by both thinking and language, with an intention to "create the quality of connection with other people and oneself that allows compassionate giving to take place. In this sense it is a spiritual practice: All actions are taken for the sole purpose of willingly contributing to the well-being of others and ourselves."[23] Rosenberg argues that people who employ nonviolent communication are concerned with two questions: What is alive in me and you? What can we do to make life more wonderful?

How do we use nonviolent communication? If the difference in cultural values is indicative of an interpersonal relationship you have, you should consider "agreeing to disagree." Perhaps the relationship offers benefits that greatly offset the problems encountered. If you have other aspects to the relationship that can "outweigh" your differences, you can choose to accept the other person as he or she is, and permit that person to value, believe, and engage in rituals that are different from you own. There are successful and happy romantic relationships in which there is significant cultural divide, but the partners have built bridges in spite of these differences. Having said that, one of your authors recalls a former female student who was romantically involved with a wealthy international student who flew her to his homeland (at his expense) in the Middle East so that she could meet his family and better understand what life is like if she married him. She did not like what she saw and decided not to marry him. She had to take a realistic look at the pros and cons of his proposal, and she made her decision. There certainly are many other cases, where the women decided that the advantages outweighed the disadvantages and are happy with their decision to marry someone from a different culture. In the example of a couple traveling in the Middle East, the unengaged couple could not agree to disagree but in other cases other couples could.

You might also find ways to combine with the other against some third force that threatens you both. Having a common enemy can end civil conflicts. Similarly, in the case of an intercultural couple, they may consider moving to a country that is not home to either of them and where a language is spoken that they do not share. They are then equal in their challenge of surviving in a different culture.

In other situations where we might encounter others in less comfortable circumstances, we should reject the use of verbal and physical aggression in our communication; threats, for example, have no place in nonviolent communication. As we learned in previous chapters, we should try to avoid judgments of the other as a person. We should try to observe without evaluating. We should take responsibility for our feelings and make requests that allow the other to say no to us. We should bring genuine presence to our listening to another person, and we should develop empathy that allows us to be vulnerable to the other. We should express anger appropriately.

Finally, we realize that even in giving a compliment, we may make a judgment. If someone has done something good for us, we tend to say something like "you're a nice person for doing that." Although the statement is positive, it is still a judgment about the person. Rosenberg argues that the most effective compliments are those where we identify:

1. the actions that have contributed to our well-being
2. the particular needs of ours that have been fulfilled
3. the pleasureful feelings engendered by the fulfillment of those needs[24]

Sometimes a simple "thank you" does all of the above. But people are more likely to appreciate acknowledgment of a particular action.

MANAGE IT!

In this chapter, we emphasized a type of issue that cannot be resolved by communication and negotiation techniques alone because it involves intractable issues, which is *central or lies at the core of our worldview and* is fueled by a general dislike and distrust of the other. An intractable issue transcends the people involved because it is a clash of their social/cultural, religious or political, and economic philosophies. We need to examine our worldviews to see if we can make room for people who are different from us.

A worldview is a composite of all the values, beliefs, and rituals one holds toward the world. The worldview for U.S. citizens is what it means to be an American. **Values** refer to what we hold dear, ranging from something of economic value, through sentimental value, to values we might die for (freedom, equal opportunity, and the love of someone dear to us). Because **beliefs** may or may not be true, they are related to knowledge such as manifest destiny (the belief in the mid-1800s that the United States had an obligation to expand to the Pacific Ocean). **Rituals** are symbolic actions like saluting the flag and singing the national anthem at athletic events.

One of the difficulties with identifying the cluster of beliefs, values, and rituals we hold as important is that we are rarely aware of them until they are challenged. Our worldview has a "taken for granted" aspect to it. We assume others believe as we do and see the world as we see it, but that is not the case. As we try to live side by side with other races, nationalities, ethnic groups, and cultures in a world that is increasingly pluralistic in its worldviews, we must learn how to live and work together to forge answers to the most pressing social, political, and economic problems in a way that neither denies nor magnifies the differences inherent in our worldviews.

Also referred to as social conflicts, societal conflicts, and moral conflicts, slogans and simple answers substitute for arguments and reasoning as each side despairs of winning the other to its way of thinking. Actions toward one another may become more violent and turn into a self-sealing pattern. In order to better understand the nature of worldview and how it can produce problematic intractable issues, we offered an example involving patriotism and nationalism, leaving it to you to decide whether or not to incorporate them in your worldview.

Two recent theories have been proposed to account for the way intractable issues are managed by the parties engaged in them. Critical theory analyzes power relations between the participants in an effort to uncover oppression, exploitation, and injustice. In order to understand patterns of domination and oppression, critical theory analyzes power relationships between groups, based on praxis, which examines ways in which people are allowed access to the expression of their ideas during a conflict.

While critical theory examines the distribution of power in a society, ripeness theory focuses the alternatives confronting conflicting parties. Proponents of ripeness theory argue that, if conflicting parties realize that the path they are following produces pain, they can seek ways to reduce that pain. If a less painful alternative is found for them, the parties may want to seek out that alternative. Ripeness occurs when participants in a conflict realize that they are involved in a mutually hurting stalemate and recognize a mutually enticing opportunity.

Both critical theory and ripeness theory suggest some methods for managing conflicts over intractable issues. We believe that at the heart of any success in ameliorating an intractable issue is the ability to approach the other who is different in ways that are honoring to that person and in using communication that is nonviolent in nature.

If we are to effectively manage conflicts over intractable issues, we must find a way to diminish the separation between the other and us. We must see those who are different as individuals, and much like the steps in forgiveness, we must not only see them as "like ourselves" but see ourselves as "like them" without denying the differences that do exist. In addition to the way in which we view the other, our language must reflect a desire to welcome the other and engage in nonviolent communication by rejecting the use of force, avoiding judgments of the other as a person, taking responsibility for our feelings and making requests that allow the other to say no to us, bringing genuine presence to our listening to another person, and developing empathy in a way that allows us to be vulnerable to the other. Finally we need to express anger appropriately.

EXERCISES

THINK ABOUT IT

1. On what issues are you likely to find yourself embroiled in an intractable issue? What happens when you argue with people who believe they have absolute Truth and do not even listen to what you have to say? How can you learn to listen to the other side of issues that are important to you?
2. Have you heard the term "worldview" before? In what context? Does it seem like a useful concept to you? Why or why not?
3. What is the place (if any) of faith (of any kind) in politics? What are the advantages of a faith-based government? The disadvantages?
4. How has the world changed for you since 9/11? How do you see the impact of that event on life in general? What would you like to see happen?
5. Is the idea of nonviolence in words and actions workable? Why or why not?

APPLY IT

1. Watch television for an hour, paying close attention to the commercials. Alternatively, go through an advertisement-heavy magazine such as *Vogue*. What are the values being sold to the viewer or reader? Are these good values? Why or why not? How do they reflect a worldview?

2. Look up information about one of these intractable issues: Sudan, Israel, Ireland, Guatemala, or another of your choice. Try to summarize the positions of the major parties to the conflict. How would you use critical theory or ripeness theory to advise those in the conflict?

3. Look at websites associated with secular humanism (e.g., *Free Inquiry* magazine at http://www.secularhumanism.org/index.php?section=fi&page=index) and evangelical Christianity (e.g., *Reasons to Believe* at http://www.reasons.org/). How does each side characterize itself? How does each side characterize the other? What would you do if you were the conflict manager in this case?

4. For one day, listen closely to what you and others say in conversation. How do you use words that are essentially violent (e.g., jokingly saying, "I'm going to smack you if you don't stop") or nonviolent? What would it take to change your language habits? Will it really change anything at all?

WORK WITH IT

Determine "your worldview" by considering your answers to the following questions. Put the answers on one page, if possible, so that you can see how they correspond to one another. Are there inconsistencies in what you believe and think? Where are they? How do you reconcile them to one another? Worldviews generally contain, either implicitly or explicitly, the answers to these questions:[25]

1. What is a human being? Where do we come from?
2. What is the ultimate reality? Is it a supernatural being?
3. What happens to people at death?
4. What is right with our society? Why do you think that is? Another way of thinking about this is to ask "what is good?"
5. What is wrong with our society? Why do you think that is? Another way of thinking about this is to ask "what is evil?"
6. What should we be striving to do in this lifetime?
7. What are your responsibilities in the various roles you play?
8. As a human being?
9. As a citizen of this country?
10. As an inhabitant of earth?
11. As a family member?
12. As a friend?
13. As an employee?
14. As a student?

DISCUSS IT

Read the case study below and discuss your answers to the questions that follow it.

When I was a sophomore in college, I got pregnant and had an abortion. It was soon after Roe vs. Wade had been decided. I went to Planned Parenthood, and when I blurted out that I wanted an abortion, no one tried to dissuade me or offer me any alternatives. I felt trapped. I didn't know that there were places I could go and have the baby and give it up for adoption. All I could think of was my high school friend who had to drop out of school when she got pregnant and carried the baby to term. I didn't want to do that. So I had the abortion. It was probably the most horrifying experience of my life. I know that some women have abortions and never feel any qualms about it. I went under the anesthetic screaming and came out weeping. It took a long time for me to forgive myself for what I had done. I felt I had taken the coward's way out of my situation. I'm married and have children and I love them to death, but I still think about that one baby and who it might have been. Well, one of my employees came to me and told me she had to have some time off. She hadn't been with us long and I asked her if it could wait until Easter because we'd be closed. She said no, that it couldn't. I asked her if something was wrong and she just said that she had to have time off. She looked nervous and upset, and it seemed like she wanted to talk to me but was afraid, so I just asked her point blank, "Are you pregnant?" At first she looked away and said she didn't want to talk about it, and then she burst into tears and said, "How did you know?" Having been down that road myself, it wasn't all that hard for me to figure out.

I talked to her and she said she was scheduled to have an abortion. I asked her if that's what she really wanted to do, and she said she thought it was all she could do. I'm not a person who would ever work to outlaw abortion because I don't think that really addresses the real issue, which is keeping people from getting pregnant to begin with. But I knew that I wanted to save her baby if I could, and I thought if she just knew that there were people who would support her and that there were alternatives that maybe she wouldn't have the abortion. We took off from work and talked all afternoon. I told her about my experiences, and why I wanted so much for her not to make the same mistake I made. I took her to my doctor and paid for the examination, because all she had taken was a urine test, and she hadn't had a physical exam yet. We went to a pregnancy counseling center where she saw *The Silent Scream*. That was probably a bit heavy-handed, but I really believe that abortion is murder and if you're going to do it, you ought to do it with your eyes open. We talked; she talked to friends. As she was wavering in her decision, she confided to me that she didn't want to have an abortion but that she was afraid to tell her parents about her problem. She was afraid they'd disown her.

She delayed the abortion a week, and during that time I found five couples who were interested in being prospective parents. None of them knew who she was, but I told her about them. There were two families who volunteered to have her stay with them during her pregnancy. One family offered to help her with her medical bills. I lined up all these people willing to help her, hoping to make her see that she wouldn't have to deal with the problem alone. Unfortunately, what mattered to her was whether she had support at least from the baby's father or from her parents. The father had taken off for parts unknown after urging her to have an abortion. She still hadn't told her parents and was afraid if she did she would lose them too.

Questions to address:

a. What is the moral issue in this case study?
b. Did both people act in ways that honored the other's point of view?
c. How would you have responded if you were the employer? The employee? Why?

SOCIETAL CONFLICT CLASS EXERCISE: THE GRAND SOCIETY

The Objective:

The objective is to discuss and decide on a perfect society and then enter into international discussions about mutual concerns with members of other nations.

Time:

Total of four class hours: one hour for each nation to develop its worldview; two hours for international meetings; and one hour for class discussion of the exercise.

Instructions:

1. Divide the class into four nations with at least three members each, so that at least one person can meet with the other three nations simultaneously. Members of each nation are

to name their society, list several values and beliefs, which guide their decisions at home and when dealing with other nations.

2. The members of each nation decide who will represent them in their meetings with members of other nations and how these representatives are to interact and cooperate with the other nations on "a mutual concern" (see below). Representatives return to discuss their meetings with the rest of the members in their nation before returning to the next meeting.

   a. Nation A is preparing to build a dam that will reduce the supply of water to neighbor B. Note that A is an industrial nation and B is agricultural.

   b. Nations C and D need to discuss the idea of creating a combined defense force to defend against the other two nations A and B. Note that C and D share a history in which they have fought against the peoples of A and B for centuries.

   c. Nations A and C need to discuss the idea of exchanging spies who were caught and jailed in both nations. Note that nation A has captured 500 people they accused of being spies with little or no proof, while nation B has captured five spies who were caught attempting to assassinate their top government officials.

   d. Nations B and D need to discuss the idea of a college student exchange program between their nations. Note that D is an industrial nation and B is agricultural.

   e. Nations A and D need to discuss protecting a species of beautiful birds that live in nation A and migrating each winter to nation D where they are hunted for their feathers. Note that this is the national bird of nation A and is used for decoration by nation D.

   f. Nations B and C speak tongues not spoken by most people in their nations, so the two nations need to meet to discuss how to exchange translators and teach the language to their populations. Note that A and B speak the same language, while C and D share another language.

3. At the end of the meetings and discussions, the members of each nation discuss their answers to Form 1 and answer the questions. This form may serve as a basis for each nation's report to the class.

4. The class meets to discuss the exercise. Based on its Form 1, each nation summarizes its meetings with the other nations and internal discussions that resulted in decisions made by the nation. They should point out if and how they applied the basic values first agreed on in their international discussions.

Form 1: A Nation's Worldview (One per Nation)

1. Describe your nation's worldview (beliefs, values/ethics, rituals).

2. Did any intractable issues arise? (Fueled by dislike of other nations; central to conflicting nations' worldviews? Conflict over who is right and who is wrong? Couldn't get past the issue?)

3. Did members of your nation or any of the other nations treat each other as "mad, bad, sick, or stupid," and say anything like "We cannot reason with people like that!"?

4. Did members of your nation or any of the other nations engage in name calling or other personal attacks (calling someone stupid, ignorant, prejudiced, etc.)?

5. Were there any issues that you thought members of your nation or any other nation should have understood, appreciated, and supported, but they did not? What was their reasoning?

6. Were the views of members of your nation or any other nation repeated more than once (or many times, over and over)? What were they?

7. How would you characterize the other nations' discourse (violent vs. nonviolent communication)? Did members of any nation make demands rather than requests, threats rather than showing compassion?

8. Did members of your nation want to change any aspects of the worldview your nation created at the beginning of this exercise?

9. Did members of your nation or any other nation want to stop meeting and quit talking? Did they think that it was pointless to meet and discuss matters of mutual concern? Was there talk of going to war against the other nation?

10. Considering ripeness theory, do you think that your nation and any of the other nations were engaged in a mutually hurting stalemate?

11. Consider a critical theory approach, and examine the dynamics that occurred in your own nation. Were any members playing a more dominant role and others less so? Were you all equally supportive of your nation's worldview? Were any members marginalized even in subtle ways? Do members of your nation believe that changing some aspects of your worldview might have enabled your nation to better work with other nations in resolving mutual problems?

NOTES

1. See John J. Macionis, *Sociology,* 10th Edition (Upper Saddle River, NJ: Pearson Prentice Hall, 2005), p. 66.

2. Dennis Hollinger, "Pluralism and Christian Ethics: Responding to the Options," *Christian Scholar's Review* 30 (2000), 164, 163–183.

3. Robert R. Agne, "Reframing Practices in Moral Conflict: Interaction Problems in the Negotiation Standoff at Waco," *Discourse and Society* 18 (2007), 549–578.

4. Shadia B. Drury, "Fascism American Style," *Free Inquiry* (April/May, 2009), 27, 26–27.

5. Ibid., p. 26

6. Sally A. Freeman, Stephen W. Littlejohn, and W. Barnett Pearce, "Communication and Moral Conflict," *Western Journal of Communication* 56 (1992), 315.

7. W. Barnett Pearce, "Keynote Address: Communication Theory," Institute for Faculty Development: Communication Theory and Research, Hope College, Holland, T, July 1992.

8. Freeman, Littlejohn, and Pearce, "Communication and Moral Conflict," p. 319.

9. Jacob Bercovitch, "Characteristics of Intractable Issues," in Guy Burgess and Heidi Burgess (Eds.), *Beyond Intractability* [electronic book] (Boulder, CO: Conflict Research Consortium, University of Colorado, Boulder) Posted: October 2003; http://www.beyondintractability.org/essay/Characteristics_IC/ (accessed May 27, 2009).

10. Julie W. Morgan and Richard K. Olsen, "Discursive Taboo in Community Discourse: Communication Competence and Biblical Wisdom," *Christian Scholar's Review* 38 (2009), 346, 341–358.

11. Eran Halperin, "Group-Based Hatred in Intractable Issue in Israel," *Journal of Conflict Resolution* 52 (2008), 718, 713–736.

12. Conflict Research Consortium, University of Colorado, Boulder, CO, Problem List 2: Core Conflict Problems, http://www.colorado.edu/conflict/peace/!core_problems.htm (accessed May 27, 2009).

13. Hollinger, "Pluralism and Christian Ethics," p. 165.

14. Toran Hansen, "Critical Conflict Resolution Theory and Practice," *Conflict Resolution Quarterly* 25 (2008), 403–427.

15. Ibid., p. 409.

16. John Drury, "'When the Mobs Are Looking for Witches to Burn, Nobody's Safe': Talking about the Reactionary Crowd," *Discourse and Society* 13 (2002), 42, 41–73.

17. Peter T. Coleman, Antony G. Hacking, Mark A. Stover, Beth Fisher-Yoshida, and Andrzej Nowak, "Reconstructing Ripeness I: A Study of Constructive Engagement in Protracted Social Conflicts," *Conflict Resolution Quarterly* 26 (2008), 3–42.

18. John Drury, "'When the Mobs Are Looking for Witches to Burn, Nobody's Safe': Talking about the Reactionary Crowd," *Discourse and Society* 13 (2002), p. 5.

19. Robert J. Schreiter, *Reconciliation* (Maryknoll, NY: Orbis Books, 2003), pp. 42–53.

20. Robert I. Sutton, *The No Asshole Rule* (New York: Warner Business Books, 2007), p. 25.

21. Lynne J. Cameron, "Patterns of Metaphor Use in Reconciliation Talk," *Discourse and Society* 18 (2007), 199, 197–222.

22. Miroslav Volf, *Exclusion and Embrace* (Nashville, TN: Abingdon Press), p. 29 (italics in original).

23. Marshall B. Rosenberg, *Speak Peace in a World of Conflict* (Encinitas, CA: PuddleDancer Press, 2005), p. 16.

24. Marshall B. Rosenberg, *Nonviolent Communication: A Language of Life,* 2nd Edition (Encinitas, CA: PuddleDancer Press, 2005), p. 186.

25. Adapted from James W. Sire, *The Universe Next Door,* 4th Edition (Downer's Grove, IL: IVP Academic, 2004); James W. Sire, *Naming the Elephant* (Downer's Grove, IL: IVP Academic, 2004); and James H. Olthuis, "On Worldviews," *Christian Scholar's Review* 14 (1985), 153–164.

INDEX